Clinical Negligence Made Clear

A Guide for Patients and Professionals

Nigel Poole QC

With a Foreword by Sir Robert Francis QC

Published October 2019

ISBN 978-1-9164315-6-0

Text © Nigel Poole

Typography © Bath Publishing

Bath Publishing Limited
27 Charmouth Road
Bath
BA1 3LJ
Tel: 01225 577810
email: info@bathpublishing.co.uk
www.bathpublishing.co.uk

Bath Publishing is a company registered in England: 5209173

Registered Office: As above

For Michael Poole

(1938 – 2019)

Foreword

This book is a welcome and much needed resource for the people the law on clinical negligence is designed to serve, namely patients who believe they have suffered avoidable harm and the loved ones who support and care for them, and in many sad cases, mourn their death. That it takes a book of over 400 pages to explain this in a comprehensive way should not put them off reading the parts which are the most relevant to their own situation. Regrettably it should also not deter them from seeking legal advice. Every case is different, and very few are sufficiently simple for a person to be able to pursue a claim effectively without legal help. The book will also be of tremendous value to all those whose job involves considering cases of avoidable harm, such as hospital managers and leaders, those who deal with adverse incidents and complaints, patient advocates, and advice services. Not least among the groups who can benefit from a clear non-technical explanation of the law are our politicians who do not always understand what the law does and does not do. A vivid example is given in a reference to the debate over Lord Saatchi's Medical Innovation Bill [page 102].

When I first encountered medical cases in practice as a barrister, rather too long ago in the 1970s and 1980s, clinical negligence cases were rare, and successful claims even more scarce. This was probably not because errors which would be classified as negligent today were less common, but because credible patients were more likely to be reassured by the mantra that they had suffered a "recognised complication" rather than being given an open and candid explanation of what had happened. Even if they suspected something had gone wrong which should not have done, it was difficult if not impossible to access the medical records which would throw light on the matter, without starting court proceedings, a step which in itself required possession of evidence suggestive of negligence. Such evidence was extremely hard to gain in any event. Doctors were hard to find who were prepared to criticise their colleagues, and there was an unfortunate tendency to castigate those who were as mavericks or in some way unreliable: whereas the defence could often find an expert willing to support the "recognised complication" argument.

Times have changed and for the better. We all have a right to see our records, whether or not we want to bring a claim; we have standard of care more capable of assessment by experts and judges and we have a far wider range of experts prepared to offer honest and objective opinions to both sides in a case. The assessment of damages, while far from perfect, is now much better equipped to reflect the reality of a claimant's needs.

However the current state of the law, civil and criminal, is far from satisfactory:

- This book rightly describes the focus of clinical negligence cases to be on the individuals who provide advice and treatment and the standards of practice applicable to their profession, rather than the organisation or organisations which employ those professionals. This may be thought to encourage compliance with good practice through the threat of accountability, but in reality encourages divisiveness between patients and those who treat them, and a reduction in trust and openness.

- Opportunities for learning quickly from mistakes and for involvement of patients in that process are lost by the encouragement given by litigation for an adversarial relationship through the claimant's search for people to blame and the professional's and their employer's reliance on every argument they can find to support a defence.

- These divisions are made worse in the most tragic cases of all, those involving a death, by the current state of the criminal law. The fear of a prosecution for gross negligence manslaughter inevitably causes healthcare professionals to be defensive rather than open about their mistakes. While the risk of prosecution is in fact very small it is very difficult for the nervous professional who has made a mistake that may have resulted in death to know. In fact the test for what is or is not a sufficiently serious mistake to amount to manslaughter is dependent on the verdict of a jury in an individual case. And the earlier decision as to whether there should be a prosecution is taken on expert evidence that inevitably is not available to the practitioner for months if not years.

- Victims of medical accidents are divided into those who can receive relatively full compensation for their injuries and losses, and those with identical needs who have to fight for and then rely on the often very variable and less effective support offered by the state. This gives rise to a sense of unfairness.

- An indefinable number of those who are entitled to compensation do not receive it because of the challenges in obtaining funding to investigate and mount a clinical negligence claim. Indeed it is likely that the claims actually made are the tip of a very large iceberg. A recent study of deaths caused or contributed to by the adverse effect of medical treatment (AEMT) [see https://jamanetwork.com/journals/jamanetworkopen/fullarticle/2720915 Sunshine, Meo, Kassebaum *Association of Adverse Effects of Medical Treatment with Mortality in the united States*, 18

January 2019] estimated the national standardised mortality rate due to AEMT as 1.45 per 100,000 population, with a total of 123,603 deaths with AEMT as the underlying cause between 1990 and 2016. The World Health Organisation estimates that 134 million adverse events contribute to 2.6 million deaths every year, and that 4 out of 10 patients in primary and ambulatory settings are harmed of which 80% of harm could be avoided [see https://www.patientsafetyinstitute.ca/en/Events/pages/world-patient-safety-day-september-17-2019-.aspx]. It has been reported that between 8 to 12% of hospitalisations (10% in the UK) in EU member states involve a medical error or healthcare related adverse event [see above]. Doubtless many of those would not pass the *Bolam/Bolitho* test of negligence but it seems highly likely that many more would do so than currently see the light of day. Therefore only a proportion of those actually entitled to compensation get it.

- A major barrier to compensation is the difficulty in proving causation. Many, if not most, claims falter because a causal link between the negligence and the injury suffered cannot be proved. The obvious difficulty is that by definition those receiving medical treatment are almost always already suffering an illness or injury. Not only can medical treatment not guarantee a cure or improvement, there are genuinely unavoidable risks that have to be taken in order to obtain the better chance of an improvement. The lingering sense of injustice that often surrounds the unsuccessful claimant in such a case would be reduced if a defendant who was found to have provided negligent treatment were to be liable to provide compensation unless they proved that the injury was not caused by the negligence.

- The barriers to a successful claim in relation to NHS provided treatment are even greater when the treatment was provided privately. As pointed out [page 313] the challenges of identifying the "right" defendant to sue can be greater: independent hospitals do not generally employ their doctors who enter into private agreements direct with their patients. An independent hospital may not provide, as the NHS does, an indemnity to such doctors who are expected to have their own professional insurance cover. It is not unknown for it to be discovered too late that an allegedly negligent doctor with insufficient resources to satisfy a judgment for damages did not have the necessary insurance. At a time when private medical treatment is obtained by increasing numbers of people, it is time that the law required insurance arrangements at least as good as those available in relation to NHS care.

- Although progress has been made in regulating the conduct of experts, as pointed out [page 104] some experts still find it difficult to separate a preference for their own practice from the question they are employed to answer, namely whether the professional accused of negligence acted in accordance with a responsible body of relevant medical opinion. The test requires a challenging degree of objectivity and in all but simple cases [simple that is for the relevant medical specialty] a comprehensive study of the learning and of any differing practices that are or were current at the time of the incident in question. As each party may well be confined to one expert each in the speciality in which the standard of care is being considered – and sometimes the court will insist on a single joint expert – there is a risk of the court being misled into believing that the experts in the case are truly representative of medical opinion more widely. As is pointed out [page 182] there is no requirement for experts to be accredited. To require accreditation would be unduly restrictive of the parties' right to choose the evidence they put before the court to support their case and would risk injustice. However the author is not alone in having wondered whether some experts would be recognised by their peers as experts. There are now many training opportunities available to aspiring experts and while they should not be compulsory if a witness has been trained in this way it is less likely that they will commit errors of subjectivity and partisan advocacy that some undoubtedly commit. I would go further and ask whether some form of quality assurance of expert reports should not be made available by professional bodies such as the Royal Colleges, not to adjudicate in difference of opinion but to audit whether an expert's reports comply with acceptable standards.

• The duty of care for healthcare professionals is put in a different position from others accused of causing injury by negligence, some say unjustifiably so. The element of self-determination in professional negligence is considered in Principle 2 in relation to the circumstances in which a professional duty of care arises. The question could equally be raised under Principle 4 or 5 in relation to the standard of care owed to a patient. Matters have improved from a patient's perspective by the reminder given in *Bolitho* that ultimately the court has to decide whether a professional opinion is rational as well as supported by the doctor's peers. However the courts have been understandably reluctant to question widely held professional views. The burden on a claimant in seeking to challenge an established "school of thought" as described by an expert to the court is considerable and depends on their being able to find an expert brave enough to challenge it. It might be wondered whether there is not scope for the court or a party to seek an intervention from some better resourced organisation with an ability to survey and analyse the range of relevant opinion.

- A question is raised about the scope of the duty of care owed by complementary or alternative medicine practitioners. The same question could equally be raised about the increasing varieties of qualified, or at least trained, practitioners such as nursing associates, associate physicians, nurse consultants, to name but a few. Some of these have as yet few defined standards around their training or skills required for the job. I suggest that for the moment at least no lower standard of care should be applied to their work than that imposed on doctors and nurses: in other words it's a medical standard in that sense by which the new ancillary workers acts and omissions should be judged.

Apart from these ways in which our current system for compensating avoidable medical harm is unsatisfactory it may be questioned whether there should not be a much better system for achieving the same results. There are many different ways outside the court process in which adverse clinical incidents are considered and investigated. These range from the informal, such as hospital mortality and morbidity reviews, to the more formal such as complaints processes, adverse incident investigations, and inquests. The formal processes tend to suffer from the same cultural defects as litigation – they place the patient and those who provided the treatment on opposite sides of a fence – the patient and their family may not feel they are genuine participants in a process designed to get at the truth [which is all that many of those who eventually resort to litigation say they want] but persons against whom a defence must be mounted if possible. I suggest that all those involved in an incident should be brought together to identify the questions that needed to be answered, and to provide the answers in processes designed to preserve rather than destroy the trust and partnership that are at the heart of all successful medical treatment. That process should include a power to provide immediate practical and financial support to the patient and the family, according to their needs rather than being dependent on a finding of blame. That would surely serve better the causes of patient safety and of the welfare of the injured patient and their family. It might reduce work for lawyers but would surely enhance the lives of those affected by the inevitable mistakes which will continue to occur so long as we need medical care.

Sir Robert Francis QC

October 2019

Acknowledgements

I would like to thank the following:

Sir Robert Francis QC for providing his foreword and for being a great example of how a barrister can have a wider influence beyond the Bar.

Alastair Forrest, who taught me so much about the law, introduced me to clinical negligence and who was a trusted friend and guide at the Bar for many years.

Jenny Urwin of Field Fisher LLP, who kindly talked me through the solicitor's role, read the first draft of the book and made helpful corrections and suggestions.

My family: Will for his help with proof reading, Sue and Alice for their suggestions, and most of all Annmarie, for her wise advice and inexhaustible patience.

David and Helen from Bath Publishing for their professionalism, encouragement and support.

And finally my thanks to the many clients solicitors, barristers, judges and medical experts it has been my privilege to work with, and to be educated by, during my career at the Bar.

Nigel Poole QC

October 2019

"This book is a comprehensive and up to date guide which should be of interest and practical use to anyone working in the field of clinical negligence".

Peter Walsh

Chief Executive, Action against Medical Accidents (AvMA)

"Healthcare practitioners may go through their careers without ever being named personally in a clinical negligence claim. Fewer still will be asked to provide expert evidence to the courts. Some will have received some basic training or professional guidelines. However, their understanding of best practice in avoiding claims or resolving complaints, before they escalate as far as the courts, of negligence law, processes around making or defending claims will vary. In particular, the scope of their own professional roles and responsibilities with regard to clinical negligence and in navigating this complexity may bewilder. Concern over rare but recent high profile cases of gross negligence manslaughter may add to that confusion.

Nigel Poole QC's *"Clinical Negligence, Made Clear"* is aimed at practitioners, managers and members of the public who are not legal experts but seek to be better informed. It is written by someone with three decades' experience litigating in this field. The book walks us through all those areas in a logical order, wonderfully referenced and illustrated with summaries from case law along the journey and despite its rich technical content is highly accessible for non-lawyers. It should be a standard text for years to come."

Professor David Oliver

Consultant Physician, Kings Fund Fellow, past Vice President Royal College of Physicians and former National Clinical Director for Older Peoples Services

Contents

Part 3: Clinical Negligence Litigation – The Anatomy of a Claim

Part 4: Particular Claims

Table of Cases

List of Useful Contacts

Association of Personal Injury Lawyers	www.apil.org.uk
AvMA – Action against Medical Accidents	www.avma.org.uk
Bar Council	www.barcouncil.org.uk
Citizens Advice	www.citizensadvice.org.uk
General Medical Council	www.gmc-uk.org
Health and Care Professions Council	www.hcpc-uk.org
Law Society	www.lawsociety.org.uk
Medical Defence Union	www.themdu.com
Ministry of Justice	www.gov.uk/government/organisations/ministry-of-justice
National Voices	www.nationalvoices.org.uk
NHS Resolution	resolution.nhs.uk
National Institute of Health and Care Excellence (NICE)	www.nice.org.uk
Nursing and Midwifery Council	www.nmc.org.uk
Patient and Advice Liaison Service	www.nhs.uk/common-health-questions/nhs-services-and-treatments/what-is-pals-patient-advice-and-liaison-service
Personal Support Unit	www.thepsu.org
Society of Clinical Injury Lawyers	www.scil.org.uk
The Patients Association	www.patients-association.org.uk

Introduction

When clinical negligence litigation makes headline news, which is often, it is usually for one of two reasons. Either a patient's life has been ended or catastrophically changed because of seemingly inexcusable medical error, or there is a new alarm about the huge cost of legal claims against the NHS. Simultaneously, the healthcare system is condemned for its failings and the legal system is condemned for exploiting those failings. How fair are those criticisms? Why do so many patients turn to lawyers when something has gone wrong, and so many medical professionals feel unfairly treated by the legal system? When the worlds of law and medicine collide, who are the winners and losers?

No patient or healthcare professional would choose to be caught up in clinical negligence litigation. It is adversarial, stressful, and costly. It is also complex and confusing for those who have no prior experience of it. Over many years as a practising barrister I have dealt with thousands of former patients and their families. I have tried to explain the legal principles and procedures to them and to guide them through the litigation process, sometimes successfully, sometimes unsuccessfully. In doing so I have encountered very many doctors and other healthcare professionals who, by different routes, have become involved in litigation. I have seen the impact, both positive and negative, that clinical negligence litigation can have.

This book is the product of that experience. It is not my purpose to impress other lawyers – had I tried to do so I would have been sure to fail. This is not a book for experienced clinical negligence litigators. My aim is to make clear the law of clinical negligence and to provide an intelligent but accessible guide for patients, doctors, nurses, therapists, expert witnesses, healthcare managers and anyone else who has an interest in medico-legal issues and practice. The book will also serve as an introduction to clinical negligence litigation for law students and practising lawyers who have not yet gained extensive professional experience in the field. It is very much a personal view rather than an instruction manual.

I do not believe that lawyers should regard themselves as holding the keys to a secret kingdom. I want lawyers to share their experience and knowledge with the wider public. The civil justice system is there to serve everyone and so it should be accessible and comprehensible. The more that patients and healthcare professionals understand how the law of clinical negligence works, the better everyone can trust in the system and work co-operatively to improve it.

Perhaps it is an over-ambitious goal to make clinical negligence clear. As I describe in Part 1, negligence is part of the law of tort and, like most tort law, it has largely been developed over many years through hundreds of judicial decisions in individual cases. The law is therefore sometimes hard to pin down. If you struggle to find a coherent set of principles you are in good company. When he was President of the Supreme Court, the highest judicial position in the country, Lord Neuberger told an audience of lawyers, "Analysis of tort cases appears to demonstrate a notable degree of disarray and a marked lack of reliable principle."

I begin in Part 1 by setting clinical negligence litigation in context, explaining its place within the justice system as a whole, and within the law of negligence in particular. How has it evolved and what is its purpose?

In Part 2 I examine ten core legal principles: to whom does a doctor owe a duty of care, what is the standard that healthcare professionals are expected to meet, and how does the law determine whether a patient has suffered avoidable harm for which a clinician is responsible? I also discuss how compensation is assessed by the courts and why sometimes the sums are so high.

Part 3 addresses the court process. How is a claim brought and what happens before, and at, trial?

Specific kinds of clinical negligence litigation are examined in Part 4. They include obstetric claims where a child has suffered cerebral palsy, wrongful birth, delay in diagnosing cancer, psychiatric cases, cosmetic surgery, and fatal cases. All of these give rise to their own particular issues.

In the Epilogue I will briefly consider the future of clinical negligence. Is the current system sustainable? What improvements or alternatives should be considered?

Clinical negligence is an important and sometimes controversial area of the law. It touches on issues of life and death, the protection of vulnerable individuals, risk, accountability, human rights, and personal autonomy. The human and financial costs of clinical negligence are considerable but it is worth putting it into some kind of perspective. The NHS claims to deal with 1.4 million patients every 24 hours – that's about 511 million patient interactions each year. The chances of any one of the millions of these interactions resulting in a clinical negligence claim are extremely low. NHS Resolution, the body that is responsible for handling such claims against NHS Trusts, reported that it had resolved 11,625 clinical negligence claims in the year 2018-19. 41% of all claims were resolved without payment of any compensation and there were only 100 or so clinical negligence trials in that year. It is very difficult to obtain statistics for claims arising out of primary healthcare practice, but the NHS Resolution report shows that the chances of treatment or management of a patient by an NHS hospital ending up at trial are vanishingly small.

The number of clinical negligence claims against the NHS is falling. The NHS Resolution report for 2019 showed that, after year on year reductions in new clinical negligence claims since 2013-14, there had been an increase of only five claims between 2017-18 and 2018-19. But whilst the number of claims has decreased, the cost of those claims to the NHS has been rising. Clinical negligence claims, including damages and legal costs, cost the NHS over £1.7 billion in 2016-17, £2.2 billion in 2017-18, and £2.34 billion in 2018-19. Most of that increase was due to a government decision to change the discount rate which is used to calculate the cost of future losses and expenses suffered by claimants. In July 2019 the rate was changed with the likely consequence that there will be some correction to that sudden increase. NHS Resolution reported in 2019 that the future costs of current and past claims against the NHS would be £83.4 billion. This is in part because higher value claims are often resolved on the basis of an agreement to make annual payments to the injured patient for as long as they live. So the future costs of current and past claims continue long into the future. The annual cost of the NHS to the taxpayer is currently about £125 billion. The annual cost of clinical negligence is £2.34 billion, which is significant, running at over 1.8% of the annual NHS budget.

Clinical negligence costs the state, and therefore the taxpayer, a large amount of money. This causes widespread resentment as shown by those front page headlines about a compensation culture and the greedy lawyers who foster it. This in turn encourages a perception amongst doctors that every error, however understandable, can result in them being dragged through the courts. There is anger within the medical profession at how the law is used to attack doctors and nurses who are trying to do their best in often stressful and under-resourced circumstances.

The fear of litigation can also affect the way medical professionals manage and treat their patients. In a survey of General Practitioners by the Medical Protection Society, 87% said they are increasingly fearful of being sued, 84% said the fear of being sued has resulted in them ordering more tests or making more referrals and 41% said it has resulted in them prescribing medication when not clinically necessary.

There is, of course, another side to the clinical negligence story. The responsibilities placed on clinicians are of a different order from those shouldered by other professionals, such as lawyers or accountants. A surgeon's professional error might have catastrophic consequences, causing life-changing injuries or death. Patients trust doctors and nurses with their lives and the lives of their loved ones and that level of trust brings with it high expectations. When things do go wrong it is understandable that patients want answers, they want accountability and they want redress. There is, after all, a lot at stake.

I have had the enormous privilege of representing many patients and their families whose lives have been thrown into crisis because of another's negligence and yet, for all the claims in which I have been involved, my perception is that people are generally very reluctant to sue their doctors or other healthcare professionals. Indeed, I suspect that only a small proportion of patients who could bring a claim, do so. The NHS remains a much loved institution and respect for medical and other healthcare professionals remains strong. They are dedicated to helping others and make hugely positive contributions to countless lives. But sometimes things do go badly wrong and sometimes patients have little option but to consult lawyers and to bring a clinical negligence claim. Perhaps they have to support a severely disabled child for the rest of their lives, or they are unable to work again but have a partner or children who depend upon them. Often those who litigate feel that their concerns have been brushed aside and they see no way other than through litigation to secure a proper investigation into what went wrong.

History is written by the victors. Whilst most litigation ends in compromise, the development of common law legal principles depends on the outcome of legal battles taken all the way to trial. For every successful party, there is a loser. The stories that tend to get re-told are those of the victors in litigation. Occasionally someone is lying in litigation: they have concocted evidence, falsified records or covered up. But the vast majority of those involved in litigation are genuine and honest. Spare a thought for those patients and their families who did not succeed but whose lives were changed forever in ways they did not expect, and for those doctors who were held responsible for life-changing injuries or deaths when they sincerely felt that they did not do anything wrong or were working under extreme pressure.

Litigation is adversarial, but no good purpose is served in encouraging hostility between healthcare professionals and their patients. Where hostility does exist it stems, I believe, from misunderstanding and poor communication. My hope is that by shedding a little light on the relevant laws and procedures, this book will increase understanding for all those who might find themselves involved in a clinical negligence claim.

Note
This book addresses the law of England and Wales. The corresponding laws in Scotland and in Northern Ireland, are outside the remit of the book.

I have included insets describing some of the key cases affecting clinical negligence litigation. At the end of any significant case the court, whether an individual judge or, in cases heard on appeal, a team of judges, gives a written judgment. These are published in law reports and, now, online. The insets are not in the form of a law report but are designed to give the reader sufficient information about the case to understand its significance. Where available, I have referred to the published report or to what lawyers call the "neutral citation number". A neutral citation number gives the year of the judgment followed by initials for the court, and a case number for that court in that year. The courts for cases referred to in this book are the England and Wales High Court (EWHC), England and Wales Court of Appeal (EWCA), and United Kingdom Supreme Court (UKSC). The High Court and Court of Appeal have divisions which, for clinical negligence cases, are respectively the Queen's Bench Division (QB) and the Civil Division (Civ). So, you might see a case name, being the names of the claimant and the defendant separated by a "v" followed by the neutral citation, such as *Smith v Jones* [2019] EWHC 123 (QB). These judgments are usually obtainable online at the website for the British and Irish Legal Information Institute ("Bailii") where there is a case search facility. Where a case has been reported in a law report, the reference will be different. The common law reports for clinical negligence cases are the Weekly Law Reports (WLR), the All England Law Reports (All ER) and Appeal Cases (AC). Where I have referred to a judgment and a reference to it in a law report you will find the year, then the law report abbreviation and a page number. Sometimes there is more than one volume of law reports for each year, so you might see: *Smith v Jones* [2019] 1 WLR 123, meaning that the judgment is found at page 123 of Volume 1 of the Weekly Law Reports for 2019.

I decided not to use footnotes in this book. Believe me, for a lawyer writing a book about law, that is a punishing self-imposed stricture. Lawyers like to back up every point they make: "My Lord this accident happened on Friday 15 March, which was the day after Thursday 14 March (see *Grind v Northern Tramways Limited* [1834] BLT, 76)." This book is not intended to be an encyclopaedic review of the law or an aid for those writing academic essays. It is meant to be a friendly guide. So, no footnotes – you will just have to trust me!

Part 1: Clinical Negligence In Context

Chapter 1: The Rule of Law

"In a world divided by differences of nationality, race, colour, religion and wealth [the rule of law] is one of the greatest unifying factors, perhaps the greatest, the nearest we are likely to approach to a universal secular religion."

Tom Bingham, The Rule of Law

Laws and the rule of law are the cornerstones of a civilised society. They bring order to human affairs where there would otherwise be chaos. They allow us to function within a community of individuals whose interests may sometimes be in common, but at other times may be in conflict. Laws give powers to the state over its citizens but also protect those citizens from the abuse of state power. Laws govern our private dealings with each other: the making and breaking of promises, the ownership and transfer of land and property, or the duty not to cause avoidable harm. Without agreement as to how laws are to be made and enforced, and consent to be bound by those laws, societies veer to the extremes of tyranny or anarchy.

The rule of law is a guiding principle or philosophy underlying our own society. It means that those who govern us must act within their powers and that the law is certain and applies equally to all. Lord Bingham, one of the greatest judges of the last 100 years, and author of *The Rule of Law*, identified eight elements of the rule of law:

(1) The law must be accessible, clear and predictable.

(2) Questions of legal rights should not be resolved by the exercise of discretion, but by the law.

(3) The law should apply equally to all, except where objective differences justify differentiation.

(4) Ministers must act within their powers and not exceed their limits.

(5) The law must afford adequate protection of fundamental human rights.

(6) The law should provide access to justice, especially where people cannot resolve inter-personal disputes themselves.

(7) Court and tribunal processes should be fair.

(8)   The state should comply with international law.

Just as doctors seek to maximize the health of their patients and to advance the practice of medicine, so lawyers seek to serve justice, uphold the law and strengthen the rule of law. Do not let the wigs, gowns and breezy self-confidence fool you. It is not, as someone once rather insensitively suggested to me, "all a bit of a game". It matters.

Our constitutional rules and conventions, developed over centuries, are designed to ensure that the rule of law is maintained. Ministers must act within their powers. Laws apply equally to all unless objective differences justify differentiation. The government should ensure that the state complies with international law and it should ensure effective access to the law. Recently the Supreme Court, the highest court in the land, took the government to task over the introduction of large fees for bringing claims in the Employment Tribunal. Without effective access to justice, it said, laws are liable to become a dead letter, the work of Parliament in creating the laws would become irrelevant and the democratic process of electing members of Parliament to create those laws, a meaningless charade. Strong stuff.

Clinical negligence law sits in one corner of a complex system of justice. Does it satisfy Lord Bingham's elements of the rule of law? Does it operate justly? I hope that after reading this book you will have a more informed view of whether the law of clinical negligence and the court processes that govern its enforcement are clear, fair and apply equally to all. I have practised in clinical negligence law for nearly 30 years but I am not blind to its failings.

Many contend that the law of clinical negligence is neither clear nor predictable. They complain that doctors, for example, cannot know in advance of embarking on a course of treatment, whether or not they are being negligent. It is also uncertain and risky for patients bringing claims. It is only after a prolonged and expensive process of investigation and litigation that the court will determine whether the treatment was negligent.

Is the court system accessible and fair? Public funding for the cost of representation has been cut right back, and in its place the government has introduced conditional fee agreements – so called "no win, no fee". Although there is a common perception that this encourages more claims to be brought, in fact lawyers are reluctant to bring any claims that have a significant risk of not succeeding. Even if a case is assessed as having a 55% chance of success, many solicitors would not agree to take it on. As a result, a significant number of patients with cases that might succeed are not given access to this part of the justice system. The lack of public funding for representation at inquests into deaths that might be due to clinical negligence is also a potential factor in impeding access to justice and the upholding of human rights.

If the rule of law mandates that the law applies equally to all, why are there special rules for clinical negligence? As we shall see, the law as to whether a motorist is negligent is quite different from the law as to whether a doctor is negligent. Should that be so? Or are there objective differences between motorists and doctors that justify differentiation in treatment before the law?

In England and Wales the rule of law is supported by a highly developed system of laws and constitutional principles. In Part 1 of this book I try to put clinical negligence in context: who makes the law; are the rules affecting doctors and other healthcare professionals different from those that apply to other people; and where does clinical negligence sit alongside other laws that govern clinicians?

The laws of England and Wales have three principal sources: the common law, legislation, and international laws. Each source is relevant to clinical negligence litigation and so it is important to understand how each source operates.

Chapter 2: The Common Law

The laws of England and Wales can be roughly divided into two categories: criminal law and civil law. Criminal law is concerned with conduct deserving of punishment. The state creates and enforces the criminal law. The police investigate, the Crown Prosecution Service prosecutes, judges and juries decide on guilt or innocence, and judges pass sentence. The prison authorities and others enforce the sentences of the courts. The victims of crimes do not decide who should be prosecuted, tried and convicted. Except in very rare cases, they cannot bring criminal proceedings against another individual. They do not determine what punishments should be passed on the guilty.

Someone who breaks the criminal law commits an offence. They are innocent until proven guilty but they can be questioned, searched, arrested, and even detained in custody before their guilt or innocence is established. They are charged with having committed alleged offences and they can plead guilty or not guilty. When criminal charges are disputed there will be a trial, either in the Magistrates Court before a team of lay magistrates or a professional judge, or in the Crown Court before a jury at a trial presided over by a professional judge. Those found guilty will then face punishment – a sentence is passed by the court.

Civil Law

Civil laws are not punitive. They are largely designed to regulate our private transactions and disputes and to put right the wrongs we do to each other. They also serve to hold public bodies to account and to ensure that their decision-making is lawful. Both Parliament and the judiciary create the rules that form the body of civil law. The state facilitates access to the civil law and the courts enforce it. Individuals can bring civil claims against other individuals. The state therefore provides a structure of civil justice within which individuals can act to enforce their legal rights and seek redress.

An individual (being a person, a partnership or a company) will typically make a claim against another seeking compensation for a past wrong and/or an order that the other party shall do, or stop doing, some harmful or unlawful act. The individual bringing the claim is called a claimant (previously "plaintiff") and the person against whom the claim is made is the defendant. The claim is issued in court and the proceedings up to and including a trial will be governed by judges in the civil courts. Except in very rare circumstances, trials are heard by a single judge, not by a jury. If the claimant succeeds then the court orders the defendant to pay compensation to the claimant, or to act, or desist from acting, in a certain way.

Areas of civil law include those of equity and trusts, land law, administrative law, contract and tort. Contract and tort law are the areas of civil law relevant to clinical negligence. Contract law is founded on the premise that some promises are intended to have binding effect. Breaches of contracts cause loss and expense for which the law of contract provides remedy. Tort law is a body of legal rights, responsibilities and remedies, developed over many years by the courts, sometimes added to or adjusted by Parliament, all designed to offer protection and redress for individuals who suffer harm through the fault of others.

The law of tort covers a number of different, specific wrongs, including trespass, nuisance and negligence. Professional negligence is simply a particular form of negligence, and clinical negligence is one kind of professional negligence. Think of civil law as a tree with a trunk, larger branches and smaller branches. Clinical negligence is a smaller branch: it has features all of its own but has grown out of and is still attached to and dependent on the still larger branches of the law of negligence and the law of tort.

Criminal justice is a different tree altogether. It stands apart from civil justice and has its own structure, rules and practices. Each serves a different purpose.

The laws of the land do not regulate every single aspect of human behaviour, thank goodness. Amongst the most difficult decisions for legislators and the courts are those that concern the extent of the law's reach. Judges are not eager to apply the laws of contract to social arrangements between friends, for example. Non-malicious, accidental injury on the sports field will not often lead to the involvement of lawyers. Nevertheless, civil laws do cover a huge range of human conduct. Indeed, they have to cover an infinite variety of possible human interaction. The activities of professionals are certainly not immune from the civil law and the courts have developed the law of negligence specifically to apply to lawyers, accountants, building surveyors and other professional groups. Clinical negligence law applies the law of negligence to healthcare professionals. What used to be called "medical negligence" has now been widened to incorporate other clinicians such as nurses, sonographers, and physiotherapists. So the term now used is clinical negligence.

Common Law

Clinical negligence law is largely the product of the common law. That means that it is judge-made.

There are different levels of judicial seniority within the civil justice system.

Fig 1 shows the judicial hierarchy within the civil justice system. Only the more senior judges make or develop the law. This happens by way of a process known as judicial precedent.

Fig 1: The Judicial Hierarchy for Clinical Negligence

When a judge decides an important case they will give a written judgment that will be published and pored over by lawyers anxious for any sign of a change or refinement of the existing law. The helpful fiction is that judges do not change the law, they simply declare what the law is. However, the law does develop over time, and it has tended to become more expansive, to have a longer reach.

Once a judgment of the higher courts has been published it is called an "authority" and lawyers may bring that judgment to the attention of another judge in a later case. They "cite" the case. They are obliged to bring a court's attention to relevant "authorities" whether or not they are helpful to their own client's case. That is part of their duty to the court. Most often, however, the lawyer at court seeks to persuade the judge that the earlier judgment represents the law on the particular issue.

Clinical negligence cases are heard by judges in the County Court and the High Court. High Court judges hear the more serious and complex cases. The decisions of County Court judges are not influential on other courts. The decisions of High Court Judges do carry weight but other judges do not have to agree with them. A few clinical negligence cases each year reach the very highest courts: the Court of Appeal and the Supreme Court. The judgments of these courts are regarded as precedent decisions that are binding on the judges hearing subsequent cases in the County Court and High Court.

Sometimes a judgment by, say, a High Court judge might be referred to with approval by a Court of Appeal judge. This can elevate the importance of the High Court judge's decision.

Common law is to be contrasted with legislative law which emanates from Parliament, but the judiciary have an important role in interpreting legislation. Hence, the process of judicial decision-making and precedent can apply equally to the application of the written laws created by or under the authority of Parliament.

When considering a judgment and deciding whether it should carry weight or be binding on a judge in a later case it is important not just to look at the seniority of the judge who wrote the judgment, but also to identify the issues that the judge decided. Not everything a judge puts in their judgment should be taken into account by other courts, only those parts of the judgment that were central to the things that the judge was deciding. Other remarks by the judge do not carry so much weight. A judge might decide that a defendant had not been negligent, but that if they had been the judge would have held that they were liable to pay compensation for the claimant's shock and distress. That second part of the decision would not be part of the issue that determined the case.

So, case by case, the courts decide how certain issues should be approached and their powers deployed. By this process, the common law, including the law of clinical negligence is developed over time.

As we shall see in Part 2, the core principles of the law of clinical negligence have been judge-made. They are products of the common law.

Who are the judges who make the law? There are 12 justices of the Supreme Court, about 40 in the Court of Appeal, and about 100 in the High Court. Statistics published in 2015 showed that about 20% of the judiciary in the Court of Appeal and High Court were women. Of all judges, 53% of those under 40 were women, but only 13% of those over 60. Of all judges who declared their ethnicity, 6% declared their background as Black or Minority Ethnic. Roughly 65% of all judges had been barristers by profession and all but one in the High Court or Court of Appeal had been barristers. It is well known that a relatively small percentage of the senior judiciary were state educated. These are the men and women who make the common law. There are clearly arguments to be had about whether they should be more representative of society, but what we do have is a judiciary that is wholly independent of political and other special interests and that, at the higher levels, consistently demonstrates intellectual rigour and honesty.

Chapter 3: Legislation and Human Rights

Domestic Legislation

The courts not only apply and develop the common law, they also have to enforce legislation: the laws created or authorised by legislative bodies, most obviously the UK Parliament but also, for example, the National Assembly for Wales. There are different tiers of laws so created or authorised. Acts of Parliament, otherwise known as primary legislation, are passed after complex but well established procedures involving both Houses of Parliament. They include the Highways Act 1980 which imposes a duty on local highway authorities to maintain the highways under their control. Breach of that duty can create a liability on the authority to compensate a person who is injured by tripping over a dangerously raised paving stone. An Act of Parliament is also known as a statute. So, we refer to statutory laws or provisions.

Parliament may also delegate powers to create laws to ministers of the Crown, such as the Secretary of State for Health and Social Care, or to public bodies. The regulations, rules and orders made under such delegated authority have the force of law, just as do Acts of Parliament, but they are known as subordinate legislation because they are not subject to the full scrutiny of Parliament. Typically, secondary legislation is in the form of statutory instruments, such as various health and safety regulations governing the provision and use of protective equipment at work.

Legislation, whether primary or secondary, may or may not provide that breaches of legislative provisions give rise to civil liability. Some legislation, such as the Highways Act 1980 mentioned above, does allow for an individual to bring a claim for redress for breach of the legislation – in that case a failure to maintain the highway. Other legislation does not allow an individual to bring a claim for what is known as a breach of statutory duty. In such cases anyone wishing to bring a claim will have to rely on the common law rather than on there having been a breach of a legislative duty.

In the field of clinical negligence, legislation has always played a minor role. As we shall see in Part 2 the greater part of the law of clinical negligence is judge-made, common law. Nevertheless, there are some important legislative provisions that shape the law of clinical negligence. Examples of relevant primary legislation include:

The Law Reform (Contributory Negligence) Act 1945: provides that a claimant's compensation might be reduced where they, as well as the defendant, were at fault and their own negligence was responsible in part for their injury and loss.

The Law Reform (Personal Injuries) Act 1948: rules that when determining the compensation payable to a claimant for expenses, the courts shall disregard the possibility of avoiding those expenses by making use of the NHS.

The Fatal Accidents Act 1976: permits certain people to bring claims for the losses they have suffered as a result of the death of another. Typically, in clinical negligence claims, a partner or child of the deceased will use the Act to bring a claim for compensation where the deceased was a patient who has died as a result of unacceptable clinical error.

The Limitation Act 1980: sets down a three year time limit for claimants to bring a clinical negligence action, subject to a court's discretion to extend that period in circumstances set out in the Act.

The Social Security (Recovery of Benefits) Act 1997: lays down a scheme allowing the government to recover, from a compensation award, the sum equivalent to the state benefits paid to the claimant in respect of their injuries.

The Mental Capacity Act 2005: provides a framework for the assessment of a person's mental capacity to litigate and to manage the proceeds of litigation.

Some examples of secondary legislation relevant to clinical negligence litigation are:

The Civil Procedure Rules 1998: govern the detailed procedures to be followed when bringing or defending a clinical negligence claim.

Damages (Personal Injury) Order 2017: fixed the rate of return claimants are expected to achieve when investing their compensation, so as to help determine how future losses and expenses should be assessed.

Human Rights

International law plays a large part in some other fields of civil law, but not in clinical negligence. Nevertheless, one aspect of international law has featured increasingly in recent years. The UK had a significant role in the drafting of the European Convention on Human Rights, and the foundation of the European Court of Human Rights. The Convention and court have nothing to do with the European Union. Britain's exit from the EU will, in principle, not affect its relationship with the European Convention on Human Rights.

The Convention comprises "Articles" that protect fundamental rights such as the right to life (Article 2), and freedom from torture (Article 3). It also provides for the right to a fair trial (Article 6), and the right to family and private life (Article 8). These rights create obligations on the state, and on public authorities, including NHS Trusts. For many years British citizens had to travel to the European Court of Human Rights in Strasbourg to seek enforcement of their rights under the Convention. However, since the commencement of the Human Rights Act 1998, the domestic courts are required to enforce Convention rights, including, where appropriate, by way of an award of damages.

In *Rabone v Pennine Care NHS Trust* [2012] UKSC 2, the parents of a 24 year old woman whose death by suicide, it was admitted, would have been avoided but for the negligent management of her psychiatric condition, were awarded damages under the Human Rights Act for breach of their daughter's right to life by the NHS Trust responsible for their daughter's care and treatment. The Fatal Accidents Act 1976 did not provide them with any remedy because their daughter had been over the age of 18 when she died. They successfully contended that the Trust knew or ought to have known that their daughter's life was at real and immediate risk, and that the Trust did not take reasonable steps to protect her from suicide. The Trust owed an obligation under Article 2 of the convention to protect the life of Ms Rabone because she was a vulnerable patient under their control. In other healthcare cases public authorities have been found to have Article 2 obligations in respect of patients detained under the Mental Health Act 1983. In *Rabone*, the obligation arose even though Ms Rabone had not been formally detained.

Damages awarded under the Human Rights Act are not intended to be compensatory. Rather, they should reflect the extent of the failing in the obligation under the Convention, and the impact of the breach.

Healthcare failings could also result in liability for breaches of rights under Article 3 or Article 8. Where, however, domestic legislation (other than the Human Rights Act) provides redress, then recourse to the Human Rights Act is unnecessary and damages will not be awarded even where there has been a failure to comply with a Convention obligation.

Chapter 4: The Law of Negligence

Good Neighbours

One Sunday in August 1928 Mrs Donoghue went with a friend to the Well-meadow Café in Paisley. Her friend bought her an ice cream float: a delightful confection of ice cream swimming in a pool of ginger beer. The ice cream was brought to the table with a bottle of Stevenson's ginger beer. The bottle was opaque. Half of its contents were poured over the ice cream and Mrs Donoghue began to eat. After a while Mrs Donoghue's friend poured the rest of the ginger beer out of the bottle, whereupon a decomposed snail fell out. Mrs Donoghue became ill. She had not purchased the ginger beer so she had no contract with its manufacturer but she succeeded in a claim against them for damages in negligence. The court observed that the rule that you are to love your neighbour becomes, in law, a rule that you must not injure your neighbour. Your neighbour is anyone who would reasonably foreseeably be likely to be harmed by your acts or omissions. This case of the snail and the ginger beer marks the beginning of the modern law of negligence (see *Donoghue v Stevenson* [1932] UKHL 100).

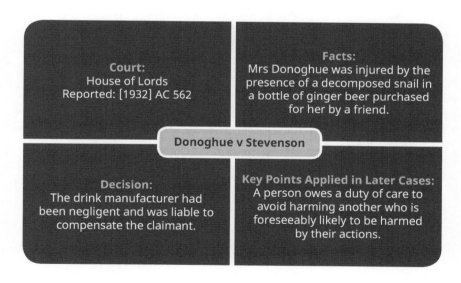

Court:
House of Lords
Reported: [1932] AC 562

Facts:
Mrs Donoghue was injured by the presence of a decomposed snail in a bottle of ginger beer purchased for her by a friend.

Donoghue v Stevenson

Decision:
The drink manufacturer had been negligent and was liable to compensate the claimant.

Key Points Applied in Later Cases:
A person owes a duty of care to avoid harming another who is foreseeably likely to be harmed by their actions.

Casenote 1

If it is reasonably foreseeable that your conduct could harm another, then you may well owe that other person a duty of care. You might then be liable to that other person in negligence if you act carelessly and thereby cause them harm.

Contracts create very specific obligations. If I purchase a car it is a term of the contract that it will be roadworthy. If you agree to pay me £500 to build a wall, and I build the wall to the agreed specifications, you cannot simply choose to pay me £250. That would be a breach of your binding promise, a breach of contract. There are many more situations in which conduct could cause harm to another without there being any contract in existence. Car drivers can harm other road users by driving carelessly, public institutions such as schools can cause harm to others for example by having unsafe premises. There are an infinite number of situations in which the neighbour principle might apply. The law of negligence allows us, as individuals, to seek redress for the civil wrongs of our fellow citizens and the institutions in society. We can use the civil justice system to put right the harm wrongfully caused to us by others. In the absence of the law of negligence we would have no personal redress against a careless driver who caused us injury. They might be fined by the criminal courts but we would have no legal means of obtaining compensation for the fact that we suffered great pain, had to have time off work, or had to be looked after for several months after the accident.

The law of negligence is therefore rooted in a fundamental principle that if we cause avoidable harm to another we should pay for it.

If we cause harm to another intentionally, we might face a criminal prosecution. At the other end of the scale we might cause harm unavoidably, even after taking great care not to do so. If so, unless the law imposes what is called "strict liability", we will not have to pay compensation to the injured person. If we cause harm negligently, however, we are liable to put right the harm caused.

Put simply, negligence is lack of care. It is always situation specific: whether a person has been negligent or not depends on all the circumstances of the case. Given the infinite variety of possible situations in which one person might unintentionally cause harm to another, the law of negligence cannot be codified. It would be impossible to set down in writing all the situations in which a person would be found to be negligent.

Instead the courts have developed a general approach, comprising a series of elements, which is then applied to the facts of each case.

The law of negligence imposes liability for financial harm in some limited circumstances but in this book we are more concerned with cases where negligence is responsible for physical harm – for what lawyers call "personal injury". Clinical negligence is a branch of personal injury law.

A person who, as a matter of law, has to provide redress to another for harm caused by their negligence is said to be liable in negligence. The necessary elements for liability in negligence are:

(i)   A duty of care ("duty");

(ii)   Breach of duty ("breach");

(iii)   Harm caused by the breach ("causation").

As we shall see, there are some tweaks, additions and caveats to those essential elements, but in every potential case of negligence, including clinical negligence, it is necessary to consider whether there was a duty, breach and causation.

A Duty of Care

The case of the snail and the ginger beer established that a duty of care may arise when it is reasonably foreseeable that your conduct is likely to cause harm to someone else. The courts apply a further test – were the parties reasonably proximate? So, where a driver carelessly collides with another road user, there will be a duty of care, but if a third person, with no connection with the injured party, comes along to the scene of the accident some time later and is so shocked by what they see as to suffer a psychiatric injury, there is insufficient proximity between the careless driver and the shocked witness. There is no duty of care.

Over time the courts have established that certain relationships give rise to a duty of care: car drivers owe a duty of care to other road users, employers owe a duty of care to employees, and doctors owe a duty of care to their patients. Where a judge is faced with a novel situation, which has not been the subject of a previous court decision, then they will ask: was there reasonable foreseeability of injury and a close or "proximate" relationship between the parties? If so, then a third question arises: would it be fair, just and reasonable to impose a duty of care? Only if all those three requirements are met will a duty of care be imposed.

The third element is important. Both in respect of those categories of cases where the courts have already established that there exists a duty of care, and those novel cases where the court has to consider whether a duty of care should be imposed, question of policy arise. When a court asks whether it is fair, just and reasonable to impose a duty of care on a person, that is a moral, political and economic question, not one of pure law. As such, and because the judiciary changes with the times, the common law has changed. There is a greater willingness to find that public officials and bodies owe duties of care. There is no absolute immunity for the police nor, regrettably, for barristers. However, when a person is carrying out a function which would be incompatible with a duty of care to a specific person affected by that function, then the courts will not impose such a duty. A barrister acting for a defendant in a criminal case will have to cross-examine witnesses. They owe certain professional duties and must adhere to a certain level of conduct when carrying out cross-examination, but their duty is to the court and to their client. They cannot be found liable in negligence for causing distress, even psychological harm, to a witness by reason of their cross-examination. And, as you have probably already guessed, judges are immune from being sued in negligence when acting in their judicial capacity. Their role is to dispense justice whether or not that causes distress or loss to someone affected by their decisions.

Similarly, a doctor who owes a duty of care to a particular patient will generally not owe a duty to another person whose interests may conflict with those of the patient. If a doctor has to assess whether a child has been abused and they do so negligently with the consequence that a parent is wrongly arrested, the doctor will not be liable to the parent. The doctor's duty is to the child not the parent and the interests of child and parent may well not coincide.

Public bodies can owe duties of care to those they serve and it is well established that NHS Hospital Trusts owe a duty of care to their patients. This liability arises because they assume responsibility for the patients they manage, and because the NHS Trust is responsible for the individual acts and omissions of its doctors, nurses and other staff (when an organisation is liable for the negligence of its staff it is said to be vicariously liable). A claim in negligence by an individual against a public body is nevertheless called a private law claim. This distinguishes it from a public law claim which is a challenge to the legality of a decision of a public body. Such challenges are usually pursued by way of a process known as judicial review. In this book, even though many clinical negligence claims are brought against public bodies within the NHS, we are not concerned with the legality of the body's decision-making but rather whether there is a liability on the body to provide compensation for the negligent performance of its functions. A challenge to a national drug pricing policy might be made by way of judicial review. When harm is allegedly caused by negligent over-prescription of a drug to an individual patient, the challenge is made by way of a private law claim for compensation.

It is always necessary to consider the scope of the duty of care. If A owes a duty of care to B, they are not liable for all the consequent damage to B, even if that damage would not have occurred but for A's negligence. A famous hypothetical example illustrating the importance of considering the scope of the duty of care is that of a mountaineer who consults his general practitioner before embarking on an expedition in the Alps. The GP negligently fails to identify a serious weakness in the mountaineer's knee. The mountaineer travels to the Alps and begins his climb only to be killed in an avalanche. The doctor owed his patient a duty of care. The doctor was negligent. Had it not been for the doctor's negligence, the mountaineer would not have met his death in the avalanche. Duty, breach and causation all seem to be present, so why is the GP not liable for the mountaineer's death? The answer is because it was not within the scope of the duty of care of the GP to protect the patient against being crushed in an avalanche. The GP was not being asked to advise about the weather forecast or the risks of avalanche in the mountains at that time of year. Even when A owes B a duty of care, it is always necessary to ask what kind of damage A must be careful to save B from suffering. The nature of the damage is relevant to the extent of the duty of care.

Certain relationships have long been held by the court to give rise to a duty of care and one of those is the relationship between a healthcare professional and their patient. It is considered axiomatic that just as a motorist owes a duty of care to other road users, so a doctor or nurse owes a duty of care to their patients. It is reasonably foreseeable that a doctor's acts or omissions are liable to harm their patients if not performed with care. There is a close relationship of proximity between doctor and patient. So, in the majority of clinical negligence cases the existence of a duty of care is not a contentious issue. Nevertheless, there are cases that test the extent of the scope of that duty, and occasionally there are questions about whether, in the circumstances of the case, the duty has arisen. Did a person actually become a patient of the doctor or of the NHS Trust he is suing? And does the duty of care extend to the relatives of patients or even further? These issues will be addressed in Part 2 of this book.

As the law of negligence has been developed by the courts, so certain general rules have emerged. Whilst the courts will more readily find a duty of care existed to avoid causing harm by actions, they have been more restrictive in relation to the duty to intervene to avoid harm. What kind of harm are we under a duty to avoid and what about those of our "neighbours" who are unusually vulnerable: do we owe duties of care to them?

Acts and Omissions

What is the nature of the duty of care? A motorist owes a duty to take care not to harm other road users. They must not perform actions that endanger others. Does the motorist also owe a duty to prevent other motorists causing harm? If it becomes clear that another motorist is not going to stop at a pedestrian crossing, do I owe a duty to sound my horn or otherwise warn the pedestrian about to cross the road?

Generally, I do not owe a duty of care to prevent harm to another that occurs through a source of danger I did not create. I might owe a moral duty to warn the endangered pedestrian, but I do not owe a legal duty to do so. However, there are exceptions to this general rule. In some circumstances I might have assumed a responsibility to protect B from the particular danger. This will often apply to doctors. If a patient comes into hospital with signs of sepsis, the doctor treating the patient did not create the danger but they assume a responsibility to take care to protect the patient from avoidable further harm. Another exception might be where a person has done something that prevents another from protecting the injured person against the danger. I might have negligently prevented an emergency 999 call being made to the fire brigade. I did not cause the fire that burned the injured person, but I prevented the fire officers from attending and putting out the fire. A third exception to the general rule that there is no duty to protect another from a danger which you have not created is where you have a special level of control or special status which creates an obligation to protect the other from that danger. This might apply to teachers who have control over young students or, in a clinical context, where a patient is under anaesthetic, or where a psychiatric patient is detained under the Mental Health Act.

What Kind of Harm?

The courts have, over time, refined their approach to liability for negligence depending on the kind of damage suffered. Where the damage liable to be suffered is bodily injury, the courts have taken a liberal approach to imposing a duty to take care to avoid causing such harm. A defendant will also be liable for the financial consequences where physical harm to another is caused. On the other hand where the damage is not physical harm but only economic loss, that is purely financial harm, the courts have restricted the potential for liability, imposing a duty of care only in cases where there is, for example, a particularly close relationship between the parties involved, an assumption of responsibility by the defendant and reliance by the claimant on the special knowledge or skills of the defendant.

The duty of care will extend to a person who was placed in physical danger by the defendant's actions and suffered a psychiatric condition but no physical harm. Where the harm is a psychiatric condition, such as Post Traumatic Stress Disorder, and the person making a claim was not physically endangered by the defendant's conduct, then the courts have imposed a particular set of conditions that have to be met before the defendant will be found liable. This applies to people witnessing a horrifying event that endangers a loved one. I shall discuss these so-called "secondary victims" within Principle 2 in Part 2. There are also cases where a defendant has been found to have owed a duty of care where the claimant was given false information which caused psychiatric injury. In one case a health authority was liable where the claimant was wrongly told that her new born baby had died. In another it was conceded that there was a duty of care when communicating information to former patients of a healthcare professional about the risk of HIV infection.

One issue that has troubled the courts has been the meaning of "harm". Where the harm suffered is only distress or is only the anticipation of possible future physical harm, the courts will not impose liability. People found to have plaques on the lining of their lungs, an indication that they have been exposed to asbestos and are therefore at risk of mesothelioma or other diseases, are not regarded as having suffered an injury. They may be anxious about the future but they have not suffered harm for which they are entitled to compensation.

Is having a child an "injury" or "harm" which a doctor, nurse or midwife has a duty of care to protect a patient against? The answer, explored in Part 2, is that they do, in certain narrowly defined situations.

Foreseeable Harm Suffered in an Unforeseeable Manner
It is not reasonable to expect people to guard against every risk of harm, however fantastical the chances of it occurring. On the other hand, if there is a foreseeable risk of harm from my conduct, it is no defence that the claimant befell such harm in an unexpected manner. If I leave an uncovered manhole in a pavement it is foreseeable that someone might fall down it and hurt themselves. It does not matter that the particular claimant fell down the manhole after having been distracted by witnessing a bank robbery on the opposite side of the road. My duty of care is to protect pedestrians against coming to harm due to my leaving an open chamber in the highway.

A Duty to Whom?
Persons
A person is under a duty of care to others when their conduct could fore-

seeably harm them. There is some circularity therefore in the question – to whom is the duty of care owed? The answer is that the duty is owed to everyone at a foreseeable risk of harm. "Everyone" means every person. Who is a person?

An unborn child is not, in law, a person. The House of Lords has held that a man who stabbed a woman in the stomach knowing her to be pregnant, was not guilty of murder when the trauma caused a very premature delivery and the child lived only a few months: *Attorney General's Reference (No. 3 of 1994)* [1998] AC 245. A stillborn baby is considered, in law, never to have lived as a legal person. Hence, although the law provides for a fixed "bereavement award" for parents of a child who, due to clinical negligence, dies only hours after birth, the award is not paid to parents of a stillborn child.

That is the position at common law, but Parliament has passed various laws which either allow the termination of the unborn child – The Abortion Act 1967 – or protect the unborn child, including the Congenital Disabilities (Civil Liability) Act 1976. Under section 1 of that Act:

"(1) If a child is born disabled as the result of such an occurrence before its birth as is mentioned in subsection (2) below, and a person (other than the child's own mother) is under this section answerable to the child in respect of the occurrence, the child's disabilities are to be regarded as damage resulting from the wrongful act of that person and actionable accordingly at the suit of the child.

(2) An occurrence to which this section applies is one which—

(a) affected either parent of the child in his or her ability to have a normal, healthy child; or

(b) affected the mother during her pregnancy, or affected her or the child in the course of its birth, so that the child is born with disabilities which would not otherwise have been present."

The Act further provides that, subject to certain exceptions, if a person would have been liable in tort to the parent, they shall be liable for injuries to the child.

Notwithstanding the common law position, in 1992 the Court of Appeal held in *Burton v Islington Health Authority* [1992] EWCA Civ 2 that a child born before the 1976 Act came into effect nevertheless had the right to sue for clinically negligent care when she was in utero, which caused her to suffer injury upon her birth. There are three elements of the tort of negligence:

duty, breach and damage. The damage occurred at birth, when the claimant became a legal person. She had a right to sue in negligence for her injuries even though the negligent acts had occurred before she was born. It appears that the court was satisfied that when the negligent acts were performed, it was reasonably foreseeable that they might result in the claimant being born damaged. Thus our "neighbours" comprise all legal persons and the unborn.

Philosophers may have contended that certain high-functioning animals have "personhood" but the courts of England and Wales would have no truck with that. It is true that in 2015 Manhattan Supreme Court Justice Barbara Jaffe granted a writ of habeas corpus on behalf of two non-human plaintiffs, Hercules and Leo, chimpanzees used for medical experiments at Stony Brook University on Long Island. However, on the following day the judge struck the words "writ of habeas corpus" from the order, in order to clarify that she had not meant to imply the chimpanzees were persons in law.

There is a duty to prevent harm to property too, and animals can be regarded as property, but personal injury can only be suffered by a person. It does not matter what age that person is, their ethnicity, gender or religion. All of us have the same legal protections. Nevertheless, not everyone is the same. Not everyone is at the same risk of suffering harm. How does the law of negligence treat those who are particularly vulnerable? And are there any people who forfeit the right to be protected from the negligence of others?

People Who Are Unusually Vulnerable to Suffering Accidental Injury
Some people might be at increased risk of coming to harm. So, a pedestrian with impaired vision might be at greater risk of falling down an open manhole. Although pedestrians with impaired vision might comprise a very small percentage of the pedestrians, it is reasonably foreseeable that they might walk along any particular pavement. Hence, the duty of care extends not only to able-bodied pedestrians but also to those who are disabled. It extends to children, to those who are not paying full attention and, if the pavement is outside a public house, to those who are drunk.

Likewise, restaurateurs have a duty to take care to avoid feeding peanuts to customers with peanut allergies, and doctors have a duty to all their patients, however rare the condition from which they are suffering.

Rescuers are not usually thought of as "vulnerable" but, through their role, they are exposed to an unusually high level of risk. If a person has created that risk negligently, for example by inadvertently setting fire to a building, and a fire officer is injured during the rescue effort, the negligent person will be found to have owed a duty of care to the fire officer.

People Who Are Unusually Vulnerable to Suffering Severe Harm if Injured

Once a duty of care is established, it is no defence to a claim for breach of that duty that the person injured suffered injury to a much greater extent than could have been anticipated. If a low hanging light fitting on a shop beam could foreseeably cause a head injury and a customer strikes their head on it, the shop owner is likely to be found liable even if the customer suffers a catastrophic injury because they have an abnormally thin skull. This is the so-called "eggshell skull" rule. Defendants have to take claimants as they find them.

On the other hand, if the adverse reaction of a person to certain conduct is so unusual as not to be reasonably foreseeable, then the defendant will not be found liable. It is foreseeable that a person mistakenly reported by a police officer as being involved in a road traffic accident might become distressed. But it would not be reasonably foreseeable that they would develop a psychotic illness. The kind of damage was not within the scope of the police officer's duty of care.

Who is Liable in Negligence?

We are all potentially liable in negligence. If the Prime Minister were negligently to run over a pedestrian whilst driving his car, he would be liable for the injuries he had caused. There are some exceptions. As we have already noted, judges have ruled that there can be no liability for the negligence of judges. To be more precise, judges cannot be sued for negligence committed in their roles as judges. The justifications for this are (i) the role of a judge is to dispense justice not to protect the parties in cases before them from distress or loss; (ii) to allow litigants to sue judges would create the potential for never-ending litigation; and (iii) there is a system of appeals against judicial decisions that are thought to have been wrong.

Barristers used to enjoy immunity from being sued in negligence in relation to court proceedings, but no longer. There is no blanket immunity for police officers. The police were recently found by the Supreme Court to be liable for injuries negligently caused to a bystander whilst officers tried to make an arrest in a public street. There is a concept of combat immunity, providing members of the armed forces with protection against being sued for their actions during combat with an enemy "on the battlefield", although the Ministry of Defence has been held liable in many other circumstances, including in relation to decisions concerning equipment and training.

The Crown Proceedings Act 1947 allowed actions in tort to be brought as of right against employees or agents of the Crown. In an article in the Guardian on 7 September 2017 Polly Toynbee aired the idea of bringing back Crown immunity for the NHS. Crown immunity represented the special social contract between citizen and service. If her suggestion were enacted then this book would not need a second edition. More seriously, it would mean that patients of private hospitals could sue for injuries caused by negligence, but not patients of the NHS. Patients who were deprived of their livelihoods due to avoidable errors by clinical practitioners in the NHS would have no recourse to compensation. Ironically this might be a boon for the private health sector. Why would patients risk suffering negligently caused harm within the NHS when they could not recover compensation for it? If they could afford to do so, they would tend to use the private sector instead.

Many of us will have signed waivers. I once did a bungee jump and signed away my right to sue the operator. However, under the Unfair Contract Terms Act 1977 any contractual term purporting to avoid liability for personal injury or death caused by negligence, is unenforceable.

Children who are too young to appreciate the consequences of their actions will not be liable in negligence. There is no specific age below which a child will have immunity, but generally it is thought that children under the age of eight do not have enough road sense to be regarded as careless if they step out in front of an oncoming car.

Vicarious Liability, Non-Delegable Duties and Joint and Several Liability
As well as humans, other entities can be treated as having legal personality, rights and liabilities. These "legal personalities" can sue and be sued. Limited companies, partnerships and other associations can have legal personality. If a shopper slips on an uncleaned floor in a Tesco supermarket, they can sue Tesco plc (public limited company).

Bodies such as limited companies or public authorities will naturally use employees or others to carry out their functions. Where an employee is negligent in carrying out a function in the course of their employment, the employer is liable for the harmful consequences of their negligence. This is the principle of "vicarious liability". In effect the courts extended the personal liability of the employer to cover the acts and omissions they required of their employees. An employer could not avoid liability by saying that it had passed responsibility over to an employee. That would create an artificial barrier to the effective enforcement of the law of negligence because employers tend to be insured or otherwise have the resources to pay compensation, but employees do not.

Over time vicarious liability has been found to apply to the negligence of employees who have not acted as required, but have carried out their role in an unauthorised manner. It has also been extended to cover non-employees, called "agents", who nevertheless have a relationship with the person who engaged them to act, their "principle", that is close to that of employee and employer.

For many years it was supposed that this principle of vicarious liability did not extend to cover the acts and omissions of third parties who were truly independent contractors. If you contract with a builder for the construction of an extension, and the builder sub-contracts the electrical work to an electrician whose negligence work later causes you to suffer serious injury through an electric shock, the builder is not liable in negligence. If the electrician has disappeared or has no resources to pay for compensation, that is bad luck on the injured person. More recently, however, the courts have found that in some cases a duty of care *is* owed and responsibility cannot be delegated to a third party so as to avoid liability. Hence, a local education authority that had a duty to provide pupils with physical education and had contracted out the provision of swimming teaching to a third party organisation did not avoid liability when a pupil suffered severe brain damage due to negligent supervision during a swimming lesson. Some duties can be delegated to others but, exceptionally, not if (i) the claimant is vulnerable or dependent; (ii) where due to the history of relations between the claimant and defendant, the defendant owes a duty to protect the claimant from harm; (iii) where the performance of that obligation has been contracted out to a third party that itself assumes custody and care of the claimant in respect of a function that is an integral part of the defendant's duty; (iv) where the claimant has no control over the exercise of the function; and (v) where the negligence was in relation to the core protective duty which the defendant delegated to another.

It is possible that more than one person can be liable for the injuries sustained by a claimant. Two defendants might have "joint liability" – they are both negligent for the same injury. Alternatively, two defendants might be liable for separate elements of the claimant's injuries – "several liability". A pedestrian is knocked over by negligent driver A and hits his head on the road surface. Driver B negligently drives over the pedestrian's legs when he is on the ground. A is liable for the head injury, B for the leg injuries. Drivers C and D each negligently enter a junction through red traffic lights and collide. C's car spins around and strikes a pedestrian causing head and leg injuries. In that case both C and D are jointly liable for all of the pedestrian's injuries.

Breach of Duty: The Standard of Care

A breach of duty can only occur if there is a duty of care. If a duty of care does exist then, as a generality, the duty is to take reasonable care to avoid causing harm. As we have already seen there may also arise a duty to take reasonable care to prevent harm. In either case the duty is to meet a standard of reasonable care. What does this standard of reasonable care entail? What does "reasonable" mean?

One of the common law's best known creations is the man on the Clapham Omnibus. He represents the reasonable person. He is prudent, he bases his decisions and judgements on all the facts available to him and he weighs all the evidence in the balance. He is a useful fiction for judges who have to decide whether the conduct of a person is reasonable or unreasonable. That is because the test of reasonableness is an objective one. It is not a test of what the claimant or the defendant thought was reasonable. Their subjective views do not determine whether the conduct in question was or was not to a reasonable standard.

The man on the Clapham Omnibus has been replaced in more recent times, sometimes with the commuter on the London Underground, but also with the less specific, more prosaic, "reasonable person". After all, this useful legal fiction should represent all people, not just men who take a certain bus route. The question for a court determining a negligence claim is whether the defendant's conduct met that of a reasonable person.

The standard of care is objective.

The standard is that of the reasonable person and it applies whether the actual person accused of negligence is timorous or bold and whatever their gender, ethnicity or religious beliefs. We are all taken to know what our duty of care is in any particular situation. A person cannot escape liability for their negligence on the grounds that they did not know that what they were doing was negligent.

The standard is that of reasonableness.

In negligence law the courts do not impose strict liability. The fact that injury resulted from A's actions does not, without more, establish that A was negligent. As an exception, in very rare circumstances, it might be that the fact of an accident speaks for itself: of course, the person driving ten miles the wrong way down a dual carriageway was negligent.

The test is applied to the particular circumstances of the case.

Whether or not a person was negligent – whether they fell below the standard of care expected of them – will depend on the facts of each particular case. The courts might consider previously decided cases where the circumstances were similar, but those cases will be guidance only and will rarely determine whether a particular defendant was or was not negligent. That is because the facts are never exactly the same in any two cases.

The defendant is not taken to be omniscient.

A defendant cannot be taken to know everything but they cannot wilfully turn a blind eye to what they do know, and they are expected to know what they ought to know. Two points can be made about a reasonable person's knowledge. First, a reasonable person should take into account everything they know, or ought to know. Ignorance is not a defence, but if a certain fact of which the defendant was ignorant would not have been known to them even had they made reasonable inquiry, then they are not to be judged on the basis of what they did not know. Second, a person's conduct will not be judged in retrospect. Naturally, their actions are in fact considered after the event, but the question is whether they acted to the standard of reasonableness given what they knew or ought to have known at the relevant time, and given the standards that applied at that time. Our conduct is not judged by later standards or with the advantage of knowledge that could only reasonably have been known after the event.

The court decides.

It is for a judge at court to decide whether a defendant was or was not negligent. Even in cases where expert evidence is required to assist the court to determine what happened and what the standards are within a profession, it is the court that decides. It decides what the facts were and it decides whether, on all the evidence, the defendant breached their duty of care.

In some cases it is easy to identify a breach of duty. If a motorist hurtles through a red traffic light at 90mph, everyone would agree that he has failed to exercise reasonable care. He has breached his duty to take care to avoid conduct that would be likely to harm other road users. In other cases, it is more difficult for the court to determine whether a person has been negligent. The task then is for the court to weigh up various relevant factors.

The reasonable person takes into account all the circumstances of the case, including:

(i)   the degree of risk that their conduct will cause harm;

(ii)   the extent of any harm that might be caused if the risk materialised;

(iii)   the importance and usefulness of the conduct in which they are engaged;

(iv)   the practicability, cost and consequences of altering their conduct so as to reduce or eliminate the risk.

For many years the courts have taken into account these four factors. It is plain to any judge or lawyer in the field of negligence law that if a person is engaged in important work, and that work carries with it a risk of injury to others, then the utility of the work is a factor to be taken into account. And so it was with some derision that the legal profession greeted the Social Action, Responsibility and Heroism Act 2015. By this Act, colloquially known as SARAH, Parliament insisted, amongst other things, that when considering whether a person has met a required standard of care, the court must take into account whether the person accused of negligence was "acting for the benefit of society". The Act was completely redundant because judges had been doing that all along. Quite obviously an assessment of whether a person is negligent will take into account whether they were acting for the benefit of society. And even if the courts had overlooked the obvious, the 2015 Act did not add very much to the earlier Compensation Act 2006 which provided that, when considering whether a person had taken steps to meet a required standard of care, the court must have regard to whether a requirement to take those steps might "prevent a desirable activity". These were statutes passed by governments of different political hues, designed to tackle the "compensation culture" but which did nothing more than articulate what the courts were already doing, and had been doing for decades. They were examples of what one legal commentator has called the "Something Must Be Done Act".

What the courts do, and have done for decades, is to determine the standard of care by reference to an objective, impersonal standard and then decide whether, as a matter of fact, the defendant has fallen below that standard and breached the duty of care that they owed to the claimant. As an example, consider the following reported case from over half a century ago.

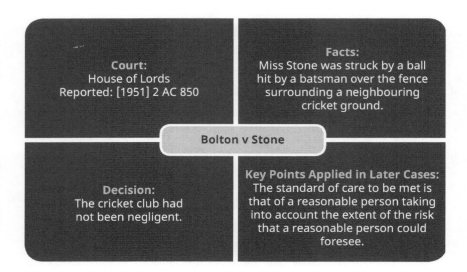

Court:
House of Lords
Reported: [1951] 2 AC 850

Facts:
Miss Stone was struck by a ball hit by a batsman over the fence surrounding a neighbouring cricket ground.

Bolton v Stone

Decision:
The cricket club had not been negligent.

Key Points Applied in Later Cases:
The standard of care to be met is that of a reasonable person taking into account the extent of the risk that a reasonable person could foresee.

Casenote 2

On 9 August 1947, during a game of cricket at the Cheetham Cricket Ground in Manchester, a batsman from the visiting team hit the ball for six. The ball flew out of the ground and hit Miss Stone, the claimant, who was standing outside her house in Cheetham Hill Road. The ball had travelled an impressive 90 metres from bat to claimant. The club had been playing cricket at the ground since 1864 and the road had been built in 1910. The ground was surrounded by a high fence. There was evidence that a ball had been hit that far out of the ground only very rarely, about six times in the previous 30 years – although some witnesses reported that balls were hit out of the ground a few times each season. The claimant argued that since the ball had been previously hit out of the ground it was reasonably foreseeable that it could happen again and that the cricket club was liable in negligence for her injuries.

The case was appealed to the highest court in the land, the House of Lords (the predecessor of the Supreme Court). The court decided that the cricket club was not liable. As one of the judges, Lord Normand, said, "It is not the law that precautions must be taken against every peril that can be foreseen by the timorous." The fact that a risk of injury could have been foreseen did not mean, of itself, that the defendant was negligent when that risk materializes. The probability of the risk occurring was highly relevant. Here, the chances of the ball being hit over the fence and so far as to reach Miss Stone's house were remote. The chances of injury occurring as a consequence were even more remote. The steps that would have to be taken to eliminate those risks would be significant and costly, or would even curtail the useful activity of playing cricket at the Cheetham Cricket Ground. Weighing those factors in the balance, there was no breach of the duty of care.

We should look at some more facets to this standard of the reasonable person.

When the Defendant is Young, Unskilled or Inexperienced
The test of reasonableness is objective but does the standard of care nevertheless vary according to certain characteristics of the person who is under a duty of care? Does the same standard apply whatever the age, experience or skills of the individual, or does the law vary the expected standard of care to reflect youth, inexperience and lack of skill or training?

As a general rule the standard is the same for everyone. It is an impersonal standard. It is useful to think of the role being performed by some generic person – driver, paediatrician, employer – rather than the individual actually fulfilling that role.

In one famous case a learner driver was held to the same standard of care as a qualified driver. Similarly, as we shall examine in Part 2, a junior doctor will be expected to meet the same standard as a consultant if they are carrying out the same role. It is no defence to a claim that a surgical procedure was negligently performed that the surgeon did not have the skills and experience to perform it. If so, they should not have undertaken the procedure at all. Naturally, not all doctors are held to exactly the same standard – the court would not judge a paediatrician by the standards of a neurosurgeon or vice versa. But it is the role that matters, not the particular characteristics or experience of the individual fulfilling the role.

Nevertheless, the standard of care is flexible and it does respond to particular factors, including some that are personal to the individual who owes the duty of care.

The age of the person can be of relevance. Indeed, as already noted, it is a rule of thumb that young children under the age of about eight, are not considered to be sufficiently mature to be able to weigh risk and understand the need to take care for the safety of others or themselves. Moreover, they are not usually insured and so are not worth suing. However, if a young person is put into a particular role, they are expected to meet the standards reasonably to be expected of someone fulfilling that role, even if they lack the experience of others.

When the Defendant is Particularly Skilled, Qualified or Experienced

This is an issue with obvious relevance to clinical negligence law. The reasonable person riding on the back of the Clapham Omnibus is not supposed to be possessed of any particular knowledge or skill. A professional, such as a lawyer or doctor, on the other hand, is expected to have a set of specialist skills and knowledge. It would be absurd for the law to require a consultant brain surgeon merely to exercise the care expected of the ordinarily prudent person on the street. Patients expect a higher level of care and skill than that. The law has therefore had to adapt the "reasonable man" test of negligence in the field of professional negligence. Clinical negligence is a branch of professional negligence and has developed its own principles, as we shall see in Part 2. Those who depend on professionals having certain skills and knowledge are entitled to expect those professionals to exercise a higher level of skill and care than non-professionals. But where there is no reliance on the special skills of the defendant, that expectation is not justified. Therefore, a car driver who has passed tests as an Advanced Motorist is not held to a higher standard of skill and care than everyone else when driving on the public road.

Identifying whether a clinician has been negligent is seldom as straightforward as identifying whether a motorist has been negligent. There is no equivalent of the Highway Code. There are no fixed, written rules applying to every situation. Even when treatment is not in accordance with clear national guidelines or local protocols, there may be a range of reasonable professional opinion as to whether departure from those guidelines and protocols is justified in certain situations. And there may be debate about what happened to a patient: what facts were available to the clinician, what was the nature of the patient's condition at the relevant time, and whether their death was due to poor treatment or to unpreventable natural causes.

Causation of Harm

The law of negligence is not punitive. It is designed to provide redress for those who suffer avoidable harm. Therefore, it is never sufficient only to establish breach of a duty of care. To succeed in a claim, the claimant also has to prove that they were harmed as a consequence of the breach.

In personal injury cases the courts require a claimant to prove that the breach of duty caused or materially contributed to their injury.

When does negligence "cause" harm? The courts answer that question by applying a "but for" test. But for the negligence, would the injury have occurred? If a pedestrian is knocked over by a car being driven at 40mph in a 30mph zone, then the court will ask whether, in the absence of the defendant driving his car at 10mph over the speed limit, the pedestrian would have safely crossed the road without suffering harm. If so, the excessive speed caused the accident and the consequential injuries. The driver was negligent in driving too fast and their negligence caused harm for which he, or his insurers, have to pay compensation.

If, however, the car would have collided with the pedestrian causing the very same injuries even if it had been driven at 30mph, then the pedestrian's claim will fail. The driver was negligent but his negligence did not cause the accidental injuries – they would have been suffered even without the negligence. The claimant cannot establish that but for the defendant's excessive speed they would not have suffered their injuries.

The courts recognise that harm is not always a case of all or nothing. The pedestrian might be able to prove that their injuries would have been less severe but for the negligence of the driver. Compensation will then be paid for the additional injuries suffered in consequence of the negligence.

As the case of the mountaineer killed by an avalanche shows, the "but for" test can result in an absurd finding of liability against a defendant unless the court also considers the scope of the defendant's duty. Just as the flutter of a butterfly's wing might ultimately cause a monsoon thousands of miles away, so a negligent action might set in train a chain of events leading to catastrophic consequences. For the want of a nail the battle was lost! As discussed earlier, the law avoids imposing liability for every consequence of an action by asking what was the scope of the defendant's duty of care.

What of "material contribution"? This is a concept that allows the courts to find a defendant liable where the established negligence made a more than negligible contribution to the claimant's injury. This is discussed in much more detail in Part 2. In the field of industrial disease the courts have adopted special rules to enable claimants suffering from asbestos related conditions to succeed in claims against their past employers, even though they cannot prove that the exposure to asbestos caused by a particular employer actually made a difference to their condition. Outside of these special rules, claimants do have to prove that they are worse off as a result of a defendant's breaches of duty, not merely that they might be worse off or that the defendant increased the risk of them being harmed. However, a claimant's condition or injury might have a number of different causes.

This can often happen in a medical context where a claimant might have had an underlying condition, but a doctor's negligence has contributed to the patient having a worse long-term outcome than would otherwise have been the case. If acts of clinical negligence made a more than negligible contribution to a claimant's avoidable injuries, then the person responsible for that negligence is taken to have caused the injuries.

Lawyers enjoy pretending to be philosophers by indulging in thought experiments about causation. Suppose two men shoot identical bullets from identical guns into a wood. A deer is killed. No-one can prove from which gun the bullet came. Is each man responsible for causing the deer's death, or neither? A person is knocked over by a negligently driven taxi in the middle of the night. There were no witnesses and all that the victim can recall is that the vehicle was a taxi and that it went through a red light on a pedestrian crossing. The town where the accident occurred has only two taxi companies. One has 20 red taxis, the other has five blue taxis. All 25 taxis were in operation in the town centre on the night in question. On the balance of probabilities was it the driver of a red taxi who was responsible for the collision, and if so, is the red taxi company liable to compensate the injured pedestrian?

There might be situations where simultaneous causes of an event each have equal causative potency. Other situations might arise where simultaneous causes have markedly different importance. On other occasions, there might be causes that are sequential rather than simultaneous. The causes might have a cumulative effect. Sometimes there might be more than one negligent causative agent. In yet others the effect of the negligent cause might be outweighed by a whole host of other non-negligent agents. And there is always the question of proof. In complex situations where scientific knowledge does not permit neat explanations, how can a court make findings that act A or omission B caused injury C?

It is beyond the bounds of this book to explore all the facets of causation in negligence law. We will however look at some of the difficult issues the courts have had to address in clinical negligence cases in Part 2.

Compensation

The outcome for a successful clinical negligence claim is an award of compensation. The object of the compensation is to put right the avoidable harm caused. Here, I shall explain the categories of compensation and then, in broad terms, the forms of awards that are made and how they are managed by or on behalf of claimants.

Categories of Compensation

If a defendant's breach of their duty of care to the claimant has caused harm to the claimant, then the defendant is said to be "liable" to the claimant. Whilst the courts have various powers, including making declarations and ordering defendants to act or cease to act in a certain way, liability in negligence invokes the court's power to order the defendant to pay compensation to the claimant.

The object of compensation is to provide restitution. Compensation – known as "damages" within the court system – is designed to put the claimant back in the position they would have been in had the negligence not occurred. Compensation is intended, as best as money can, to repair the avoidable harm caused to the injured party. Awards of compensation are not "payouts" or "wins" for claimants, let alone a "windfall" as sometimes described. They make good the damage suffered by the claimant.

If the claimant's injury has caused them to lose eight month's pay, then the defendant will be ordered to compensate for that loss by paying the equivalent net earnings to the claimant. The claimant has not gained anything at all but their lost earnings are restored to them.

Not all losses are so easily identified and calculated. In negligence claims compensation falls into three categories: damages for the injuries themselves, for the losses and expenses consequent on the injuries which have been suffered in the past, and for the consequential losses and expenses that the claimant will suffer in the future. In each case the claimant has to prove that the injury, loss and expense has been caused by the negligence. In clinical negligence cases that can be particularly hard to prove. Most clinical negligence claimants had an injury, illness or disability before the negligence that is the subject of the claim. It might be that they would not have returned to their usual occupation even if the negligence had not occurred. A claimant has to prove that their future need for help cleaning their house is due to the negligent management of their cardiac arrest, not the cardiac arrest itself. Disentangling the consequences of negligence clinical treatment from those of the underlying condition or illness can be very difficult, particularly when some underlying conditions have variable effects – they may wax and wane, or they may lead to deterioration with age.

Pain, suffering and loss of amenity

Compensation for the avoidable injuries themselves is awarded in accordance with convention. The levels of awards for different kinds of injury have developed over time in a similar way to how the common law itself has developed. If a claimant has suffered a severe hip fracture then the court will look at the amounts that have previously been awarded for severe hip fractures.

In the jargon used by litigators, compensation for the injuries themselves is called "general damages for pain, suffering and loss of amenity." "Pain" is intended to cover all physical injuries and disability. "Suffering" encompasses psychiatric injury and mental distress. "Loss of amenity" is the impairment of quality of life. Technically "general damages" includes not just compensation for the injuries themselves, but all future and other losses and expenses that cannot be precisely calculated. However, many litigators refer to "general damages" when they mean to refer to damages for pain, suffering and loss of amenity.

No two cases are identical even minor whiplash injuries, let alone in complex clinical negligence cases, but reports of previous awards are a very helpful guide. Judges will consider how many years have passed since the award made in a previous case, and take into account the effect of inflation. A judge also should consider how an award of compensation in the case before them would compare with awards in other cases where the injuries were different: does an award of compensation sit well within the whole structure of compensation awards for the range of different injuries? Would it be fair to award the claimant with a severe hip fracture more compensation than a claim who had lost an eye, for example? Judges do not merely consider the injuries in the abstract, they look at the practical impact of the injuries. Where the claimant has suffered multiple injuries then the judge will take into account that some of the damaging effects of each individual injury might overlap, and they will consider whether the overall award is a fair one. Clearly, the same injury might affect two claimants in very different ways. Will the individual claimant suffer harm from their injuries for two years or 20 years? What will be the effect of the injuries on their pastimes, their leisure activities, and their family and social lives?

In 2000 a book was published that has greatly assisted judges and litigants in the task of assessing, and predicting the assessment of, compensation for injuries. Now in its fourteenth edition, the punchily titled *"Judicial College Guidelines for the Assessment of General Damages in Personal Injury Cases"* is a short book, costing about £20, that sets out the ranges of awards that the courts make for injuries from a broken tooth to tetraplegia.

Referring to our earlier example of a hip fracture, the guidelines suggest compensation of between about £34,000 and £46,000 for a fracture resulting in a hip replacement which is only partially successful and will be likely to require revision surgery. If the claimant in the case before a judge was young, and likely to need two revision procedures, then they might award compensation towards the higher end of this range.

It is sometimes observed that the level of compensation for negligently caused injury is deliberately set at amounts that no rational person would exchange for enduring the injury in question. I doubt whether any reader would choose to have both legs amputated above the knee in exchange of compensation of between £211,000 and £247,000 (the range set out in the 14th edition of the Judicial College Guidelines).

The highest figure within the 14th edition of the Guidelines is £354,260. This is the top of the range of awards considered suitable for the most severe injuries, including someone who has suffered total blindness and deafness, for example.

A person who suffers lifelong severe cerebral palsy affecting all four limbs as a result of clinical negligence might receive an award of compensation for their injuries in the region of between £250,000 and £300,000.

Past losses and expenses

These are the losses and expenses, consequent on the avoidable injuries that have already been incurred at the date of the assessment of compensation. Typically, they include loss of earnings, expenses incurred travelling to and from medical appointments, the cost of any care and assistance the claimant has received, and the cost of equipment such as a wheelchair.

The claimant should keep an account of all the additional expenditure they have incurred, and of the losses they have suffered as a result of their avoidable injuries. They should keep receipts and other proof of the losses and expenses. Claimants are entitled to claim interest on these past losses and expenses, because they have been out of pocket as a result of having to incur them whilst not recovering compensation until later. The interest rate is set by statute and is the court's Special Account interest rate, currently only 0.5% per annum.

Where the claimant has received certain state benefits as a result of the injuries which are the subject of a claim, then a certificate of those benefits is produced which is called a Compensation Recovery Unit (CRU) certificate. Only those benefits that are received by the claimant up to the point of resolution of the claim or, if earlier, up to five years of the injury being sustained, appear on the certificate. The benefits on the CRU certificate have to be paid to the Department of Work and Pensions by the defendant. The defendant offsets those payments from the corresponding claims for past losses and expenses damages. If a claimant claims past loss of earnings of £20,000 but has had income support or a similar benefit related to loss of employment of £5,000, then the defendant is liable for damages of £20,000 but pays £5,000 to the DWP and £15,000 to the claimant.

Future losses and expenses

These are the losses and expenses that it is predicted, on the balance of probabilities, the claimant will suffer in the future as a result of their avoidable injuries. In a very serious injury case the categories of future loss may include the following: loss of earnings, the cost of care, a claim for the additional costs of suitable accommodation, aids and equipment, additional costs of going on holiday, the cost of physiotherapy, occupational therapy, and any other necessary therapeutic input. There is no interest claim for these costs because they have not yet been incurred. Very often, expert evidence is required to establish what the future costs are likely to be. It is common in larger claims to have an expert in care and occupational therapy to advise the court and the parties on the claimant's needs and the likely cost of providing, say, a care assistant for four hours a day, or the cost of a wheelchair and hoist. Where the claimant's current home is unsuitable because, for example, they can no longer use the stairs and access a toilet or bathroom, then an expert may be needed to advise on the costs of purchasing and adapting alternative accommodation.

In the next section I shall refer to the different forms of award for future losses and expenses, but in general the court needs to know: (i) how much the claimant is likely to spend or lose each year in the future as a result of the avoidable injuries; and (ii) over how many years those losses and expenses are likely to continue. In some cases, the injuries might have resolved by the time of the assessment of compensation, in which case there will be no future losses and expenses. In others, the expert evidence might point to a fixed time in the future by which it is expected the injuries will have resolved. That makes it easier to predict the future impact of the claimant's injuries. But if the injuries are permanent, then they will have consequences for the rest of the claimant's life and so the court will need to know for how long the claimant is likely to live.

The assessment of compensation for future losses and expenses not only has to take into account the claimant's life expectancy, but also the likely future variations in their condition, the risks of complications, deterioration and treatment. If compensation is designed to meet future costs of aids and equipment, how much will that equipment cost in the future? Indeed, what equipment will be available to purchase in, say, 40 years from now? And if the compensation is to be paid as a single lump sum, how will it be invested by the claimant and what returns will they enjoy on that investment?

The traditional approach to assessing compensation for future losses is on what is called a multiplier/multiplicand approach. The multiplicand is the annual expense or loss. The multiplier is a figure, arrived at with the assistance of actuarial calculations, by which the multiplicand must be multiplied to produce a single lump sum sufficient to meet those annual payments for the period needed. So, if a 40 year old woman with normal life expectancy needs £10,000 a year to pay for her care, then the multiplicand is £10,000. That's the easy bit. For the multiplier we have to turn to a set of tables, known as the Ogden tables, named after Sir Michael Ogden QC, a lawyer who chaired the working party that first produced them. To find the correct multiplier for a future lifetime loss we have to know: the gender of the claimant (female), their age (40) and the discount rate. The discount rate is a percentage figure, fixed by order of the Lord Chancellor, which is intended to reflect the real rate of return (that is the rate above inflation) that a claimant will enjoy on investing the award of compensation. There are various important assumptions that lie behind the setting of the discount rate such as whether the claimant is expected to invest in no or very low risk products, or whether they will be expected to have the benefit of investment advice and to take a little more risk with their investments.

For many years the discount rate was 2.5%. In 2017 the then Lord Chancellor determined that claimants investing compensation awards would receive negative real rates of return on their investments and set the rate at -0.75%. This change in the discount rate created shockwaves through the insurance industry and the NHS because it gave rise to a very large increase in the levels of compensation paid to claimants. In July 2019 the government revised the rate but kept it as a negative figure of -0.25%. Returning to our example, the multiplier for a 40 year old woman at a discount rate of -0.25% is 52.64, and the award becomes £526,400.

Forms of Award
The traditional form of award is a single lump sum payment.

Awards of compensation are assessed on a particular day, be it at the time of settlement of the claim or at trial, yet they have to meet the claimant's needs for the remainder of their lives. Therefore, they involve predictions: not only of the claimant's life expectancy, but also of the returns they will enjoy when investing their compensation award, and the likely future costs of care and equipment 20, 40, even sometimes 80 years ahead. An award of compensation has to cover variations in the claimant's condition and needs, including the risk of significant deterioration or the chance of substantial improvement.

Once compensation has been agreed or ordered by the court, the case is over. The compensation award is final and cannot be re-visited if some of the predictions that informed the assessment of the award prove to have been incorrect. A claimant cannot ask for more compensation if they deteriorate more than anticipated, or if they fail to secure alternative employment as had been expected. Likewise, a defendant cannot ask for reimbursement if the claimant enjoys an unexpected recovery, or secures a job with remuneration well above that which was foreseen at the time of the assessment of damages.

In large claims for lifelong injuries, if the claimant lives longer than expected, then the award of compensation will prove to have been insufficient. But if they die sooner than expected, even if it is for a reason unrelated to the negligence, then they will have been over-compensated and others who were not intended to be compensated – the beneficiaries of their estates – will receive the balance of any compensation award.

The only thing we can be certain of when trying to predict the future is that many of the predictions will be wrong. A single lump sum award of compensation is a blunt and inflexible instrument for meeting all future uncertainties and variables. Hence, some alternatives to the traditional form of award have been introduced. They are provisional damages, periodical payments and variable periodical payments.

Provisional Damages: this form of award is suitable where a claimant is at a material risk of a serious deterioration in their condition. For example, a claimant with a severe head injury might have a small but significant additional risk of developing uncontrolled epilepsy. If they did so, their uncontrolled epilepsy would result in significant increased future losses and expenses. Under a provisional damages award, a single lump sum award would be paid at the conclusion of the case on the assumption that the risk will not materialise, but the claimant would be entitled to return to court to seek further damages in the event that they were to develop uncontrolled epilepsy as a result of the defendant's negligence. The triggering deterioration or change must be identified at the time of the initial assessment of damages. So, provisional damages awards can only cover known unknowns – measurable risks of deterioration known to be a future possibility at the time of the resolution of the claim.

Periodical Payments: under this form of damages, items of future losses are agreed to be paid on an annual (or other regular) basis rather than by way of a single lump sum. Using again the example above of a 40 year old woman who will need to pay for care costing £10,000 per year for the rest of her life, the lump sum award, using actuarial tables, called the Ogden Tables, with the current discount rate set by the Lord Chancellor, was £526,400. Instead of making a lump sum payment for that amount, the parties might agree to the defendant making annual payments of £10,000 for as long as the claimant is alive. If she were run over by a bus four years after the award, the payments would cease. The defendant will have paid only £40,000, and have saved itself £486,400. But the claimant will have been fully compensated for her care needs during her life. On the other hand if the claimant were to outlive average life expectancy for 40 year old women, surviving to say age 100, then the defendant will end up paying much more than £526,400. But, again, the claimant will have been fully compensated for her care needs during her life. Periodical payment orders are carefully designed so that annual payments are index-linked. It is not the case, therefore, that the defendant would pay £10,000 annually to the claimant. Each year the amount would be re-calculated to reflect wage inflation for carers. Furthermore it is possible to build in more substantial future increases in the periodical payments. Where it is reasonably predictable that the claimant's future losses and expenses will rise or fall significantly at some point in the future, then a step change in the periodical payments can be agreed or ordered at the time of the assessment of compensation. If, therefore, the claimant in our example is likely to need increased care, costing £30,000 per annum from the age of 70, then a periodical payments order could be made for index-linked payments of £10,000 annually to the age of 70 and £30,000 annually thereafter for the remainder of her life. If she dies at 69, the defendant will never make a payment of £30,000 to her. If she lives to 100, the defendant will make 30 payments of £30,000, as well as 30 of £10,000 (subject to indexation).

Variable Periodical Payments: this form of award represents a combination of provisional damages and periodical payments, with a twist. Future losses are paid periodically rather than as a final award and on the assumption that the claimant will not suffer a serious deterioration in their condition, such as uncontrolled epilepsy, but with an entitlement to apply to the court for a variation in the periodical payments should that deterioration occur as a result of the defendant's negligence. Those changes which might trigger a variation must be identified in advance at the time of the assessment of damages, but the amount of the variation would be determined on later application, if the triggering change is then found to have occurred. The twist is that the defendant can also apply for a variation of the periodical payments in the event that the claimant enjoys a significant improvement in their condition. This is not a provision that applies to a provisional damages award. It only applies to a variable periodical payments award. On the face of it this very flexible form of award should be very useful in many cases, but it is very rarely used. Indeed, no case in which I have been involved has ever been resolved with the making of a variable periodical payments order.

Managing Awards of Compensation

Most claimants who receive awards of compensation are left to manage those awards for themselves. If they receive a very large amount of compensation, intended to meet their needs for the rest of their lives, they will need to invest the money wisely, but the defendant and the courts give no assistance in that regard. Claimants cannot claim money from the defendant to pay for the costs of taking investment advice. They are left either to manage the money themselves or to pay for advice out of the compensation which was in fact designed to meet their other costs and losses.

The fact that a claimant has received compensation for an injury through a negligence claim does not prohibit them from seeking state-funded provision for their needs in the future. Indeed, where a large award is made, claimants might be well advised to put the money in a personal injury trust so that the money will be disregarded for the purpose of assessing entitlement to any means-tested state benefits. The prospect of a defendant paying compensation to meet the costs of future care but then finding that the claimant receives similar care through the state resulted in a spate of cases in which defendants sought orders or other means by which claimants would be prevented from seeking, or would have to account to defendants for the receipt of, any future state provision. Those attempts have largely failed, the main reason being that the courts cannot be sure of the extent and quality of any state provision that might be made available to an injured or disabled claimant in the future. However, it might be true to say that many members of the public would think it odd that the NHS should be ordered to pay compensation for, say, additional transport costs caused by its negligence, and then the claimant could claim benefits from the state for their reduced mobility.

Where the claimant is a child under the age of 18, or where the claimant is an adult who lacks the mental capacity to manage their own affairs, then the compensation has to be managed on their behalf. For large awards, the compensation is most often managed under the supervision of the Court of Protection. This is a part of the court system that is concerned solely with the best interests of persons who do not have the capacity to make decisions for themselves about their own welfare, or about their finances. Adults over the age of 18 are all assumed to have capacity unless otherwise proved. The Mental Capacity Act 2005 sets out the criteria for assessing capacity. The principles underlying the Act are set out in section 1:

"The principles

(1) The following principles apply for the purposes of this Act.

(2) A person must be assumed to have capacity unless it is established that he lacks capacity.

(3) A person is not to be treated as unable to make a decision unless all practicable steps to help him to do so have been taken without success.

(4) A person is not to be treated as unable to make a decision merely because he makes an unwise decision.

(5) An act done, or decision made, under this Act for or on behalf of a person who lacks capacity must be done, or made, in his best interests.

(6) Before the act is done, or the decision is made, regard must be had to whether the purpose for which it is needed can be as effectively achieved in a way that is less restrictive of the person's rights and freedom of action."

A person's ability to make a decision for themselves, including in relation to managing money paid to them by way of compensation, is determined by reference to criteria set out in section 3:

"Inability to make decisions

(1) ... a person is unable to make a decision for himself if he is unable—

(a) to understand the information relevant to the decision,

(b) to retain that information,

(c) to use or weigh that information as part of the process of making the decision, or

(d) to communicate his decision (whether by talking, using sign language or any other means).

(2) A person is not to be regarded as unable to understand the information relevant to a decision if he is able to understand an explanation of it given to him in a way that is appropriate to his circumstances (using simple language, visual aids or any other means)."

As can be seen, there will be many claimants with brain injuries or mental illness who, whilst their decision-making capacity is impaired, will not be found to lack the capacity to make financial decisions for themselves. Thus, many claimants who might find it difficult to manage an award of compensation of, say, £500,000, or even as much as £5 million, will be left to manage that money for themselves. It is particularly important for solicitors to give the right advice to those litigants about how to manage their compensation.

I have long been struck by the paucity of research evidence as to how awards of compensation are actually spent. How often do claimants run out of money long before their need for continued expenditure ends? How many claimants invest their money unwisely? How often do claimants find they spend significantly more or less than was anticipated on their future care or accommodation? It is very difficult to find any evidence or research that provides convincing answers to these and other questions about what actually happens to compensation payments made in negligence claims.

Proving Liability in Negligence
The Burden of Proof
In negligence litigation, including clinical negligence cases, the claimant has to prove all the elements of their case: the existence of a duty of care, breach of that duty, and causation of injury. A defendant can defend the claim by defeating any one of these essential elements. If the claimant proves duty of care and breach but not causation, the claim fails.

Lawyers say that the burden of proof lies on the claimant. A defendant does not have to prove anything. It is the claimant who brings the claim and the claimant who has to prove it.

A claim, or any element of it, is proved by bringing evidence before the court. In some negligence cases this will be factual evidence only. In the vast majority of cases of negligent driving, the court will decide the case after hearing the accounts of the accident from those involved and any other witnesses, seeing photographs of the scene and perhaps some evidence about the damage to the vehicles involved. If the claimant suffered injuries there will be a medical report or two on the harm suffered.

In clinical negligence cases the court will hear evidence as to what happened (evidence of fact) and expert opinion evidence both as to whether the defendant has been negligent and as to whether the negligence has caused the claimant's injuries. The evidence of fact might include witness evidence – the recollections of the patient, healthcare professionals and others as to what was said at a consultation, what symptoms the claimant was feeling at a particular time and so on. It will also include documentary evidence from the medical records kept at the time. The extent of the expert opinion evidence will depend on what issues require to be determined.

A defendant might choose to admit part or all of a claimant's case. What a defendant admits, the claimant no longer has to prove. Alternatively, a defendant might contest all of a claimant's case. When contesting the claimant's case, a defendant can elect to deny an allegation, or not to admit it. A denial is stronger than a non-admission. A defendant will deny an allegation it thinks is wrong. It will not admit an allegation where perhaps it does not know, or cannot say, whether the allegation is right or wrong but requires the claimant to prove it.

The Standard of Proof

Whether an allegation is denied or not admitted, a claimant has to prove it. The standard of proof in negligence cases is the balance of probabilities. This is a lower standard of proof than the well-known criminal standard "beyond reasonable doubt". A claimant has to prove that, say, a doctor's negligence probably caused his below-knee amputation. It is more likely than not that the negligence caused the injury.

The civil standard of proof, on the balance of probabilities, means that it is never sufficient for a claimant to establish that a doctor "might have" been negligent, or that there was a "reasonable chance" that poor treatment caused their injuries. I have seen too many expert medical reports with the conclusions along the lines of "on the balance of probabilities the doctor's negligence may have resulted in the claimant's cardiac arrest." To a lawyer, that is a contradictory statement. "May have" indicates a degree of probability below 50%, whereas "on the balance of probabilities" indicates a probability over 50%.

This standard applies to past facts as well as to issues such as causation. There may be a dispute as to whether a surgeon warned a patient of a 5% risk that a proposed facelift operation would result in unsightly and permanent scarring around the ears. The patient says no such warning was given, the surgeon says it was. The judge at trial will have to determine, on the balance or probabilities, what was said. The patient has to prove, to that level of probability, that the warning was not given.

When it comes to issues such as causation, the court is often dealing in speculation. What would have happened if the warning had been given? Would the claimant have elected not to proceed with the facelift? It would be very difficult, in most cases, to prove beyond reasonable doubt what would have occurred in the absence of a defendant's negligence. The lower standard of the balance of probabilities is a more realistic level of proof, but it is not an easy hurdle to overcome.

When seeking to prove that a defendant was negligent the courts judge their conduct by what they knew or ought to have known at the time. In contrast, when assessing what actually occurred and whether the negligence caused injury, the courts will consider all the available evidence, even if it would not have been available at the time. Some evidence may come to light long after the events in question, but if it is relevant to determining what happened and whether the negligence caused the injury, it will be taken into account.

Defences to Negligence

Given that the burden of proving the essential elements of negligence – duty, breach and causation – lies with the claimant, defendants will often successfully defend a claim because the claimant fails to reach the standard of proof in relation to one or more elements of their case. The defendant may persuade the court that the evidence on which the claimant relies does not prove one or more of those elements, or the defendant may bring before the court its own evidence undermining the claimant's case on a key element. However, there are also some specific defences that a defendant can deploy to defeat a claim even if the claimant can prove the main elements. These specific defences require separate consideration.

Limitation

A negligence claim for compensation for injury must be begun no later than three years after the right to bring the claim has arisen. This is why those daytime television advertisements often ask: "Have you had an accident that was not your fault in the last three years?" I address the question of "Limitation" in more detail in Part 3.

The reason for having what is called a "limitation period" is that it would be unfair to potential defendants to have to defend claims going back many years when memories would not be fresh and documents might have gone missing. The limitation clock starts ticking once the right to bring a claim exists. That will often be the date of the negligence but not necessarily so. Thinking of the three elements of a negligence claim, the third – causation of harm – might not arise until days, weeks or even years after the breach of duty. A mechanic fails fully to tighten a wheel nut on 1 February, and the wheel comes off causing an accident on 28 April. In that case the right to bring a claim in negligence would not arise until 28 April. The claimant would have three years from 28 April to bring a claim.

Generally, in law ignorance is never a defence. What about the claimant who knows they are suffering pain or disability but does not know whether that is due to negligence? In such cases the limitation clock does not begin ticking until the person knows that they have suffered a serious injury (one that would be worth suing for) which is capable of being attributed to something the proposed defendant has done or has omitted to do. The claimant does not have to know that the conduct of the defendant was negligent. That, after all, may be something to be determined by the court after a trial. The parties will not necessarily know in advance of the court case what was or was not negligent. Knowledge of whether the act or omission was in fact negligent is irrelevant. But if the claimant has knowledge that their suffering is capable of being attributed to another's acts and omissions, then the clock will start ticking. The court will also assume that a claimant will make reasonable efforts to obtain professional help, for example from a solicitor, to find out whether their condition or injury might be attributable to another's conduct. Claimants have three years from the date when they had such knowledge, to bring a claim.

The time limit only applies to adults aged 18 or over. Therefore, a child injured at birth has until their 21st birthday to bring a claim. Nor does the time limit apply to adults who do not have the mental capacity, through brain damage or mental illness, to make decisions for themselves about matters such as whether to bring a claim for compensation. The limitation clock simply stops for such adults. Therefore there is, in effect, no limitation period for a child injured at birth who has suffered such severe brain damage that they will never be able to understand concepts such as a legal claim or that their condition might be due to the conduct of another person.

These rules about limitation periods come from an Act of Parliament – the Limitation Act 1980. The Act provides a safety net provision for claimants who miss the three year deadline. Section 33 of the Limitation Act provides that the court may disapply the three year limitation period if it is "equitable" to do so. In deciding whether it is equitable to allow a claim to be brought more than three years after the right to bring the claim arose, the court will consider all the circumstances including the strength of the claim, the effect of delay on the quality of the evidence in the case, and the conduct of the defendant after the right to bring the claim arose, including whether they have co-operated in any investigations.

Where someone dies as a result of another's negligence, their loved ones have three years from their death to bring a claim, but if the deceased's own claim for compensation for injury was already "out of time" before they died, then the right of their loved ones to claim dies with them and it cannot be resurrected by using the discretion to disapply under section 33.

The Claim Has Already Been Decided

It is a defence to a claim in negligence that a court has already decided it. Claimants cannot have the proverbial second bite at the cherry. This applies to particular issues in a case as well as the whole of the claim itself. If four passengers are injured in a road traffic accident and the first brings a claim in which the court decides at trial that drivers A and B are equally to blame for the accident, then the other three passengers are bound by that judgment. They cannot separately re-open the question of the liability of the drivers.

Consent

Very rarely a claimant will have fully consented not to bring a claim in negligence if they are harmed by the negligence of the defendant. The courts will not lightly make such a finding, but where that has been found to be the case, it provides the defendant with an absolute defence. This defence is usually referred to by a Latin phrase meaning "to a willing person, injury is not done". There are other legal principles that are often referred to by their Latin tags. Tempting though it is to use them, this book is about making the law clear, and so I will resist the temptation.

The claimant's knowledge of risk is not sufficient to make out the defence. They must also be willing to forego the right to make a claim if the risk materializes. So, a man who voluntarily rode pillion on a motorcycle ridden by an obviously very drunk rider, could not claim compensation for injuries sustained when the motorcyclist lost control and crashed into a tree.

Illegality

There are two aspects to this defence. If a person is engaged in illegal conduct when injured by the negligence of another, this can provide the defendant with a defence to an otherwise valid claim. So, if two bank robbers are engaged in blowing open a safe and one negligently sets off the explosives thereby injuring the other, the injured one will have difficulty in claiming compensation for their injuries. In one case that was decided at court, two burglars A and B were in a getaway car that crashed due to A's negligent driving. B's claim in negligence failed because of the defence of illegality. Illegality can also present a bar to a claim for compensation where the claimant seeks damages for the consequences of an illegal act committed by them but which would not have been committed had it not been for the defendant's negligence. If a negligently caused accident results in psychiatric injury to a claimant who, as a result of that injury, kills someone, then they are barred from recovering compensation for the time they spend in prison as a result of that killing. This defence is a matter of what is sometimes called "public policy". The court system, as a whole, should not take away liberty with one hand and give compensation for the loss of that liberty with the other. Even if the claimant had diminished responsibility because of the psychiatric injury caused by the defendant's negligence, the law may determine that they should be detained as a result of their act of manslaughter. As a question of policy therefore, the law should not compensate them for that detention.

Fundamental Dishonesty

In any negligence claim where the evidence is disputed, there is the potential for a judge to find that one or more witness has deliberately exaggerated or lied to bolster their case. Far more often than not, disputed evidence is resolved without a finding that a witness has been dishonest – it is much more common for witnesses to make honest mistakes – but some witnesses, including claimants, do give dishonest evidence to the court. A finding that a claimant has given dishonest evidence has always had two obvious consequences. First, the claimant will not succeed in that part of their claim that relies on the dishonest evidence. If that evidence concerns the very happening of an accident, say, then the whole claim will collapse. It is well known that road traffic accidents have been staged or fabricated purely for the purpose of bringing a compensation claim. The extent to which this is happening within the legal system is contested, but no-one would dispute that it does happen. A finding that the claimant is lying about having been involved in a genuine accident will lead to the claim being dismissed, usually with costs penalties and possibly referral of the claimant to the authorities with a view to criminal proceedings being brought against them. Similarly, even if the claimant has genuinely suffered injury as a result of the defendant's negligence, if they are then dishonest about the extent of their injuries or a particular aspect of their claim for compensation, then clearly they have put that part of their claim in jeopardy.

There is a second consequence of dishonesty: the impact of a finding of dishonesty on the credibility of the rest of a witness' evidence. If a judge cannot trust the claimant's word that their back pain has prevented them from working, why should they trust their word that the pain has prevented them from doing any housework? A finding that the claimant's evidence has been dishonest in relation to a part of their evidence can adversely affect the credibility of the whole of their evidence.

The extent to which a claimant's dishonesty adversely affects their credibility and their claim as a whole has always been left to the trial judge. Or it was, until section 57 of the Criminal Justice and Courts Act 2015 was enacted. By section 57, in a personal injury claim in which the claimant would otherwise be entitled to compensation, the court may dismiss their whole claim if the claimant has been "fundamentally dishonest in relation to the primary claim or a related claim".

Under this provision, the whole claim will be dismissed, including those claims that were honestly made. Claimants are punished for their dishonesty not merely by their dishonest claims being dismissed, but by their honest claims being dismissed also.

As you can imagine, lawyers have seized upon the phrase "fundamentally dishonest". What does it mean? When is dishonesty "fundamental"? Given that Parliament introduced the concept of fundamental dishonesty in the Act, you might expect it to have included a definition, but it did not. It has fallen to the courts to define the meaning of the phrase. The Court of Appeal has accepted a definition that fundamental dishonesty goes to the root of either the whole of the claim or a substantial part of the claim. The claim will have substantially depended upon dishonesty.

The court only has to be satisfied that there was dishonesty on the balance of probabilities, not beyond reasonable doubt. There is no similar sanction against defendants: a defendant who has been fundamentally dishonest in relation to their defence of part of the claim does not forfeit their entitlement to defend the remainder of the claim.

Contributory Negligence
The Law Reform (Contributory Negligence) Act 1945 provides that where a claim is made in negligence and the injuries suffered are partly the result of the fault of the claimant, then their claim shall not be defeated by reason of that fault, but the damages shall be reduced *"to such extent as the court thinks just and equitable having regard to the claimant's share in the responsibility for the damage."* Thus, contributory negligence is a partial defence and it arises only if the defendant is itself liable to the claimant. If a claimant's own negligence contributed to their injuries then their compensation will be reduced. In determining to what extent the damages should be reduced the court will consider both the blameworthiness of the conduct of each party and the causative potency of their conduct in relation to the injuries suffered. This will be reflected in a determination of a percentage reduction in the damages. In relation to road traffic accidents a rule of thumb has developed that an injured person who was not wearing a seatbelt will have their compensation reduced by 25% if they would have avoided all injury

had they worn one, and by 15% if they would have had less severe injuries. In other situations, the extent of the reduction will be very much within a judge's discretion. Lawyers will seek to predict what that reduction might be, if any, but there is no precise science to that exercise. It is not unheard of, but rare, for compensation to be reduced by more than 50% for contributory negligence.

I will discuss contributory negligence in the field of clinical negligence in Part 2 – it is a controversial issue.

Chapter 5: Other Branches of the Legal System

Acts and omissions that might constitute clinical negligence can also engage other branches of the legal system. These distinct forms of legal control include statutory provisions about defective products, the use of the criminal law, systems of regulation and Coroners' Inquests.

Clinical Negligence and Defective Products

Healthcare professionals often use drugs, prostheses, devices and other "products" which they trust are of satisfactory quality. What happens if a defect in one of those products causes harm?

The Medicines and Healthcare Products Regulatory Agency (MHRA) oversees the safety of medical products. It is beyond the scope of my duty, in this book, to set out all the rules and regulations governing the introduction of new drugs and devices, but a patient injured by a defective product can claim damages under the Consumer Protection Act 1987 which implements in England and Wales the Product Liability Directive 1985 (85/374/EEC) ("the Directive").

By section 2 of the Act, *"where any damage is caused wholly or partly by a defect in a product, every person to whom subsection (2) below applies shall be liable for the damage."* Those persons include the producer of the product. By section 3 of the Act, *"there is a defect in a product for the purposes of this Part if the safety of the product is not such as persons generally are entitled to expect; and for those purposes "safety", in relation to a product, shall include safety with respect to products comprised in that product and safety in the context of risk of damage to property, as well as in the context of risks of death or personal injury."* In considering what persons generally are entitled to expect the Act refers to a number of circumstances including how the product would be expected to be used and how it was marketed, but "all circumstances" should be taken into account, not just those specifically described in the Act.

What the public is entitled to expect may not accord with an individual's actual expectation, nor even general expectation. An entitlement to expect something is not necessarily the same as the actual expectation. It is for the court to decide, in all the circumstances, what the persons generally are entitled to expect. In *A v National Blood Authority* [2001] EWHC QB 446; [2001] 3 All ER 289, Mr Justice Burton said at [31]:

> *"the court decides what the public is entitled to expect... such objectively assessed...expectation may accord with actual expectation; but it may be more than the public actually expects, thus imposing a*

> *higher standard of safety, or it may be less than the public actually expects. Alternatively, the public may have no actual expectation – e.g. in relation to a new product."*

If the criteria in the Act are established, then liability follows even if there has been no negligence by the producer.

In a recent High Court case, *Gee and others v DePuy International Ltd* [2018] EWHC 1208 (QB), the 1987 Act was considered in the context of so-called "metal on metal" hip prostheses. Over 300 claimants brought a group action against the producers of a hip prosthesis, called Pinnacle Ultamet, alleging that it was "defective" within the meaning of the Act because it had a tendency to cause a soft tissue reaction around the hip known as an Adverse Reaction to Metal Debris ("ARMD"). The court warned against rigidity when determining whether a circumstance could be relevant to what the public was entitled to expect. The circumstances which could in appropriate cases be relevant included the avoidability of the harmful characteristic, the product's benefits, the involvement of a surgeon in selecting the product and advising the patient, regulatory compliance and warnings provided with the product. The public is not entitled to expect that a product which is known to have a potentially harmful characteristic will not cause that harm, especially if the product cannot be used for its intended purpose without incurring the risk of that harm materialising, as was the case with the Pinnacle hip. It created a risk but, compared with other prostheses that were on the market, there was no abnormal risk of damage associated with the defendant's product.

Product liability claims are often brought on behalf of a large group of affected patients. This is usually because: (i) it can take repeated failures of a product before it is recognised that there might be a defect; and (ii) the economics of litigation against large companies that produce drugs and medical devices mean that a claimant is unlikely to take on such a claim by themselves.

Clinical Negligence and the Criminal Law

The law of negligence is designed to compensate those harmed by the avoidable acts and omissions of others. If a doctor is found to have been negligent, they are not punished for it: they are ordered to compensate the victim to make good the harm they have caused. For hospital doctors and nurses, it is usually the Trust they work for that is the named defendant liable to pay the compensation.

Like everyone else, doctors and other clinicians are also subject to the criminal law. If a doctor intentionally kills someone they may be charged with murder. If they thump someone in the face they may be tried for assault. If they cause the death of another by being grossly negligent they may be found guilty of manslaughter. It matters not whether the victim of the crime is a patient or someone else, the criminal law applies equally.

The most infamous medical practitioner of modern times was Harold Shipman, a general practitioner found guilty of murdering 15 patients, but considered to be responsible for up to 250 deaths by the Inquiry chaired by Dame Janet Smith. He is the only British doctor to have been found guilty of murdering a patient.

An unwanted or unconsented to touching may be an assault. So, an operation performed without consent may constitute a serious criminal offence such as an assault causing grievous bodily harm. However, it is exceedingly rare for the criminal law to be deployed in such cases. If a patient contends that they did not consent to a particular operation they might bring a claim for compensation for negligent pre-operative advice, but it is unlikely that the police would be interested in making any arrests. Nevertheless, Ian Paterson, Breast Surgeon, was convicted of 17 counts of Wounding with Intent, contrary to section 18 of the Offences Against the Person Act 1861, together with three counts of Unlawful Wounding. He was sentenced to 15 years imprisonment, increased on appeal to 20 years.

In recent years the most controversial use of the criminal law in a clinical setting has been in relation to the offence of gross negligence manslaughter. This criminal offence is committed when a person is guilty of gross negligence – mistakes that are not simply honest errors or mere negligence, but are "truly exceptionally bad" – causing the death of another. Below, I look at the recent, controversial case of the death of a young boy, Jack Adcock, and the subsequent conviction of Dr Bawa-Garba for gross negligence manslaughter and her treatment by the regulatory authorities. Other high profile manslaughter prosecutions involving doctors have included those of Dr Adomako and Mr Sellu.

Dr Adomako's case went to the House of Lords and is reported at *R v Adomako* [1994] UKHL 6. He was an anaesthetist who, for six minutes during an operation, failed to notice that the oxygen supply to the patient had become disconnected from the ventilator. As a result, the patient suffered a cardiac arrest and died. The House of Lords upheld his conviction for gross negligence manslaughter, confirming that the elements of the offence that the prosecution had to prove were that:

- The defendant owed the victim a duty of care – this is the same test as for civil liability in negligence. Therefore, in the case of a doctor/patient relationship there will almost certainly have existed a duty of care.

- The defendant breached that duty – again, this test is the same as for civil liability.

- The breach caused (or significantly contributed to) the victim's death – this is not an unusual situation in clinical negligence cases.

- The breach was grossly negligent. This final element marks the difference between civil liability for negligence and criminal liability for manslaughter. The defendant's conduct must fall so far below the expected standard of care as to warrant criminal sanction. The terminology currently favoured by the courts is that the conduct must be truly exceptionally bad. Mere "honest errors" do not constitute gross negligence.

The other marked differences between civil and criminal liability in this context are: (i) anyone prosecuted for gross negligence manslaughter has the right to trial by jury, whereas civil liability is determined at trial by a judge alone; and (ii) whereas the standard of proof at a civil trial is "the balance of probabilities", at a criminal trial it is "beyond reasonable doubt". Judges now direct juries that they must be certain that the defendant is guilty before they can convict. Thus, for a doctor to be convicted of gross negligence manslaughter, a jury of 12 members of the public must be certain that a defendant's conduct was a breach of the duty of care they owed to the victim that was exceptionally bad.

Mr Sellu's case involved a patient, James Hughes, admitted to a private unit for a knee replacement. Post-operatively the patient developed abdominal symptoms and Mr Sellu was asked to review the patient. The patient subsequently died following a laparotomy, and it was alleged that there had been an inappropriate delay in the diagnosis and treatment of a perforated bowel. The experts for the prosecution and the defence disagreed over whether Mr Sellu's actions were reasonable in the circumstances. Nevertheless, the jury convicted him of gross negligence manslaughter and the trial judge sentenced him to two and a half years imprisonment.

Mr Sellu's conviction was quashed (overturned) on appeal to the Court of Appeal. Hence he was ultimately found to be innocent of the crime of manslaughter. The case is reported at *Sellu v The Crown* [2016] EWCA Crim 1716; [2017] 4 WLR 64. At a criminal trial the jury decides the guilt of the defendant, but the judge directs the jury as to the law. At Mr Sellu's trial the judge had directed the jury as follows:

> *"But your task is not just to decide whether Mr Sellu fell below the standard of a reasonably competent consultant colorectal surgeon, but whether he did so in a way that was gross or severe. Start with what Mr Sellu knew or ought reasonably to have known about the risk to Mr Hughes' life if the proper standards were not observed. Then ask yourselves, did Mr Sellu's behaviour or failure to act fall so far below those standards that his conduct and omissions deserves to be characterised as gross? When we want to weigh a physical object we can use scales marked in ounces or grams. There is nothing similar which I can give you to measure or weigh whether any negligence was 'gross'. As in many other contexts we leave it to juries to apply their own common and good sense to decide whether the line has been crossed. Using that good and common sense, it is for you to decide whether Mr Sellu acted in a way that was grossly negligent. If you conclude he was then it will mean that his behaviour was potentially criminal."*

The Court of Appeal determined that the direction was insufficient and had rendered unsafe the jury's subsequent guilty verdict. The jury had in fact passed a note to the judge after a day's deliberations. It read:

> *"Two questions: one, could we please be reminded of what we must or are to be deliberating on (evidence)? Two, are we to be deliberating legalities or are to be judging as human beings, lay people?"*

This note tended to expose a confusion as to the test the jury were being directed to apply. The Court of Appeal gave two examples of directions that trial judges might give in such cases.

> *"The first refers to "something which was truly exceptionally bad which showed such an indifference to an obviously serious risk of death of the deceased and such a departure from the standard to be expected as to amount to a criminal act and omission and so to be the very serious crime of manslaughter". The second similarly expresses the test in clear terms as follows:*

> *"It is not enough to found guilt that Dr [X] was negligent. You must be sure of gross negligence.*

> *Mistakes, even very serious mistakes, and errors of judgment, even very serious errors of judgment, and the like, are not enough for a*

*crime as serious as manslaughter to be committed. You must go on
to consider the nature of the carelessness or negligence, as you find it
to be. . . .*

*Over the years, in relation to the crime of gross negligence man-
slaughter, the courts have used a number of expressions to describe
the additional element which is encompassed in question five. The
key is that the breach of duty must be gross. It must have been so bad,
so obviously wrong, that, having regard to the risk of death involved
in it, it can properly be condemned as criminal, not in some technical
sense of the word like somebody might be regarded as a criminal if
they didn't have a light on the back of their bicycle, but in the ordinary language of men and women of the world. So, in this case,
when you are considering the conduct of Dr [X], you may find it
helpful to concentrate on whether the prosecution have made you sure
that the conduct of Dr [X], in all the circumstances you have heard
about and as you find them to be, fell so far below the standard to be
expected of a reasonably competent General Practitioner that, in your
assessment, his breach of duty – his negligence – should be characterised as gross in the sense that it was truly exceptionally bad and was
such a departure from that standard that it consequently amounted
to it being criminal and thus the criminal offence of gross negligence
manslaughter."''*

This phrase, "truly exceptionally bad" was adopted by the judge in the later
trial of Dr Bawa-Garba, discussed below, leading the Court of Appeal in
the appeal against conviction in that case to observe: *"Suffice to say that this
jury was (and all juries considering this offence should be) left in no doubt as to the
truly exceptional degree of negligence which must be established if it is to be made
out."* (see *Bawa-Garba v R* [2016] EWCA Crim 1841).

The crime of gross negligence manslaughter does not, of course, apply only
to doctors and other healthcare professionals. Mr David Duckenfield has
been tried for gross negligence manslaughter as a result of his role in the
management of the crowd at the 1989 FA Cup semi-final at Hillsborough
stadium in Sheffield. At the time of writing he is awaiting a re-trial after the
jury at his first trial could not agree on a verdict.

By the Corporate Manslaughter and Corporate Homicide Act 2007, Parliament created a criminal offence of corporate manslaughter whereby companies and organisations can be found guilty of corporate manslaughter
if serious management failures result in a gross breach of a duty of care
causing death. The Act provides that

"s. 1(1) An organisation to which this section applies is guilty of an offence if the way in which its activities are managed or organised—

(a) causes a person's death, and

(b) amounts to a gross breach of a relevant duty of care owed by the organisation to the deceased.

s. 1(3) An organisation is guilty of an offence under this section only if the way in which its activities are managed or organised by its senior management is a substantial element in the breach referred to in subsection (1)."

"Duty of care" and "breach" in the context of the Act have the same meaning as in common law negligence. The question of whether the breach was "gross" mirrors the test of that which applies to individuals charged with gross negligence manslaughter, but there is the additional requirement under section 1(3).

An NHS Trust can be charged with corporate manslaughter. In 2016 a criminal trial took place following the death of a patient, Mrs Cappuccini. The defendants were her anaesthetist, Errol Cornish, charged with gross negligence manslaughter, and the Maidstone and Tunbridge Wells NHS Trust, charged with corporate manslaughter. Both were acquitted on the trial judge's direction.

There have been few successful prosecutions under the 2007 Act, and fewer still convictions against large organisations such as an NHS Trust. The inherent difficulty in prosecuting a large corporate structure with manslaughter is that the "senior management" are further removed from the acts and omissions that might cause a death. Criminal convictions have been secured for "lesser" offences under Health and Safety legislation. In 2018 Southern Health NHS Foundation Trust was fined after the deaths of two patients Teresa Colvin and Connor Sparrowhawk. The Trust pleaded guilty to breaches of section 3(1) of the Health and Safety at Work etc. Act 1974. By section 3(1):

"It shall be the duty of every employer to conduct his undertaking in such a way as to ensure, so far as is reasonably practicable, that persons not in his employment who may be affected thereby are not thereby exposed to risks to their health or safety".

It is much easier for the prosecution to establish this offence than one of gross negligence manslaughter or corporate manslaughter. However, the fines imposed on Southern Health were considerable. For the breach relating to Teresa Colvin, the sentence was a £950,000 fine. For the breach relating to Connor Sparrowhawk's death, the sentence was a fine of £1,050,000. The fines are not payable to the patients' families, they go to the Treasury.

Clinical Negligence and Professional Regulation

Clinicians, be they surgeons, physicians, pathologists, nurses or physiotherapists, are "professionals". It is not as easy as it once was neatly to define what constitutes a professional, but the following characteristics apply to most professions. First, a profession usually has some entry requirements in the form of specific training or formal qualifications. Second, a profession will have a body or organisational structure to which members of the profession must belong. Third, professionals are usually expected to exercise independent judgement and to take responsibility for their decisions and actions – they are not required to complete routine tasks according to a prepared set of instructions. Many professionals will claim that this aspect of their role has been eroded in recent years: commercialisation and a managerial culture have served to marginalise the importance of the exercise of individual skill and judgement. Finally, professionals have to adhere to a set of rules and ethics, and can expect to be sanctioned or even barred from the profession for breaching them.

The table below shows the regulators for each clinical profession. Generally, the regulators have the power to control registration of members of the profession and to "erase" practitioners from the register that they control. The regulators below are overseen by the Professional Standards Authority.

Role	Regulator
Medical Practitioners	General Medical Council
Dental Practitioners	General Dental Council
Nurses and Midwives	Nursing and Midwifery Council
Art therapists, biomedical scientists, chiropodists/podiatrists, clinical scientists, dietitians, hearing aid dispensers, occupational therapists, operating department practitioners, orthoptists, paramedics, physiotherapists, practitioner psychologists, prosthetists/orthotists, radiographers, social workers in England, speech and language therapists	Health and Care Professions Council
Pharmacists	General Pharmaceutical Council
Opticians	General Optical Council
Osteopaths	General Osteopathic Council
Chiropractors	General Chiropractic Council

Taking the General Medical Council as an example, its functions and powers are set out in the Medical Act 1983. It controls a register of doctors that anyone can search online. The register not only shows whether the doctor is registered but also where and when they qualified, whether they are on a specialist register, such as for general surgery, and whether there are any conditions on their registration.

If a complaint against a doctor is made to the GMC which it considers relates to the doctor's fitness to practise or to public confidence in the profession, then the GMC may investigate the complaint and, ultimately, it may refer the matter to the Medical Practitioners Tribunal Service. This is an independent tribunal. Where allegations against a doctor are disputed the tribunal will hear evidence and determine whether the allegations are proved. The GMC brings the allegations, rather like a prosecutor at a criminal trial, and it has the burden of proof – the doctor does not have to prove that the allegations are untrue. However, unlike at a criminal trial, the standard of proof is the civil standard, on the balance of probabilities, not the criminal standard of certainty or beyond reasonable doubt. Therefore, there is no logical inconsistency in a doctor being acquitted of gross negligence manslaughter at a criminal trial, but being found guilty of gross negligence, on the same evidence, before the tribunal.

If the allegations are admitted or proved after a hearing, the tribunal will then determine whether, as a result of those admissions and findings, the doctor's fitness to practise is impaired.

An allegation of negligence might result in the doctor facing a fitness to practise hearing before the tribunal, but the GMC should only refer a doctor to the tribunal where the negligence had been gross or, perhaps, where there had been a series of negligent errors that, if proved, would demonstrate that the doctor's fitness to practise was impaired. Single acts of negligence, regarded as "honest errors", may not have ramifications for a doctor's general fitness to practise.

If a medical practitioners tribunal hearing finds that a doctor's fitness to practise is impaired, it can respond in a number of different ways depending on the seriousness of the findings and the steps needed to protect the public. It can elect to take no action, it can accept promises, known as "undertakings" from the doctor at the hearing or it can impose sanctions on the doctor, including putting conditions on their registration, controlling their activities as a practitioner, suspending them from practice, or erasing them from the register.

Clinical Negligence and Coroners' Inquests

The Coroners Court is a somewhat idiosyncratic corner of our legal system. Firstly, coroners are not chosen by the judicial appointments commission as judges are – they are appointed by local authorities. Secondly, coroners inquests are inquisitorial not adversarial. The coroner decides how to investigate a death, which witnesses to call and in what order. The coroner questions the witnesses before allowing any "interested parties" to do so. Coroners investigate deaths where there is reason to suspect that death was violent or unnatural, the cause of death is unknown, or the deceased died while in state detention. The coroner has to determine who the deceased was, where and when they died, and how they died.

Coroners sometimes sit with a jury and sometimes seek the assistance of an expert assessor, but most often they sit alone. They are not permitted to apportion criminal or civil liability for a death. However, amongst the conclusions a coroner is entitled to reach about how a person died is "unlawful killing". Coroners may also find that a death was aggravated by neglect – a term that means that there was a failure to give basic support necessary for life, not that there was negligence. Other conclusions include accident, natural causes or suicide. Alternatively, coroners may give a narrative conclusion, usually a paragraph or two describing how the deceased died, where a short form conclusion will not suffice.

There are several ways in which coroners might find themselves inquiring into deaths related to clinical negligence. Firstly, prisoners are detained persons who might die as a result of clinical negligence. Their deaths must be investigated by a coroner. Secondly, a detained psychiatric patient might die as a result of clinical negligence and a coroner should investigate their death. Thirdly, there may be many different circumstances in which a person suffers a violent or unnatural death, or their cause of death is unknown, where they have or may have died as a result of clinical negligence.

There is a strained relationship between clinical negligence litigation and Coroners Courts. This is because of a number of factors:

(1)   There is no automatic public funding for the representation of bereaved families at inquests. Indeed, at the time of writing, it is extremely rare for such funding to be provided although this is under review. This lack of support is all the more striking because state funding is, in effect, given for legal representation for NHS trusts or other public bodies. Hence, it is not at all unusual for an NHS Trust to have legal representation by a solicitor and barrister at an inquest at which the bereaved family has no representation, even in cases involving detailed and technical medical evidence.

(2)   Bereaved families may have engaged solicitors to represent them for a potential claim for compensation for clinical negligence. If so, it is highly likely to be on a conditional fee basis – no win, no fee. As such, the solicitor might represent the family at the inquest, but:

(a)   If the subsequent litigation is unsuccessful the solicitor will not be paid for their services, including those of representing the family at the inquest. Hence, many solicitors will not offer representation at an inquest unless and until they know there is a reasonably good chance of winning the subsequent litigation – something they are unlikely to know before there has been a proper investigation into the cause of death.

63

(b)   Even if the subsequent litigation is successful, the courts may well not order the defendant (for example an NHS Trust) to pay the family's costs of representation at the inquest. The courts are reluctant to order the payment of costs for representation at inquests unless it can be shown to have been necessary to the conduct of the litigation.

(c)   In cases where it is clear that there has been clinical negligence, an admission of negligence by the defendant prior to an inquest will mean that the family cannot show in subsequent clinical negligence litigation, that it was necessary to have representation at the inquest: the admission may leave the family with no need to prove that the acts or omissions they believe were negligent, did in fact cause the patient's death. I have known a few cases where an NHS Trust has made an admission of liability in a clinical negligence case on the eve of an inquest, leaving the family's representatives having to advise them that they would be unlikely to recover the costs of legal representation at the hearing. Families may therefore find themselves with no representation at very short notice.

(d)   The bereaved family may well want to probe the evidence of medical and other witnesses at an inquest in order to establish negligence, but the coroner (encouraged by representatives of other interested parties such as an NHS Trust) will prevent such questioning if it is designed to establish civil or criminal liability.

(e)   Interested parties at inquests can, with permission of the coroner, ask questions of witnesses but are not permitted to make submissions to the coroner about the evidence. For example, they cannot seek to persuade the coroner that one witness' evidence should be preferred over another's. This can lead to shorter submissions but more protracted questioning.

(f)   Coroners are generally loath to introduce expert evidence and are certainly adverse to a multiplicity of experts. Hence, there can be a tendency at inquests to rely on the opinions of doctors and other healthcare professionals who are also witnesses of fact and who are employed or engaged by one of the interested parties at the inquest. I have seen a clinical director of an NHS Trust give several opinions about the management by the Trust's employees of the deceased patient. This is not unusual at an inquest but it would be frowned upon at the trial of a clinical negligence claim, where opinion evidence may only be given by independent witnesses.

A coroner's conclusion is not binding on a court determining a clinical negligence claim. The evidence given at an inquest can be relevant at a later clinical negligence trial, but a witness might give different evidence at a trial and be able to explain why they have done so. Nevertheless, an inquest can be a very important influence on the course of a subsequent clinical negligence claim. Therefore, the parties at an inquest do try to probe and expose evidence not only with a view to persuading the coroner to reach a particular conclusion, but also to help establish their credentials for the pending clinical negligence action. Inquests can become a dry run of the trial to come. They are not intended to be adversarial contests between warring parties, but that is what they can easily become. The fact that one party does not have legal representation does not prevent an inquest becoming a contest, it just makes the battle more one-sided.

Chapter 6: Case Study – Dr Bawa-Garba:
Negligence, Inquest, Manslaughter and Erasure

Introduction

The case of Dr Bawa-Garba and the death of her young patient, Jack Adcock, has provided many headlines and opinion pieces, both in professional journals and in newspapers. This case demonstrates how acts of clinical negligence can lead to other court proceedings such as inquests, criminal prosecutions, and professional regulatory processes. The case has divided opinion, seemingly pitching many in the medical profession against patients and patients' advocates, and exposing a wide rift in mutual understanding. Alongside many well-informed publicised opinions on the case, there have been as many that have been ill-informed. There has been widespread confusion about the role of the criminal courts, regulators and the civil justice system of compensation for negligence. It seems fitting therefore to conclude Part 1 by exploring the details of this tragic case.

The facts

Jack Adcock, aged six, was admitted to the Children's Assessment Unit (CAU) at Leicester Royal Infirmary on 18 February 2011 following a referral from his GP. Jack had Down's syndrome and a known heart condition. He had been having diarrhoea and vomiting, difficulty breathing and his lips were blue.

Dr Hadiza Bawa-Garba was a specialist registrar in year six of her postgraduate training (ST6). She had an unblemished record. She had only recently returned from maternity leave and this was her first shift in an acute setting. She was the most senior doctor covering the CAU, the emergency department and the CAU ward that day. She was working a double shift.

Dr Bawa-Garba saw Jack on the CAU at 10:30. He was receiving supplementary oxygen and Dr Bawa-Garba prescribed a fluid bolus and arranged for blood tests and a chest x-ray. At 10:44 the first blood gas test was available and showed a high lactate reading. The x-ray was available at around 12:30 and showed evidence of a chest infection.

Dr Bawa-Garba was heavily involved in treating other children, including a baby that needed a lumbar puncture. At 15:00 Dr Bawa-Garba reviewed Jack's x-ray and prescribed a dose of antibiotics which were administered by nurses about an hour later.

Dr Bawa-Garba had requested blood tests at 10:45 but did not receive the results until about 16:15. This was due to a failure in the hospital's electronic computer system. Dr Bawa-Garba spoke to a consultant – a more senior doctor – at about 16:30 and she raised with him the fact that Jack's blood results had included a high level of CRP. She raised the diagnosis of pneumonia but did not ask the consultant to review Jack in person and he did not do so. She told the consultant that Jack's condition had improved and he was bouncing about.

Jack was on enalapril for his heart condition and it ought to have been discontinued. When she wrote up the initial notes Dr Bawa-Garba neglected to record that it should be stopped and he was given his usual evening dose by his mother at about 19:00.

At about 19:45 Jack collapsed and a little later a 'crash call' went out. Dr Bawa-Garba responded and on attending mistakenly thought Jack was another patient and called off the resuscitation. Within two minutes her mistake was identified and resuscitation was recommenced.

At 21:20 Jack died.

The Cause of Death

I take this from the judgment of the Court of Appeal, criminal division ([2016] EWCA Crim 1841):

> *"When Jack arrived and was admitted to the Unit at about 10.15 am, he was unresponsive and limp. He was seen by Sister Taylor, who immediately asked that he be assessed by the applicant, then the most senior junior doctor on duty. For the following 8-9 hours, he was in the Unit, under the care of three members of staff; at about 7.00 pm, he was transferred to a ward. During his time at the Unit, he was initially treated for acute gastro-enteritis (a stomach bug) and dehydration. After an x-ray he was subsequently treated for a chest infection (pneumonia) with antibiotics. The responsible staff were Dr Bawa-Garba and her two co-accused* [two nurses].

> *In fact, when Jack was admitted to hospital, he was suffering from pneumonia (a Group A Streptococcal infection, also referred to as a "GAS" infection) which caused his body to go into septic shock. The sepsis resulted in organ failure and, at 7.45 pm, caused his heart to fail. Despite efforts to resuscitate him (which were initially hampered by the mistaken belief that Jack was a child in the "do not resuscitate" or DNR category), at 9.20 pm, Jack died.*

It was accepted that even on his admission to hospital, Jack was at risk of death from this condition (quantified as being in the range 4-20.8%). The expert evidence, however, revealed the clinical signs of septic shock which were present in Jack (cold peripheries, slow capillary relief time, breathlessness and cyanosis, lethargy and unresponsiveness). In addition, raised temperature, diarrhoea and breathlessness all pointed to infection being the cause.

The cause of death given after the post mortem was systemic sepsis complicating a streptococcal lower respiratory infection (pneumonia) combined with Down's syndrome and the repaired hole in the heart."

Clinical Negligence

Although there is no public record of any judgment in civil proceedings for clinical negligence, there would be a strong claim that there were breaches of the duty of care owed to Jack Adcock during the hours before his death, and that those breaches were causative of his death. Any civil claim would be made against the NHS Trust that employed or engaged Dr Bawa-Garba and the other nursing and medical personnel. The Trust would also be responsible for any failings in the computer system insofar as they affected Jack's care. On the facts set out above most if not all judges in a civil claim would have found the NHS Trust liable. However, the claim would have been for a bereavement award under the Fatal Accidents Act and funeral expenses – total compensation of less than £20,000 for the avoidable death of a young child. The case, if brought (and I have no idea whether any claim was brought) would be likely to be resolved by an admission and offer from the defendant Trust at an early stage and without any exploration of the evidence or issues at court. As we have seen a claim for compensation against the Trust, even if admitted, would not constitute any inquiry into what had gone wrong. It would not constitute a disciplinary process against those responsible or lead to a determination of guilt.

The Inquest, Criminal Charges and Interim Regulatory Proceedings

It seems that although the matter was referred to the police, initially Dr Bawa-Garba was informed by the police that she would not face any criminal charges.

On 23 July 2013 a coroner's inquest began into Jack Adcock's death. It was adjourned after evidence was adduced at the inquest that prompted a change of heart by the police and a decision to commence a criminal investigation. As noted above, a coroner must not attribute civil or criminal liability. Nor should an inquest prejudice potential criminal proceedings. Once the police decided to investigate the coroner rightly adjourned the inquest.

On 1 December 2014, after a lengthy investigation, the Crown Prosecution Service brought charges for gross negligence manslaughter against Dr Bawa-Garba and two nurses involved in Jack's care: Isabel Amaro and Theresa Taylor. Dr Bawa-Garba was then subject to regulatory proceedings. These were not on a final basis – that would await the outcome of the criminal process. In the interim she was initially suspended for 18 months, but following review by the High Court that was reduced and she was allowed to practise but subject to conditions. The Nursing and Midwifery Council took interim action against Nurse Isabel Amaro.

The Criminal Trial

The criminal trial of the doctor and two nurses took place at Nottingham Crown Court in October and November 2015. As we have noted, at a criminal trial the prosecution has to prove the defendant's guilt beyond reasonable doubt. A jury decides whether the defendants are guilty. The judge directs the jury as to the law to be applied. There has been much comment on the evidence given at trial, mostly by people who were not present. An objective but short account can be found in the judgment of the Court of Appeal referred to above. The court set out the prosecution case against the doctor as follows:

> " .... the case for the Crown was that all three members of staff contributed to, or caused Jack's death, by serious neglect which fell so far below the standard of care expected by competent professionals that it amounted to the criminal offence of gross negligence manslaughter.

> In respect of Dr Bawa-Garba, the Crown relied on the evidence of Dr Simon Nadel, a consultant in paediatric intensive care. He considered that when Jack, as a seriously ill child, was referred to her by the nursing staff, Dr Bawa-Garba had responded, in part, appropriately in her initial assessment. His original view was that her preliminary diagnosis of gastro-enteritis was negligent but he later changed that opinion on the basis that the misdiagnosis did not amount to negligence until the point she received the results of the initial blood tests, which would have provided clear evidence that Jack was in shock. As to the position at that time, however, Dr Nadel's evidence was that any competent junior doctor would have realised that condition. His conclusion was that had Jack subsequently been properly diagnosed and treated, he would not have died at the time and in the circumstances which he did.

To prove gross negligence, the Crown therefore relied on Dr Bawa-Garba's treatment of Jack in light of those clinical findings and the obvious continuing deterioration in his condition which she failed to properly reassess and her failure to seek advice from a consultant at any stage. Although it was never suggested as causative, the Crown pointed to her attitude as demonstrated by the error as to whether a DNR ('do not resuscitate') notice applied to Jack.

In somewhat greater detail, the particular failings on which the prosecution case rested were, first, what was said to be Dr Bawa-Garba's initial and hasty assessment of Jack (at about 10.45-11 am) after receiving the results of blood tests which ignored obvious clinical findings and symptoms, namely:

i) a history of diarrhoea and vomiting for about 12 hours;

ii) a patient who was lethargic and unresponsive;

iii) a young child who did not flinch when a cannula was inserted (to administer fluids);

iv) raised body temperature (fever) but cold hands and feet;

v) poor perfusion of the skin (a test which sees how long it takes the skin to return to its normal colour when pressed);

vi) blood gas reading showing he was acidotic (had a high measure of acid in his blood indicative of shock);

vii) significant lactate reading from the same blood gas test, which was extremely high (a key warning sign of a critical illness);

viii) the fact that all this was in a patient with a history which made him particularly vulnerable.

The second set of failings on which the prosecution rested related to subsequent consultations and the proper reassessment of Jack's condition. More particularly, these were that Dr Bawa-Garba:

i) did not properly review a chest x-ray taken at 12.01 pm which would have confirmed pneumonia much earlier;

ii) at 12.12 pm, did not obtain enough blood from Jack to properly repeat the blood gas test and that the results she did obtain were, in any event, clearly abnormal but she then failed to act upon them;

iii) failed to make proper clinical notes recording times of treatments and assessments;

iv) failed to ensure that Jack was given appropriate antibiotics time-ously (more particularly, until four hours after the x-ray);

v) failed to obtain the results from the blood tests she ordered on her initial examination until about 4.15 pm and then failed properly to act on the obvious clinical findings and markedly increased test re-sults. These results indicated both infection and organ failure from septic shock (CRP measurement of proteins in the blood indicative of infection, along with creatinine and urea measurements both indica-tive of kidney failure).

Furthermore, at 4.30 pm, when the senior consultant, Dr Stephen O'Riordan arrived on the ward for the normal staff/shift handover, Dr Bawa-Garba failed to raise any concerns other than flagging the high level of CRP and diagnosis of pneumonia. She said Jack had been much improved and was bouncing about. At 6.30 pm, she spoke to the consultant a second time but did not raise any concerns.

Before parting from the history, two further details need to be added, neither of which caused Jack's death. First, having been transferred to a ward (Ward 28) and, thus, out of Dr Bawa-Garba's care, Jack received what had been his usual dose of enalapril (for his unrelated conditions) from his mother shortly before he fatally collapsed. This was entirely understandable and known to the medical staff on the ward. In fact, Dr Bawa-Garba had deliberately not prescribed enal-april as she was aware (accurately) that it could lower blood pressure, particularly in a dehydrated child. It was agreed at trial that enal-april should not have been given and may have contributed to Jack's death although it did not cause his death.

The second detail is that for a short while, Dr Bawa-Garba had a mistaken belief that Jack was a child for whom a decision had been made not to resuscitate: this was because she mistook Jack's mother for the mother of another child. Although this was said to be indica-tive of the degree of attention or care that Jack was receiving, it was underlined that this had no material or causative impact."

Therefore, the most eye-catching error – the direction to stop resuscitation – was not part of the prosecution case against Dr Bawa-Garba for manslaughter because it did not contribute to Jack Adcock's death.

As for the administration of enalapril, the judge directed the jury that if it thought that the administration had caused Jack's death, irrespective of any acts or omissions of the defendants, then none of the defendants were guilty of manslaughter.

The Court of Appeal's judgment also sets out the doctor's defence to the charge of manslaughter. She denied any gross negligence. In particular:

> *"i) Dr Bawa-Garba had taken a full history of the patient and carried out the necessary tests on his admission;*
>
> *ii) At 11.30-11.45 am, Jack was showing signs of improvement as a result of having been given fluids (although it was agreed that this improvement had not been documented). There were also clinical signs of improvement from the second blood gas results which were available at 12.12 pm; Jack had been sitting up and laughing during the x-ray and reacted to having his finger pricked.*
>
> *iii) Dr Bawa-Garba was correct to be cautious about introducing too much fluid into Jack because of his heart condition.*
>
> *iv) A failure in the hospital's electronic computer system that day meant that although she had ordered blood tests at about 10.45am, she did not receive the blood test results from the hospital laboratory in the normal way and she was without the assistance of a senior house officer as a consequence. The results were delayed despite her best endeavours to obtain them. She finally received them at about 4.15pm.*
>
> *v) Dr Bawa-Garba had flagged up the increased CRP infection markers in Jack's blood to the consultant, Dr O'Riordan, together with the patient's history and treatment at the handover meeting at 4.30pm. The consultant had overall responsibility for Jack.*
>
> *vi) A shortage of permanent nurses meant that agency nurses (who included Nurse Amaro) were being used more extensively.*
>
> *vii) Nurse Amaro had failed properly to observe the patient and to communicate Jack's deterioration to her, particularly as Dr Bawa-Garba was heavily involved in treating other children between*

> *12 and 3pm (including a baby that needed a lumbar puncture). The nurse also turned off the oxygen saturation monitoring equipment without telling Dr Bawa-Garba and, at 3 pm, when Jack was looking better, the nurse did not tell her about Jack's high temperature 40 minutes earlier or the extensive changing of the nappies.*

> *viii) Dr Bawa-Garba had prescribed antibiotics for Jack at 3pm as soon as she saw the x-ray (which she agreed she should have seen earlier), but the Nurses failed to inform her that the x-rays were ready previously and then failed to administer the antibiotics until much after she had prescribed them (an hour later).*

> *ix) At 7 pm, the decision to transfer Jack to Ward 28 was not hers and she bore no responsibility for the administration of enalapril:*

> *x) The mistaken belief that Jack was a "DNR" was made towards the end of her 12/13 hour double shift and was very quickly corrected. It was agreed that her actions in attending with the resuscitation team and communicating this made no difference, although that incident would have been highly traumatic for Jack's family."*

Dr Bawa-Garba gave evidence in her own defence and the jury was informed of the fact that she had an unblemished record and no criminal convictions. She relied on references as to her character. Evidence was given that she had worked a double shift that day (12/13 hours straight) without any breaks and had been doing her clinical best, despite the demands placed upon her. She also relied on supportive expert evidence to the effect that septic shock was difficult to diagnose and Jack's case was complicated because the symptoms of sepsis were subtle and not all the classic signs and symptoms were present. Dr Bawa-Garba also relied on the fact that Nurse Amaro had delayed in administering antibiotics, that there had been problems with the computer system, and that it was not she who had administered the enalapril.

A great deal of concern has been expressed by doctors and others about the use at trial of Dr Bawa-Garba's own written reflections on the tragic events of Jack Adcock's deaths. Doctors are encouraged to keep written reflections in a so-called e-portfolio as part of their learning process, but if those reflections can be used as evidence against them in a criminal trial then that would provide an obvious incentive not to commit anything into writing. Such a practice might protect the doctor but it would hinder opportunities to learn from mistakes. However, Dr Pallavi Bradshaw from the Medical Protection Society which represented Dr Bawa-Garba, wrote on GP Online in February 2018 that: *"at no time during Dr Bawa-Garba's criminal trial was her e-portfolio reflection statement presented to the court or jury as evidence."* Further, the judge at the criminal trial: *"was clear from the start that reflections were irrelevant to the facts of the case and that no weight should be given to any remarks documented after the event."*

Other commentators have expressed concern that an investigation into the failings in Jack Adcock's care, which identified systemic failings and errors by other healthcare professionals, was not put before the jury. However, failings by others do not absolve a defendant of guilt. Dr Bawa-Garba's own barrister agreed that this report should not go before the jury. As the trial judge directed the jury:

> *"You may or may not think that the hospital itself was at fault, but you must set those feelings aside. Your role is not to choose between various people who may have played a part in Jack's death. It is not your job to decide whether these three defendants or any of them come top of that list or to try to rank them. Rather you must focus on the specific elements of manslaughter which the Crown must prove in relation to each of the defendants."*

The jury was directed by the court that to convict Dr Bawa-Garba and the other two defendants, they had to be sure, in relation to each, that they had been guilty of gross negligence and that their negligence had caused or significantly contributed to the shortening of Jack's life. In directing the jury as to the test of gross negligence the Court of Appeal was fully satisfied that the jury had been *"left in no doubt as to the truly exceptional degree of negligence which must be established if it is to be made out."* Indeed, Dr Bawa-Garba, who was represented by a QC throughout the criminal proceedings, did not ultimately seek to appeal the judge's direction as to what constituted gross negligence.

The jury at the criminal trial returned guilty verdicts against Dr Bawa-Garba and Ms Amaro. The ward sister, Ms Taylor, was found not guilty. The Court of Appeal refused permission for Dr Bawa-Garba to appeal the verdict because there was no arguable case that there had been any errors of law.

Dr Bawa-Garba was sentenced for the offence of gross negligence manslaughter. The judge took into account all the mitigation put forward on her behalf and passed a sentence of two years imprisonment suspended for two years. This meant that provided the doctor did not commit any further crimes within two years, her sentence of imprisonment would not be triggered. However, if she were to commit a further criminal offence then she would not only be sentenced for that offence, but also the suspended prison sentence for manslaughter would be enforced.

Suspension and Erasure

The criminal proceedings having been concluded, the GMC brought professional regulation charges against Dr Bawa-Garba to a final hearing before the Medical Practitioners Tribunal. The tribunal was faced with a doctor who had been found guilty by a jury of gross negligence manslaughter. The first question for the tribunal was whether Dr Bawa-Garba's fitness to practise was thereby impaired. It does not appear that this was disputed by the doctor and the tribunal found that her fitness to practise was impaired. Accordingly, the tribunal went on to consider what sanction it should impose on her. It will be recalled that sanctions include imposing conditions on practice, suspension from the register or erasure from the register (striking the doctor off the register). The tribunal determined that the appropriate sanction was one of 12 months suspension subject to review. It rejected the GMC's contention that Dr Bawa-Garba's name should be erased from the register, deciding that "striking the doctor off" would be a disproportionate sanction.

The GMC has a right to appeal decisions of the Medical Practitioners Tribunal to the Divisional Court – part of the Queen's Bench Division of the High Court – and it did so. The judgment of the Divisional Court is at *General Medical Council v Bawa-Garba* [2018] EWHC 76 (Admin). The court held that the tribunal had been wrong to impose a sanction less than erasure. The court noted that under the Medical Act 1983 the GMC must pursue the objective of protection of the public which involves maintaining public confidence in the profession and promoting and maintaining proper professional standards. The court held that in addressing the question of sanction the tribunal failed to give due respect to the jury's finding at the criminal trial. It held:

> *"Full respect had to be given by the Tribunal to the jury's verdict: that Dr Bawa-Garba's failures that day were not simply honest errors or mere negligence, but were truly exceptionally bad. This is no mere emotive phrase ... nor were her mistakes mere mistakes with terrible consequences. The degree of error, applying the legal test, was that her own failings were, in the circumstances, "truly exceptionally bad" failings. The crucial issue on sanction, in such a case, is whether any sanction short of erasure can maintain public confidence in the profession and maintain its proper professional standards and conduct. We consider that ... the Tribunal's approach did not respect the true*

force of the jury's verdict nor did it give it the weight required when considering the need to maintain public confidence in the profession and proper standards."

Instead, the court held, the tribunal:

"... reached its own and less severe view of the degree of Dr Bawa-Garba's personal culpability. It did so as a result of considering the systemic failings or failings of others and personal mitigation which had already been considered by the jury; and then came to its own, albeit unstated, view that she was less culpable than the verdict of the jury established."

It was not for the tribunal to re-run the criminal trial and to reach a different conclusion from the jury. The jury's finding was determinative of the doctor's guilt for an offence of gross negligence manslaughter. She was guilty of truly exceptionally bad failings, even given all the mitigating circumstances. The tribunal should have imposed a sanction on that basis and nothing short of erasure would meet the gravity of the failings and the case.

Dr Bawa-Garba appealed that decision to the Court of Appeal. Her appeal was successful. The case is reported as *Bawa-Garba v The General Medical Council & Ors* [2018] EWCA Civ 1879. The Court of Appeal began its judgment by saying that: *"The central issue on this appeal is the proper approach to the conviction of a medical practitioner for gross negligence manslaughter in the context of fitness to practise sanctions under the Medical Act 1983 ("MA 1983") where the registrant does not present a continuing risk to patients."* Notwithstanding her errors, and the jury's finding that they had constituted gross negligence, it was agreed that Dr Bawa-Garba did not present a continuing risk to patients. The Court of Appeal noted that there was a significant difference between the role of the criminal court, and the role of the regulatory tribunal:

"... there was a fundamental difference between the task and necessary approach of the jury, on the one hand, and that of the Tribunal, on the other. The task of the jury was to decide on the guilt or absence of guilt of Dr Bawa-Garba having regard to her past conduct. The task of the Tribunal, looking to the future, was to decide what sanction would most appropriately meet the statutory objective of protecting the public pursuant to the over-arching objectives in section 1(1A) and 1(B) of Medical Act 1983, namely to protect, promote and maintain the health, safety and well-being of the public, to promote and maintain public confidence in the medical profession, and to promote and maintain proper professional standards and conduct for members

of the profession."

The Court of Appeal held that the Divisional Court had been wrong to suppose that the tribunal had ignored or undermined the jury's verdict by imposing a sanction to suspension rather than erasure.

> *"Undoubtedly, there are some cases where the facts are such that the most severe sanction, erasure, is the only proper and reasonable sanction. This is not one of them. Once it is understood that it was permissible for the Tribunal to take into account the full context of Jack's death, including the range of persons bearing responsibility for that tragedy and the systemic failings of the Trust, as well as the other matters relied upon by Dr Bawa-Garba, and that the Tribunal plainly had in mind its overriding obligation to protect the public for the future ... it is impossible to say that the suspension sanction imposed by the Tribunal was not one properly open to it and that the only sanction properly and reasonably available was erasure."*

Therefore, the Divisional Court had been wrong to interfere with the decision by the tribunal to suspend Dr Bawa-Garba. The tribunal's decision should stand.

Aftermath of the Case

This case prompted Jeremy Hunt, then Secretary of State for Health, to order a review of gross negligence manslaughter led by Professor Sir Norman Williams. The report was published in June 2018, before the Court of Appeal's decision to uphold the tribunal's suspension of Dr Bawa-Garba. The recommendations included removal of the power of the GMC to appeal decisions of the Medical Practitioners' Tribunal, and steps to achieve consistency of approach to cases of suspected gross negligence manslaughter by healthcare professionals.

Speaking to the House of Commons Health Select Committee in October 2018, Sir Robert Francis QC raised a more fundamental point about gross negligence manslaughter. It was, he observed, a criminal offence where the courts relied entirely on the jury to determine whether the facts constituted a crime. Remember the jury's questions at the trial of John Sellu? That jury was clearly troubled by the same point. At a trial of theft, the jury would be directed as to what elements of the crime had to be proved for them to return a guilty verdict. If, after hearing the evidence, the jury found that the defendant had taken property belonging to another, intending permanently to deprive the other of that property, and had done so dishonesty, then they would find the defendant guilty of theft. The jury would not have to decide whether overall the defendant's conduct was worthy of being treated as a crime. At a trial of gross negligence manslaughter, the jury does have to determine some of the facts – did the defendant fail to follow up an abnormal blood test or fail to administer medication when they should have done so? But, they are then asked to determine whether the conduct of the defendant fell so far below an acceptable standard as to be "truly exceptionally bad", and therefore to constitute the crime of gross negligence manslaughter. This is a judgement, and it is bound to lead to variation from jury to jury. It might be added that when someone has died as a consequence of the conduct of a healthcare professional, and the jury is asked whether the conduct was "truly exceptionally bad", then in one sense, the obvious answer is *"of course it was: someone died"*. The very fact that someone died who should not have died might well lead some jurors to conclude that what happened was indeed "truly exceptionally bad".

In reaction to this case many from the medical profession have implied that the actions of Dr Bawa-Garba, if not common, were not so exceptional. *"I know of no colleague who hasn't reacted with the thought: "There but for the grace of God go I.""* wrote Phil Whitaker in the New Statesman. The BBC reported that Dr Peter Wilmshurst, a Midlands-based cardiologist, wrote to the GMC to ask them to investigate him. *"I've made clinical mistakes including delayed diagnosis and errors in treatment,"* he said. *"Some sick patients died. I suspect that many would have died anyway but in some cases my errors are likely to have contributed to poor outcomes and some patient deaths ... I therefore feel obliged to ask the GMC to investigate my clinical practice over the last 40 years to see whether I should be struck off the medical register."*

This reaction demonstrates a view from the profession that is very distant from the view of the jury in Dr Bawa-Garba's case. Perhaps a jury is more representative of the views of the public as a whole. If the profession would not condemn the failings of a doctor whom a jury has found guilty of truly, exceptionally bad negligence, that suggests a gulf between public expectations and professional perception. Many doctors view Dr Bawa-Garba's failings as being "honest mistakes" which should not have resulted in criminal prosecution. Clearly, Dr Bawa-Garba did not intend to cause harm, let alone to cause the death of Jack Adcock. To that extent her failings might be described as "honest mistakes". But if we are to have an offence of gross negligence manslaughter – such as was used in 2018 successfully to prosecute food retailers who caused the death of a young woman to whom they supplied food containing nuts after they had been warned that she was allergic to nuts – then it will cover those who did not intend to cause harm but whose conduct was so negligent as to deserve criminal sanction.

Perhaps the offence should only apply to someone who is found to have had no regard to the life of another? The concept of "not caring" whether someone's life is imperilled by one's actions carries with it the right degree of culpability that should be needed for a criminal conviction of manslaughter. However, it is very difficult to prove a state of mind of wholesale disregard for the safety of others.

Some in the profession have suggested that juries should not be trusted with "complicated" cases involving negligence in a healthcare setting, or that there should be immunity from prosecution for gross negligence manslaughter for healthcare professionals. But why should the healthcare profession enjoy special treatment? Shouldn't the rule of law apply equally to all? Surely there has to be a role for the criminal law in the field of healthcare, and not just for murderers such as Harold Shipman? There must be cases where a healthcare professional has been so reckless as to the life of their patient that gross negligence manslaughter is an appropriate charge. The difficulty is in exercising a discretion as to which cases merit prosecution for manslaughter, and which do not.

Gross negligence manslaughter is an offence that is only committed if a certain consequence arises from the conduct of the defendant. A doctor whose gross negligence causes no harm, will not have their collar felt by the local police. It is only if death follows from the doctor's conduct that criminal investigation and prosecution are considered. When an avoidable death occurs, feelings may run very high, and there is a strong desire to hold someone accountable. I have to say that I have handled more than a few cases where patients have died following repeated acts of negligence of the kind that were identified throughout Jack Adcock's management and care. None of those cases resulted in criminal prosecution. If Dr Bawa-Garba's conduct merited criminal charges, then a consistent approach would lead to very many more doctors standing in the dock. The unpalatable truth is that mistakes of the kind she made are made more frequently than many members of the public realise. This is not a state of affairs to be condoned, but it is surely not in the public interest to have increasing numbers of healthcare professionals brought before the criminal courts for incompetent rather than malicious conduct.

As it happens, very, very few healthcare professionals are prosecuted for gross negligence manslaughter. Recent decisions to prosecute doctors for manslaughter have led to concerns that the bar to prosecuting healthcare professionals has being lowered. If Dr Bawa-Garba was to be prosecuted, then so would many other doctors, most of them working in very difficult circumstances. Such an approach on the part of the police and the Crown prosecution Service would discourage students from pursuing a career in the medical profession, encourage defensive practice, and dissuade healthcare professionals from being open about their mistakes, when candour rather than secrecy is more likely to promote good practice and patient safety.

The more doctors own up to their mistakes, the more they and their peers can learn from those mistakes, and the more realistic public expectations of the medical profession will become. Personally, I would put more trust in a doctor who was accepting of their fallibilities than one who assumed a posture of god-like infallibility. The jury may have found Dr Bawa-Garba's conduct to be exceptionally bad because of an unrealistic expectation of what standards of care are achievable in an over-stretched hospital setting. More honesty about the limits of what the healthcare professions can do might lead to a more sympathetic understanding when things go wrong.

Part 2: The Principles of Clinical Negligence

In this Part I set out ten core principles that apply to all clinical negligence cases. An understanding of these principles will give the reader a good understanding of the law governing such claims. Some of these principles are specific to clinical negligence claims, others apply to all personal injury cases. In Part 1 I looked at the law of negligence. In this Part I will examine some of those in more detail and explain how they apply to clinical negligence litigation. As always in law, for every principle there are exceptions and I shall discuss those which are the most important. All ten principles have developed through the common law processes described in Part 1 and so I refer to some of the key judgments that have helped to establish or confirm them.

Principle 1: The purpose of clinical negligence law is to compensate the injured or bereaved, not to punish those responsible for causing injury

In Part 1 I explained that clinical negligence litigation belongs to the tort and contract branches of civil law, and is distinct from both the criminal and regulatory legal systems. It is not designed to punish healthcare professionals or to protect the public and improve patient safety, but to compensate people who have suffered avoidable injury. Those responsible for causing the avoidable injuries must pay the compensation but a court's order to compensate is not a punishment, like the imposition of a fine in the criminal courts. It is an order to make good the harm that has been caused.

The aim of compensatory damages in tort is to place the claimant, so far as money can do so, in the same position as they would have been in had they not suffered the wrong for which they are entitled to be compensated. The object is "full compensation" for both financial and non-financial losses. The claimant is entitled to damages sufficient to meet their reasonable needs resulting from their injuries. In principle the claimant's compensation monies should run out on the day they die. They will have had sufficient compensation to meet their reasonable needs arising out of their avoidable injuries – no more, no less. When considering any particular claim – often referred to in litigation as a "head of claim" – the court should assess the reasonableness of the head of loss and its amount. The court will ask whether the need for the head of claim arose as a consequence of the injury, and whether the claim is reasonable. The court may also consider whether the claim is proportionate: could the same need be met by another, less expensive means?

In relation to future losses and expenses, the court will not only consider whether the claimed cost will have been caused by the avoidable injury, whether it is reasonable and whether it will be proportionate, but also whether the cost is one that the claimant is likely to incur. Suppose a young injured person claims for the cost of private hip replacement surgery in their 50's. They will need expert evidence to establish that the surgery is likely to be required, and that it would not have been required but for the negligence of the defendant. They will also have to prove that they will be likely to pay for the surgery in the private sector, rather than relying on the

NHS. Finally, they will have to prove what the likely costs of the surgery will be. By an act of Parliament – section 2(4) of the Law Reform (Personal Injuries) Act 1948 – the court must disregard the fact that the surgery would be available free of charge through the NHS. The court must be persuaded that the claimant will use private healthcare provision before compensation is awarded to pay for that provision. However, it is no defence to a claim for future medical or surgical costs to say that the provision will be available free of charge and therefore that the defendant should not be obliged to pay for the care or treatment to be given privately. Nor, for that matter, is there any means by which a defendant can seek recoupment after the litigation has been concluded. So, a claimant may genuinely intend to have hip replacement surgery performed privately in their 50's, but find that when that moment arises, there is a highly reputable local NHS hospital offering hip replacement surgery with a very short waiting list. The claimant may have been awarded £30,000 for the future need for private hip replacement surgery, but later choose to undergo the surgery through the NHS. Their clinical negligence claim will have been concluded many years earlier and they have no obligation to inform the defendant of the change, let alone to reimburse them.

The compensation principle means that where there is no injury, there is no claim. It is not intended as a flippant observation, but there will be thousands of negligent acts and omissions every day in the NHS that do not cause anyone any harm. Just as a car driver might exceed the speed limit without causing injury, so a doctor's carelessness might not result in any harm to their patients. A patient cannot bring a negligence claim for a "near miss".

The compensation principle means that the injured patient is only entitled to be compensated for any injuries they would not have suffered had it not been for the negligence concerned. In most clinical negligence cases the patient had been suffering from some injury, disease or condition prior to the negligence: that is why they were being treated. Therefore, it is necessary to work out what their condition would have been without the negligence and to compare that with the outcome as it has been after the negligent acts and omissions. Broadly speaking, the difference between those two outcomes represents the avoidable injury. Since one of those outcomes is hypothetical, the court has to speculate: what would have been the probable outcome for the patient without the negligence?

The law of tort does provide for limited exceptions to the compensatory principle. In very narrowly defined cases damages can be awarded against a defendant that are designed to go beyond the purpose of compensating the claimant. "Exemplary damages" may be awarded to reflect a defendant's oppressive or arbitrary misuse of public office or powers, or actions designed to profit the perpetrator. These are unheard of in clinical negligence cases but could in principle apply, for example against a private sector healthcare provider. "Aggravated damages" may be awarded in principle where the defendant's conduct was malicious or otherwise designed to cause particular distress and humiliation to the claimant. Arguably, however, aggravated damages are still compensatory – it is just that the compensation is for hurt feelings or a loss of dignity that goes beyond physical or psychiatric injury.

Some acts of clinical negligence by public bodies providing healthcare can, when certain additional criteria are met, amount to contraventions of the European Convention on Human Rights. Following the introduction of the Human Rights Act 1998 the courts here can award damages for such contraventions. For example, the Supreme Court has held that damages should be payable to parents of a 24 year old woman who took her own life after a hospital failed to protect her when it knew or ought to have known that her life was at real and immediate risk and she was under its control and particularly vulnerable. Damages in such cases may reflect the seriousness of the default by the defendant as well as the impact of the default on the claimants. Therefore, they are not compensatory.

Where a claim is for bereavement damages under the Fatal Accidents Act 1976, the award is not designed to meet the loss and grief suffered: it is a notional sum set under the statute. It does not vary according to the impact of the death on those entitled to the award. It is not therefore a compensatory award but a nominal sum fixed by legislation.

Principle 2: Healthcare professionals owe their patients a duty to exercise reasonable care and skill in their management and treatment

---

In Part 1 I looked at the "neighbour principle" established in the case of *Donoghue v Stevenson*. When applied in a medical or clinical setting, it is well established that a patient is a "neighbour" of the healthcare professional who is caring for them. Quite obviously it is foreseeable to a doctor that their patient might be harmed if they do not manage or treat them with due care. My GP, my consultant, the nurses on my ward, the paramedics who take me to hospital and the physiotherapist who visits me at home, all owe me a duty to take care. Furthermore, because I rely on them not merely as fellow human beings but as people who purport to have particular training and knowledge, I rely on them exercising professional skill as well as care.

Whilst it is obvious that a qualified medical or nursing professional is a healthcare professional, where are the limits of this category of person drawn? Certain professions have regulatory bodies and thresholds including training or qualification requirements for membership. At the fringes of medicine there are therapists, some self-styled, who may very well not come under the umbrella term "healthcare professional". Nevertheless, they will owe a duty of care to any client or patient, and they ought to exercise the standard of skill that the client or patient is entitled to expect. So, if they purport to have a special skill to perform chakra acupuncture for example, they are obliged to exercise that skill.

Note that the duty to exercise care and skill extends not just to specific treatment such as the administration of medicine or the performance of surgery, but to the whole care and management of the patient, from giving advice to arranging a follow up review. Care and skill must be exercised in taking histories from patients, examining them, carrying out investigations, reaching diagnoses, obtaining consent to procedures and deciding on the timing of interventions. A surgeon must not only take care when wielding a scalpel but also when reviewing the patient on the ward after an operation.

To Whom is the Duty Owed?
The duty is owed to patients. Those might be the patients of a named healthcare professional, or the patients at a hospital for which an NHS Trust is responsible.

In most cases it is obvious to a healthcare professional that someone is their patient. If a GP is examining a child with a stethoscope in their surgery, that is a good clue that the child is the patient to whom they owe a duty of care. But if the child is with their father, does the GP owe a duty to him as well? The answer – a typical lawyer's answer – is that it depends on the circumstances.

Suppose the GP suspects that the child is very young and may have TB? In those circumstances, the GP might well owe a duty of care to the father, present in the surgery, to give certain advice. The father is a "neighbour" of the GP at that point. He might foreseeably come to harm if the GP does not exercise appropriate care and skill in giving advice to the father. In different circumstances the GP might well not owe a duty of care to the father. The courts have held that where a doctor was examining a child to determine whether the child had been sexually abused, the doctor did not owe a duty of care to the parent of that child. A doctor who negligently diagnosed the child as having been sexually abused with harmful results for the parent was not liable to compensate the parent. The doctor's duty to the child might conflict with the interest of the parent. The court should not impose potentially conflicting duties on the doctor.

The field of genetics throws up difficult questions about the extent of the duty of care on healthcare professionals to people who are manifestly not their patients. In a case called *ABC v St George's Healthcare NHS Trust & Ors* [2017] EWCA Civ 336, the Court of Appeal decided that healthcare professionals might owe a duty of care to the daughter of their patient. The patient in question had been diagnosed with Huntington's disease. He was being treated as a patient detained under the Mental Health Act 1983 after he had killed the mother of his daughter (who was the claimant in the case). The daughter's complaint was that she should have been informed of her father's diagnosis because there was a 50% chance that she had inherited the condition. Her father had told his treating doctors that he did not want his daughter to be informed. They decided that they should not override his wishes and breach patient confidentiality. They maintained that position even when they knew that the claimant was pregnant and that there was a chance that her own child would inherit the condition. In fact, the claimant was inadvertently informed of her father's diagnosis. It transpired that she had inherited the condition and she sued the Trust responsible for treating her father. The Trust tried to have the case struck out as having no reasonable prospects of success but the Court of Appeal ordered that the daughter's claim was arguable. So, a doctor might owe a duty to inform someone of a diagnosis of a genetic condition, even though that person was not their patient and even though their own patient had told them not to disclose the information.

Given that there are very many hereditary conditions and that relatives affected might include not only children and grandchildren, but siblings, nieces, nephews and beyond, this case has very wide potential ramifications.

The law also recognises what are called "secondary victims". A patient harmed by a healthcare professional's negligence is a "primary victim". In certain narrowly defined circumstances, a healthcare professional may also owe a duty of care to someone who suffers psychiatric injury as a result of their witnessing harm to a primary victim. The Hillsborough disaster spawned the leading judgments in this field. Those scores of Liverpool FC fans who were killed or physically injured at the ground were the "primary victims" of any negligent policing. But what of those who suffered distress or psychological trauma as a result of watching the terrible events of 15 April 1989 unfold? These included those present in the ground aware that loved ones were in significant danger. They also included those present who saw the events at close hand but who did not know anyone in the affected area. There would be others watching on television or listening to the radio. The courts drew a line, and narrowly defined the category of person who was not at risk of physical harm but to whom a negligent defendant might nevertheless be liable. The principles apply in clinical negligence too.

The courts have set down the following rules. A secondary victim – someone not at risk of physical injury but to whom a negligent healthcare practitioner may owe a duty of care – is someone who has a close tie of love and affection with a person who is physically harmed or endangered as a result of the defendant's negligence. They must be in close proximity in time and space to the event in question that caused the physical injury; they must have suffered a recognised psychiatric injury (not merely distress); and their own injury must have been caused by the sudden apprehension of a horrifying event that caused injury to the other.

The emphasis is on "shock" – a sudden traumatic event jolting the witness and causing psychiatric injury. Therefore, a widow who suffers from an abnormal grief reaction after the prolonged terminal illness and then death of her husband after a negligent delay in diagnosis of cancer would not come within the category of "secondary victim". A father who witnesses the birth of his baby, born with unexpectedly severe injury, may qualify as a secondary victim. The mother is generally treated as a primary victim provided the injury to her baby was caused when the baby was as yet unborn.

The courts have been reluctant to find that events in hospitals carry the required element of "sudden shock" to enable those who have witnessed harm to others to recover compensation. In one Court of Appeal case a sympathetic court held that the deterioration and death of a baby witnessed by her mother was an "event" although it took place over a 36 hour period. In other cases, however, a tougher line has been taken in relation to secondary victim claims following clinical negligence. One argument has been that hospitals are places where people are conditioned to expect serious illness, traumatic deteriorations, even death. Therefore, the illness or death of a loved one whilst being treated in hospital is not readily found by the courts to be a sudden and horrifying event. A further difficulty for claimants claiming to be secondary victims of clinical negligence is that the effects of negligent omission often occur days, weeks, even months later. A negligent failure to prescribe anti-psychotic medication to a patient might result in their suicide several weeks later. The patient's mother might come upon the body and suffer psychiatric injury as a consequence. Is she a "secondary victim"? Lawyers have argued about what is the "event" in such a case: is it the original negligence or the suicide? And heartless distinctions are made between a parent who discovers the body within minutes of the suicide, and a parent who discovers the body a week later. Only one of those may be sufficiently proximate to the event to recover compensation.

This is an area of the law where artificial rules are laid down as a matter of policy, attempting to keep a balance between allowing claims to be brought by those whose lives have been blighted by witnessing horrifying trauma to loved ones, and preventing a flood of claims by a much wider group of people.

Who is a Healthcare Professional?

The neighbour principle means that anyone who has physical contact with another owes them a duty to exercise care. The more particular questions are when does a duty to exercise *professional skill* arise, and when do the principles of clinical negligence law set out in this Part apply to someone who has dealings with a "patient"? There is no dispute that the principles of clinical negligence apply to all medical practitioners registered with the General Medical Council, to nurses and to midwives. They also apply to other professionals who work within mainstream medicine, such as radiographers, sonographers and physiotherapists. A more difficult question is whether practitioners of complementary and alternative medicine (CAM) are healthcare professionals to whom the principles of clinical negligence law apply.

The NHS website lists the following as being CAM services that are sometimes provided within the NHS: acupuncture, aromatherapy, massage and osteopathy. Other alternative practices include homeopathy and Chinese herbal medicine. As explained in more detail later in this Part, the expected standard of care and skill of a neurosurgeon is that of all responsible bodies of neurosurgeons. A general practitioner is not negligent if they act in a way that would be considered acceptable by a responsible body of general practitioners. Is an osteopath to be judged by the standards of other osteopaths? Should the management of a patient by a homeopath be assessed by the standards of other homeopaths or by reference to the standards of mainstream healthcare professionals experienced in treating such patients with the same conditions?

In a High Court case called *Shakoor v Situ* [2001] 1 WLR 410, the judge considered a claim arising out of allegedly negligent and fatal treatment given to a patient by a practitioner of Chinese herbal medicine. The judge posed the question of whether: *"those who practice "in the same art" as the practitioner are able to dictate to the court the standards in accordance with which he is to be judged?"* The judge concluded that:

> *"when a court has to adjudicate on the standard of care given by an alternative medical practitioner it will ... often (perhaps invariably) not be enough to judge him by the standard of the ordinary practitioner "skilled in that particular art"; it will often be necessary to have regard to the act that the practitioner is practicing his art alongside orthodox medicine; the court will need to consider whether the standard of care adopted by the alternative practitioner has taken account of the implications of this fact."*

A claimant might therefore adduce evidence before the court that an osteopath failed to act in accordance with a responsible body of osteopaths, or that the practice adopted by the particular osteopath, and other practitioners of the same "art", was negligent. That would be assessed, the judge held, by reference to *"the risks that were not and should have been taken into account."* If this approach is adopted then the ordinary principles of negligence will apply to CAM practitioners as well as the particular principles of clinical negligence.

The judgment in *Shakoor v Situ* indicates that the courts will consider CAM practitioners as being healthcare professionals but subject to an additional layer of scrutiny. They must both act within the accepted standards of the "profession" and they must act reasonably having regard to a rational assessment of the benefits and risks of what they are doing to a patient.

Contract

Where a healthcare professional treats a patient within the NHS there is no direct charge for the service. There is no contract between patient and professional. The duty of care arises in tort (see Part 1). Does Principle 2 above apply also to relationships within the private sector?

A contract arises where there are promises offered and accepted. I promise to pay £100 for goods which the seller agrees to provide. The terms of the contract might include that I shall pay £100 before I take possession of the goods and that the goods will be in a reasonable condition. In a contract for services a typical term will be that the service will be performed with reasonable care. Sometimes contractual terms are put in writing, sometimes they are not. In a contract for medical services there will often be written standard terms and conditions. But even if those do not include an obligation to perform the services with reasonable care and skill, the courts will find that there was an implied term to that effect. Therefore Principle 2 applies equally to most contracts for clinical services as it does where no contract arises. Healthcare professionals acting under contract with their patients owe a duty of care to those patients just as much as they would were they treating them within the NHS.

In any event the existence of a contract does not prevent a duty of care arising in tort. The cosmetic surgeon who agrees to perform a procedure on a patient for money may have a contract with the patient, but they will also owe a duty of care to the patient in tort. That is so whether the contract is directly with the patient, or the contract is between the patient and a third party, such as a private clinic. The contractual arrangements do not absolve the surgeon of their duty of care to the patient.

The courts will nearly always find an "implied" contractual term to exercise reasonable skill and care but in some contractual cases the circumstances and wording of an offer to provide the service might give rise to an even more onerous duty. There might be circumstances whereby a surgeon has held themselves out to exercise a very high level of skill in relation to a particular procedure, and a patient has been induced to enter into a contract for that procedure in reliance on the surgeon having an exceptional, not a reasonable, level of skill. The surgeon might then be liable for damages for breach of contract if they exercised reasonable but not exceptional skill and care when operating on the patient.

Principle 3: The extent of a healthcare professional's legal duty of care is to save their patients from avoidable harm attributable to their wrongful acts and omissions

---

"It is never sufficient to ask simply whether A owes B a duty of care. It is always necessary to determine the scope of the duty by reference to the kind of damage from which A must take care to save B harmless."

Lord Bridge in Caparo Industries plc v Dickman [1990] 2 AC 605.

The duty of care must have substance. It is unhelpful to inform a doctor that they have a duty of care to their patients without telling them what it is they are obliged to do.

Just as physicians are told: "First, do no harm", so the law of clinical negligence enjoins them to save their patients from avoidable harm. "Harm" includes physical and psychological or psychiatric harm. It must have been avoidable. Medical treatment sometimes inevitably involves causing pain or discomfort, even harm, to patients, usually with the intention of preventing even greater harm from an injury or a naturally occurring condition. A negligent act or omission might create harm, or it might prevent the occurrence of harm, but in either case the duty is only to protect against the harm that would be avoidable with the exercise of reasonable care and skill.

A recurrent issue in clinical negligence law is the scope of a healthcare professional's duty. All sorts of avoidable harm might be foreseeable following a doctor's negligent act or omission, but the doctor is not liable to compensate their patient for all such avoidable harm. I have already referred to the famous example of the mountaineer's knee. This illustration of the importance of the scope of the duty of care was given by Lord Hoffmann in the (non-medical) case of *South Australia Asset Management Corpn v York Montague Ltd* [1997] AC 191, commonly referred to as "SAAMCO".

> *"A mountaineer about to undertake a difficult climb is concerned about the fitness of his knee. He goes to a doctor who negligently makes a superficial examination and pronounces the knee fit. The climber goes on the expedition, which he would not have undertaken if the doctor had told him the true state of his knee. He suffers an injury which is an entirely foreseeable consequence of mountaineering but has nothing to do with his knee."*

Suppose the mountaineer was injured in an avalanche. They would not have been in the path of the avalanche were it not for the doctor's negligence, but the doctor's duty of care did not extend to warning their patient of avalanches let alone preventing the avalanche. The scope of the doctor's duty is not to prevent all avoidable harm. It is to protect the patient from avoidable harm attributable to that which made the act or omission wrongful.

This might seem to be a circular test. A doctor may ask, before acting negligently: *"What harm do I have to protect my patient against?"* The lawyer answers: *"You have to protect your patients against harm that is attributable to your negligence."* The doctor asks: *"How do I know what that harm is going to be when I have not yet been negligent?"* The lawyer says: *"Let's wait and find out."*

In truth, doctors cannot always know in advance what their liabilities may be in clinical negligence law. It is obvious that doctors must save their patients from harm such as having the wrong limb amputated. But there may be consequences of negligence which were not foreseen. Suppose the mountaineer was caught up in an avalanche but would have been unharmed but for the fact that his knee gave way due to an undiagnosed weakness, and he could not climb out of the way. The mountaineer is injured in an unusual manner, but the harm is connected with the doctor's failure to examine the knee properly and pronounce the mountaineer unfit for the expedition.

Principle 4: The law requires healthcare professionals to exercise a reasonable standard of care and skill

A claimant will not establish liability in a clinical negligence claim merely by proving that things could have been done differently. It is not even sufficient to show that things could have been done better. Negligence only occurs when a healthcare professional falls below an acceptable level of competence and fails to meet a *reasonable* standard of care.

I have seen many medical experts' reports in clinical negligence litigation where the writer has stated that the standard of care was "sub-optimal", "not what I would have expected", "below par", or "lower than would be hoped for." Those experts have not applied the basic principle that a healthcare professional is required only to exercise a reasonable degree of care and skill.

The law does not demand gold standard performance. So, "sub-optimal" performance is acceptable in law and compensation will not be awarded to a patient who has suffered harm that would have been avoided had their surgeon exercised the best level of skill and care that could be expected. The fact that a doctor could have acted differently, or that other doctors would have done better, does not prove negligence.

As will be shown in more depth below, the law of clinical negligence does not even demand average competence. If "par" is average then "below par" care is not necessarily negligent care. A doctor can perform worse than half of their peers and not be negligent. Indeed, there is a range of competence, the bottom end of which is well below the average standard. Negligent management of a patient is so poor that it falls outside this range of ordinary competence. Think of an exam where grades A* to E constitute a pass. Some students are in the top 10% who achieve an A*. Another group do well with an A grade, and still more perform above average at B. Those with an E grade are in the lowest performing group of those who pass, but they still pass. Their performance will be well below the A and A* students, and below the average C graders. But they have still passed – they have exceeded the bottom line of what is considered to be acceptable. Only those below E grade have failed. So it is with negligence – only those professionals that fall below the bottom line of acceptable performance will be considered to have been negligent.

It is therefore a high hurdle for a claimant to overcome to prove clinical negligence.

Gross negligence, in a criminal context, is therefore conduct that has fallen so far below an unacceptably poor level, such that it is truly, exceptionally bad. This is not just a "fail" in the exam analogy, but a truly exceptionally bad fail.

Whilst conduct amounting to gross negligence will always raise a question about a healthcare professional's competence more generally, a finding of negligence does not necessarily do so. It is true that an act of negligence might be a signal of wider failings in professional competence, but it is more often the case that a usually competent, even skilled practitioner, has simply failed to meet the required standard on a particular occasion. The question for a court is not whether a practitioner is generally incompetent, but whether they fell below a reasonable standard in relation to their management of a particular patient at a particular time. This simple point is difficult for some healthcare professionals to accept. They feel that their general level of competence is under attack when a claimant brings a claim for clinical negligence arising out of their treatment and care. In fact, in my experience, the courts are more often inclined to disbelieve that a professional has been negligent on a certain occasion if they are shown to be generally skilled and proficient. An individual claimant is unlikely to be able to obtain evidence that a healthcare professional is incompetent generally. Therefore, the default assumption for some trial judges is that the professional alleged to have been negligent will usually be competent and skilled and so would have been unlikely to have been negligent on the alleged occasion. Most judges do as they should and focus on the particular circumstances. It is always inherently unlikely that a doctor or other healthcare professional will have been negligent – negligence is very uncommon – but that is not something that should be given great probative value when assessing what happened to a particular patient.

The role of national guidelines and hospital protocols is relevant to this principle of "reasonable care". The National Institute of Health and Care Excellence ("NICE") publishes guidelines setting out standards for the management and treatment of patients, including those for the recognition and referral for suspected cancer. Under those particular guidelines, general practitioners are given advice about referring patients urgently, non-urgently or occasionally on an emergency basis, when certain signs or symptoms are present. So, a woman over 30 with an unexplained breast lump should be referred to be seen within a breast clinic within two weeks. These guidelines might therefore be thought to set a standard of what is reasonable such that a failure to follow the guidelines would be considered unacceptable and negligent.

That is not necessarily the case. The particular guidelines about referring patients with suspected cancer say:

> "these recommendations are recommendations, not requirements, and they are not intended to override clinical judgement".

It should not be forgotten that written guidelines cannot cover every eventuality. Each patient is unique and doctors have to make professional judgements depending on all the circumstances. Guidelines do not have the force of law. There may be good reason why a practitioner has not followed the recommendations within a guideline. Conversely, it might be negligent to fail to refer a patient for investigation even though the guideline does not expressly say that referral should be made. A patient who does not meet the criteria for referral within the guidelines might nevertheless have some other feature of their personal or family history that makes it mandatory to refer them.

Even so, national guidelines are of importance in helping to establish what is a reasonable standard of care and skill in clinical negligence litigation. In one case concerning delay in diagnosing cancer from 2007, called *Adshead v Tottle*, Mr Justice Gray held that a GP was negligent for failing to follow the recommendations within national guidelines:

> "In the case of a patient who presents with a potentially life-threatening symptom, I do not accept that a responsible general practitioner would delay referring her, even for a short period, in circumstances where the recommendation made unambiguously in the guidelines is

to refer immediately."

NHS Trusts produce their own protocols covering certain diagnostic investigations, or medical or surgical treatment. These protocols provide good evidence of the expected standard of care within the Trust, and failure to follow them, without good reason, will often be found to be unacceptable and negligent.

Principle 5: If a healthcare professional acts in accordance with the practice of a reasonable body of relevant professional opinion, they are not negligent

---

The *Bolam* Test

This principle was established in the most important clinical negligence case of all: *Bolam v Friern Hospital Management Committee* [1957] 1 WLR 582. This was not a decision of the Court of Appeal or the House of Lords, but of a single High Court Judge, Mr Justice McNair. In fact, the decision in the case was made by a jury (the use of civil juries has, with a few exceptions, since ceased) upon the direction of McNair J, but it is his direction to the jury that has been applied in so very many subsequent cases. The case did not necessarily break new ground – the judge enunciated a principle that had already been established in previous cases. Nevertheless, McNair J's direction has been so often repeated and adopted in later judgments that it has established itself as the most important judicial statement ever made on breach of duty in clinical negligence cases. The test of whether a doctor or other healthcare professional has met the required standard of reasonable care and skill is now known as the *Bolam* test.

Mr Bolam was being treated for psychiatric illness. He elected to undergo electro-convulsive treatment. When being given the treatment he suffered from fractures and claimed that: (i) he should have been given relaxant drugs; (ii) failing that he should have been restrained with strapping etc; (iii) he was not warned of the risks of fractures in the absence of relaxants or restraint; and (iv) his injuries would have been avoided but for those breaches of duty. There was evidence before the jury that some psychiatric units did use relaxants and/or restraint, and some did not.

Court:
High Court – McNair J
(sitting with a jury)
Reported: [1957] 1 WLR 582

Facts:
Mr Bolam suffered acetabular fractures when given electro-convulsive treatment (ECT) for a psychiatric condition. He had not been given relaxant drugs prior to the ECT, and no restraints had been applied during the treatment.

Bolam v Friern Hospital Management Committee

Decision:
Whilst some practitioners would have given relaxants or applied restraints, there was a responsible body of opinion that it was not necessary to do so. Accordingly the doctor had not been negligent to fail to give relaxants or to apply restraints. On the same basis it had not been negligent to fail to warn Mr Bolam of the risk of injury from not using relaxants or applying restraints.

Key Points Applied in Later Cases:
A doctor who acts in accordance with a responsible body of relevant medical opinion is not negligent, notwithstanding that there may be other bodies of opinion that would have acted differently.

Casenote 3

McNair J gave a direction to the jury about how it should approach the allegations of negligence made by the claimant:

> "How do you test whether this act or failure is negligent? In an ordinary case it is generally said you judge it by the action of the man in the street. He is the ordinary man. In one case it has been said you judge it by the conduct of the man on the top of a Clapham omnibus. He is the ordinary man. But where you get a situation which involves the use of some special skill or competence, then the test as to whether there has been negligence or not is not the test of the man on the top of a Clapham omnibus, because he has not got this special skill. The test is the standard of the ordinary skilled man exercising and professing to have that special skill. A man need not possess the highest expert skill; it is well established law that it is sufficient if he exercises the ordinary skill of an ordinary competent man exercising

> *that particular art."*

He went on to direct the jury that it should approach the question of whether a doctor has exercised such ordinary skill as follows:

> "[A doctor] *is not guilty of negligence if he has acted in accordance with a practice accepted as proper by a responsible body of medical men skilled in that particular art . . . Putting it the other way round, a man is not negligent, if he is acting in accordance with such a practice, merely because there is a body of opinion who would take a contrary view."*

This has become known as the "*Bolam* test".

The *Bolam* test recognises that there may be a range of reasonable professional opinion on how to interpret a patient's history, signs and symptoms, and on how to manage or respond to a particular set of circumstances. It does not mandate adherence to some particular "standard" treatment. Perhaps there are some tenets of medical practice that are so well established that no responsible body of doctors would consider it proper not to follow them. But doctors are professionals, not automatons, and there will be many situations where they have to exercise their judgement, or to adopt one of several reasonable options for the management of a patient.

Earlier I explained that the courts do not require gold standard, nor even average, care. Nor do they require that all healthcare professionals act in a uniform way. The *Bolam* test shows that to be the case. 95% of doctors might have done better than the defendant doctor who treated the claimant, but if the defendant doctor acted in accordance with a practice accepted as proper by 5% of their peers, and that 5% constitutes a responsible body of relevant professional opinion, then they have not been negligent.

Lawyers love nothing better than to take apart a seemingly simple, concisely worded statement, so let's examine this statement of the *Bolam* test in more detail. Think of it as legal dissection. Several aspects of the statement of principle require further consideration.

– **responsible "body"**. A responsible "body" is not necessarily an organised or formal body of practitioners. It does not have to be a Royal College or a recognised professional corps. "Body" simply describes a group or number of practitioners. It might be a very small group, particularly if the practice with which the court is concerned is highly specialised. Perhaps there are only 20 practitioners in the country who would perform a certain kind of surgery. If three of them are considered to be competent surgeons within that field, with a sound basis for their mode of practice, they might well constitute a "responsible body". There is no threshold for when a number of practitioners comprise a "body" – the court will exercise its sense and judgement in that respect. In practice, the courts do not demand actual evidence that, say, 50 orthopaedic surgeons would condone the defendant surgeon's surgical technique. Litigants do not present the courts with surveys of opinion. One reason why that is not done, is that each case is fact sensitive, and the precise facts may not be known, or determined, until the judge gives their decision at the conclusion of the trial. Instead, as explained below, the courts rely on expert advice, usually limited to one expert per relevant field of practice, as to what opinions are held within the profession and how they would apply to the particular circumstances of the case.

– **"practice"**. The *Bolam* test was clearly intended to apply to the manner in which treatment is delivered. Mr Justice McNair would have anticipated his statement of principle being applied to the way an operation is performed, the mix of drugs used to anaesthetise a patient, or the timing of the use of antibiotics for a suspected infection. All those activities would comfortably come under the umbrella of "practice". But the *Bolam* test has also been applied to other aspects of a healthcare professional's work – the interpretation of x-rays or biopsies for example. In a recent case a High Court judge questioned whether the *Bolam* test ought to apply to, say, an examination of a pathology slide to determine whether it contained malignant cells. The argument goes that this kind of exercise has a right and a wrong outcome – if the sample did contain malignant cells, and the histopathologist reported that it did not, they would be wrong, and it would be odd to find that a responsible body of histopathologists would consider it proper to be report malignant cells as non-malignant. Having raised those doubts the judge then held that he was bound by precedent cases to adopt the *Bolam* test. In fact, in my experience, it is not that unusual, in difficult cases, to find a range of opinion amongst experts as to what a histopathological sample, a CT scan or an x-ray reveals. With hindsight there may be a right or wrong answer, but in some cases there may be grey areas where more than one interpretation is reasonable. The courts' focus is on what is acceptable practice, not necessarily on what is an acceptable outcome.

One area of practice where the *Bolam* test does not apply is in relation to the obtaining of consent to treatment. A different principle applies, as explained below. Although the *Bolam* test is known to every student and practitioner of clinical negligence, it is sometimes overlooked that there were two strands to Mr Bolam's claim. First, he alleged that it had been negligent not to have used relaxants or, failing that, not to have applied restraints during the ECT. The *Bolam* test would apply to the same allegations were they made today. Second, he alleged that it had been negligent not to have warned him of the risks involved with the treatment as it was proposed to be given. McNair J advised the jury to take the same approach – what we now call the *Bolam* test – to that second allegation. In fact, now, the *Bolam* test is not applied to determine whether a practitioner should have warned a patient about a relevant risk. It is tempting to say that the *Bolam* test should not have been applied in the *Bolam* case (or at least in the part dealing with consent)!

– **"that particular art"** refers to the need for the body of opinion to be relevant to the conduct under consideration. It is no use asking what a body of GPs would have done if you are considering the conduct of an orthopaedic surgeon. Likewise, it is not relevant to ask an orthopaedic surgeon whether a GP's conduct was proper, even if the GP was managing a patient with a possible fracture. The healthcare professional's acts and omissions are to be assessed by reference to a responsible body of practitioners who practise in the same field at the same level.

– **"accepted"**. In the great majority of cases the court will hear evidence of what is accepted practice. The practice will be already established, even if it has only been established relatively recently. Sometimes, at the time of the alleged negligence, professional opinion is undergoing change – perhaps the received wisdom is under threat or a new practice is emerging. The *Bolam* test still works well in that situation. But what of wholly innovative practice? Can the *Bolam* test apply where the practice adopted is not "accepted" in the sense of tried, tested and approved? When Lord Saatchi was trying to introduce his Medical Innovation Bill through Parliament, he complained to a largely credulous House of Lords that the *Bolam* test requires doctors to adhere to the tried and tested standard practice, however often that practice has failed patients in the past. He was wrong. The *Bolam* test is flexible. It moves with the times. Just as a previously accepted practice might become unacceptable, so the *Bolam* test allows for wholly innovative treatment to be accepted as proper, and therefore non-negligent. A brilliant brain surgeon might adopt a new technique when operating on a fully consenting patient. If the technique would be considered acceptable by a responsible body of brain surgeons then it was not negligent to have used it, even if it resulted in serious injury, and even if the majority of surgeons would not have deployed it. On the other hand, a "quack" doctor, whose innovative practices have no rational or reasonable basis, will likely fail to find a body of colleagues who consider those practices to be proper.

An interesting argument concerning changing practice was raised recently by defence counsel in the case of *Jones v Taunton and Somerset NHS Foundation Trust* [2019] EWHC 1408 (QB). He argued that if a doctor was *Bolam* negligent by the standards of the profession at the time when they provided treatment, but in fact their conduct would have been in accordance with later or current standards – in other words they were ahead of their time – then they should not be considered to have been negligent. The judge did not have to decide the issue and so left it to be considered by another court in a future case, but logically it would be difficult for a court to find a doctor to have been negligent just because of a more general ignorance amongst their profession at the time. If advances in knowledge and practice reveal their conduct to have been justified, surely the court would not find them to have been negligent? We will look at the case of *Bolitho* below, which requires the court to scrutinise medical practice for rationality. If a doctor's conduct at the time was out of kilter with the practice of all responsible bodies of professional opinion but was nevertheless subsequently shown to have been rational and logical, then the court would be unlikely to find them to have been negligent. This would be a qualification to the rule that retrospectoscopes are not allowed (see below). They are not allowed to be used to condemn a practitioner, but they may be used to exonerate them.

– **"proper"** does not introduce any concept of propriety or ethical behaviour. In this context it means the same as "reasonable". Sometimes litigators refer to a "competent" or "ordinary" standard, which again means the same. The point of the *Bolam* test is that what is considered to be reasonable is to be judged by the standards considered competent or "proper" within the relevant profession.

– **"not guilty of negligence"**: the test is put negatively. A doctor is not negligent if they act in accordance with the practice of a responsible body of opinion. Incidentally, the words "guilty of" are not used to indicate guilt for a criminal offence, but are synonymous for "responsible for". Were the *Bolam* test put positively it would be: *"a doctor is negligent if they fail to act in accordance with a practice accepted as proper by any responsible body of medical men skilled in that particular art."*

In contested litigation, each party – the claimant and the defendant – will obtain expert opinion as to the standard of care that was exercised when the claimant was treated or managed. In those cases where breach of duty is contested at trial, the judge will usually be faced with contrasting opinions. The claimant's expert will advise the court that the defendant doctor's management of their patient was below an acceptable level of care. The defendant's expert will advise the court that it was not. As Lord Scarman explained in *Maynard v West Midlands Regional Health Authority* [1984] 1 WLR 634, the *Bolam* test requires the court to do more than simply choose which expert's advice it finds more compelling.

> *"... I have to say that a judge's 'preference' for one body of distinguished professional opinion to another also professionally distinguished is not sufficient to establish negligence in a practitioner whose actions have received the seal of approval of those whose opinions, truthfully expressed, honestly held, were not preferred. If this was the real reason for the judge's finding, he erred in law even though elsewhere in his judgment he stated the law correctly. For in the realm of diagnosis and treatment negligence is not established by preferring one respectable body of professional opinion to another. Failure to exercise the ordinary skill of a doctor (in the appropriate speciality, if he be a specialist) is necessary."*

In my experience some expert witnesses seem to think that a doctor is negligent if they fail to act as would a particular responsible body of opinion, usually the body of which the expert would consider themselves to belong. That is clearly not the *Bolam* test. For a healthcare professional to be negligent there must have been no responsible body of relevant opinion that would have considered what they did to be proper. It matters not that some doctors would have thought that what the defendant doctor did was unreasonable.

Retrospectoscopes Are Banned

Of necessity, the court assesses whether an act or omission was negligent only after the act has been committed or the omission has occurred. It is only then that the full circumstances can be assessed, and a judgement made as to whether avoidable harm has been suffered. Indeed, many litigated cases come before a judge at trial several years after the events in question. By the time a judge considers a doctor's conduct, and whether it has been harmful, they know much more than the healthcare professional involved knew at the time. All evidence is relevant to the court's determination. Nevertheless, the court must not assess the standard of care with the benefit of hindsight. There must be no use of the retrospectoscope when applying the *Bolam* test. This important condition has two aspects.

First, the court should assess the standard of care provided to the patient by reference to events as they occurred. The court may know that the patient developed sepsis after an operation, but the surgeon would not have known that when advising the patient pre-operatively. Doctors – even surgeons – are not omniscient. Likewise, although a particular blood test result was in fact the first sign of post-operative internal bleeding, at the time that it was reported to the treating doctor it might have been indicative of one of a number of possible diagnoses. The doctor's management of the patient is judged by reference to what they knew or ought to have known at the time, as events unfolded.

The second aspect of the condition that the *Bolam* test is not applied retrospectively is that the professional's conduct is assessed by reference to the standards that applied at the relevant time. If a baby was born in 2001, then the standard of care and skill to be expected of a midwife is that which pertained in 2001, not the current standard. If there were national guidelines issued in 2008, then those guidelines are not in themselves relevant to the standards in 2001. The evidence behind the 2008 guidelines might have been relevant in 2001 if it was evidence that had been published or was widely known in 2001, but the guidelines would not be helpful to the court. Practices change over time, techniques develop and knowledge is shared. What might be acceptable at one time, might be anathema at another. Practitioners' conduct is judged by the standards of the time, whether or not they would now be considered to have been negligent by current standards.

It is quite a different matter when the question for the court is causation. When asking whether a breach of duty caused the patient to suffer injury, all evidence is relevant, whether or not it was known to the treating medical personnel at the time. Indeed, the state of medical knowledge might have developed apace since the events in question, allowing the court to determine that A caused B, when, at the time the injury was suffered, no-one could have known that A caused B.

The Importance of the Role
The required standard of care and skill is that applicable to the role that the healthcare professional is fulfilling.

I have heard it said of trainee surgeons that they "See one. Do one. Teach one." I am sure that surgical training has moved beyond that caricature, but the fact remains that we all have to start somewhere: a ski jumper has to make their first jump and a surgeon has to perform their first cholecystectomy. Would it be fair to judge the novice surgeon by the standards of their supervising consultant? Should a first year trainee doctor on their first shift be held to the same standards as a much more experienced colleague?

The short answer is "yes". The courts do not make allowances for the inexperience or experience of the healthcare professional. The required standard of skill and care is the same for all healthcare professionals fulfilling the particular role. It is the nature of the role that dictates the expected standard, not the personal characteristics of the person performing that role. Lord Justice Jackson put it this way in the case of *FB v Rana and Princess Alexandra Hospital NHS Trust* [2017] EWCA Civ 334:

> *"Whether doctors are performing their normal role or 'acting up', they are judged by reference to the post which they are fulfilling at the material time. The health authority or health trust is liable if the doctor whom it puts into a particular position does not possess (and therefore does not exercise) the requisite degree of skill for the task in hand."*

The same principle applies, incidentally, to learner drivers. In the well-known case of *Nettleship v Weston* [1971] EWCA Civ 6, the court held that a learner driver is expected to exercise the same level of care and skill as every other driver permitted to drive on the public highway.

Remember that clinical negligence law is compensatory not punitive. The principle stated above underlines the point that a patient is entitled to expect a certain level of skill and care to be exercised. A junior doctor is not being punished for their lack of experience – the patient is being compensated because the doctor did not perform their role to the expected standard.

Clearly, however, healthcare professionals of differing seniority and experience will tend to perform different roles. A first year trainee doctor needs to know when to "refer up" to their registrar, and the registrar needs to know when to seek the opinion of their consultant.

Where a healthcare professional's role is to exercise a particularly high degree of care and skill, then the standard is set accordingly. A surgeon at a specialist centre who carries out intestinal surgery on a patient referred to them by another surgeon from a general hospital will be expected to exercise a higher degree of skill than the referring surgeon.

Conversely, the practice of a general radiologist interpreting a CT scan of a brain should not be judged by the standards of a specialist neuro-radiologist. It would be an error to ask a breast surgeon whether a GP had been negligent in failing to spot a cancerous lump on examination.

Where the claim is brought against an NHS Trust, then it is legitimate to ask whether the roles of those involved in a patient's care were appropriately filled. Should the CT brain scan have been reviewed by a specialist rather than a generalist radiologist? Should an inexperienced trainee have been left in charge of two wards of post-operative patients? It is no defence to a claim in negligence against an organisation simply to say that the particular professional lacked the necessary qualifications or experience to perform the role that needed to be performed.

Collective Negligence and the *Bolam* Test

Two cases involving misinformation given by a receptionist at the then Mayday Hospital in Croydon reached the High Court within a year of each other. They are discussed in Part 4, Chapter 3. One was *Darnley v Croydon Health Services NHS Trust* and the other was *McCauley v Croydon Health Services NHS Trust*. Mr Darnley's case ended up in the Supreme Court. Ultimately each claimant succeeded in establishing liability against the Trust, but in each case it was a receptionist who had been negligent. Receptionists are not healthcare professionals and so the *Bolam* test would not apply to their conduct. What the courts emphasised in each case was that it was the Trust that owed the duty of care to the respective patients. It was for the Trust to take reasonable steps to protect the patients from harm. It did not matter so much how the Trust decided to deploy staff, and whether it used medically qualified staff for particular roles, so long as the duty of care was fulfilled.

This emphasis on the adequacy of the system of care in place at an NHS Trust chimes with the views of many healthcare professionals that the focus should be on systems to protect patient safety, rather than on the acts and omissions of individual personnel who work within the system. All of us make errors, but sometimes deficient or unsafe systems of work create additional risk of error, and fail to protect against the consequences of error.

How does the *Bolam* test apply if the court is assessing the adequacy of a system of care? The *Bolam* test provides an approach to assessing the standard of care of a professional, judging them by reference to the standards of the profession. It naturally tends to an individualistic rather that systemic view. Is it suited to a broader assessment of a Trust's care for a patient, or an ambulance service's management of someone needing emergency treatment?

These questions are likely to be tested in the higher courts in the next few years. The Mayday hospital cases have focused attention on the importance of examining the duty of care of the NHS body involved, rather than the duty imposed on each individual working for that organisation. It is a macroscopic, not a microscopic analysis. However, the Supreme Court in *Darn-*

ley did look at the standard of care of the particular person who fulfilled the role of first point of contact, and who gave misinformation to the patient which resulted in him leaving the hospital and suffering avoidable injury. It did not ask whether the Trust had been in breach of duty, but whether the receptionist had failed to meet the expected standard of care. The standard of care of a receptionist is not judged using the *Bolam* test but the Supreme Court did not say what kind of test for breach of duty it had applied. Furthermore, it did not ask what the scope of the duty of care was on the receptionist, only what the scope of the duty of care was on the Trust. It might have been more consistent to ask, as did Lord Justice McCombe who gave a judgment in the Court of Appeal, whether the Trust had breached its duty of care, rather than whether the receptionist, in her role, had been in breach.

In cases where the duty of care is on an NHS body such as a Trust, but the court has to look at whether individuals within the system were negligent, there are some potential difficulties for those involved in litigation. First, it may not be straightforward to identify which individual failed to act to an acceptable standard, and whether they were a professional or not. Suppose a blood test is not followed up and acted upon. Is that the responsibility of the clinician who ordered it, the clinician who should have expected to receive it, the nurse whose job it was to send it to the lab, the lab technician, or someone else? If you cannot identify the person who failed, and the role they were employed to fulfil, how do you know whether they fell below the expected standard of care, and whether that standard was a *Bolam* standard or not?

A second difficulty, arising from the first, is that if there is a breakdown in the system, and you cannot identify a particular person's error, then by what standards do you judge the system as a whole? The *Bolam* test does not seem well suited to a macroscopic approach. In *Darnley* it was clear who had made the error alleged to have been negligent. It was a receptionist. In many other cases it will not be so obvious, but it might be clear that there had been a systemic failing. If an NHS Trust owes a duty to protect A&E patients from harm, and it seeks to fulfil that duty with a team of professional and non-professional employees, then in many cases the test of whether the duty has been breached does not reduce to an analysis of individual standards of care.

Principle 6: Even if a practice is considered proper by a recognised body of professional opinion, the court should determine whether it is logical, rational and reasonable

"They would say that wouldn't they?"

Many an injured patient has said that to me on learning that other medical professionals have given supportive opinions of a doctor's practice. In fact, as I usually reply, my experience is that healthcare professionals are perfectly prepared to call out unacceptably poor practice when they see it. However, the courts are aware of the danger of the profession having exclusive control over the question of what standards of practice that patients are entitled to expect. It is not sufficient, therefore, for a defendant to a clinical negligence claim merely to produce an expert to say that the defendant's practice was acceptable. Whether or not the practice was acceptable is a matter for the court to decide. The court will examine whether there is a body of opinion to that effect, and whether that body is reasonable, rational and responsible.

In the case of *Bolitho v City and Hackney Health Authority* [1997] UKHL 46; [1998] AC 232, the House of Lords accepted that when determining whether a doctor has acted in accordance with a responsible body of opinion, the court should consider whether the body of opinion in question is truly responsible, reasonable and rational. It should consider whether the practice said to be acceptable was logical. When applying the *Bolam* test,

> *"the court had to be satisfied that the exponents of a body of professional opinion relied upon had demonstrated that such opinion had a logical basis and in particular had directed their minds where appropriate to the question of comparative risks and benefits and had reached a defensible conclusion; that if, in a rare case, it had been demonstrated that the professional opinion was incapable of withstanding logical analysis, the judge was entitled to hold that it could not provide the benchmark by reference to which the doctor's conduct fell to be assessed, but that in most cases the fact that distinguished experts in the field were of a particular opinion would demonstrate the reasonableness of that opinion."*

This is an important passage. It asserts judicial authority over the medical and related professions. Ultimately, the court, not the relevant healthcare profession, will decide whether the practice adopted by the defendant was or was not rational and reasonable. *Bolitho* (some say Bol-eye-tho; some say Bol-ee-tho) also points to how judges might approach the question of assessing the logical basis for a particular treatment or management choice. The courts will weigh the risks and benefits. This will remind the reader of the approach in *Bolton v Stone* (the flying cricket ball case) mentioned in Part 1. It is the standard approach to assessment of the standard of care in cases of negligence that do not involve the professions. It is the approach that might be more suited than the *Bolam* test when the courts examine the adequacy of a system of patient care, rather than the acts and omissions of individual practitioners.

The passage in *Bolitho* ends with a reminder that the courts will pay great respect to the fact that there is a body of opinion in accordance with which the defendant doctor acted. In most cases a judge will not need to enquire much further if persuaded that there is a respected body of professional opinion that would regard what the defendant did as proper practice. The judge will not usually be medically qualified. They will not have the experience of treating patients that has been gained by the experts giving evidence at trial. Some judicial humility is therefore called for. However, ultimately, the judge should consider for themselves whether the practice adopted by a body of medical opinion is rational.

Typically, a clinical negligence judgment after trial includes a quote from *Bolam* and a quote from *Bolitho*. It is, however, rare for a judge to accept that there is a recognised body of medical opinion that would consider what the defendant did to be proper, but expressly to say that the practice it would consider acceptable was in fact irrational or illogical. More often, a judge who finds it difficult to accept that the practice supported by the defendant's expert witness makes logical sense given the risks and benefits involved will simply say that they prefer the other party's expert's opinion that the practice would not be supported by any responsible body of medical opinion.

The case of *Bolitho* also concerned an important question of causation following a negligent omission, but that is relevant to the ninth principle set out below.

Court:
House of Lords
Reported: [1998] 2 AC 232

Facts:
A doctor failed to attend to a child suffering from respiratory difficulties. The child developed respiratory failure and suffered brain damage. The court had to determine what consequences flowed from the doctor's non-attendance and in particular whether the child would have been intubated, thereby avoiding brain damage.

Bolitho v City and Hackney Health Authority

Decision:
The claimant lost. The doctor would not have intubated had he attended and it would not have been negligent not to have intubated.

Key Points Applied in Later Cases:
(i) When applying the *Bolam* test, the court must consider whether the opinion on which the defendant relies is logical. If not, it cannot be relied upon, even if it is the practice of a body of practitioners.
(ii) When considering the consequences of a negligent omission, the first question is what would have happened – a question of fact. But a defendant cannot avoid liability by saying that injury would have occurred in any event because they would have acted negligently.

Casenote 4

Principle 7: When obtaining a patient's consent to treatment, a healthcare professional has to take reasonable care to ensure that the patient is aware of any material risks involved in any recommended treatment, and of any reasonable alternative or variant treatments

The courts anxiously protect the right of autonomy of adults who have the mental capacity to make decisions about their own health and welfare. If I choose not to undergo potentially curative chemotherapy, that is my right. If I choose to submit to hazardous surgery rather than conservative treatment, that is my right. I cannot insist on the NHS making available to me all possible treatments – there are resource implications – but I have the right to choose from the viable treatments that are available. The healthcare professional's role is not to choose my treatment for me, but to advise as to the risks and benefits of the available options. Doctors advise, patients decide.

We have seen that in the case of *Bolam v Friern Hospital Management Committee*, the claimant alleged both negligent performance of the treatment he was given and negligent advice about the risks of the treatment. Whereas the *Bolam* test still applies to clinical performance, whether in the form of investigations, diagnosis or treatment, a different approach has since been adopted to clinical advice and the obtaining of consent to treatment.

In *Sidaway v Board of Governors of the Bethlem Royal Hospital* [1985] UKHL 1, the claimant failed to prove that a neurosurgeon had been negligent in failing to advise her of the very small risk of spinal cord damage inherent in proposed surgery to alleviate her neck pain. The very rare risk materialised and she sued for damages. Her claim went all the way to the House of Lords. Although the court dismissed her claim, the judges in the House of Lords gave differing opinions about whether the *Bolam* test should be applied to the question of pre-operative advice. Lord Scarman held that the *Bolam* test should not be applied and that the courts should focus on the right of the patient to make informed decisions about their treatment, the duty on the doctor being to give the prudent patient the information they needed to make an informed decision. Other judges, including Lord Bridge preferred to apply the *Bolam* test but with the qualifications that: (i) the court should exercise an oversight role, ensuring that patients should be informed of risks that are obviously relevant to their decision whether to proceed with treatment; and (ii) doctors must give honest answers when asked specific questions by their patient.

In a later case, *Pearce & Anor v United Bristol Healthcare NHS Trust* [1998] EWCA Civ 865, an expectant mother had carried her baby over term. Her consultant obstetrician advised that she should allow nature to take its course and to have a vaginal delivery at that time, rather than to choose to have a Caesarean section at an earlier date. In the event, the baby died in utero. The Court of Appeal had to determine whether the mother should have been warned of that risk. Lord Woolf, then Master of the Rolls (the senior civil judge), picked up on Lord Bridge's qualification of *Bolam* and said:

> "In a case where it is being alleged that a plaintiff has been deprived of the opportunity to make a proper decision as to what course he or she should take in relation to treatment, it seems to me to be the law, as indicated in the cases to which I have just referred, that if there is a significant risk which would affect the judgment of a reasonable patient, then in the normal course it is the responsibility of a doctor to inform the patient of that significant risk, if the information is needed so that the patient can determine for him or herself as to what course he or she should adopt."

More recently, in 2015, the Supreme Court considered an appeal from the Scottish courts concerning advice given to another expectant mother about the risks that might be involved in the delivery of her baby, in particular the risks associated with shoulder dystocia (where a shoulder becomes stuck, obstructing or even preventing vaginal delivery of the body after delivery of the head). This was the case of *Montgomery v Lanarkshire Health Board* [2015] UKSC 11.

Montgomery is perhaps the most important clinical negligence judgment since *Bolitho*. Its ramifications are still being worked out, and I shall discuss some of the subsequent case law below. In Part 1 I explained how the common law develops incrementally, case by case. This process can be seen in the changes from *Bolam* to *Montgomery*, via *Sidaway* and *Pearce*. The courts have gradually moved over nearly 60 years from deference to professional judgment, to an assertion of patient autonomy.

The Supreme Court in *Montgomery* explained why the *Bolam* approach was not entirely appropriate to the question of pre-treatment advice to patients. There is:

> *"... a duty on the part of doctors to take reasonable care to ensure that a patient is aware of material risks of injury that are inherent in treatment. This can be understood, within the traditional framework of negligence, as a duty of care to avoid exposing a person to a risk of injury which she would otherwise have avoided, but it is also the counterpart of the patient's entitlement to decide whether or not to incur that risk. The existence of that entitlement, and the fact that its exercise does not depend exclusively on medical considerations, are important. They point to a fundamental distinction between, on the one hand, the doctor's role when considering possible investigatory or treatment options and, on the other, her role in discussing with the patient any recommended treatment and possible alternatives, and the risks of injury which may be involved."*

The importance of patient autonomy – the right to decide what happens to one's own person – means that it is inappropriate to consider only what the profession regards as necessary in terms of warnings to patients. Each patient will have their own views as to what is important and what risks are relevant to their decision-making.

The Supreme Court set out the approach that the courts should take to a doctor's duty to obtain a patient's consent to treatment:

> *"An adult person of sound mind is entitled to decide which, if any, of the available forms of treatment to undergo, and her consent must be obtained before treatment interfering with her bodily integrity is undertaken. The doctor is therefore under a duty to take reasonable care to ensure that the patient is aware of any material risks involved in any recommended treatment, and of any reasonable alternative or variant treatments. The test of materiality is whether, in the circumstances of the particular case, a reasonable person in the patient's position would be likely to attach significance to the risk, or the doctor is or should reasonably be aware that the particular patient would be likely to attach significance to it."*

There is an exception to this rule – sometimes called the "therapeutic exception". Very rarely a doctor would be justified in withholding information about a particular risk if they reasonably consider that its disclosure would be "seriously detrimental to the patient's health".

The courts also recognise that in some circumstances it is necessary to proceed with treatment without obtaining prior express consent from the patient. This might be so in a case of emergency, or where the patient is unconscious and cannot give express consent.

Court:
Supreme Court
Reported: [2015] UKSC 11;
[2015] 1 AC 1430

Facts:
A mother was not given advice about the respective risks and benefits involved in proceeding to vaginal delivery as opposed to elective Caesarean delivery of a child when there was a particular risk of vaginal delivery being complicated by shoulder dystocia. Had the mother been so advised she would have elected to have a Caesarean section, thus avoiding the permanent brain damage and physical injury suffered by her child as a result of those complications.

Montgomery v Lanarkshire Health Board

Decision:
The doctor was negligent in that she failed to give the mother information about the options for treatment to allow her to give her informed consent to proceeding to vaginal delivery.

Key Points Applied in Later Cases:
The *Bolam* test does not apply to determine whether advice to a patient about the risks and benefits of treatment was adequate. The test to be applied is as follows: the doctor is under a duty to take reasonable care to ensure that the patient is aware of any material risks involved in any recommended treatment, and of any reasonable alternative or variant treatments. The test of materiality is whether, in the circumstances of the particular case, a reasonable person in the patient's position would be likely to attach significance to the risk, or the doctor is or should reasonably be aware that the particular patient would be likely to attach significance to it.

Casenote 5

115

Only patients who are adults and have the mental capacity to make decisions about their own treatment, can give consent. So where there are disputes between parents of a child and medical professionals about major treatment decisions, the courts may be asked to intervene to decide what is in the child's best interests. This has given rise to high profile and controversial decisions such as those concerning the withdrawal of life-sustaining treatment to the babies Alfie Evans and Charlie Gard. Similar principles govern treatment decisions for adults without capacity. These are not clinical negligence cases, but "best interest" decisions.

The Supreme Court referred to three important matters in relation to the standard of care to be exercised when obtaining consent to treatment from adults with the capacity to make decisions about their own treatment.

(i)   There is no particular, universally applicable threshold for the extent of risk beyond which the risk will be considered material. The *"assessment of whether a risk is material cannot be reduced to percentages. The significance of a given risk is likely to reflect a variety of factors besides its magnitude: for example, the nature of the risk, the effect which its occurrence would have upon the life of the patient, the importance to the patient of the benefits sought to be achieved by the treatment, the alternatives available, and the risks involved in those alternatives. The assessment is therefore fact-sensitive, and sensitive also to the characteristics of the patient."*

(ii)   Advising a patient and obtaining consent is not a tick-box exercise. Form-filling is no substitute for genuine dialogue. *"The doctor's advisory role involves dialogue, the aim of which is to ensure that the patient understands the seriousness of her condition, and the anticipated benefits and risks of the proposed treatment and any reasonable alternatives, so that she is then in a position to make an informed decision. This role will only be performed effectively if the information provided is comprehensible. The doctor's duty is not therefore fulfilled by bombarding the patient with technical information which she cannot reasonably be expected to grasp, let alone by routinely demanding her signature on a consent form."*

(iii)   The therapeutic exception must not be abused by healthcare professionals. It will be applicable in limited cases and is not a licence to keep information from a patient because the doctor believes the patient will make the "wrong" decision or one that is not in their own best interests: *"... it is not intended to subvert that principle by enabling the doctor to prevent the patient from making an informed choice where she is liable to make a choice which the doctor considers to be contrary to her best interests."*

Many medical professionals have expressed deep concerns about the *Montgomery* decision. They have feared that it mandates long conversations about all manner of possible risks and complications, for which there is insufficient time in a GP's or out-patient list. Subsequent cases, in which *Montgomery* has been applied, may or may not have calmed their nerves.

One line of cases shows that *Bolam* was not killed off entirely in this field of clinical negligence.

In *Duce v Worcestershire Acute Hospitals NHS Trust* [2018] EWCA Civ 1307 the Court of Appeal held that the *Montgomery* approach involved a two-fold test:

> *"(1) What risks associated with an operation were or should have been known to the medical professional in question. That is a matter falling within the expertise of medical professionals.*
>
> *(2) Whether the patient should have been told about such risks by reference to whether they were material. That is a matter for the Court to determine [83]. This issue is not therefore the subject of the Bolam test and not something that can be determined by reference to expert evidence alone."*

The claimant suffered nerve damage and chronic post-surgical pain following a total abdominal hysterectomy and bilateral salpingo-oophorectomy. The surgery was performed competently but it was alleged that there had been negligent pre-operative counselling in that the claimant was not adequately warned of the risk of pain. The claimant lost at trial and appealed, alleging that the trial judge had failed to apply the materiality test from *Montgomery*. The Court of Appeal rejected that complaint, holding that: *"the reason that the judge did not address the issue of materiality is that he had found that the claim failed at the first hurdle: proof that gynaecologists were or should have been aware of the relevant risks, which is a matter for expert evidence."* The reliance on expert evidence indicates that the *Bolam* test still applies to the first stage of the *Montgomery* approach.

Duce concerned advice about the risks of the recommended treatment. *Bayley v George Eliot Hospital* [2017] EWHC 3398 (QB) (HHJ Worster sitting as Deputy High Court Judge) concerned advice about alternatives to the recommended treatment. This judgment preceded *Duce* but the judge adopted a similar approach. The claimant unsuccessfully alleged that there had been a negligent failure to advise her of the possibility of an alternative to the treatment she actually underwent for her deep vein thrombosis, namely the insertion of an ilio-femoral venous stent. The judge noted that the *Montgomery* obligation was to advise as to *"any reasonable alternative or variant treatments"*. HHJ Worster discussed what test should be applied to determine whether an alternative treatment was "reasonable". He said that the matter must be judged by what was known or ought to have been known about the alternative treatment at the relevant time. The question of reasonableness had to be approached by reference to all the circumstances including the particular patient, their condition and prognosis. In the circumstances of the case before him, the judge found that the evidence did not establish that a reasonably competent vascular surgeon would or ought to have known about the particular alternative treatment the claimant alleged she should have been offered. In any event, the judge found, the option was not feasible for this claimant at the relevant time – the opportunity to use stenting had passed. The judge appears to have treated the question of what is a "reasonable alternative" as a *Bolam* question – would any responsible body of surgeons have been aware of and considered reasonable, any particular alternative treatment?

The findings that the judge recorded – that the alternative was not viable, and that it was not negligent to have been unaware of it – made easier the task of concluding that stenting was not a "reasonable" alternative. But what would the situation be where the clinician did know of an alternative and potentially feasible treatment but did not consider it to be a *reasonable* alternative? There is a risk that allowing (*Bolam* reasonable) professional judgement to dictate what is a reasonable alternative treatment undermines the sovereignty of patient autonomy and the purpose behind the second part of the *Montgomery* "two-fold" test. Suppose there is an innovative treatment being used by 10% of clinicians in a particular field, and that the patient's clinician knows about it but considers it not to be a reasonable alternative because it has not been sufficiently tried and tested. If the *Bolam* test applies then the court might well find that it was not negligent to have failed to have mentioned the alternative to the patient. Is that not the very paternalism that the Supreme Court in *Montgomery* was striving to end?

On the other hand, if clinicians are obliged to advise as to the risks and benefits of every alternative treatment of which they are, or should be, aware, however unreasonable they believe it to be, then a great deal of valuable clinic time will be spent running through the many alternatives to the recommended treatment, even when some of those alternatives are on the fringes of reasonable clinical understanding and practice.

One interesting question that arises is whether a doctor owes a duty to advise the patient about treatments that are not available within the NHS, but might be available, at cost, in the private sector, including treatments only available abroad. Does the possibility of paying tens of thousands of dollars for innovative treatment in Florida fall under the category of "reasonable alternative or variant treatments"? Who decides what is a reasonable alternative: the doctor or the patient?

Recent case law also suggests that the courts will look closely at the difference between giving information to a patient, and giving advice. Patients may make decisions in reliance on a whole host of factors, only one of which is information provided by a healthcare professional. In contrast sometimes patients rely on a professional to take over the decision-making process for them. In a wrongful birth claim (see Part 4) called *Khan v MNX* [2018] EWCA Civ 2609, the Court of Appeal held that a doctor who negligently misinformed a woman that she was not a carrier of haemophilia, was liable only for the additional costs attributable to the subsequent child having haemophilia, not those due to his also having autism. The doctor had not taken over the decision whether the woman should become pregnant. The doctor had not assumed responsibility for all the potential risks associated with pregnancy and congenital or other problems that a subsequent child might have. The doctor was responsible only for the misinformation he had negligently given. Professionals are not liable to compensate patients for everything that happens after they give negligent information to patients.

Following *Montgomery*, courts have had to grapple with the question of what is a "material" risk for the particular patient. Clinical negligence defendants often seek to emphasise the remoteness of a risk. Surely a 1 in 1,000 risk is not material? How would the dialogue between doctor and patient ever end if they have to discuss risks as low as that?

Mrs A v East Kent Hospitals University NHS Foundation Trust [2015] EWHC 1038 (QB) was another wrongful birth claim. The claimant alleged that she should have been advised of a risk of a chromosomal abnormality affecting her unborn child. Had she been warned, she would have elected to terminate the pregnancy. Dingemans J drew a distinction between a 1% to 3% risk of an abnormality, which would have been "material" and a 1 in 1,000 risk which was not. Mr Justice Jay adopted a similar approach in *Tasmin v Barts Health NHS Trust* [2015] EWHC 3135 (QB) holding that when advising expectant parents in that case, a 1 in 1,000 risk was too low to be material. However, when considering a 1 in 1,000 to 1 in 500 risk of paralysis with proposed spinal surgery in *Hassell v Hillingdon Hospitals NHS Foundation Trust* [2018] EWHC 164 (QB), Dingemans J held that that was a material risk. The experts agreed that the risk is usually communicated as a 1 in 1,000 risk but in was fact between 1 in 1,000 and 1 in 500. Had the claimant been advised effectively of that risk and of the reasonable alternative of conservative treatment, she would not have elected to undergo the surgery. It should not be surprising that the same judge found that a 1 in 1,000 risk was not material in one case (*Mrs A*) and was material in another (*Hassell*) because it all depends on the context. The Supreme Court in *Montgomery* expressly said that materiality cannot be reduced to a simple statement of percentage.

The importance of genuine dialogue rather than form-filling was underlined by Mr Justice Green in *Thefaut v Johnston* [2017] EWHC 497 (QB). The defendant sought to rely on the fact that they had obtained "consent" from the patient shortly before the surgery. The judge was not impressed:

> "It is routine for a surgeon immediately prior to surgery to see the patient and to ensure that they remain wedded to the procedure. But this is neither the place nor the occasion for a surgeon for the first time to explain to a patient undergoing elective surgery the relevant risks and benefits. At this point, on the very cusp of the procedure itself, the surgeon is likely to be under considerable pressure of time (to see all patients on the list and get to surgery) and the patient is psychologically committed to going ahead. There is a mutual momentum towards surgery which is hard to halt. There is no "adequate time and space" for a sensible dialogue to occur and for free choice to be exercised. In making this comment I am not of course referring to emergency situations where the position might be quite different."

Standardised consent forms may provide some evidence that there was a discussion about risks and benefits, but they are of limited evidential use in litigation. The common practice is to enter on the form a list of possible complications, such as infection, bleeding, scarring, general anaesthetic risk, nerve damage etc. That is no evidence that the patient was properly advised of the extent of the risk materialising, the consequences if it did materialise and so on. Written information in the form of a leaflet or information sheet is more helpful. Nevertheless, a doctor should ensure that the patient has understood what has been written down. It could be that hospitals could begin to use IT more effectively – an App or a website page could include an explanation of the proposed treatment and alternatives, with an interactive question and answer section to follow. This would not suit all patients, but it might help many, as well as freeing up the time of healthcare professionals.

Whilst pro-forma consent documents have limited evidential weight in clinical negligence litigation, they do nonetheless provide some evidence about what was and what was not said at a pre-treatment consultation. Other evidence will include a doctor's own clinical notes, and the recollections of those who were present. Where recollections conflict, the contemporaneous notes can be very important evidence, but they can cut both ways. If a surgeon has noted that they have advised the patient of a small but significant risk of visible, raised scarring following a facelift procedure, then that is good evidence to set against the patient's recollection that they were not told anything about that risk. On the other hand, if the surgeon asserts that they warned of the risk of the need for revision surgery, but the patient denies it, and there is no record of such a warning, then the very absence of a note might weigh heavily against the surgeon at court. Whilst healthcare professionals make contemporaneous notes, patients rarely do. Of course, there is nothing to stop a patient making notes during a consultation, keeping them, and relying on them at trial as evidence of what was or was not said. In fact, it is surprising that more patients do not take notes because it is difficult to take in everything at a consultation, and useful to have something in writing as a reminder. There may yet come a day when it is routine for audio or film recordings to be made at consultations.

As we have seen, claimants have brought clinical negligence claims arising out of an alleged failure to obtain informed consent to treatment for decades, including in the case of *Bolam* itself. The courts have always regarded these as negligence claims, rather than claims for trespass against the person, a different form of tort. Trespass is an intentional, unconsented to, interference with the person. Operating on a person without their consent might seem to fall within that definition, but the courts have held that where a patient knows in broad terms the treatment they will be undergoing and agrees to it, even if not given the proper information about the proposed treatment (and alternatives), then the allegation is one of negligent advice rather than trespass to the person.

As with any claim in negligence, the claimant has not only to prove negligence but also causation. It can be particularly difficult to prove causation in "consent" cases. This is discussed below under the ninth principle.

Principle 8: NHS Trusts are liable for the negligent acts and omissions of their employees and other staff concerning the management and treatment of patients

Where a patient alleges negligent treatment at an NHS hospital, the appropriate defendant is the NHS Trust responsible for managing the hospital. The Trust owes a duty of care to their patients. The Trust must take reasonable care to ensure that systems are in place adequately to manage, care and treat patients. It must take reasonable care to employ and engage personnel who are suitably qualified and trained. In addition, even if the Trust is not itself negligent in carrying out these functions, it may be fixed with liability for the negligence of those it employs or engages to care and manage its patients.

Vicarious Liability

A patient who attends the A&E department at a hospital with a head injury might be seen and managed by a triage nurse, an A&E doctor, a radiologist, a neuroradiologist, a neurosurgery ward nurse, and a neurosurgeon. All of these healthcare professionals will be employed or engaged by the NHS Trust responsible for running the hospital. In law, the Trust is directly liable for the negligent acts and omissions of all those personnel concerning their care, management and treatment of the patients at the hospital.

This is the principle of vicarious liability. The Trust is liable to the injured patient by reason of the negligence of an employee or an agent who is acting in a role in which they are required to act by the Trust.

Suppose a factory worker loses a finger because of the negligent operation of machinery by a colleague. It would be of little benefit to the injured worker to sue his colleague for compensation. His colleague would not have insurance and would be unlikely to meet an award for damages against him. But his employer, the owner of the factory, would very probably have insurance and would be very likely to be able to make a payment of compensation if ordered to do so. The factory owner might themselves have been negligent in relation to the provision of the machinery or protective equipment, or the training of employees in the safe use of the machinery. But they are also directly liable as the employer of the negligent worker who was acting in the course of their employment when they negligently caused another worker's finger to be cut off in a machine in the factory premises.

Clearly an NHS Trust does not require doctors and nurses to act negligently. Vicarious liability arises when the medical and nursing staff act negligently when performing duties they are required to perform as part of their employment or engagement by the Trust.

This principle of vicarious liability gives protection for injured patients – they can be assured that an NHS Trust will meet the compensation bill. It also provides some protection for healthcare professionals – the NHS Trust will organise the defence of any claim and the payment of compensation. The negligent doctor or nurse will not personally have to pay the compensation flowing from their errors.

Although a patient can sue the NHS Trust responsible for running a particular hospital, they could, in principle, also sue the individual who was negligent. In reality this is virtually unheard of. Why would a patient sue an individual and the Trust for the same negligence and the same potential compensation? The litigation costs would be increased in return for no additional benefit.

For general medical practitioners, GPs, the position may be somewhat different. A GP will often not have the shelter of vicarious liability. They may do so if they were acting as an employee or agent of a Primary Care Trust or other NHS organisation, but much more often a GP will be sued either in their own name, or as a member of a partnership. Traditionally, therefore, GPs have taken out professional indemnity insurance, usually either with the Medical Defence Union or the Medical Protection Society. The MDU or MPS have arranged to handle any claim on the GP's behalf and to meet the damages that may ultimately be payable to the injured patient. Where a GP is in a partnership with other GPs then they are jointly and severally liable for each other's negligence. It is all for one and one for all. As a partner of Dr Wright, Dr Smith is liable for Dr Wright's negligence. However, a new scheme was introduced in 2019: the Clinical Negligence Scheme for General Practice. This applies to all claims for clinical negligence in relation to primary healthcare in England which come within the scope of the scheme, provided that the act or omission alleged to have been negligent occurred on or after 1 April 2019. NHS Resolution operates this new scheme. There is guidance available as to the scope and application of the scheme on the NHS Resolution website. It covers not just GPs who run a practice, but also locums, practice nurses and others. A similar scheme called the Clinical Negligence Scheme for Trusts is operated by NHSR for NHS hospital Trusts. It is fair to say that the GP scheme has not got off to a promising start. The Medical Defence Organisations are not happy with the scheme. Nevertheless, if their objections are resolved, in a few years, nearly all defendants to clinical negligence claims within the NHS in England will be indemnified by schemes operated by a single body. It is not yet clear whether this will lead to substantial changes in the litigation process.

Where a healthcare professional is in private practice they might be employed by an organisation in which case that organisation will be vicariously liable for their negligence, or they might be engaged as what is called an independent contractor. If, say, a cosmetic surgeon, is contracted by a cosmetic clinic to provide surgery to patients, then they may very well not be employed by the clinic but might be paid for their services under a different kind of contract. The contract might specify that the surgeon has to have certain qualifications and training, that they have to use certain facilities and complete certain forms etc, but the surgeon will not be under the kind of control of the clinic as would be an employee. In such cases the clinic will argue that it is not vicariously liable for the negligence of a cosmetic surgeon. This defence to a claim brought against the clinic for negligent surgery can be a surprise to patients who have paid money to the clinic for the surgery performed. I will address this a little further in Part 4. For present purposes it suffices to note that the boundaries of vicarious liability are not easily drawn. In some recent cases schools have been found to be vicariously liable for acts of sexual abuse of teachers on children. A bank was recently held to be vicariously liable for the sexual assaults of a doctor engaged, but not employed, by the bank to carry out examinations of prospective employees. At the time of writing the Supreme Court has given permission to appeal that decision and will be considering the case in the near future.

Non-Delegable Duty

There is another principle, similar to that of vicarious liability, that has featured in more recent claims for personal injury, including clinical negligence, and that is the principle of non-delegable duty. It has a similar end result to vicarious liability but reaches it through different reasoning. In the leading case on non-delegable duty, a child suffered catastrophic injury in a swimming pool during a school swimming lesson. The local authority responsible for the school did not, however, employ the swimming teacher but had delegated responsibility for the lessons to a company – it had contracted out the service. The case is called *Woodland v Essex County Council* [2013] UKSC 66; [2013] 3 WLR 1227. The defendant local authority argued that it should not be held responsible for the negligent acts and omissions of the independent contractor it had relied upon to provide the swimming teaching and supervision. The local authority was not vicariously liable for the swimming teacher's negligence – he was employed by the company that it had contracted to provide the service. The question for the Supreme Court was whether nevertheless the local authority had a personal liability to the claimant.

Lord Sumption, giving the lead judgment of the Supreme Court, held that it did. He noted the following features of cases in which a non-delegable duty will be held to exist:

> "(1) The claimant is a patient or a child, or for some other reason is especially vulnerable or dependent on the protection of the defendant against the risk of injury. Other examples are likely to be prisoners and residents in care homes.
>
> (2) There is an antecedent relationship between the claimant and the defendant, independent of the negligent act or omission itself, (i) which places the claimant in the actual custody, charge or care of the defendant, and (ii) from which it is possible to impute to the defendant the assumption of a positive duty to protect the claimant from harm, and not just a duty to refrain from conduct which will foreseeably damage the claimant. It is characteristic of such relationships that they involve an element of control over the claimant, which varies in intensity from one situation to another, but is clearly very substantial in the case of schoolchildren.
>
> (3) The claimant has no control over how the defendant chooses to perform those obligations, i.e. whether personally or through employees or through third parties.
>
> (4) The defendant has delegated to a third party some function which is an integral part of the positive duty which he has assumed towards the claimant; and the third party is exercising, for the purpose of the function thus delegated to him, the defendant's custody or care of the claimant and the element of control that goes with it.
>
> (5) The third party has been negligent not in some collateral respect but in the performance of the very function assumed by the defendant and delegated by the defendant to him."

Lord Sumption noted previous cases involving hospitals. In *Cassidy v Ministry of Health* [1951] 2 KB 343 at the Court of Appeal, Lord Denning agreed with the other two members of the court that liability attached to the defendant, but whereas they had decided the case on the basis of vicarious liability, he went further:

> *"when hospital authorities undertake to treat a patient, and themselves select and appoint and employ the professional men and women who are to give the treatment, then they are responsible for the negligence of those persons in failing to give proper treatment, no matter whether they are doctors, surgeons, nurses, or anyone else... where the doctor or surgeon, be he a consultant or not, is employed and paid, not by the patient but by the hospital authorities, I am of opinion that the hospital authorities are liable for his negligence in treating the patient. It does not depend on whether the contract under which he was employed was a contract of service or a contract for services. That is a fine distinction which is sometimes of importance; but not in cases such as the present, where the hospital authorities are themselves under a duty to use care in treating the patient."*

This is an assertion that the hospital authority (now the NHS Trust) owes a personal duty to patients and is directly liable to them, as well as vicariously liable for the acts and omissions of employees or agents. Lord Sumption said that Lord Denning had correctly identified the underlying principle.

The application of this principle to the clinical management of patients by NHS Trusts is yet to be fully worked out through the common law system of case law and precedent. In one recent case the Ministry of Justice was held not to owe a non-delegable duty for the healthcare of a prisoner. The healthcare services were provided by the local Primary Healthcare Trust and the judge held that the Ministry of Justice's core activity or functions did not include providing healthcare to its prisoners. That decision is not without controversy. In *Farraj v King's Healthcare NHS Trust* [2008] EWHC 2468 (QB) Burnett J doubted that the Trust owed a non-delegable duty of care to expectant parents who had a DNA test performed. The Trust contracted out the DNA testing service to an independent clinic. After *Woodland*, perhaps a different decision would now be reached. Certainly, where a core service of the hospital is contracted out, it is very arguable that the Trust will not avoid liability simply by asserting that the only responsibility for negligence is that of the independent contractor. This is an increasingly important principle now that there is a trend for public services to contract out functions, including some core activities, to the private sector.

Principle 9: Liability only arises where negligence causes or materially contributes to injury or death

There is no civil liability for negligence that does not cause harm. A doctor might face regulatory sanction for harmless negligence – for the purpose of protecting the public – but they could not be sued for compensation. The purpose of the law of clinical negligence is to compensate for avoidable harm, therefore liability only arises if negligence has caused harm.

It is for the person bringing a claim for compensation to prove that on the balance of probabilities the negligence caused harm. "Harm" means any physical or psychiatric injury, or death, and the financial consequences of that injury or death. As we saw in Part 1, the courts typically ask whether the claimed injury or death would have occurred "but for" the negligence. If, in the absence of the negligence, the patient would have suffered the same outcome, or would have died at the same time in any event, then the negligence was not causative of the harm for which the claim is made. In that case there is no liability, however egregious the negligence.

The "But For" Test

This so-called "but for" test can be applied to most clinical negligence claims. But for the negligent failure to decide to proceed to an emergency Caesarean section, would the baby have been delivered without neurological injury? But for the decision to discharge the patient before performing blood tests, they would have been diagnosed with sepsis, commenced on intravenous antibiotics, and have avoided the worst effects of their meningitis.

In clinical negligence cases it is always necessary to consider what the claimant's illness or condition was that brought them to the GP, hospital or other healthcare provider in the first place. What would have been the progress of that condition had non-negligent care and treatment been given?

I have had many clients who have fallen into the trap of thinking that they would always have been as fit and healthy as they were immediately prior to the negligent treatment they were given, when in fact they had an underlying condition which, even if treated non-negligently, would have restricted their activities in any event. That is not to say that someone who would in any event have been disabled, is incapable of suffering more injury and disability as a result of a defendant's clinical negligence. It does mean that the defendant is not liable for what would have been suffered in any event. Sometimes the additional injury can cause disproportionately severe injury and consequential loss. Take the one-eyed patient who loses sight in his remaining eye as a result of clinical negligence. The loss of vision in one eye would be much more devastating for them than for a person who previously had two functioning eyes. On the other hand, a potentially very serious injury might not have the financial consequences for a previously disabled claimant as it would for someone without a pre-existing disability.

Disentangling the effects of the condition, injury or illness that required treatment from the effects of negligent treatment can be very difficult. As ever, the onus is on the claimant to prove that it was the negligence that was causative of the harm for which compensation is claimed. The harsh consequences of that rule can be seen in two well known cases.

In *Hotson v East Berkshire Area Health Authority* [1988] UKHL 1 the claimant fell from a tree and fractured his left femoral epiphysis. He was taken to hospital, where there was a failure properly to diagnose or treat his condition for several days. He suffered avascular necrosis of the epiphysis, leaving him with a permanent disability. The House of Lords held that on the evidence the avascular necrosis must have been caused either by irreparable rupture of the blood vessels to the epiphysis at the moment of the fall, or by later pressure within the joint from bruising or internal bleeding (for which the defendant was potentially liable). There was no room for finding that the avascular necrosis was caused by a combination of the two factors. The trial judge's findings were to the effect that on the balance of probabilities the cause was the original traumatic injury. The claim therefore failed.

In *Wilsher v Essex Area Health Authority* [1987] UKHL 11 the injury was a condition known as retrolental fibroplasia or RLF, to which premature babies are vulnerable. The condition may be caused by various factors, one of which is an oversupply of oxygen. The claimant was born prematurely and as a result of clinical negligence he was given too much oxygen. He developed RLF, but it was held by the House of Lords that it was not enough to show that the defendant's negligence added to the list of factors that could have caused RLF. The claimant's RLF was capable of being caused by any one of a number of factors that existed at the relevant time. The fact that one of them had been negligently brought about did not mean that it was the likely cause of the condition. The claim failed.

Application of the "but for" test always involves speculation. In relation to every head of claim, the court has to ask "but for" the negligence, what would the claimant's position have been to date, now and in the future? For example, "but for" the loss of two fingers, would the claimant have been able to continue in work? What work would they have done and how much would they have earned? When would they have retired? What would their pension have been? The claimant has to establish the answers to all those, and very many more questions relevant to "causation", and to establish them to the required standard or proof: on the balance of probabilities.

In some cases, there needs to be a series of "but for" questions. Take, as an example, a failure to refer a patient for further assessment of a breast lump. The court will need to consider:

– But for the failure to refer, when would the claimant have been seen in a breast clinic?

– Had they been seen in a breast clinic, what investigations and examinations would probably have been performed?

– What would have been the outcome of those investigations and examinations: would breast cancer have been diagnosed and when?

– If so, what would the size, stage and grade of the cancer have been at that time?

– What treatment would the claimant have been offered?

– What treatment would the claimant have elected to undergo?

– What would have been the outcome of the treatment? What would have been the claimant's condition and prognosis at the conclusion of treatment?

– Having regard to those matters, but for the failure to refer would the claimant have avoided the mastectomy she in fact underwent after she was diagnosed? Would she have a better prognosis than she now has?

Each question is a link in the chain of causation. The claimant has to establish each and every link to the court's satisfaction on the balance of probabilities. It is insufficient for a claimant to establish, for example, that but for the failure to diagnose and treat her breast cancer at an earlier stage, she *might have* avoided a mastectomy, or that the chances of her avoiding a mastectomy would have been somewhat higher.

The "but for" test can, if applied mechanistically and without keeping in mind the important question of the scope of the duty of care, lead to peculiar outcomes. I negligently drive through a red light. But for that careless driving, I would have arrived at the top of the road where I live one minute later and I would have avoided the tree which was blown over in the storm and onto my car, killing my passenger. But for my negligence the passenger would not have died – am I liable in negligence?

The answer is "no". It was not within the scope of my duty as a driver to be at the top of my road at a certain time. It was not within the scope of my duty to avoid the wind blowing over a tree. We have seen how the unthinking application of the "but for" test can lead to an unfair outcome, as illustrated by Lord Hoffman's mountaineer's knee example.

One important assumption underlies the "but for" test, namely that in the absence of the negligent act or omission, the defendant would have acted non-negligently. This was underlined in the case of *Bolitho* to which I have already referred. Suppose that a midwife has negligently failed to report to an obstetrician that a CTG trace recording the fetal heart rate is showing clear signs of significant fetal distress. The claimant has to prove that but for that negligence, the birth would have been accelerated and loss of oxygen to the baby's brain at around the time of delivery would have been avoided, and with it the cerebral palsy from which the claimant now suffers. Suppose the obstetrician gives evidence that had they been informed of the abnormal fetal heart trace, they would not have elected to accelerate the birth but would have proceeded to manage the labour in the same way as it was in fact managed. The baby would have suffered the same brain damage in any event. Even in the absence of the negligence, the same injuries would have been suffered.

In such a case the claimant may yet succeed in establishing liability if they can prove that the actions of the obstetrician would also have been negligent. The defendant Trust cannot rely on behaviour that would itself have been negligent, to defeat the claim. If what would have happened would have resulted in injury being avoided but for the negligence, the claimant has succeeded. If what would have happened would not have avoided the injury but would itself have been negligent, then the claimant may yet succeed. In the example of the obstetric case, the claimant would have to establish what would in fact have happened had the obstetrician been told of the abnormal CTG trace, and had responded to that information in a non-negligent manner. It is not a question then of what would have happened, but of what should have happened.

Causation and Negligent Advice

We have seen that the *Bolam* test no longer applies to pre-treatment advice and obtaining a patient's consent to treatment. Instead, the approach in *Montgomery* applies. This change in approach has affected questions of causation, and the "but for" test. In *Webster v Burton Hospitals NHS Foundation Trust* [2017] EWCA Civ 62, the Court of Appeal considered a case where the claimant had been born at over 40 weeks gestation. Had he been born at term he would have avoided severe neurological injuries. It was admitted that it had been negligent, following an antenatal scan at 34 weeks, to fail to follow up with fortnightly scans thereafter. However, the trial judge held that it would not have been *Bolam* negligent to keep to the plan that was in fact followed, leading to delivery at "term + 2", i.e. at 42 weeks gestation, and therefore the claimant's injuries would not have been avoided. The Court of Appeal allowed the claimant's appeal. It held that the proper approach to the "but for" question was that in *Montgomery*, not *Bolam*. The court should consider what advice ought to have been given to the claimant's mother after the 34 week scan, and then ask what decision would the claimant's mother have made in the light of that advice? She would have been advised of the material risks and benefits of the proposed management to allow the pregnancy to continue past "term", and of the reasonable alternative of electing earlier delivery. As a matter of fact, on the evidence before the court, she would have chosen elective delivery at term. Hence the claimant's injuries would have been avoided. The question as to what would have happened but for the negligence was not what the doctors would have decided to do, but what advice they would or should have given, and what the mother would then have decided to do on the basis of that advice.

In all cases, including those involving negligent advice, the claimant has to prove that they suffered harm as a result of the negligence. Where a claimant persuades the court that, but for negligent advice, they would have elected not to undergo surgery, then it follows that they would have avoided the surgery, and the risks associated with the surgery. The surgery might well constitute an injury in itself. What about the risks of complications? A risk is not an injury: it is only if the risk materialises that an injury is sustained. It matters not, in this context, whether the risk materialises due to negligent performance of the surgery, or due to a non-negligent complication.

Where a claimant suffers from, say, a 1 in 500 risk of nerve damage following surgery which, if properly advised about material risks they would have elected to avoid, then their injuries comprise having undergone surgery and having suffered the nerve damage. Of course, the court will also have to consider: (i) what the claimant would have elected to do had they been given non-negligent advice; and (ii) what the probable outcome of that chosen option would have been. If the claimant would have elected to have physiotherapy, how effective would that have been in alleviating their condition? Had they decided to have no treatment at all, would their condition probably have deteriorated, causing significant disability?

In one famous and controversial case, *Chester v Afshar* [2004] UKHL 41, the House of Lords, by a majority of 3 to 2, held that a claimant was entitled to damages where the defendant had negligently failed to warn her of a *"small (1% to 2%) but unavoidable risk that the proposed operation, however expertly performed, might lead to a seriously adverse result, known in medical parlance as cauda equina syndrome"*, but where *"if duly warned, Miss Chester would not have undergone surgery three days after her first consultation with Mr Afshar, but would, very understandably, have wished to discuss the matter with others and explore other options. But he did not find (and was not invited to find) that she would probably not have undergone the surgery or that there was any way of minimising the small degree of risk inherent in surgery."*

The claimant had not proved that she would never have undergone the surgery. The most that could be said was that she would not have had it on the day she did. She would have taken more time to think about whether to proceed. Since the burden of proof is on the claimant, she had failed to prove that she would not have had the surgery later.

Should the court award damages where "but for" the negligent advice the claimant would not have avoided the surgery, but may have undergone the same procedure at a later date? The timing of the operation would not have affected the extent of the risk. Two of the judges in the House of Lords thought the claim was without merit. Lord Hoffmann dismissed the claimant's contentions that the defendant should be held liable in a few short paragraphs and said:

> *"In my opinion this argument is about as logical as saying that if one had been told, on entering a casino, that the odds on No 7 coming up at roulette were only 1 in 37, one would have gone away and come back next week or gone to a different casino. The question is whether one would have taken the opportunity to avoid or reduce the risk, not whether one would have changed the scenario in some irrelevant detail. The judge found as a fact that the risk would have been precisely the same whether it was done then or later or by that competent surgeon or by another."*

But three of the judges held that the defendant should be liable for damages for the cauda equina syndrome. This was surely a departure from the "but for" approach but Lord Steyn said:

> *"Standing back from the detailed arguments, I have come to the conclusion that, as a result of the surgeon's failure to warn the patient, she cannot be said to have given informed consent to the surgery in the full legal sense. Her right of autonomy and dignity can and ought to be vindicated by a narrow and modest departure from traditional causation principles.*

> *"On a broader basis I am glad to have arrived at the conclusion that the claimant is entitled in law to succeed. This result is in accord with one of the most basic aspirations of the law, namely to right wrongs. Moreover, the decision announced by the House today reflects the reasonable expectations of the public in contemporary society."*

This was indeed a controversial decision. Nevertheless, it has stood for over 14 years. It has been applied in a number of cases to allow claimants to recover damages where surgery would not have taken place on the same day but for the defendant's negligence. For example, in one case surgery took place about three months earlier than it would have done but for a negligent failure to try a period of physiotherapy prior to a decision to proceed to surgery. In fact, it was agreed evidence that the physiotherapy would not have been effective and the patient would have come to surgery, with the same risk of complication, in any event. It might be asked, what injury did the claimant suffer as a result of the negligence? On one view they benefited from avoiding three months of ineffective physiotherapy. However, if you ask: "would the 1% to 2% risk which did materialise have probably materialised had surgery been performed on a different date?" the answer is clearly "no", because it was only a 1% to 2% risk. Thus, there was a 98% to 99% probability that if the surgery had been performed at another time, the complication would not have arisen. On the other hand, if you reduce this argument to absurdity, you could argue that if the surgery had taken place one minute earlier then the risk would probably not have materialised. In these cases, the timing of the surgery was irrelevant to the complication occurring. The risk of the complication was the same whenever the surgery was performed and the surgeon was not negligent when performing the operation.

Recently, Lord Justice Leggatt in the Court of Appeal in *Duce* (see above) commented that *Chester v Afshar* is:

> *"... problematic because on the facts, applying the normal burden of proof, the surgeon's failure to warn did not expose the claimant to a*

risk which she would not willingly have accepted. In law as in every-
day life A's wrongful act is not normally regarded as having caused
B's injury if the act made no difference to the probability of the injury
occurring. In such a case the fact that the injury would not have oc-
curred but for the wrongful act is merely a coincidence."

He effectively issued an open invitation for litigants to challenge *Chester v Afshar* in the future, which is all well and good if you have the resources to take a case to trial and then to the appellate courts.

It is helpful to view such cases through the prism of the "scope of duty". It is not within the scope of duty of a surgeon deciding when surgery should take place, to avoid a non-negligent complication of the surgery when that risk is not affected by the timing of the operation. A patient ought to know of the material risks and benefits, but if they would have been subject to the same risks irrespective of the timing of the treatment, then why should the defendant be liable?

Notwithstanding the decision in *Chester v Afshar*, it is usually difficult for a claimant to establish causation in a claim for negligent clinical advice. Claimants alleging that they would have chosen to avoid the surgery that gave rise to the complication that has ruined their lives, often face the Mandy Rice Davies response – they would say that wouldn't they? The courts have an understandable scepticism that a claimant's evidence that they would not have accepted the small risk of a complication had they been told about it, is unduly influenced by retrospect. By definition most of these claimants will have experienced the complication. They are living with cauda equina syndrome or some other serious adverse consequence of the treatment. Of course, says the defendant, the claimant will say that had they been warned that there was a 1 in 100 risk of suffering that con-sequence, they would not have gone ahead with the surgery. We are much more likely to accept a small risk, even of a serious complication, prior to treatment, because it is just a theoretical risk. Furthermore, the patient has a disability, pain or condition that merits consideration of surgery. They have to weigh the small theoretical risk against the potential benefit of alleviating their pain or disability. It is probably true that most patients elect to have the surgery notwithstanding advice about risks, even risks of quite serious complications. The courts therefore look for compelling evidence that the claimant, who has in fact suffered the complication, would be amongst a minority of patients who would have elected to avoid the surgery and con-tinue to live with their condition.

Material Contribution

Contrary to popular opinion, good lawyers and judges like to keep things simple. It is just that the evidence sometimes thwarts that ambition. It is all very well applying a "but for" test to causation "on the balance of probabilities", but sometimes the evidence does not supply a neat answer. In one area of personal injury law – cases of mesothelioma due to exposure to asbestos – the courts have bent the existing law to allow for claimants to recover compensation even when they cannot prove that but for a particular defendant's negligence they would have avoided the illness. In clinical negligence cases it is not uncommon to find experts advising that they just cannot say whether or not the injury would have been avoided but for the negligence, but that the negligence probably did contribute to it.

In the case of *Bailey v The Ministry of Defence & Anor* [2008] EWCA Civ 883; [2009] 1 WLR 1052 the Court of Appeal considered the case of a female patient who, after undergoing surgery, aspirated her vomit leading to a cardiac arrest that caused her to suffer hypoxic brain damage. The court identified the question for it to determine as follows: *"What caused her to aspirate her vomit? In particular, to what extent, if at all, was it due to lack of care while she was at hospital?"* There was a non-negligent cause of her weakness – the fact that she had pancreatitis following her surgery – and a negligent cause – a lack of proper care for her in the post-operative period. So what did cause the aspiration of vomit? The expert evidence in the case did not resolve this question neatly on a "but for" approach. The negligent and non-negligent causes acted in conjunction, or "cumulatively", to produce the injury. This was in contrast to the position in *Hotson* or in *Wilsher* (see above) where the potential causes under consideration would have acted independently of each other. The Court of Appeal in *Bailey* said that the test was whether the negligence "caused or materially contributed to" the claimant's injury. Lord Justice Waller held as follows:

> *"I would summarise the position in relation to cumulative cause cases as follows. If the evidence demonstrates on a balance of probabilities that the injury would have occurred as a result of the non-tortious cause or causes in any event, the claimant will have failed to establish that the tortious cause contributed. Hotson exemplifies such a situation. If the evidence demonstrates that 'but for' the contribution of the tortious cause the injury would probably not have occurred, the claimant will (obviously) have discharged the burden. In a case where medical science cannot establish the probability that 'but for' an act of negligence the injury would not have happened but can establish that the contribution of the negligent cause was more than negligible, the 'but for' test is modified, and the claimant will succeed."*

> *"The instant case involved cumulative causes acting so as to create a weakness and thus the judge in my view applied the right test, and was entitled to reach the conclusion he did."*

A contribution is "more than negligible" if it is more than minimal, or it is "material" or "of substance". These are synonymous terms.

The judgment in *Bailey v MOD* has been criticised in some quarters as being too generous to claimants who cannot in fact prove that negligence caused their injuries. A few years after *Bailey*, an opportunity arose for the Privy Council to consider the thorny question of "material contribution" in clinical negligence cases. The Judicial Committee of the Privy Council sits as a court hearing appeals from judgments in some Commonwealth countries. In *Williams v The Bermuda Hospitals Board* [2016] UKPC 4, the Judicial Committee considered an appeal from the Bermuda Court of Appeal involving a claimant who had suffered complications following a ruptured appendix. There was negligent delay in investigating and treating him at hospital but the septic process would have been underway before any such negligence. The complications comprised injury to his heart and lungs. The additional period when the septic process due to the ruptured appendix continued due to negligence was two hours and 20 minutes. The Judicial Committee was presented with detailed legal argument about the issue of material contribution, with many cases cited to it. However, as is clear from a very succinct judgment, it was not troubled by the apparent complexities of the issue. Giving the judgment, Lord Toulson said,

> *"In the present case the judge found that injury to the heart and lungs was caused by a single known agent, sepsis from the ruptured appendix. The sepsis developed incrementally over a period of approximately six hours, progressively causing myocardial ischaemia. (The greater the accumulation of sepsis, the greater the oxygen requirement.) The sepsis was not divided into separate components causing separate damage to the heart and lungs. Its development and effect on the heart and lungs was a single continuous process, during which the sufficiency of the supply of oxygen to the heart steadily reduced.*

> *"On the trial judge's findings, that process continued for a minimum period of two hours 20 minutes longer than it should have done. In the judgment of the Board, it is right to infer on the balance of probabilities that the hospital board's negligence materially contributed to the process, and therefore materially contributed to the injury to the heart and lungs."*

Likewise, in *Bailey v MOD*, there was no departure from the usual "but for" rule, observed Lord Toulson. Ms Bailey suffered aspiration of vomit due to weakness. That was the cause, and the failure to give adequate post-operative care contributed to that weakness.

This approach is adaptable to many cases of clinical negligence where there is a process that is exacerbated or materially contributed to by negligence, but as yet its application to cases such as delay in diagnosing cancer have not been definitively addressed by the higher courts. Generally, the point now reached at common law is that the claimant must prove that, on the balance of probabilities, the defendant's clinical negligence made more than a negligible contribution to a process which, on the balance of probabilities, caused injury or death. If, however, injury or death would probably have occurred without the contribution, then the claim will fail.

In amusement arcades you will nearly always find a coin pusher game, now used in the daytime TV show "Tipping Point". A pile of coins is spread out on a horizontal surface with some of the coins precariously close to the edge of a drop. Behind the coins is a sliding block moving backwards and forwards. The player drops a new coin into the slot and watches it fall onto the pile below. As the block slides, the new coin is pushed into the pile and the player hopes that it pushes forward other coins so that some fall of the edge and into their waiting hand. Why am I painfully trying to describe an arcade game? It is because it helps to illustrate the theory of material contribution. Suppose there is a mix of 10 pence and 2 pence coins resting in the machine. Then you add a 2 pence coin and as a result coins are tipped over into the drop. There was a process during which the pile of coins grew until a tipping point was reached and a payout achieved. This was not caused by the 10 pence coins alone nor by the 2 pence coins alone. The tipping point would not have been reached when it was had there only been 2 pence coins or only 10 pence coins in the machine. Suppose that the 10 pence coins represent negligent acts, and the 2 pence coins represent non-negligent acts. The payout represents injury. The process of adding negligent and non-negligent acts creates a tipping point causing injury. The extent of the injury did not depend solely on the number of negligent 10 pence coins nor solely on the number of non-negligent 2 pence coins, but upon the combination of both. The negligent 10 pence coins made a more than minimal contribution to the injury.

In *Bailey* and *Williams* the causative factors, both negligent and non-negligent, resulted in the same injury – aspiration of vomit leading to brain damage in the case of *Bailey*, and heart and lung damage in the case of *Williams*. It could not be said that the injury could be divided up so that a particular

137

part of it was attributable to one or the other cause. In other cases, there may be injuries that can be divided up and attributed to different causes. An arm injury might be due to negligent insertion of an intravenous line, and a leg injury due to non-negligently caused ischaemia. In those cases the negligent defendant is liable only for that part of the injury that is attributable to the negligence. There is no question of the defendant being liable for all the injury because it made a contribution to all the injuries. This distinction – between injuries that are divisible and those that are indivisible – can lead to some difficult decisions for claimants in litigation. Suppose that there was a non-negligent process of the brain damage due to starvation of oxygen, but the process was significantly prolonged by negligent delay. The claimant suffers permanent neurological injury due to brain damage caused by a period of loss of oxygen to the brain. This looks like the sort of process that was under consideration in *Williams*. There has been a single process causing the brain damage, and negligence resulted in that process being prolonged or exacerbated to a more than minimal extent. The claimant might therefore claim that the defendant's negligence materially contributed to the permanent brain damage and is liable for all of the claimant's brain damage. But what if the expert witnesses in the case give evidence that the brain damage suffered is proportionate to the period of hypoxia (lack of oxygen) and that the negligent delay cause the claimant to 35% worse brain damage that they would have had without the delay. Is the claim for 35% of the injury, rather than 100%? Is the injury divisible or indivisible? And suppose that there is other expert evidence showing that even with 65% of the total brain damage suffered, the claimant would still have required 24 hour care, would have been unable to work, unable to manage their own affairs and unable to live independently. Would the claimant have no right to recovery of compensation for any of their care, loss of earnings etc? It can be seen that the case is now on a knife edge. If the injury is viewed as being indivisible, the claimant might recover 100% of compensation for all their care needs, loss of earnings and other losses and expenses. If the injury is seen as divisible, they will recover some compensation but may receive nothing for future care, loss of earnings and any other losses and expenses that would have been suffered even with 65% of the brain damage they have incurred.

When the outcome of a case is uncertain, and the consequences of success or defeat on an issue such as that just described can mean a difference in compensation of several millions of pounds, very often the parties reach a compromise rather than taking the risks involved in leaving it to a court to determine who is right and who is wrong. There is too much at stake. The upshot is that only rarely does a High Court Judge, or an appellate court have the opportunity to give a judgment on these difficult issues. When they do, such as in *Williams v Bermuda*, the judgment can still leave questions as to how the approach set out by the court should be applied to different factual scenarios. These are the uncertainties with which litigants and their advisers have to contend.

Intervening Cause and Shared Liability

Life can be complicated. Even where there is clear evidence of negligence causing injury, it might be that "events" intervene and cause further harm. In some cases, it is easy to distinguish between the effects of the subsequent event and the consequences of the clinical negligence. If a claimant has suffered a leg amputation due to a negligent failure to manage their lower limb ischaemia, but three months later they suffer a broken arm as a passenger in a road traffic accident, the clinical negligence defendant is not liable for the arm injury or the care needed during the recovery from that injury. In other cases, the subsequent event is more closely connected to the original negligence and injury. Sometimes, the subsequent event is of such significance that it terminates the liability of the clinical negligence defendant for any further losses after the event. It breaks the chain of causation between the negligence and any further injury, loss and damage. This used to be known by the Latin term but is now known as an "intervening cause".

An intervening cause might be an "act of God" or have been caused by another person. The acts of a third party might be deliberate or accidental.

If a patient suffers a spinal injury due to negligent neurosurgery but three years later is struck by a bolt of lightning and killed, then clearly the clinical negligence defendant will only be liable for the patient's injuries up to the point that they die. The spinal injury was not the cause of death. The death put an end to the suffering and loss due to the spinal injury. The lightning strike was not a foreseeable consequence of the spinal injury – it had nothing to do with it.

A similar approach would be taken where the patient had been attacked and killed on the street three years after their spinal injury. The deliberate and malicious intervention of a third party would break the chain of causation.

A more difficult issue arises where the subsequent event is due to human intervention resulting from the original negligence, where that intervention was not with intent to cause harm. A leading case on such a situation is *Webb v Barclays Bank Plc* [2001] EWCA Civ 1141; [2002] PIQR P8.

Mrs Webb had polio as a child. In adulthood she injured her affected knee in a fall at work caused by the breach of duty of her employer, Barclays Bank. She later underwent an above knee amputation of her left lower limb

Court:
Court of Appeal, Civil Division
[2001] EWCA Civ 1141;
[2002] PIQR P8

Facts:
Mrs Webb suffered a fall at work injuring her knee. Surgical above knee amputation was performed on advice. The fall was caused by negligence. The advice to have a surgical amputation was negligent.

Webb v Barclays Bank

Decision:
Medical negligence did not break the chain of causation between the negligence causing the fall and the injury of having an amputated limb. Gross negligence might well do so. However, the negligent employer responsible for the fall was only 25% liable for injuries after the amputation. The Trust responsible for the medical negligence was 75% liable.

Key Points Applied in Later Cases:
Simple, not gross, clinical negligence in treating an injury caused by another's negligence will not prevent the originally negligent person remaining at least partially liable for the claimant's injuries.

Casenote 6

but the advice of her surgical team to have an amputation was itself negligent. She sought compensation from her employer, but the Bank alleged that the surgeon's negligent advice had broken the chain of causation – it was an intervening cause. So, she joined the relevant Trust as a second defendant. The Bank also sought a contribution from the Trust.

The Court of Appeal held that the surgeon's negligence had itself caused injury, but it had not broken the chain of causation between the employer's original negligence, and the claimant's injuries after the amputation. The court held that the Bank was liable for all of the damage attributable to the initial fall, up to the point of the amputation, and for 25% of the damage attributable to the amputation. Whilst there had been clinical negligence, it was not so grossly negligent as to be an unpredictable or unforeseeable consequence of the original negligence and injury. It did not break the chain of causation. However, after the amputation, they shared liability with the Trust for the ongoing injuries. The Trust had the most responsibility after the amputation, but the employer was still 25% responsible.

As a general rule, the courts are very reluctant to find that negligence by a third party who is trying to respond to mitigate the consequences of the defendant's negligence will extinguish the liability of the defendant. If a defendant's negligence causes someone to seek to rescue the claimant, and they perform the rescue negligently, that will very rarely be found to have terminated the liability of the defendant who caused the rescuer to act. To break the chain of causation, a later, negligent act by a third party has to be so negligent and unforeseeable that it obliterates the effect of the original negligence – it makes the original negligence merely part of the history of events, rather than something that has ongoing consequences.

Wright v Cambridge Medical Group [2011] EWCA Civ 669 concerned sequential acts of clinical negligence by different healthcare professionals – did the later negligence break the chain of causation between the negligence of the first professional and the claimant's continuing injuries? In this case a GP negligently delayed referring an 11 month old child to hospital. The child had a bacterial infection which ought to have resulted in the GP referring her to hospital on 14 April. In fact the child was not referred until 17 April, but on referral there was further negligent delay by the hospital staff until appropriate treatment was commenced on 20 April. The claimant suffered permanent injury affecting her mobility as a result of the delays. Had she been treated properly on 17 April, then her injuries would have been substantially avoided. Was the GP liable given that the permanent injuries would have been avoided had the Trust acted non-negligently?

For whatever reason, the Trust was not made a defendant to the claim, only the GP. At trial before a High Court Judge, the claim was defeated, the finding of the court being that the GP's negligence had not caused any loss. But for the negligence of the GP, the Trust would still have been negligent and the same injuries would have resulted. On appeal however the decision was overturned and the claimant succeeded. Lord Neuberger said:

> *"The mere fact that, if the second party had not been negligent, the damage which subsequently ensued would not have occurred, by no means automatically exonerates the first party's negligence from being causative of that damage."*

> *"... in a case where a doctor has negligently failed to refer his patient to a hospital, and, as a consequence, she has lost the opportunity to be treated as she should have been by a hospital, the doctor cannot escape liability by establishing that the hospital would have negligently failed to treat the patient appropriately, even if he had promptly referred her. Even if the doctor established this, it would not enable him*

> *to escape liability, because, by negligently failing to refer the patient promptly, he deprived her of the opportunity to be treated properly by the hospital, and, if they had not treated her properly, that opportunity would be reflected by the fact that she would have been able to recover damages from them."*

In any event, held Lord Neuberger, there should be a presumption that a third party, here the Trust, would have acted properly (non-negligently) on earlier referral. That presumption was either irrebuttable or would require very clear evidence to rebut it.

Shared Liability

As seen in relation to the case of *Webb v Barclays Bank*, it is possible for two or more defendants to share liability for negligently caused injury. In such cases the defendant is liable only for the share of the injury which it is found to have caused.

The Civil Liability (Contribution) Act 1978 provides – so far as relevant to clinical negligence cases – that a person liable to another for damages for personal injury may seek a contribution towards that liability from another. By section 2, *"the amount of the contribution recoverable from any person shall be such as may be found by the court to be just and equitable having regard to the extent of that person's responsibility for the damage in question."* This gives courts a free hand to "do justice" as between the negligent parties. The third person may be brought into the claim by the claimant as a defendant, in which case liability may be apportioned between the defendants. Alternatively, a defendant might bring proceedings against the third person seeking a contribution. These are called "Part 20" claims. They used to be called Third Party claims. There can in fact be fourth, fifth, sixth or more parties.

Patients do not sue "the NHS". The NHS is organised into different structures or bodies, such as Trusts or commissioning groups. If five doctors at a single Trust are negligent then the patient will sue the Trust alone, relying on the principle of vicarious liability explained above. If, however, the patient is transferred between hospitals run by different Trusts, and they allege negligence in both hospitals, they may have to sue both Trusts – there would be two defendants to their claim. This can give rise to significant litigation disadvantages to a claimant who has to incur the risk of paying costs twice over if they lose their claim. Furthermore, usually each defendant is entitled to adduce evidence from expert witnesses so the claimant may find their own experts outnumbered.

Where only one of two defendants is ultimately found liable, the claimant will usually be ordered to pay the costs of the successful defendant. This can mean that a claimant who recovers, say, £100,000 in compensation from the (negligent) Trust has to use £50,000 of that to pay for the legal costs of the (non-negligent) GP. But where two or more defendants are found liable to the claimant, then the court will apportion liability between (or amongst) them.

It may seem odd that two different people or organisations, both parts of the NHS, might operate a "cut-throat" defence to a clinical negligence claim by an injured patient – each blaming the other. It might be admitted that there was negligence within the NHS and that the patient suffered injury as a result, but neither organisation within the NHS will accept responsibility. The NHS is negligent but there is a contested case. That is a result of the way the NHS is organised. It would, however, be possible to pass legislation to allow the NHS as a whole to be sued rather than its component bodies. That way, if two or more parts of the NHS had combined negligently to injure a patient, then money would not have to be wasted seeking to show whether one part or another had been causatively negligent. I discuss this in the Epilogue.

> # Principle 10: A negligently injured claimant's entitlement to compensation may be reduced or extinguished by their own fault, dishonesty or criminality

Just as the deliberate and malicious intervention of a third party can break the chain of causation between the initial clinical negligence and later injury, loss and damage, so the claimant's own actions can extinguish a defendant's liability. And just as two negligent parties can share liability for a claimant's injuries, so blame can be apportioned between the negligent defendant and a negligent claimant. A claimant who proves that clinical negligence caused them injury may not recover 100% of damages, or even any damages at all, if they themselves have been at fault or public policy considerations mean that it would be unconscionable for them to receive compensation.

Contributory Negligence

The Law Reform (Contributory Negligence) Act 1945 provides:

"1. Apportionment of liability in case of contributory negligence.

(1) Where any person suffers damage as the result partly of his own fault and partly of the fault of any other person or persons, a claim in respect of that damage shall not be defeated by reason of the fault of the person suffering the damage, but the damages recoverable in respect thereof shall be reduced to such extent as the court thinks just and equitable having regard to the claimant's share in the responsibility for the damage."

...

(4) "fault" means negligence, breach of statutory duty or other act or omission which gives rise to a liability in tort"

Contributory negligence applies, in principle, to deceased patients just as it does to those who are still alive at the time of the litigation. If, during their lives, the patient was guilty of contributory negligence, that will reduce the liability of the defendant to the patient's estate and their dependants.

Over time the courts have developed an approach to this statutory test that involves consideration both of the relative blameworthiness of the parties, and the causative potency of their conduct.

In a road traffic accident claim, it can readily be seen that if a claimant is a car driver injured in an accident with another vehicle, and both drivers are equally to blame for causing the accident at a junction, then it would be fair and just to order the other driver to pay only 50% of the damages to which the claimant would otherwise have been entitled. Where a speeding car driver knocks over a pedestrian who was not keeping a proper lookout whilst crossing the road, it is not uncommon for the court to hold that the driver should have the greater share of liability. A car is likely to do more damage to a pedestrian than vice versa. The causative potency of the driver's negligence may well therefore make it just and equitable to order them to pay more than 50% of the damages otherwise due to the claimant pedestrian. Of course, each case turns on its own facts.

The principles are the same in clinical negligence cases, but in fact there are very few reported cases in which the courts have held that a patient, injured by clinical negligence, has been contributorily negligent. This is an area which might develop in the future but, until recently, clinical negligence defendants have been reluctant to allege contributory negligence and the courts have been loath to reduce awards of damages by reason of the negligent conduct of patients.

The issue of contributory negligence in clinical negligence litigation is loaded with potential ethical and policy questions. Perhaps that is why defendants have been reluctant to defend claims in that way.

One reported judgment where a defendant did allege contributory negligence is *Pidgeon v Doncaster Health Authority* [2002] Lloyd's Rep Med 130. The claimant underwent a cervical smear test which was wrongly evaluated as 'negative' by the defendant in 1988. In fact, it was abnormal and showed a pre-cancerous condition. In 1997 the claimant was diagnosed with cervical carcinoma. The defendant accepted that it had been negligent when misreporting the 1988 test but the claimant had failed to undergo a further smear test between 1988 and 1997 even though she had been urged to do so on seven occasions by her GP and, by letter, by the screening authority. The defendant argued that the claimant's own conduct broke the chain of causation between its breach in 1988 and the injury she suffered due to delay in diagnosis of her cancer. Alternatively, it argued, the claimant had been guilty of contributory negligence. The judge held that the claimant had been negligent but that her conduct did not amount to an intervening cause (see above). However, her negligence had itself contributed to the delay in diagnosis and she should be regarded as two-thirds to blame for her own injuries. The liability of the defendant was therefore for one-third of the compensation that would be assessed by the court or agreed by the parties. On the facts of the particular case the claimant had not agreed to enter into a screening programme and her failure to attend for further tests was in part as a result of the false reassurance given by the initial test result (whether that feeling of reassurance was logical or not).

You may or may not think that that was a fair judgment on the facts of the case, but if, in principle, the courts can reduce liability for damages due to a patient's non-attendance for medical tests, examinations and consultations, then that could be fertile ground for the NHS and other defendants to reduce their litigation bills. After all, huge numbers of patients do not attend appointments. Suppose a man has arranged a blood test for PSA. An elevated PSA might indicate the presence of prostate cancer, or a number of benign prostate conditions. The test result does show an elevated PSA but the GP's surgery negligently advises him to have a re-test in one year, rather than referring him for specialist advice or re-testing in three months with advice that the PSA was raised. The man then fails to attend for a re-test at one year, and another three years pass before his next test by which time his PSA is very elevated and he has advanced prostate cancer. The practice was negligent, but was the patient also? Should the compensation he might recover from the practice be reduced for his negligence in not attending for a re-test after 12 months? If so, by how much? Perhaps he was falsely re-assured by the failure to tell him that his PSA was elevated and he needed referral or a re-test within three months?

There is another way of looking at the example given. Should the practice be liable only for the delay of nine months? If it would have been non-negligent to have advised a re-test in three months, and advice was given to re-test at 12 months, was the only culpable delay over a period of nine months? The claimant did not give the defendant an opportunity to mitigate the effects of its negligence. However, in the case of *Pidgeon*, an example of much more serious failure by a patient, the court held that the causative effects of the defendant's negligence were not brought to an end by the patient's non-attendances or non-compliance.

There is a (loose) analogy with the case of a car driver and a pedestrian. Just as the causative potency of the car driver's negligence is generally much greater than that of a pedestrian because the vehicle is capable of causing much more damage, so a healthcare professional's failures to advise clearly on the need for follow-up or re-examination can be much more causatively potent than the default of a patient missing an appointment.

Generally, the courts will not condemn a claimant in contributory negligence for a single failure to attend. I doubt whether the defendant in the PSA test example would allege contributory negligence, or that the court would find in favour of such an argument if it were raised. On the other hand, repeated, unjustifiable non-attendances or non-compliance with advice might well result in a finding of contributory negligence against a patient.

That said, an example of the court finding that a single failure to follow advice, or attend for a test, is found in the case of *Sims v MacLennan* [2015] EWHC 2739 (QB). The judge held that a doctor conducting an independent medical examination had not failed to advise the patient to follow up a high blood pressure reading with his own GP. Even if he had, the failure was not causative of the patient's death from a stroke nine years later, when the "but for" test was applied. In any event, held the judge, had he found the defendant to have been causatively negligent, he would have reduced damages by 25% for contributory negligence: about five years after the examination, the deceased had been advised by his GP to have his blood pressure tested but had failed to do so. This case shows that the court might well reduce damages for an isolated failure to attend by a patient. It also shows that the claimant's negligence does not have to be in relation to their interactions with the defendant.

Non-compliance with clear advice might well constitute contributory negligence. In an unreported case called *Turner v Caver* from 2016, a trial judge held that a cosmetic surgeon had not been negligent in their pre-operative advice to a patient electing to have breast augmentation surgery. The patient suffered from haematoma formation after the operation and the court held that this was due to her engaging in vigorous physical exercise at a gym notwithstanding very clear advice to avoid such activity in the post-operative period. The judge held that if he had found the defendant to have been negligent, he would have reduced damages for the haematoma by 66% to reflect the claimant's own contributory negligence in failing to comply with advice.

What about cases where a patient deliberately harms themselves?

In *Reeves v Commissioner of Police of the Metropolis* [1999] UKHL 35, a prisoner, Mr Lynch, had died by suicide in a police cell at Kentish Town police station. His estate and family brought a claim against the police for negligently failing to protect his life. He had made two earlier attempts at suicide whilst in custody, one on the same day. A doctor had examined Mr Lynch shortly before his last attempt and had found no other evidence of mental disturbance, but advised the officers that he was a suicide risk and should be frequently observed. Mr Lynch was checked by an officer at 1:57pm and the wicket hatch in his cell door was left open. When another officer checked him at 2:05pm it was found that Mr Lynch had hanged himself by tying his shirt through the open wicket hatch. The court found that there had been negligence by the police officers in leaving the wicket hatch open. On appeal to the House of Lords, the question was whether Mr Lynch's own actions precluded the defendant from being liable for the consequences of his death.

The House of Lords held that the police had been under a duty to take reasonable care to prevent a deliberate act of self-harm. The officers had a particular duty of care because they exercised strong control over the deceased, detaining him in a cell, and he was especially vulnerable. The suicide was a foreseeable consequence of the failure of the duty. The duty was owed whether the prisoner was mentally well or unwell at the time. The suicide was the very thing against which the duty had been directed. The suicide did not prevent the breach of duty by the police from being a cause of death, however that did not mean that the suicide was not also a cause of the death. Both the police and the deceased had been responsible for the death and a division of damages under the Law Reform (Contributory Negligence) Act 1945 was required. Section 1 of the 1945 Act required the court to apportion responsibility and not merely degrees of carelessness.

The definition of "fault" in section 4 of the 1945 Act was wide enough to extend to a claimant's deliberate acts as well as to his negligent acts. It might seem odd to talk of suicide or self-harm as "negligent" but even deliberate acts would come within the ambit of the Act. Even though the defendant had a duty to guard against a deliberate act – here self-harm or suicide – that did not preclude a finding of contributory negligence.

The House of Lords, and the lower courts that had heard the case referred to the distinction between a person of "sound mind" and one of "unsound mind", using terminology that might well not be used today. The deceased, it was found, had been of "sound mind" when he took his own life. This was based on the medical assessment made at the police station. Lord Hoffmann considered whether there ought to be an apportionment under the 1945 Act:

> "...*whatever views one may have about suicide in general, a 100 per cent. apportionment of responsibility to Mr. Lynch gives no weight at all to the policy of the law in imposing a duty of care upon the police. It is another different way of saying that the police should not have owed Mr. Lynch a duty of care. The law of torts is not just a matter of simple morality but contains many strands of policy, not all of them consistent with each other, which reflect the complexity of life. An apportionment of responsibility "as the court thinks just and equitable" will sometimes require a balancing of different goals. It is at this point that I think that Buxton L.J.'s reference to the cases on the Factories Acts is very pertinent. The apportionment must recognise that a purpose of the duty accepted by the Commissioner in this case is to demonstrate publicly that the police do have a responsibility for taking reasonable care to prevent prisoners from [dying by] suicide. On the other hand, respect must be paid to the finding of fact that Mr. Lynch was "of sound mind." I confess to my unease about this finding, based on a seven minute interview with a doctor of unstated qualifications, but there was no other evidence and the judge was entitled to come to the conclusion which he did. I therefore think it would be wrong to attribute no responsibility to Mr. Lynch and compensate the plaintiff as if the police had simply killed him.*"

The House of Lords determined that the equitable position would be to reduce damages by 50% to reflect the deceased's contributory negligence.

I have conducted a few cases where a patient under the care of an NHS Trust or a private hospital for a psychiatric condition has suffered serious injury after an act of attempted suicide or self-harm, and where the defendant has alleged contributory negligence. In none of those cases has the issue been argued at trial. In one case the NHS Trust withdrew its allegation that the claimant was responsible for his own injuries on the first day of the trial, having maintained its position for many months leading up to that point. Where such an allegation is raised, the court will need to have expert evidence on the state of mind of the claimant (or deceased) at the time of self-harm or suicide. Did the individual have capacity to make decisions about their own health and welfare? Experts will generally acknowledge that not everyone who tries to take their own life lacks the mental capacity to make a decision about their own health and welfare. But where the individual suffered from a psychiatric condition that so overwhelmed their reasoning that they did not have capacity, then the court will be highly unlikely to find

Court:
House of Lords
[2000] 1 AC 360

Facts:
A prisoner died by suicide in a police cell having made two attempts earlier whilst in custody. A doctor warned the police as to the risk of suicide. A hatch in the cell door was left open which the prisoner used to tie clothing to and then to hang himself.

Reeves v Commissioner of Police of the Metropolis

Decision:
The fact that the deceased chose to take his own life did not preclude the defendant from being liable for the death, but the deceased was guilty of contributory negligence to the extent of 50%.

Key Points For Application in Later Cases:
If a defendant owes a duty of care to protect a person from suicide then it is unlikely that the act of suicide by that person will prevent the defendant from being liable in negligence.
An act of deliberate self-harm or suicide can lead to a reduction in damages for contributory negligence. A person of "sound mind" is responsible for their actions and so a finding of contributory negligence is not precluded.

Casenote 7

that they were guilty of contributory negligence.

Until very recently I was not aware of any judgment in a clinical negligence case in which a patient had been found contributorily negligent for self-harming or attempting suicide. However, in 2019 Mrs Justice Whipple did comment in *PPX v Aulakh* [2019] EWHC 717 (QB) that had she found the defendant GP liable in negligence, she would have reduced damages by 25% for contributory negligence. The claimant had tried to hang himself after a GP had failed to refer him to a mental health crisis team. The judge referred to the case of *Reeves* but there is no discussion in the judgment of whether clinical negligence cases concerning the management of patients with mental health problems differ from cases where the police or other authorities are looking after someone in custody.

Many people act in ways that harm their own health – they smoke, or drink too much alcohol, eat too much sugar, take illegal drugs, drive too fast, or participate in dangerous sports. Where an individual drives negligently, injures themselves, but is then negligently treated in hospital, the Trust responsible for the negligent treatment is only responsible for the additional injuries caused by the clinical negligence, not for the injuries caused in the road traffic accident. Similarly, a hospital Trust is not responsible for the respiratory condition caused by smoking, or the liver failure caused by excessive alcohol consumption. There is no question of contributory negligence in those instances because the healthcare provider is only responsible for the additional injury caused by its negligence and the prior conduct of the claimant did not cause the additional injury. Might it be otherwise, where the patient continues to drink excessively, or smoke or take illegal drugs after the negligent treatment?

Usually defendants in clinical negligence claims have regarded these continuing lifestyle activities as "givens" affecting causation rather than as potential reasons to make a finding of contributory negligence. Thus, the claimant who continues to smoke after surgery to remove part of his lung due to cancer is not generally regarded as contributorily negligent; rather their life expectancy and condition, in the absence of any original clinical negligence, is assessed in the light of their continuing smoking. They would not have lived for as long or have been able to function as well as they would had they stopped smoking. Nevertheless, as we have seen in the case of the breast augmented gym enthusiast, failures to abide by clear medical advice might lead to a finding of contributory negligence. My impression – not supported by any objective evidence – is that clinical negligence defendants are now more willing than they have ever been to allege contributory negligence than in the past. Perhaps this will be an issue that will trouble the courts more frequently in the future.

Illegality

In theory there can be a finding of 100% contributory negligence, but I have never been involved in such a case. Contributory negligence may include deliberate conduct by the claimant, but even deliberate acts rarely extinguish completely the defendant's liability. In those rare cases, however, they may do so. One such example is where the claimant is guilty of illegal conduct connected with the claim such that the court will not permit them to recover damages they would otherwise be entitled to receive.

In *Henderson v Dorset Healthcare University NHS Foundation Trust* [2018] EWCA Civ 1841, the claimant, who lacked capacity to litigate and who proceeded by a litigation friend, had stabbed her mother to death. She suffered from a severe psychiatric disorder and, at the time of the killing, had been under the care of a community mental health service operated by the defendant Trust. As the Court of Appeal recorded, it was *"common ground between the parties that this tragic event would not have happened but for the Trust's breaches of duty in failing to respond in an appropriate way to Ms Henderson's mental collapse."* Nevertheless, her claim was dismissed on the grounds of illegality. The Court of Appeal noted that Ms Henderson had been charged with murder but after considering expert psychiatric evidence the prosecution accepted a plea to manslaughter on the grounds of diminished responsibility. In other words, this was a deliberate killing but Ms Henderson had lacked the capacity to intend to kill her mother or fully to control her actions. The judge presiding over the criminal proceedings made an order for her detention in hospital under the Mental Health Act.

The Court of Appeal reviewed previous court decisions and identified two rules governing how illegality affects claims.

The first is a narrow rule: *"a person who has been convicted of a serious criminal offence cannot recover damage in tort which is the consequence of a sentence of detention imposed upon that person for the criminal act whereas the latter is authority for the proposition that such a person cannot recover for damage which is the consequence of that person's criminal act."*

So, a clinical negligence claimant cannot claim damages for their detention – even under a hospital order rather than a sentence of imprisonment – following the commission of a crime, even if that crime would not have been committed but for the negligence of the defendant. The reason, as touched on in Part 1, is that the law, through the criminal courts, has imposed the "harm" for which compensation is being sought. It would be inconsistent for another branch of the legal system to award compensation for the legal imposition of a sanction. This rule applies to a claim for damages for the detention itself, and the consequences of the detention such as loss of earnings.

The second is a wider rule: *"you cannot recover compensation for loss which you have suffered in consequence of your own criminal act."* This rule is founded on public policy, as explained by Lord Hoffman in an earlier case called *Clunis v Camden and Islington Health Authority* [1997] EWCA Civ 2918. It is, he said, offensive to public notions of the fair distribution of resources that a claimant should be compensated (usually out of public funds) for the consequences of his own criminal conduct. Thus, a claim for compensation to meet the claimant's own liabilities to the relatives of the person they killed, or for their own injuries due to remorse for their conduct, would be defeated by application of the wider rule of illegality. Lord Hoffman thought that the question was really one of causation:

> *"... can one say that, although the damage would not have happened but for the tortious conduct of the defendant, it was caused by the criminal act of the claimant? Or is the position that although the damage would not have happened without the criminal act of the claimant, it was caused by the tortious act of the defendant?"*

A nice statement of principle, but one that might be difficult to apply in a borderline case.

Fundamental Dishonesty
Parliament has passed a statutory provision that may also operate to deprive a claimant of compensation to which they would otherwise be entitled, where their claim is fundamentally dishonest.

Section 57 of the Criminal Justice and Courts Act 2015:

"applies where, in proceedings on a claim for damages in respect of personal injury ("the primary claim") –

(a) the court finds that the claimant is entitled to damages in respect of the claim, but

(b) on an application by the defendant for the dismissal of the claim under this section, the court is satisfied on the balance of probabilities that the claimant has been fundamentally dishonest in relation to the primary claim or a related claim."

Section 57 goes on:

"(2) The court must dismiss the primary claim, unless it is satisfied that the claimant would suffer substantial injustice if the claim were dismissed.

(3) The duty under subsection (2) includes the dismissal of any element of the primary claim in respect of which the claimant has not been dishonest."

Hence, it is not just the dishonest parts of a claim that will be dismissed if section 57 applies, but the whole of the claim, unless to do so would cause the claimant to suffer substantial injustice.

Then, for good measure, section 57(4) provides:

"(4) The court's order dismissing the claim must record the amount of damages that the court would have awarded to the claimant in respect of the primary claim but for the dismissal of the claim."

As Jim Bowen used to say on Bullseye: *"Look at what you could have won ..."*.

As I noted in Part 1, unhelpfully the key term, "fundamentally dishonest" is not defined within the Act. So the courts have had to interpret and apply the term. This was done in a clinical negligence claim brought by a prison inmate against the Ministry of Justice in *Razumas v Ministry of Justice* [2018] EWHC 215 (QB). The claimant alleged delay in diagnosis of a soft tissue sarcoma by various medical professionals who had seen him during various periods of imprisonment. Due to the delay he underwent an amputation and suffered metastatic spread of the cancer. Although it was conceded that there had been clinical negligence, his claim was defeated for various reasons, but the judge also considered whether he had been fundamentally dishonest within the meaning of section 57. The claimant alleged that during a period out of prison he had sought medical advice and had been referred for surgery. He said, further, that upon returning to prison prior to that referral taking effect, he advised the prison medical staff accordingly, but still they did not treat his condition with the seriousness it merited. The judge found this evidence to have been false and dishonest. He had not been referred for surgery and he had lied about that to prison staff.

The judge, Mrs Justice Cockerill, adopted a formulation set out by Mr Justice Julian Knowles in an earlier case: *London Organising Committee of the Olympic and Paralympic Games v Haydn Sinfield* [2018] EWHC 51 (QB) in which the appropriately named Mr Sinfield, who had suffered an injury for which the defendant was liable, claimed a significant amount of compensation for gardening expenses for a large plot of land he owned. The claim for these expenses was found to have been advanced dishonestly, supported by faked invoices. Mr Justice Julian Knowles said:

> *"In my judgment, a claimant should be found to be fundamentally dishonest within the meaning of s 57(1)(b) if the defendant proves on a balance of probabilities that the claimant has acted dishonestly in relation to the primary claim and/or a related claim (as defined in s 57(8)), and that he has thus substantially affected the presentation of his case, either in respects of liability or quantum, in a way which potentially adversely affected the defendant in a significant way, judged in the context of the particular facts and circumstances of the litigation. Dishonesty is to be judged according to the test set out by the Supreme Court in Ivey v Genting Casinos Limited (t/a Crockfords Club)."*

That test of dishonesty in *Ivey* was a new approach set out by the Supreme Court. A court must ascertain the individual's own knowledge or belief as to the facts and then determine whether their conduct was honest or dishonest by the standards of ordinary decent people. There is no requirement that the defendant must appreciate that what they have done is, by those standards, dishonest. Mr Justice Julian Knowles continued:

> *"By using the formulation 'substantially affects' I am intending to convey the same idea as the expressions 'going to the root' or 'going to the heart' of the claim. By potentially affecting the defendant's liability in a significant way 'in the context of the particular facts and circumstances of the litigation' I mean (for example) that a dishonest claim for special damages of £9,000 in a claim worth £10,000 in its entirety should be judged to significantly affect the defendant's interests, notwithstanding that the defendant may be a multi-billion pound insurer to whom £9,000 is a trivial sum."*

Counsel for Mr Razumas submitted that far from going to the root of the claim, his dishonest conduct barely "scratched the bark". Mrs Justice Cockerill disagreed. He had been fundamentally dishonest in his claim against the MOJ and it would not cause substantial injustice to dismiss his claim under section 57 of the Act.

As if to underline this robust judicial approach to dishonest claimants, a clinical negligence defendant was jailed in 2018 for making a dishonest claim for damages. DJ Atwal (a disc jockey not a district judge) was sent to prison for three months for contempt of court having dishonestly exaggerated elements of his claim against a healthcare provider. Mr Atwal suffered injury as a result of clinical negligence. He had been assaulted with a baseball bat but injuries to his fingers and lip were negligently managed and the NHS Trust responsible admitted liability and offered to settle his claim for £30,000. He did not accept the offer but instead commenced proceedings and ultimately claimed over £830,000 including substantial claims for loss of earnings and care.

The claimant had worked as a DJ and as a courier. He claimed that his lip deformation affected his speech and made him self-conscious such that he could not perform in front of people. His hand injuries prevented him from lifting heavy items when working as a courier and adversely affected his dexterity when working as a DJ. He was, he claimed to experts and in court documents, out of work and in need of substantial care and assistance. The defendant Trust became suspicious of the claims and carried out video surveillance which showed the claimant working for long periods as a courier lifting items in and out of vehicles. The Trust also made a search of social media posts by and of the claimant showing him working as a DJ, even releasing a single and video. The evidence was disclosed to the claimant and ultimately an agreement was reached for him to accept the much earlier offer of £30,000.

Contempt of court proceedings were brought against Mr Atwal arising out of his claims that he had suffered injuries preventing him from working and resulting in him requiring substantial care and assistance. The case came before Mr Justice Spencer: *Calderdale and Huddersfield NHS Foundation Trust v Atwal* [2018] EWHC 961 (QB). The contempt allegations fell into two categories – making false statements, mostly to medical experts, and making false statements in documents verified by statements of truth. 14 counts of contempt were found proved.

Following the *Sinfield* and *Razumas* cases, clinical negligence claimants know that their claims may be dismissed for fundamental dishonesty, even if the dishonesty relates to an element of compensation rather than going to liability. As some commentators have pointed out, there is no corresponding provision that a fundamentally dishonest defendant should have judgment entered against them, even on those parts of the claim that they might otherwise have defeated. That is not to say that a defendant to a clinical negligence action will be immune if they act dishonestly. A doctor or other healthcare professional making a false statement in court proceedings might be found guilty of contempt of court and could certainly face professional regulatory proceedings and sanctions. Such conduct would also potentially affect their continued employment as it might well constitute gross misconduct. Where a trial judge finds that a defendant has been fundamentally dishonest in their evidence, the case is unlikely to be decided in that person's favour.

Nevertheless, the courts need to see compelling evidence of dishonesty before they will act. Some patients and their families may be convinced that medical records have been altered or removed, but unless there is cogent evidence to support those suspicions, the courts will not make any findings to that effect. As can be imagined, it is not easy to provide evidence of such conduct, but it is possible that someone will have seen or referred to a medical record that is now claimed not to exist, and there are means of "interrogating" computer records to see when they were made or amended.

Even those who take the view that when it comes to dishonesty and exaggeration, the focus should be on defendants just as much as claimants, and that the law in this area is too weighted in favour of the former, would surely concede that the law is right to withhold compensation from those who abuse the court system in such a way that their claims are fundamentally dishonest.

Part 3: Clinical Negligence Litigation – The Anatomy of a Claim

How does a clinical negligence case proceed from the first complaint to the final trial? In this Part I shall examine the process by which a claim is litigated. This is not a detailed procedural guide – the annotated civil procedure rules, published as The White Book, themselves run to about 6,000 pages of very small print and cost several hundreds of pounds to purchase – but I shall discuss how some of the most important rules and procedures apply as a clinical negligence case progresses. I shall look at how evidence is gathered, and the roles of witnesses, experts, solicitors, barristers, and judges. We shall see how clinical negligence disputes come to be litigated and how they can be resolved.

The formal rules that govern the process by which all civil claims are conducted are called the Civil Procedure Rules (CPR). They are broken down into Parts, with each Part comprising a set of rules. In addition there are Practice Directions (PD) which accompany most of the Parts. Therefore a rule might be referred to as CPR Part 7.1. A provision in a Practice Direction might be referred to as CPR PD 21.5.

Chapter 1: Complaint and Investigation

Realisation

It might be thought that the obvious starting point of a clinical negligence claim is the first complaint, but in order to make a complaint a patient or relative of a patient must realise that there is something to complain about. There must be very many cases in which mistakes cause injury but the patient concerned does not realise that they have suffered avoidable harm. In others, the realisation comes many months, even years, after the negligence occurred.

Some patients recognise that they might have suffered avoidable injury immediately after the allegedly negligent treatment. A paraplegic patient develops a sacral sore after having been dressed by a nurse and then left sitting on a belt buckle for several hours. Sometimes the realisation comes after further investigation: a patient suffers prolonged pain after a hip replacement operation and a post-operative x-ray shows that the hip prosthesis has not been secured correctly. On many occasions clients of mine have told me that they went to solicitors after having been told by a nurse or other healthcare professional that they ought to do so. This advice might come from a practitioner who was themselves at fault. More commonly it comes from another professional who was involved in the patient's care at the time, or at a later stage. This sort of advice, from a professional who was not involved in the patient's care at the time, cannot be relied upon as evidence of clinical negligence. It is akin to the clichéd question: *"Which cowboy put that in?"* asked by a tradesperson! Sometimes the patient will have spoken to a friend or read something in the newspaper about another patient and will realise that they might have suffered avoidable harm.

In short, it is not always obvious that a patient has suffered an injury that they ought not to have suffered. Firstly, it is difficult to draw a neat line between non-negligent and negligently caused complications of an illness or procedure. Secondly, the professionals responsible for delivering treatment or managing a patient will rarely inform a patient that they have made errors let alone that they think they have been negligent. This is not necessarily due to a "cover up" but rather because the professional does not believe or recognise that they have done anything wrong. After all, negligence is nearly always inadvertent. It is not the deliberate or reckless infliction of harm. It is usually an honest mistake or a systemic failing. And if a professional did realise that they had been negligent then they would immediately try to prevent any harm occurring or try to mitigate the harm already caused. In many cases the failings have been a result of a series of mistakes or systemic problems. Individual healthcare professionals will tend to have a limited view of the case of an individual patient. In an obstetric negligence case, for example, the midwives may reflect on their roles, the obstetrician on their actions, and the neonatologists and paediatricians on the outcome for the child. None of the healthcare professionals has the responsibility of forming an overview of the whole process. Unless there has been a glaring error or failing or a healthcare professional raises a specific concern, it is not unusual to find that there is no realisation of an overall failing, no investigation, no overview of the management by the Trust as a whole and no feedback to the patient or family on the care given.

If the healthcare professionals and organisations often do not realise that there has been negligence, it is unsurprising that many patients do not either.

As noted, in some cases it can take a very long time before a patient realises that they have suffered injury because of negligence. Think of a patient who suffers abdominal infection due to a swab left inside them following surgery years earlier. Or a missed thoracic fracture that leads to the development of complications many years later. In those cases, patients may not bring a complaint at all, but rather go straight to a solicitor to see if they will investigate.

As we shall see, any contested clinical negligence case that is brought to court will require expert evidence to be adduced. Prior to obtaining expert advice, many patients may have a broad idea of what has gone wrong to have caused them injury, but will not know specifically what failings constituted negligence.

Alongside, or as an alternative to the realisation that "something has gone wrong", there might be a realisation that the patient, or their family, has not been given the full story. Many patients worry that they have not been given all the information that they should have been given. They do not know whether anyone has made mistakes but they suspect that they have not been told the full truth.

There must be thousands of cases every year when a patient has suffered an injury that they believe was just a non-negligent complication or "one of those things". They accept what they have been told by way of explanation and they do not raise any concerns. No-one investigates and no-one realises that the injury could and should have been avoided. But all those cases that do eventually result in litigation begin with a realisation that something had gone wrong or that there is more information to give than has been given. Once that realisation has hit, what happens next?

Complaint and Investigation

The decision whether to bring a complaint is in the hands of the patient or their family. Not all patients or their families who realise that something has gone wrong choose to do something about it. For example, some parents of children born with severe disabilities choose not to prompt investigations into what "went wrong". They may fear the answers they might be given if they raise questions. They may feel, however misguidedly, some personal blame for what has happened. They may simply wish to avoid examining events that are a source of distress to them. As a result, there will be some cases that are never looked at even though there is a realisation that things had not turned out as they should.

If the patient or the patient's family does not raise questions or make a complaint, then the odds are that no-one else will do so. An NHS trust might start an internal investigation without there having been a complaint and where there is no inkling that a complaint might follow, where it is obvious that the outcome for a patient has been far different from what would usually be expected. It is true that forms might be completed without any complaint having been made – untoward incident reports for example. But in most cases the impetus to investigate more fully will come from patients or their loved ones raising concerns.

In cases where a child has suffered from severe injury at or around the time of their birth, then it may be years before the child or their family raise questions of the NHS about what happened. I tried to make an opening speech at a trial in one case involving a birth injury, only for the judge immediately to ask: *"Why has it taken over 20 years for this case to come to court?"* In fact, the claimant's parents had not sought to make any complaint. It was only when the child had become an adult themselves that they decided to look into why they had been born with a disability, and they had eventually been advised by experts looking into their case that it had been a result of negligent management of their delivery. The judge disagreed and the case was dismissed after trial. The claimant gained the unfortunate impression that the judge was against him from the start of the trial because of the delay. But the delay had not been their responsibility.

Complaints are sometimes raised by patients or their families, not because they have identified a shortcoming in the standard of care provided but simply because they feel it is the only way that they will actually find out the full information they ought to be given about their condition or their care. As Ann Clwyd MP and Professor Tricia Hart wrote in their *"Review of the NHS Hospitals Complaints System - Putting Patients Back in the Picture"* in October 2013:

> *"Lack of information was one of the main reasons for dissatisfaction. Patients, their family, carers and friends often felt inadequately informed about the patient's condition, prognosis and expected treatment. Doctors were seen infrequently and nurses were evasive about matters they considered the province of the doctor. 'The process is too complicated, there is a lack of information, it's designed to put people off.' (Patient comment at meeting) Patients did not know who to ask for information, and often only saw the same member of staff once or twice. There was insufficient communication between staff, so that questions or concerns were not passed on and dealt with, and patients had to repeat the same things several times. Members of staff to whom they did speak were often ill informed about their situation. There were instances where staff did not consult medical notes and others when medical notes were inadequate or missing. We formed the impression that this sense of confusion caused by lack of information made people fear that they or their relative had not received the right care. As a result, they were more likely to question the treatment or make a formal complaint."*

Most NHS hospital trusts will have a Patient Advice and Liaison Service (PALS). If a patient or their family has misgivings about the care given at an NHS Trust's hospital, then they can of course raise this directly with the doctors or nurses involved, or they might wish to contact PALS to discuss their concerns and how to raise them. PALS provide a very important service and any patients concerned about the treatment and care they have received should try to make contact with that service. NHS bodies are obliged under The Local Authority Social Services and National Health Service Complaints (England) Regulations 2009 to receive, investigate and respond to complaints in the prescribed manner. However, those Regulations are not particularly specific. NHS England has published a Complaints Policy setting out who can make a complaint, how it should be made and how it should be responded to. The expectation is that a complaint should be made within 12 months of when the matter occurred or, if later, within 12 months of when the matter came to the knowledge of the complainant. If the complaint is not resolved by way of the internal complaint system, then it can be taken to the Parliamentary and Health Service Ombudsman. The complaint form on the PHSO's website includes the following statement:

Legal action

Generally, we cannot investigate a complaint if it is or was reasonable for you to take legal action to get an answer to it. This could include going to court or to a tribunal. We will look at whether legal action would be able to fully answer your complaint or give you what you want.

So, a complaint that might be a suitable subject for litigation is not generally regarded as a suitable subject of complaint to the Ombudsman. Some might argue that it should be the object of the complaints system to prevent avoidable litigation against the NHS, i.e. to resolve complaints that might otherwise proceed to litigation. That does not appear to be the goal of the current system for handling complaints.

After a severe injury it is understandable that a patient will focus on dealing with the aftermath of the injury, going through any further treatment or rehabilitation, and on getting back to work or making an adjustment to a new kind of life. Making a complaint may not be a priority. By the time the complaint is raised, it may feel too late to talk to the professionals who were directly involved at the time when the harm was caused.

In cases where patients or their families do raise questions or concerns at the time, it would be expected that the clinicians involved would speak to them and try to explain what has happened. In some cases, a member of the management team at a Trust and a senior member of the clinical staff will meet with a patient or their family to answer their questions.

Sometimes a Trust will itself launch an investigation. These may take various forms. Sometimes a "Serious Untoward Incident" (SUI) report is conducted. In others a "Root Cause Analysis" is performed. These will usually involve some evidence being taken from the healthcare professionals involved. They will be written by someone not directly involved in the events, but usually – not always – from within the same Trust. The object of such reports is to identify procedures or practices that could be improved or training requirements for members of the clinical team. They are not investigations designed to identify clinical negligence, or to attribute culpability. They are for internal purposes and are not designed as investigations to provide explanations to the patient or family affected.

All healthcare professionals have a professional duty of candour – a responsibility to be honest with patients when things go wrong. This has long been part of any professional's duty but it has been underscored by a "statutory duty of candour" introduced by section 20 of the Health and Social Care Act 2008 (Regulated Activities) Regulations 2014. This was introduced following recommendations by Sir Robert Francis QC in his report into failings at the Mid Staffordshire NHS Trust. The statutory duty applies to healthcare providers registered with the Care Quality Commission (CQC), requiring them to:

- Act in an open and transparent way in relation to care and treatment provided to service users;

- As soon as reasonably practicable after becoming aware of a notifiable safety incident, providers must notify the service user and/or their representative that the incident has occurred.

For a health service body, registered with the CQC, a "notifiable safety incident" is defined as:

> "any unintended or unexpected incident that occurred in respect of a service user during the provision of a regulated activity that, in the reasonable opinion of a health care professional, could result in, or appears to have resulted in -
>
> a) the death of the service user, where the death relates directly to the incident rather than to the natural course of the service user's illness or underlying condition, or
>
> b) severe harm, moderate harm or prolonged psychological harm to the service user."

It should be noted that it is the Trust that would be bound by this statutory duty, not the individual professionals. The CQC can warn, prosecute or take regulatory action against a registered body for failure to comply with the duty.

A new system involving Medical Examiners is being introduced which should cover all deaths within the health service by April 2021. A pilot over 10 years in Sheffield covered 25,000 deaths. The wording on the death certificate was changed in an astonishing 87% of cases, with 33% of cases involving major changes in the wording. Medical Examiners, assisted by Medical Examiner Officers, will check the cause of death and certification, perhaps contact families to see whether they have any concerns, decide whether the death needs to be reported to the Coroner and raise any clinical governance concerns with the appropriate authority, often the relevant hospital Trust.

Chapter 2: Turning to the Law

Contacting a Solicitor

Not all patients who are or become dissatisfied with their treatment make a complaint to the healthcare provider, and not all who do complain are satisfied with the response they receive. Thoughts of litigation may be the first consideration or the last resort. They may follow immediately from the answer to a complaint, or years afterwards.

For every clinical negligence claim in which I have been involved where a patient has contacted a solicitor after an admission by an NHS Trust or other healthcare provider that they have been harmed by negligent care, there must have been at least ten where a solicitor has been contacted after a denial that anything untoward has happened.

Not all solicitors conduct clinical negligence litigation but those who do are for the most part experienced and skilled in this area of law, and work constructively with lawyers for the NHS and individual healthcare professionals to resolve disputes. They are distributed around the country – there is no need to go to London to find a good clinical negligence solicitor. There are directories such as Chambers UK, and the Legal 500 that list and rank reputable lawyers in different specialist fields of practice including clinical negligence. There are also organisations such as AvMA (Action against Medical Accidents) who can provide a list of solicitors in a geographical area who are qualified and skilled in clinical negligence litigation. AvMA has a well-established and respected process of accrediting solicitors as specialists in clinical negligence. Looking for the AvMA panel quality mark is one way of assuring oneself of a solicitor's credentials. AvMA is an organisation that many who have suffered harm due to clinical negligence find very helpful. It can give advice on what questions to ask of the clinicians and the management at a hospital trust, how NHS investigations work, and how to make a complaint, as well as providing information on how to find a trusted solicitor. AvMA produces self-help guides available online and can provide support and advice in relation to Inquests. Some charities that specialise in certain conditions will also be able to make recommendations for lawyers.

Generally, AvMA or another specialist organisation would be a preferred source of information about which solicitor to contact. It is unwise to rely on a recommendation from a "man down the pub". However, word of mouth is also important, particularly if the patient knows someone who has had a similar claim and has been happy with their solicitor's conduct of their claim.

Lawyers talk of being "instructed" in a claim. It is another word for being engaged or contracted to represent a client. We also talk of "acting" for a client, which means that we represent them in relation to a specific claim or matter. Patients would instruct a solicitor to conduct their claim and, at a later stage, the solicitor instructs a barrister to act on behalf of their client, the patient. However, typically a patient considering engaging a solicitor will have an opportunity, free of charge, to meet that solicitor to discuss their concerns and to find out whether and, if so, on what terms the solicitor would be prepared to represent them.

If a patient has suffered a serious injury and the claim appears at first sight to be a strong one, then a patient should know that many solicitors would be willing to take on their claim. In such cases, most solicitors would come out to visit the patient at home and would be willing to waive their entitlement to some of the extra fees they might charge in other weaker or less serious cases.

A large clinical negligence claim in which damages were, say, over £250,000 might eventually generate over £100,000 in fees for a solicitor's firm. Of course, if the case is resolved at an early stage following an admission by the defendant then the fees would be significantly lower. However, solicitors make a living out of attracting and then conducting cases. Some patients can therefore have their pick of solicitors and should take care to choose one they trust and respect, and who is specialised and experienced in clinical negligence litigation. They should look for a firm of solicitors where there is more than one specialist in this field, so that if anything should happen to the individual solicitor handling their claim, then there will be someone else suitable to take over.

An initial discussion about the case might take a couple of hours but patients should not expect to be charged for it. It might result in the solicitor offering to take on the case, or to decline to do so, or to look into the case further before making a decision whether they will act. But the patient has the choice whether to instruct any solicitor who is willing to act for them.

The reason a solicitor might decline to act for a patient is financial. In the vast majority of cases, the solicitor is paid under a conditional fee agreement ("CFA"). If the claim is ultimately successful, then the solicitor gets paid – the defendant will pay the legal costs reasonably incurred by the successful claimant. If the claim fails, then the solicitor is not paid. They receive nothing for the hours of work they have done on the case. As will be appreciated, it is not at all obvious at the outset which claims will succeed and which will fail. A solicitor meeting a dissatisfied patient for the first time will not have medical records, witness statements or expert reports. They have to trust their judgement as to whether to commit to the claim. There is no entitlement to legal representation in all clinical negligence claims – there is a market. Patients who appear to have strong and valuable claims are in a better position in that market than those with speculative or low value claims.

Whilst most cases are funded by CFAs, there remain a few cases, for children injured around the time of birth, that may be funded by public funding – legal aid. Not all clinical negligence solicitors are authorised to do legal aid work. It is not that those solicitors who are not so authorised are any less competent, it is just that some firms of solicitors do not think it worthwhile conducting legal aid work. It involves a considerable additional administrative burden; there are delays caused by applying for and being granted certificates of public funding, and then extending or amending them; there are narrow eligibility criteria so that few clients are entitled to public funding; and there are restrictive costs conditions including limits on the amount of money that can be paid to experts through public funding. Some solicitors will advise that this will restrict their ability to conduct the claim effectively. Parents of a baby negligently injured at birth may choose a solicitor who is not authorised to conduct legal aid work. They will then enter into a CFA with that solicitor.

Those with significant personal wealth can privately fund their litigation, paying legal bills and experts' fees as the case progressed. Many experienced clinical negligence lawyers will never have had a client who has funded a clinical negligence claim in that way. Other people have insurance policies that cover legal costs for clinical negligence claims. Before entering a CFA, a potential litigant should be asked to check whether they have any insurance cover – known as "before the event" insurance. Such policies tend to have limited cover well below the amount needed to fund a claim of this nature. In the absence of such cover, the great majority of litigants enter into a conditional fee agreement. Even with such cover, most transfer to a CFA once the insured costs limit is reached and legal aid costs conditions have been exhausted.

Insurance is needed even if a CFA is entered into. The rules governing the payment of legal fees for clinical negligence cases have changed radically over the last 20 to 30 years. The current regime effectively provides the overwhelming majority of claimants an immunity from paying legal fees to defendants. A claimant who brings a fundamentally dishonest claim, or who acts unreasonably when pursuing their claim, might be ordered to pay the other side's costs. But this happens only very rarely. For the most part, a defendant who loses a claim will have to pay the claimant's legal costs, experts' fees etc. However there will be an irrecoverable element of the claimant's ATE insurance premium. Even if a claimant wins a claim they will be responsible for paying that element of their insurance costs. A claimant who loses a claim will not have to pay the defendant's costs, but will have to pay their own experts' fees and court fees. To cover that potential liability, they will take out "after the event" insurance. A premium is payable for that insurance but is usually payable only if the claim is successful, not if it is unsuccessful.

Whilst a CFA is between the solicitor and their client, legal costs are controlled by the court. The solicitor who acts for claimants under a CFA will be paid nothing if the case is unsuccessful but they will only be entitled to their reasonable fees if the claim succeeds. To ensure those fees are reasonable they have to be either agreed by the defendant or, if the defendant does not agree them, they have to be assessed as reasonable by the court. Recently the courts have adopted a system of budgeting costs at an early stage of the litigation. Thus, if a claimant's solicitor claims costs at the end of the case that are within budget, they will more likely be agreed, or be ordered to be paid by the court. The reasonableness of the fees that may be charged by a solicitor in any one case is not fixed by reference to how many other cases they have on their books, or how many of those are likely to succeed or fail. So, solicitors get paid a reasonable fee for the cases that succeed, and no fee for the cases that do not succeed. The only recompense for taking the risk that a case will not succeed is the chance to charge the claimant a success fee which is limited to the value of 25% of general damages for pain, suffering and loss of amenity, and past losses and expenses. That is the most it can be. A lower figure may be agreed. The law requires the court to assess the right level of compensation for the claimant, but expects the solicitor to take a percentage of that compensation away from the claimant as recompense for the solicitor taking the risk of not being paid at all on the case. In practice, some solicitors conducting larger value clinical negligence claims do not take any success fee from their clients. Firstly, it can feel very uncomfortable taking money from compensation assessed as being needed for a severely injured client, especially a child, Secondly, in a competitive market, clients may be put off engaging a firm that wants to take a substantial chunk of the compensation to which they are entitled

Under previous arrangements success fees were paid by the unsuccessful defendant rather than the successful claimant, and they were not capped at 25% of general damages and past losses, as they are now. As a barrister I have never been offered nor have I had the benefit of any success fee under the current CFA arrangements. Barristers acting for claimants receive "reasonable" fees for working on successful cases and no fees for working on unsuccessful cases. The fees are either agreed by the losing defendant or assessed as reasonable by the court. The reasonableness of the fees is not assessed by reference to the chance of winning or losing, or by reference to the fact that I am bound to conduct a number of cases for no payment at all. Barristers acting for defendants are paid whether the case is successful or unsuccessful. However, the NHS and other organisations defending clinical negligence claims tend to offer work to lawyers at lower rates than the courts agree as reasonable for claimant lawyers.

The fee arrangements will be the subject of discussion at the first meeting with a solicitor, but they will not be the only, nor even the most important, topic. The solicitor will want to know why the patient or their family is dissatisfied or concerned with the treatment received, and what evidence there might be to show negligence and causation of injury. They will want to obtain medical records. Medical records can be obtained directly by the patients themselves, or they can be obtained, on authorisation, by the solicitor.

Making contact and entering into terms with a solicitor does not preclude a complaint being made. A patient can pursue a complaint and legal action at the same time.

Coroner's Inquest

When a patient dies in circumstances that could give rise to a clinical negligence claim, there is a particular investigation that might take place: a Coroner's Inquest. A doctor may report a death to a coroner if the cause of death is unknown, or the death was violent or unnatural, or sudden and unexplained. A coroner would usually be informed of intra-operative deaths or apparent suicides by patients under treatment for psychiatric illness, for example. If the coroner is satisfied that the cause of death is clear, and it was not violent or unnatural, and the deceased was not in detention at the time of death, then they can release the body and the death can be registered. If the coroner considers that an investigation is needed then they may decide that a post-mortem is needed to find out how the person died. The relatives of the deceased cannot object to a post-mortem but can ask where and when it will take place. The body will be released once the coroner is satisfied that no further examinations are required.

If, following investigation, the coroner decides that an inquest is necessary, then the death cannot be registered until the conclusion of the inquest.

Coroners are appointed and employed by local authorities rather than centrally by the Ministry of Justice. Most of them have a legal background but some are medically trained. Their powers and procedures are governed by The Coroners and Justice Act 2009 and the Coroners (Inquest) Rules 2013. There is very helpful guidance about all aspects of the Coronial system given by the Coroners' Courts Support Service.

I mention the role of inquests at this stage because, in case of fatalities which may be due to clinical negligence, inquests can play a very important part in the process leading to resolution of a claim for compensation.

Coroners can require the production of documentary evidence, such as medical records. They have officers who will take statements from relevant witnesses. If they deem it necessary, a coroner can instruct an expert to give an opinion on the clinical management of the deceased and/or the cause of death. An inquest hearing may allow members of the deceased's family or their representatives to question healthcare professionals who treated and cared for their loved one. Sometimes inquests are heard with a jury. They can give rise to disclosure of highly important evidence and allow for an independent person, the coroner, publicly to draw conclusions on that evidence after an independent and formal process of investigation.

However, an inquest is not an open-ended inquiry into the treatment given to the deceased. The coroner's role is limited to investigating who was the deceased and where, when and how they died. They must not, in deciding those questions, ascribe criminal or civil liability to any individual. Hence questioning by a lawyer or a member of the deceased's family designed to show that a particular person is guilty of negligence is not permitted. It is the coroner alone who decides what evidence shall be called at the inquest, and in what order. Only interested persons can ask questions and be represented at the inquest, and there is no right to public funding to pay for representation for bereaved families. Some lawyers will agree to act for bereaved families free of charge. Others will try to recover legal fees for representation at inquests as a necessary part of the handling of the related civil claim for compensation. But if there is no subsequent successful claim, or if there has already been an admission of liability prior to the inquest, then fees cannot be recovered by that means. Hence, many bereaved families find themselves without legal representation at coroner's inquests where the deceased has died in sudden or unexplained circumstances whilst receiving medical treatment. In contrast, the relevant NHS Trust or individual doctors and other clinicians who might be directly involved with the death of the patient will usually be represented. Many regard this inequality as unjust.

The inquest will end with the coroner or jury reaching a conclusion. The most common short form conclusions include natural causes, accident or misadventure; suicide, unlawful killing or an open conclusion (where there is insufficient evidence for any other conclusion). The coroner is not obliged to adopt a short-form conclusion. They may give a narrative conclusion in which they briefly set out the circumstances and cause of the death. In rare cases the coroner might add a "rider" to their conclusion, that the death was contributed to by "neglect". "Neglect" does not have the same meaning as "negligence", but indicates a complete failure to give even basic medical care.

If there is a need for a death to be investigated by the police then generally the coroner will suspend their investigation and inquest pending the outcome of the police inquiries, including any criminal proceedings.

The conclusions reached by a coroner after an inquest are not binding on the parties to subsequent clinical negligence litigation, but they can be highly influential on the parties' approach to that litigation.

Gathering Evidence
Medical Records
Whether an inquest is arranged or a living patient wishes to investigate whether they have been injured as a result of negligence, one of the first steps to take is to obtain the relevant medical records. These are contemporaneous records that are kept by the GP surgery, hospital Trust or other body providing healthcare. They may be handwritten or computerised. They include notes made by healthcare professionals of consultations, correspondence between professionals or with the patient, observation charts plotting temperature, pulse and other vital signs, results of tests on blood, swabs, urine or other samples, reports on investigations such as MRI scans and x-rays, and accounts of procedures such as operation notes.

You cannot bring or defend a clinical negligence claim without obtaining the relevant medical records.

Medical records contain data about a patient. The EU General Data Protection Regulations (GDPR) now govern the way in which such data is handled. The regulations give patients certain rights including the right to information about what data an organisation such as their GP surgery or an NHS Trust holds about them, and a right of access to such information. You, as a patient, are a "data subject". The regulations give individuals (i.e. the data subjects) the right to request, and in most cases to be given, a copy of the information which a healthcare organisation holds about them. This is called a Subject Access Request (SAR).

The right is to see or to be given a copy of information about the subject only. There is no right under GDPR to see information held about another data subject, even if they are a spouse or child.

Most NHS Trusts and other bodies will have pro-forma Subject Access Request forms to complete. The person making the request does not have to say why they are doing so, but they should seek to identify the information they seek (the kind of records to which they want access). Bodies such as NHS Trusts are obliged to provide copies of information free of charge, but may charge a 'reasonable fee' when the request is deemed 'manifestly unfounded or excessive' and particularly if it is repetitive. A Trust can also charge a 'reasonable fee' to comply with a request for further copies of the same information.

Where records are being sought in the context of potential clinical negligence litigation, there is a Pre-Action Protocol for the Resolution of Clinical Disputes which sets out the expected practice. At paragraph 3.2 it provides:

"Obtaining health records

3.2 Any request for records by the claimant should–

(a) provide sufficient information to alert the defendant where an adverse outcome has been serious or has had serious consequences or may constitute a notifiable safety incident;

(b) be as specific as possible about the records which are required for an initial investigation of the claim (including, for example, a continuous copy of the CTG trace in birth injury cases); and

(c) include a request for any relevant guidelines, analyses, protocols or policies and any documents created in relation to an adverse incident, notifiable safety incident or complaint.

The Pre-Action Protocol, which is available online on the Ministry of Justice website, provides that requests for copies of the claimant's clinical records should be made using the Law Society and Department of Health approved standard forms which are attached at Annex B of the Protocol, adapted as necessary.

It is the Protocol that sets out that the requested information should be provided without delay and at least within 40 days of receipt of the request. However, under GDPR, the body holding the data can seek to extend the period of compliance.

On making a request for access to medical records, a person will be asked to verify their identity.

If someone wants access to the health records of someone who has died, they can apply in writing to the record holder under the Access to Health Records Act (1990). Under the terms of the Act, they will only be able to access the deceased's health records if they are either:

- a personal representative (the executor or administrator of the deceased person's estate), or

- someone who has a claim resulting from the death (this could be a relative or another person).

Only information directly relevant to a claim will be disclosed. A deceased person's GP health records should be passed to Primary Care Support England for storage. There will be a records manager for the local area to whom application can be made. The GP surgery should be able to assist in providing contact details. Alternatively, there is a Primary Care Support England website. The GP records are usually retained for ten years after a patient's death. For hospital records the application should be made to the records manager at the relevant hospital(s). A fee might apply.

Where someone wants to access another living person's medical records then they will only be entitled if they are acting with the other's consent and on their behalf, or they have legal authority to make decisions on that other's behalf such as under a power of attorney, or they have some other legal basis for being entitled to the records. Again, an application should be made to the relevant GP practice or NHS Trust (contact for the records manager) and usually a form will be provided. Proof of identity and authority to access the other's records will be required and a fee may be charged.

Anyone who is the data subject, or who has the requisite authority, can ask for access to and copies of medical records. This does not have to be done by a solicitor. However, most solicitors will offer to carry out this task as part of their service. Some will do it prior to making a decision whether to enter into a conditional fee agreement with the potential claimant.

A person's medical records can be voluminous. Once they are obtained it is beneficial – indeed necessary if a claim is to be pursued – to put the records in a comprehensible order and to paginate them, and to prepare a chronology of events relevant to the issues in the case cross-referenced to the paginated records. That way anyone involved in the case, from expert witnesses, to the judge at trial, has a common set of records and a means of identifying to which page from the records reference is being made. There are businesses that exist just to carry out the sorting and pagination of medical records. Increasingly records are scanned so that an electronic version is used by all those involved in the case. This is of considerable benefit to the environment and to the back muscles of lawyers and medical experts.

Witness Statements and Expert Opinion

There are two kinds of witness in a clinical negligence claim – witnesses of fact and witnesses of opinion. A witness of fact gives evidence as to what they saw or heard in person. Their statements must be verified by a declaration that they believe that the facts stated are true. This is a requirement of Part 22 of the Civil Procedure Rules ("CPR"). These witnesses are sometimes referred to as "lay witnesses" although they include professionals such as doctors and nurses. When a doctor gives evidence of fact, such as the dosage of antibiotics they gave, they are not permitted to give the court their opinions about those facts. They may tell the court that they thought they were giving the appropriate dosage and that their judgement as to the appropriate dosage was based on experience, instruction or reading, but their evidence that the dosage was in accordance with a responsible body of opinion would not be admissible. Witnesses of opinion give evidence for the purpose of informing the court of their opinions. They are not witnesses of fact but they give opinions based on the facts. These are called "expert witnesses" because they must possess expertise in relation to the matters on which they are giving their opinions.

Lay Witnesses

It is perfectly proper for a lawyer to help a lay witness prepare their statement, but it is the witness who has responsibility for ensuring that the statement contains their own evidence and that it is all true. A witness should not adopt a form of wording suggested by a solicitor if they do not understand it, or if they do understand it but it does not quite fit the truth as they know it to be. Statements should be written in the witness' own words. A statement of fact should be based on what they know, not on what they have been told by someone else. *"I measured my son's temperature as 40.5°C"*, is wholly different from: *"My husband measured my son's temperature and told me it was 40.5°C."* If the statement says: *"My son's temperature was 40.5°C"*, then it will not be the whole truth and it will invite the question at court: *"Who measured your son's temperature?"*

As a barrister who has cross-examined countless lay witnesses and observed many other witnesses cross-examined by other barristers, I have seen the common traps into which witnesses fall, and which could have been avoided had more care been taken when drafting their witness statements. Above all, lay witness statements must be true. It can be a contempt of court, punishable with imprisonment, to make a false statement in civil litigation. And, provided they are consistent with the truth, statements should also be relevant, comprehensive and consistent. Lay witness statements should be relevant to the issues in the case, comprehensive so that they include all the relevant evidence that the witness can give on those issues, and consistent both internally and with other evidence in the case.

Failure to abide by these simple principles can lead to trouble at trial. For example, if a witness provides some important piece of evidence in oral evidence at court but which is absent from their statement, they will inevitably be asked why it was not within their statement. The, not unfamiliar, response that they did not think it was relevant, rarely impresses the judge. The other frequent response: *"My solicitor wrote the statement and I just signed it"*, sounds even worse. Why should a judge place any trust in the evidence of such a witness? Statements should include all the important relevant evidence.

At the other extreme are the statements that contain paragraph after paragraph of irrelevant detail. It may be that a witness thought that a particular nurse rudely interrupted a family conversation at the bedside of the claimant, but if that is not relevant to the issues of negligence and causation that the court will have to decide, then there is little point in including it in the statement. The risk of fighting unnecessary battles in litigation is that you may lose them. If a witness is found not to be reliable about an unimportant matter, they risk being found unreliable about an important one. When giving evidence at trial witnesses must tell the "truth, the whole truth and nothing but the truth." The requirement to tell the "whole truth" is not a licence to tell the court everything you think about everything that happened. The court is not carrying out an unlimited inquiry – it is determining issues in dispute that could lead to a finding of liability against the defendant. That is all.

A lay witness may well have acquired a great deal of medical knowledge but if they have not, then it is best not to litter their statement with complex terminology. A judge wants to rely on a witness but may harbour doubts about their credibility if they have verified that their statement is true but manifestly do not understand its contents.

A badly drafted witness statement will put a witness' credibility under scrutiny in many different ways, but most obviously the statement should avoid inconsistency. A statement should be internally consistent – it is no good saying that pain was in the right leg in paragraph 6 of the statement, but alleging that it was in the left leg at paragraph 8. It should also, preferably, be consistent with other evidence: from other witnesses called by the same party and the evidence contained in the medical notes. Sometimes, inevitably, a witness' evidence is inconsistent with what was recorded at the time. If so, then that inconsistency needs to be addressed. Perhaps a claimant will say that the doctor misunderstood what was being said at the time, and so made a misleading record. Or a doctor may say that they wrote down something at the time that they now know to be wrong. Whatever the reason for the inconsistency, it needs addressing and should not be ignored. Where a witness has made more than one statement, the statements should be consistent with each other unless there is good reason otherwise.

There is no obligation on either party to call particular lay witnesses, but the absence of a witness may lead to adverse inferences being drawn. No such inference could be drawn if there is a good reason why the person is not giving evidence. They might lack capacity to give evidence due to their young age or infirmity, they might have died, or they might live abroad. If a party wants to rely on a statement made by a witness but is unable to call them to give oral evidence at trial, then they should serve notice on the opposing party stating their intention to rely on the statement made out of court. If, on the other hand, they have not been able to reach that witness at all, even to take a statement, then again, if there is good reason for that failure, the court will not draw adverse inferences.

If, however, a key potential witness is not called by a party and there is no reason given, the court may be invited by the opposing party to infer that the evidence from that witness would not have been helpful to the party that would have been expected to call them. Generally, a party to civil litigation can call which witnesses they want to and leave aside those witnesses they do not want, including those who they know would give evidence unhelpful to their case. That is why the right of the court to draw an adverse inference is a useful corrective. In recent times many courts have taken to giving standard directions that a defendant, say an NHS Trust, must adduce witness evidence from all the healthcare professionals who had conduct of the claimant's care and treatment. Arguably if this requirement is placed on the defendant, then a parallel requirement should be placed on the claimant. For example, in many cases a claimant's partner may have been with them in hospital at times relevant to the litigation – should they be obliged in a similar way to give evidence? In an adversarial system it seems to me to be odd for the court to require a party to rely on this witness or that witness. It should be for the party to decide.

The process of the parties providing copies of witness statements and expert report to each other is called "exchange". As we shall see, the usual procedure within litigation is for the parties to exchange lay witness statements prior to exchanging expert opinion evidence. The reason is obvious: the experts need to base their opinions on the evidence of fact. They cannot give opinions about the standard of care given to a patient without knowing what the evidence is about the care that was actually given.

Expert Witness Evidence

Expert witnesses will not have been present when patient management decisions were taken or treatment administered. Indeed, if they were present, they would not be suitable to give expert evidence in the subsequent litigation. Expert witnesses should be independent. An expert should not be employed by the Trust that might be a defendant in proceedings, nor should they have treated, or be treating, the claimant. They are not utilised in litigation to inform the court what they saw or heard, but to give their opinions, based on the evidence of fact, about the standards of clinical care that would be expected by all responsible bodies of relevant opinion, and the consequences of any failings in the care, management and treatment of the patient in question.

Expert witnesses should not give opinions on matters that are outside their field of expertise. They are required to set out in a written report their qualifications for giving an opinion and the material on which they have based their opinion. They must declare on the face of their reports:

> *"I confirm that I have made clear which facts and matters referred to in this report are within my own knowledge and which are not. Those that are within my own knowledge I confirm to be true. The opinions I have expressed represent my true and complete professional opinions on the matters to which they refer."*

Expert witnesses are instructed by the parties to litigation, but the court controls what expert evidence may be relied upon, and the CPR sets out the rules governing such expert evidence.

By CPR Part 35.3

"(1) It is the duty of experts to help the court on matters within their expertise.

(2) This duty overrides any obligation to the person from whom experts have

received instructions or by whom they are paid."

There is a Practice Direction to Part 35 that provides, amongst other things that:

"2.2 Experts should assist the court by providing objective, unbiased opinions on matters within their expertise, and should not assume the role of an advocate.

2.3 Experts should consider all material facts, including those which might detract from their opinions".

A party who instructs an expert to provide opinion evidence may correspond with the expert and may discuss the expert's opinion with them but the expert's opinion must be their own and their ultimate duty is to provide objective opinions to the court, not to give evidence to suit the party who instructed them.

To "instruct" an expert in litigation does not mean that the party can tell the expert what to say. It is a piece of legal jargon meaning that the party invites the expert to give an opinion. As noted above we also talk of Counsel (barristers) being "instructed", but whereas a barrister represents a client, the expert witness does not give evidence to help the person who instructed them – they give evidence to help the court to determine the issues in the case.

A good letter of instruction to an expert will set out the terms on which the expert is being engaged, include a background to the case with some of the relevant facts, list the documents being provided to the expert, provide a list of issues for the expert to consider, and remind the expert of the tests for establishing breach of duty and causation, and of the expert's duties to the court. These letters of instructions are most usually drafted by the party's solicitors. The solicitor will also provide the experts with a copy of the set of medical records. Increasingly these are now provided electronically, but many a tree has been felled to provide the voluminous paperwork involved in copying medical records to a number of different experts.

A doctor is more qualified than a lay person to give an opinion on medical matters, but the courts look for more focused expertise than that. If the issue in a case is the technique used in brain surgery, then the parties will need to instruct a neurosurgeon to give an opinion as to the standard of care to be expected. It may be that the particular brain surgery that was performed was within the expertise of a subset of neurosurgeons. It would be of limited help to the court to provide an opinion on the technique used from a neurosurgeon who had never used it, or who had never performed an operation of that kind. In very rare cases where the surgical technique was very innovative, it might be appropriate to rely on a neurosurgeon who, whilst they had not performed the technique in question, nevertheless had sufficient expertise in the field to offer an opinion on it. The need for specialist opinion evidence means that it can be time-consuming and expensive to obtain. These experts tend to be busy people with many calls on their time. It might take several months between instructing them and receiving their first draft report. And they do not come cheap. Like most experienced barristers, the majority of expert witnesses in all but the simplest clinical negligence claims, will charge at least £200 per hour. The alternative would be to compel the parties to such litigation to rely on "experts" who did not in fact have the relevant experience and expertise to offer reliable opinions on the matters in hand. That would be a strange way to try to achieve justice.

Most often each party will instruct their own experts. Therefore, in a case of one claimant and one defendant there will be two neurosurgeons, or other relevant experts, giving evidence. Sometimes, however, the parties will agree, or the court will order, that expert evidence on an issue should be given by a single, jointly instructed expert. The parties' solicitors will agree a letter of instruction. They will each receive the expert's written report at the same time. Neither party will be able to discuss the expert's evidence with them, but they may ask written questions of the expert, providing a copy of the questions to the other party when they do so.

Where an expert is instructed by one party, rather than jointly, the expert will send their draft report back to their instructing solicitor, not to both parties. An experienced solicitor will then thoroughly check the document for any obvious errors, such as a mis-transcription of a medical note, or a typing error. They will also seek to explore any issues that require further elucidation, and press the expert further on any important matters that have not been fully addressed. This way, the expert's report is refined and clarified. Usually the solicitor will send a copy of the draft report to their client who may have their own corrections and questions to be addressed. Where the expert is jointly instructed, this luxury is not afforded to the parties. A more formal process of questioning the expert is adopted, known as Part 35 questioning. Under that procedure the questions for the expert are written out and shared with the other parties. The expert is given a set time to answer the questions. These Part 35 questions and answers are conducted openly. Everyone sees them. A party can use the same process to ask questions of the other party's experts, once their reports have been disclosed. In contrast, correspondence and discussions with a party's "own" expert are "privileged", meaning that the party is entitled to keep them confidential. When the time comes, as set down by the court, to disclose an expert's opinion, the party instructing and relying on that expert must disclose the substance of their evidence – they cannot pick and choose what the expert has written down so as to give a misleading account of that expert's true opinion. However, there is no obligation to reveal the contents of the expert's first draft report. It is their final, settled opinion that is disclosable. Perhaps the expert has changed their mind following discussions with lawyers or other experts. There is no requirement to show to the other party and the court the written opinions of the expert from both before and after they changed their minds. The only requirement is to reveal their written reports containing their true opinions as they now are.

Nevertheless, a party might choose to reveal earlier, different opinions. They are free to do so. For example, an expert might have changed their mind because of further evidence disclosed by the opposing party. In such a case it might be useful to show the court that the further evidence was sufficiently important to change the expert's views.

As we will see later, the court controls expert evidence. There is nothing in principle to stop a party instructing, say, six experts on the issue of breach of duty, albeit that would be a potentially very costly exercise. But if the court determined that only two of them were needed for the court fairly to determine the issue of breach, then four of those experts will be redundant and the costs spent on them wasted. Nor should a party indulge in "expert shopping". The court uses its case management powers to try to prevent parties from shopping around to find a supportive expert. I address this below in Chapter 4 below.

Expert reports vary in style and length. I have seen expert reports run to fewer than five pages, and others extend to more than one hundred. Some experts include lengthy appendices with diagrams, published papers and a glossary, whilst others simply précis the evidence and then give a short opinion on the issues. In my experience, whilst it is necessary to obtain expert opinion evidence appropriate to the issues in dispute and so there will usually be a need for experts from a number of different disciplines, the litigation process does produce avoidable duplication. Three experts, instructed by the same party, may each write out extensive extracts from the medical records in their reports. The reason that this is accepted as normal practice is that it serves to show that each expert has considered all the relevant evidence, and has not taken into account anything that is irrelevant. Nevertheless, the judge at trial often ends up with lengthy expert reports of which 80% of the contents are repetition. The most important part of the expert's report is that containing their opinion. This may take up only the last 10% or so of the written report.

The other feature of expert evidence that anyone involved in clinical negligence litigation will have noticed is that, even though experts have a duty to the court to provide objective and unbiased opinions, there are many cases where two experts from the same discipline come to opposing views, and those views happen to coincide with the interests of the parties who instructed them. Parties can select their experts. Suppose you were a solicitor who acts for claimants who have suffered injury following brain surgery and you need to instruct an expert neurosurgeon 20 times a year. You need to identify an expert who can be relied upon to answer correspondence within a reasonable time, who is capable of writing a clear and compelling report, and who will be able to give cogent evidence at a trial. You identify Professor Broad and he possesses all of the qualities required but his first five reports are unsupportive of your client's cases and you have to discontinue those claims. You do not get paid for the work you have done and you have five clients who have not recovered any compensation. You then contact another neurosurgeon Professor Long who also possesses the same qualities but who gives supportive opinion evidence in four of the first five cases you send to him. When the next post-brain surgery client comes to you with what you believe to be a strong case, would you be inclined to instruct Professor Broad or Professor Long? There is, I believe, a natural tendency for some solicitors to prefer to instruct experts who tend to be more, rather than less, supportive of their clients' cases. That is not to say that expert witnesses are being biased. Some experts are a little more willing to "call out" negligence when they see it than others. Some are simply more conservative than others. I very much respect expert witnesses who are prepared to give unpalatable advice to the party who instructed them. This is a feature of their objectivity. It is in fact much better to give honest and well-reasoned advice, however negative the consequences for the party to litigation, than to strain to be "helpful". No-one benefits from an expert who gives bland reassurances early on in the litigation process, only to change their opinions later as trial approaches or, worse, during the trial. Actually, the only person who does benefit is the expert themselves. Experts are paid their fees whatever the outcome of the litigation.

It is essential that expert witnesses understand what they are being asked to do. They should be familiar with the *Bolam* test and the *Bolitho* case. They should know about the law on consent to treatment. In clinical negligence litigation an expert on an issue of breach of duty should not be asked what they would have done in the same circumstances. Evidence of their own practice is of use only by way of illustration – it is not conclusive of whether or not there was negligence. An expert who reports that they would not have done what the defendant's doctor did is giving evidence of only limited assistance to the court. Experts give opinions but the courts decide cases on all the evidence. The expert may give an opinion that a particular healthcare professional fell below a standard of care that would be considered acceptable by all reasonable bodies of opinion within the relevant field of practice, but the court determines whether there was a breach of duty.

There is no requirement for expert witnesses to be selected from a pre-approved panel or to have undergone any specific training requirements. The only time when an expert witness' credentials are openly tested is at trial. This means that some experts manage to make a living by offering opinions on matters that are not properly within their field of expertise. The system relies on lawyers scrutinising the qualifications and knowledge of expert witnesses to ensure that experts of the right calibre and experience are deployed in each case. I suspect that I am not alone amongst my colleagues in having had occasion to wonder whether the expert witnesses in a clinical negligence case would be recognised as true experts by their peers.

For all these reservations, my experience of experts has been largely positive – probably more positive than their experience of me! They usually take great care to ensure that their opinions are fair, balanced and comprehensible. When pressed they will seek to back up their opinions with published material and further reasoning. They will patiently answer questions from lawyers like me that must seem to them to be stupid or irrelevant.

Kinds of Expert Evidence

Expert medical evidence will usually be required to cover issues of breach of duty, causation and the claimant's condition and prognosis. Expert non-medical evidence may be required as to the consequences of the claimant's injuries. By way of illustration of the kinds of expert evidence that may be required in a serious clinical negligence case, consider a claim on behalf of a child with cerebral palsy alleged to have been caused by obstetric negligence during labour. To establish negligence and causation of the cerebral palsy, typically a claimant will require expert evidence from an obstetrician, a midwife, a neuroradiologist, a neonatologist and a paediatric neurologist. The paediatric neurologist will also give essential evidence on the nature and extent of the injuries, but this will need to be supplemented, in most cases, with further evidence from a variety of witnesses including experts in care, occupational therapy, educational psychology, physiotherapy, speech and language therapy, accommodation, and assistive technology. In addition, evidence will usually be required from a professional "deputy" (of the Court of Protection) as to the costs of managing a substantial award for compensation, and from an independent financial adviser as to the advantages and disadvantages of a periodical payment award as opposed to a lump sum award. Including the financial experts, that is a total of 14 experts. If there are two parties to the litigation and they each instruct their own experts, there will be 28 involved in the litigation.

The medical experts on liability will be at consultant level. The experts on quantum issues will all have to be experienced and competent to give authoritative evidence to the court under scrutiny from the other party to the litigation. Experts like these do not come cheap. Nor are they freely available to assist with the parties at the drop of a hat. They tend to have long waiting lists and many other calls on their time. Arranging a meeting of, say, five liability experts and the lawyers for a party to litigation can take many months. The need for a high level of expertise covering all issues in a complex case is one of the main reasons why clinical negligence litigation can be particularly protracted.

In a simpler case, for example a missed scaphoid fracture in A&E, the claimant might instruct an A&E consultant to advise on the standard of care and an orthopaedic surgeon to advise on causation, condition and prognosis. However, suppose that the claimant has a permanent impairment of function in their dominant right hand as a result of the failure to diagnose the scaphoid fracture on first presentation and they are a self-employed plumber who is unable to perform all the usual functions required for that role. In such a case, it may be necessary to instruct a forensic accountant – often the most costly experts of all – to provide evidence of the impact of the injuries on the claimant's earnings from their business.

In my time I have had consultations with experts in career progression in the armed forces, ultrasonography, medical statistics, horse riding for the disabled, educational psychology, hydrotherapy, adapted transport, and genetics. In many cases the issue on which the expert is asked to advise can make a difference of tens of thousands of pounds, or more, to the value of the claim.

Other Evidence
Not all the evidence that would ultimately be relied upon at a trial will be gathered at this stage. In some instances a court order will be required to force a party to disclose some of the evidence referred to below, and a court order will most usually follow the commencement of proceedings, although in rare cases a pre-action order for disclosure of documentation or other evidence can be sought from a judge. However, since it is best to gather as much relevant evidence at an early stage – to allow for a proper assessment

of the merits of bringing the claim to court – I shall set out now some of the evidence that may be relevant to a clinical negligence claim alongside the medical records and the lay and expert evidence.

National Guidance and Local Protocols

National guidance, published by the time of the events in question in the proposed litigation, can be very helpful to show: (i) the standard of care to be expected; and (ii) what would or should have occurred but for the negligent failings of the clinicians in the claimant's case. It is important, therefore, that the experts who are advising are aware of and analyse the application of any national guidance to the particular events in the case in question.

Most NHS Trusts will have devised or adopted, and implemented, protocols or policies for various aspects of the management and treatment of patients. For example, there may be a protocol for the administration of prophylactic antibiotics prior to different kinds of surgery. Again, it is very important that the expert witnesses are aware of and take into account such protocols. If the defendant has failed to abide by its own standards as set out in a written protocol, then that is good evidence, at first sight, of a failure to exercise reasonable care.

Evidence of Local Practice

Aside from protocols and policies, there may be other evidence available that will help to prove what the usual standard or expectation would have been within the defendant Trust. In obstetric negligence cases it might be important to know how long it would have taken for a baby to have been delivered by Caesarean section following a decision to proceed to an emergency delivery by that method. If no such decision was made in the case, then how can that likely period of time be established? There are national guidelines that indicate that it would not be negligent to deliver within 30 minutes of an emergency Caesarean section call. But it does not follow that it would probably take 30 minutes in every case in every Trust in the land. The parties might want to look at a plan of the layout of the maternity unit, showing the distance from the labour or delivery suite to the theatre, for example. In one recent case the claimant cleverly obtained useful evidence from the defendant Trust of actual times taken in the previous months and years between a call out for an emergency Caesarean section and the time of delivery. That was very good evidence to support a case as to the time it would have probably taken had an emergency call out being made in the claimant's own case. Similarly, a claimant in a delay in cancer diagnosis claim might seek to obtain evidence as to the waiting times from a routine referral to an appointment at a local breast clinic.

The local organisation of NHS services may be important to a case. Where would or should the claimant have been referred for specialist care? Where was the local specialist neurosurgical unit, and how long would it have taken to transfer the claimant there by ambulance for brain surgery? Should the local hospital have administered a specialist form of chemotherapy or should they have referred the patient to the regional specialist cancer unit? This kind of evidence will not necessarily be manifest from the medical records or the claimant's own witness evidence. If, as is usual practice, the experts instructed are not connected to the Trust alleged to have been negligent, then they may be unaware of local practice. Hence, the lawyers for the claimant need to be aware of the need to look for this kind of additional evidence. Of course, the defendant should already be aware of and have ready access to this information.

Telephone Logs, Texts and Transcripts

Contemporaneous evidence – made or set down at or about the time of the events in question – is not necessarily truthful or accurate but it is often given particular weight in a clinical negligence claim. It includes the medical records but there may be other forms of contemporaneous evidence available. Take, for example, a case of delayed diagnosis of meningitis. A concerned parent calls an out of hours service and then takes their child to the A&E department of the nearest hospital but is reassured that the child has a viral illness that can be managed with Calpol, sipping water and keeping a careful look out for any deterioration. They go home only to re-attend several hours later by which time the child has obvious signs of meningitis, collapses soon afterwards and is left with permanent, life-changing injuries. The medical note made in the A&E department does not refer to a history of high temperature, or whether the child was drowsy and irritable when handled. The parent recalls that the temperature had been high for five days and that the child was constantly sleepy and hated being touched or handled. In such a case it would be very important to obtain the transcript of the telephone call to the out of hours service. Suppose that in answer to basic questions by the call-handler, the parent had said that the child had had a temperature of over 39°C for a week, and cried a piercing cry whenever handled. That would be strong contemporaneous evidence that: (i) the parent's recollections were accurate and (ii) unless the parent gave the A&E doctor misleading information at the time of attendance, then the A&E doctor either failed to ask basic questions or failed accurately to recognise the significance, and to record, the answers given.

Sometimes no transcript is available but the time when a call was made is important. It is often possible to obtain telephone records for a particular day and to determine when calls were made to, say, a GP or a local hospital.

A GP's surgery reception may keep a log of attendances and calls, even if there is no other record of the reason for the attendances or the contents of the call.

Another source of contemporaneous evidence is found in electronic communications such as texts and emails. In one case of mine the client had texted his son after a consultation with a doctor saying, *"Apparently all OK"*. This is not definitive evidence that the doctor reassured the patient, but it is useful corroborative evidence for the patient's own recollection that they were reassured.

For those readers worried about the concept of "hearsay evidence", this example of a text is instructive. Hearsay is an out of court statement offered to prove the truth of the matter asserted. In clinical negligence litigation the courts are much less worried about admitting (that is allowing in evidence) hearsay statements than in criminal cases. As noted above, a notice should be given if a witness statement is being relied upon for the truth of its contents but the witness cannot be called to give oral evidence at trial. However, it is not general practice to give notice of intention to rely on statements in medical records, even if they are being relied on to establish the truth of their contents. The text referred to earlier is a contemporaneous communication which is being offered as evidence that the patient believed that the doctor had reassured him. That is not quite the same as an assertion that the doctor had said *"everything is OK"*. It is however a self-supporting statement by the claimant. There are detailed rules about the admissibility of evidence, including hearsay evidence, partly within statute, partly developed by common law, but, at the risk of being blasé about it, they need not trouble the reader. Usually, evidence that is relevant to an issue in the case, such that it helps the court to determine that issue, is treated as "admissible" evidence, meaning that a party is allowed to rely on it. It is not quite the case that all relevant evidence is admissible in clinical negligence litigation but it is not far short of it.

Interrogating Computer Entries and Earlier Records and Statements
In a number of cases that I have conducted, we have had computerised medical records "interrogated". In one case this involved nothing more than various screenshots being taken of computerised records with the mouse hovering over an entry thereby revealing more detail for that entry than appeared on the initially disclosed print-out. So, a haemoglobin record entered at between 18:00 and 19:00 was revealed to have been taken from a sample collected at 18:03 and entered on the record at 18:46.

In another case, an expert carried out much more sophisticated analysis of a GP's computerised records to reveal who had made the records and when. Sometimes it is possible to see earlier versions of records that may have been changed.

In a similar, but less technological way, a witness may have made an earlier statement, or kept notes for themselves which may not be entirely consistent with a disclosed statement. There may have been an internal investigation during which statements were made by clinicians which are materially different from later statements used for the purpose of litigation. Or they may be the same, which might add weight to the witness' evidence. Lawyers love nothing more than inconsistent statements from witnesses for the other party, but there are limits to the forensic archaeology that can be practised to unearth earlier evidence. A party is not entitled to see a first draft of a witness statement that was later changed, finalised and signed. On the other hand, if a midwife made some contemporaneous notes from which they later completed a retrospective entry in the labour record, then a claimant would be entitled to ask to see them. Imagine if they were materially inconsistent with the retrospective record and that were not disclosed – it would look like a cover-up.

Some medical records have obviously been altered. It may be necessary to look at the original documents to see what has been over-written or changed. This may have been done crudely, with different coloured ink for example. Such alterations are not necessarily, indeed are rarely, suspicious of wrongdoing. It might be perfectly natural to write something down and then change it, even to come back to it a few minutes later and make a correction. Best practice might be to initial the change, but in a busy medical setting it is understandable if there is not a clear "audit trail". If there were a dishonest change in the notes it would be unlikely to be done crudely so that the changes were obvious on examination of the original notes.

Claimants have to be very wary of alleging that notes have been dishonestly altered. Firstly, it is very difficult to prove. A mere suspicion that notes have been altered is not sufficient to establish dishonesty. There really has to be a "smoking gun" – something that very strongly indicates malpractice. On the other hand, if there are missing records and no reasonable explanation for their absence, or if the only explanations would be deliberate suppression or negligence in keeping and making available relevant documentation, then the courts may well make adverse inferences, just as they would if a relevant witness were inexplicably not called to give evidence at trial.

Similar Fact Evidence
A person wishing to bring a clinical negligence claim may have heard from

others that the practitioner involved has been negligent on other occasions. That evidence will not be in the medical records for the particular patient, nor in the witness statements. The claimant themselves cannot speak to the truth of those other allegations. Is there anything that can be done to obtain evidence of their truth, and is such evidence relevant?

As often in litigation, it depends! If there is evidence that establishes that a surgeon, say, has made the same or similar mistakes when treating other patients, then that evidence might be admissible as so-called "similar fact evidence". If, on the other hand, the evidence relating to cases other than that of the claimant is of negligence in relation to other types of operation or other errors, then the evidence will not be considered relevant. In a Court of Appeal case called *Laughton v Shalaly* [2014] EWCA Civ 1450, it was held that evidence of extraneous matters should be confined to cases of similar fact for the reason that, unless it was similar fact evidence, it was not probative of the issue to be determined. A finding in a General Medical Council report into the surgeon was said to be a damning general comment but, of itself, it could not prove that the surgeon had been negligent in the claimant's operation, particularly since the injury suffered by the claimant did not necessarily indicate negligence.

Photographs and Film
In the age of the smart phone, it is common to see photographs of patients in hospital, or of bruises, bedsores and other injuries suffered by a claimant. A picture, they say, is worth a thousand words, and photograph evidence is valuable in litigation. Additional evidence might be required to prove when and where a photograph was taken. In one case of mine some family photographs, not taken with a view to litigation or with a view to showing any injury or abnormality, were important in establishing that a health visitor had missed obvious signs of developmental dysplasia of an infant's hip. The photographs showed classic signs of dysplasia, the significance of which would not necessarily have been obvious to the family, but which would or should have been obvious to a health visitor carrying out a reasonable assessment of the child. We had to prove when the photographs were taken so that we could show that the child's appearance on the photographs would have been what the health visitor would have seen when she examined her.

In certain cases, film (I still want to call it video) provides valuable evidence. Most often, this comprises footage of the claimant showing the extent of their disability. In cerebral palsy cases, a "day in the life" film of the claimant showing them being dressed, sitting if they are able, using their hands, eating, mobilising etc. can be very helpful evidence for a judge assessing the extent and impact of the claimant's neurological injuries. In other cases, the film of a claimant is taken on behalf of the defendant and without the claimant's knowledge. This is called covert surveillance evidence. Such evidence has been commonplace for many years in personal injury cases arising out of road traffic accidents or injuries at work. It has been rarer in clinical negligence cases, but that seems to be changing. I mentioned earlier one recent case a clinical negligence claimant who said he could not function as a courier was filmed loading boxes into a van and working as normal. He was later sent to prison for contempt of court.

More often surveillance footage is very dull and demonstrates that the work of a private detective is not all glamour – I have sat through hours of surveillance film showing nothing but a closed front door. A relatively exciting minute follows showing the door opening and a man emerging, to roll a black bin to outside the front gate, before returning inside. There then follows another hour of film of the closed front door.

The camera never lies but it can sometimes be used to mislead. If surveillance evidence is disclosed, it is important to ensure that the totality of the film taken has been provided. Edited highlights might give the wrong impression of the level of activity of which a claimant is capable. Undisclosed footage might just show the claimant limping or provide other evidence that is corroborative of their case.

Whilst it is unpleasant to know that you have been filmed secretly, and there are limits – tricks to induce a claimant to carry out an activity should not be used, and covert filming within the claimant's home is not done – it seems to me that the use of covert surveillance evidence is a legitimate tool to defend certain cases. How else could a defendant prove that a claimant had significantly exaggerated or even concocted their disabilities?

Social Media

In fact – to answer the question with which I closed the last section – remarkably claimants themselves often provide clear evidence that they have exaggerated or made up their disabilities! If you bring a large claim for compensation, you might expect someone acting for the defendant to do a sweep of your social media activity. In a 2019 case, a claimant who said that as a result of her injuries she could not attend a family event abroad was filmed at the event and the film was posted on social media. She was later jailed for contempt of court having dishonestly exaggerated her injuries for the purpose of attracting increased compensation.

I heard of one case where a claimant, who claimed that they had a disabling spinal injury, was filmed for a Facebook post making a charity bungee jump from a crane. When shown the footage he said that the jump was therapeutic – it applied traction to his spine!

Quantification Evidence

A claimant wishing to establish various losses and expenses consequent upon their avoidable injuries needs to do more than simply provide a statement saying what they have lost and incurred. They need documentary evidence by way of payslips, receipts, invoices etc. Anyone contemplating bringing a substantial injury claim should organise themselves at an early stage to ask for and keep receipts, to make records of journeys taken to and from hospital appointments and even to keep a record of when a partner, parent, child or friend has provided them with care and assistance. I often suggest to parents of a disabled child that they keep a diary for, say, a two week period, recording the times they attended to the child at night, and what they did when they attended, what trips out of the house they made and how they managed them, what medical appointments were required, etc. In some cases where the injuries are very severe, and where the funding is available, a case manager might be engaged to organise care workers or nursing, therapies etc, and the case manager will keep an account of expenditure. In most cases, however, this is work for the claimant, their family and their solicitor.

Not all this evidence will be gathered at the outset of the investigation into a potential claim. Most of the quantification evidence will be obtained as the case progresses and will continue to be added right up to the date of trial. But once the medical records have been obtained, preliminary statements taken and initial expert reports obtained, it is time to take stock and assess whether the intended claim is worthwhile pursuing further.

Deciding Whether to Bring a Claim
Assessing the Evidence

Once the medical records have been produced and collated, key witness statements taken and expert medical opinions obtained, it is necessary to assess the evidence. At this stage a clinical negligence lawyer acting for a potential claimant will use their experience to analyse the evidence and determine whether it is sufficient, on the face of it, to establish that a healthcare professional or body owed a duty of care to the patient, whether there was a breach of the duty of care and whether the breach caused or materially contributed to the injuries suffered by the patient. Is the evidence robust? Have the experts addressed the issues they need to address? Is there a gap in the witness evidence that would need to be filled? What further evidence will be required to establish the necessary components of the proposed claim? If the claim were to succeed, what would be the likely level of compensation and would it be sufficient to justify the costs of litigation?

Conference with Counsel

Both solicitors and barristers are lawyers, but each have a different role. Traditionally members of the public could not instruct barristers directly – they had to go through a solicitor – and the court room was the exclusive preserve of the barrister. Only barristers could act as advocates because solicitors did not have "rights of audience", i.e. they were not permitted to address the courts. It has been said that solicitors should be good listeners and barristers should be good talkers. These clear lines of demarcation have faded with changes to the regulation of the legal profession. Solicitors can now gain rights of audience in all courts, and very commonly do act as advocates in lower level courts. Barristers may undertake direct access and public access work, allowing professional and lay clients to instruct them directly rather than through a firm of solicitors. Nevertheless, in clinical negligence litigation by far the most common arrangement is that a client will instruct a solicitor who will investigate the claim, gather the evidence, obtain expert reports and then engage a barrister. The barrister will advise on the evidence and strategy, assess the value of the claim, conduct any face to face negotiations and act as the advocate at important court hearings including trial.

Solicitors and barristers tend to have different but complementary skills. There ought not to be duplication of work. Barristers mostly work as self-employed individuals who collect together in "chambers" to share premises, staff and other overheads. They engage clerks who act rather like an actor's agent, promoting their principal, taking bookings, negotiating fees and so on. A barrister who wishes to, may, after about 15 years of professional practice, apply to become a Queen's Counsel. They have to pay a heavy fee to apply and they will seek the support of a large number of referees including judges, other barristers and solicitors. They are subjected to interview. If they are successful in the application then it is said that they have "taken silk". Annually about one hundred silks are appointed at an elaborate ceremony in Westminster Hall. When King Charles III succeeds Queen Elizabeth II they will become KCs. Approximately 10% of barristers are QCs and they tend to conduct the larger and more complex cases.

In clinical negligence litigation it is preferable for the barrister who will conduct any trial in the case to be involved at an early stage, whether for the claimant or defendant. The litigation process is adversarial. There can be a lot at stake, and it is important that the evidence is tested, plans drawn up for how the case is presented, and a strategy adopted as to the gathering of further evidence as soon as practicable. It is also helpful to the parties to litigation to establish and develop a strong trust in those representing them. In an important case it is very undesirable for parties to meet their barrister for the first time shortly before, or even at, the trial of their claim.

In my experience from representing claimants in clinical negligence litigation, it is common to hold a first conference with counsel, the claimant, and those experts who have been instructed after receipt of the first draft expert reports. This is likely to be prior to letting the proposed defendant know what the nature of the claimant's case is (see Pre-Action Protocol below). My role, as counsel, is to question the claimant to ensure that their evidence is clear and credible, and to question the experts to ensure that: (i) I understand their evidence and could explain it to a judge at court; and (ii) their evidence is supportive of the issues the claimant would need to prove to succeed in the proposed litigation. After questioning the experts, I will give my views to the client about what further evidence is needed, and the prospects for success in the proposed claim.

These meetings, called "conferences", can be a strange experience for claimants – and not just because of my involvement. My client or their child may have experienced life-changing injury or they may be bereaved as a result of allegedly negligent clinical care. The issues under discussion are deeply personal to them and yet I am meeting them for the first time and talking about those issues in detail to experts who may also be wholly unknown to them. Sometimes these discussions are conducted via a telephone on speaker mode. I might have to discuss the life expectancy of my client with an oncologist, or whether my client's baby would have been spared brain damage had a midwife made a different decision during labour. I try to conduct these conferences sensitively but they inevitably provide a foretaste of the de-personalizing nature of litigation.

For defendants, first conferences with counsel will usually take place at a later stage. The claimant has to investigate whether there is a claim to pursue. Hence, a claimant's solicitor may have been working on a case for months or years before the proposed defendant is made aware that a claim is likely to be brought. Only when the defendant knows the case against it can it meaningfully take witness statements, obtain expert reports and instruct counsel to advise. Whilst the sensitivities involved in a conference with counsel for the defence are different from those at a claimant's conference, they are nevertheless very real. A doctor who is alleged to have been negligent, and thereby to have caused death or serious injury, is liable to feel under considerable, stressful scrutiny. They will have to hear other medical practitioners, instructed as expert witnesses, give their opinions about their standards of care and skill. They may strongly disagree with the conclusions reached by those experts. They may feel wrongly accused of negligence. They may disagree with the lawyers' advice about the prospects of successfully defending the claim. It would be natural for a doctor whose patient has come to harm to feel very sorry, even guilty, about the outcome, even though they do not believe that they did anything wrong, let alone anything negligent. The question, *"would you do the same again, doctor?"* can often be an unfair one: of course a doctor would not wish the patient to suffer harm again, yet they might think that they were justified in doing what they did, even though harm resulted.

Whether the conference with counsel is for a claimant or a defendant, the object is to identify the issues in dispute, the evidence relevant to those issues, what further evidence is required and the strengths and weaknesses of the evidence for and against the party on those issues. Counsel will often be asked to advise at this stage on the prospects of success. Given that this advice is being sought before exchange of statements and expert reports, it is necessarily provisional. Furthermore, the prediction of the outcome of litigation is certainly not a precise science. I challenge any barrister, however experienced, to explain why a case has a 70% chance of success rather than a 75% chance. Only a broad assessment can really be made of the prospects of success, particularly at this early stage. The key for a claimant, however, is to determine whether the prospects are, or are ever going to be, better than 50%. If there is further evidence to be obtained, or if it is necessary to know what answer the defendant will give to the allegations once put to them, then it may be reasonable to continue the investigations and to put the allegations to the defendant before making a firm determination of the prospects of success. If, however, it is clear on the evidence already obtained, and without knowing what the defendant's response is going to be, that the prospects of success in the case are below 50%, then that will usually spell the end of the process.

For a defendant who has seen the claimant's allegations and has obtained lay and expert evidence in response, their counsel might well advise that liability, or some issues relevant to liability, should be openly admitted. Perhaps an expert witness says that on the basis of the medical records themselves it is obvious that a doctor's care fell below an acceptable standard and that no responsible body of practitioners in that field at that time would condone what was done. Prior to litigation being brought there is no obligation on a defendant to divulge that expert's opinion to the claimant's lawyers, but if it is clear that the claimant will prove negligence, then why would a defendant not admit as much? It will save time and costs by making an early admission.

I do not doubt that sometimes parties to litigation will try to bluff each other. So, a defendant holding an expert report advising that it was clearly negligent, but not being obliged to disclose that report to the claimant, might seek to resolve the case for say 80% of damages to be assessed. It knows that if the case proceeded it would be fixed with liability for 100% of damages, but there are some risks in litigation, and the claimant might be anxious to have the certainty of a resolution, even at the cost of a reduction in their damages of 20% by way of an agreement. Claimants might play the same game in different circumstances. This might shock some readers who believe that what matters most is the truth. However, the common law has developed the present system of litigation as the fairest way of finding a just solution where different parties have different views of what constitutes the truth. This is an adversarial process and it is why parties need access to good and experienced lawyers to advise them from the very beginning. I would say that wouldn't I, but I do have concerns about alternative processes in which one side has legal representation and the other does not.

Pre-Action Protocol
If the proposed claimant's advisers believe that there are or may be sufficient grounds for bringing a claim then, in the vast majority of cases, the next step is not to commence legal proceedings but rather to write a letter of claim to the proposed defendants.

The Pre-Action Protocol for the Resolution of Clinical Disputes, available on the Ministry of Justice website, is *"intended to apply to all claims against hospitals, GPs, dentists and other healthcare providers (both NHS and private) which involve an injury that is alleged to be the result of clinical negligence."* It sets out a standard for the conduct of a proposed clinical negligence claim which the courts expect to be followed. Whilst a potential claimant could simply issue proceedings without following the steps set out in the pre-action protocol, the courts are encouraged by the Civil Procedure Rules to impose costs sanctions for so acting.

Paragraph 1.3 of the Pre-Action Protocol says:

"It is important that each party to a clinical dispute has sufficient information and understanding of the other's perspective and case to be able to investigate a claim efficiently and, where appropriate, to resolve it. This Protocol encourages a cards-on-the-table approach when something has gone wrong with a claimant's treatment or the claimant is dissatisfied with that treatment and/or the outcome."

It expressly applies to litigants who do not have legal representation as much as to those who do.

We have seen already that the Protocol sets out expected practice in relation to requests for medical records. If, after obtaining such records and perhaps an initial expert report, a potential claimant considers that it is likely that they will bring a claim and they wish to do so, they can send a Letter of Notification to the proposed defendant. A copy of the Letter of Notification should also be sent to the NHSLA or, where known, another relevant medical defence organisation or indemnity provider. The purpose of the Letter of Notification is to alert the proposed defendant that a Letter of Claim is likely to be sent in due course, and to provide contact details. In return, on receipt of a Letter of Notification, a defendant should acknowledge the letter within 14 days of receipt, identify who will be dealing with the matter and to whom any Letter of Claim should be sent, consider whether to commence investigations and/or to obtain factual and expert evidence, and consider whether any information could be passed to the claimant which might narrow the issues in dispute or lead to an early resolution of the claim.

In an ideal world the proposed defendant would, even at this early stage, engage with the potential claim and claimant, obtain some independent evidence, and take a view of the potential for a finding of liability. More often, potential defendants bide their time and wait for a formal Letter of Claim. Thus, Letters of Notification seem in practice to serve no real purpose.

A Letter of Claim should be a carefully worded, formal letter setting out the matters listed in the Pre-Action Protocol, namely:

"(a) a clear summary of the facts on which the claim is based, including the alleged adverse outcome, and the main allegations of negligence;

(b) a description of the claimant's injuries, and present condition and prognosis;

(c) an outline of the financial loss incurred by the claimant, with an indication of the heads of damage to be claimed and the scale of the loss, unless this is impracticable;

(d) confirmation of the method of funding and whether any funding arrangement was entered into before or after April 2013; and

(e) the discipline of any expert from whom evidence has already been obtained."

The Letter of Claim should refer to relevant medical records and *"sufficient information must be given to enable the defendant to focus investigations and to put an initial valuation on the claim."* Proceedings should not be commenced within four months of sending the Letter of Claim, the idea being to give a proposed defendant sufficient time to investigate and respond to the letter and thereby, potentially, to avoid the need for proceedings to be issued.

Sometimes, as Counsel, I am asked to draft Particulars of Claim to be served in place of a Letter of Claim. As I explain below, Particulars of Claim are the formal court document in which the claimant sets out their claim. It is known as a "pleading". But a draft of what might become the formal pleading in subsequent litigation can be sent instead of a Letter of Claim. It will tell the proposed defendant what it needs to know and, together with a covering letter, will comply with the requirements of the Pre-Action Protocol as set out above.

In some cases, it might benefit a claimant to serve some expert or other evidence together with their Letter of Claim. This might be done on a "without prejudice" basis, meaning that the evidence is served on the defendant only for the purpose of their considering the issues raised in the Letter of Claim and the potential resolution of the claim. Evidence served "without prejudice" cannot be alluded to or used in subsequent litigation without the permission of the party serving it. In some cases when a claimant believes that they have a particularly strong case on one or more issues, or if they want to expedite the process, perhaps because they have a short life expectancy, then serving evidence "without prejudice" at this stage can be effective. It can show a defendant that the claimant has strong backing for their claims and is serious about proceeding to litigation, and doing so swiftly, unless pre-action admissions are made and resolution achieved.

There is no point in using the Pre-Action Protocol procedure if a claimant fails to include in their Letter of Claim the allegations they intend to make in any subsequent litigation. The Protocol should be followed in good faith and the Letter of Claim should provide a potential defendant with sufficient information to allow them meaningfully to investigate. It is not in the spirit of the Protocol for a proposed claimant to keep some of their cards up their sleeve. That said, if a claimant does subsequently embark on litigation, then the allegations they make in the formal court pleadings can vary from those set out in the Letter of Claim and they may be informed by and adjusted in reaction to the defendant's response to the Letter.

The Pre-Action Protocol provides that the proposed defendant should, within four months of the Letter of Claim, provide a reasoned answer in the form of a Letter of Response. The Letter of Response should include the following:

"(a) if the claim is admitted, say so in clear terms;

(b) if only part of the claim is admitted, make clear which issues of breach of duty and/or causation are admitted and which are denied and why;

(c) state whether it is intended that any admissions will be binding;

(d) if the claim is denied, include specific comments on the allegations of negligence and, if a synopsis or chronology of relevant events has been provided and is disputed, the defendant's version of those events;

(e) if supportive expert evidence has been obtained, identify which disciplines of expert evidence have been relied upon and whether they relate to breach of duty and/or causation;

(f) if known, state whether the defendant requires copies of any relevant medical records obtained by the claimant (to be supplied for a reasonable copying charge);

(g) provide copies of any additional documents relied upon, e.g. an internal protocol;

(h) if not indemnified by the NHS, supply details of the relevant indemnity insurer; and

(i) inform the claimant of any other potential defendants to the claim."

In cases of any complexity – which are many in clinical negligence – proposed defendants almost invariably request an extension of time to serve a Letter of Response. In some cases, it can take over a year for NHS bodies to respond. Claimants are nearly always advised to agree an extension of time because if they do not, and they commence litigation, then the court will almost always grant the defendant an extension of time to respond to the court proceedings. It seems pragmatic and sensible to wait to see what the proposed defendant is going to say by way of response before deciding whether to litigate.

Some Letters of Response are detailed, supported by independent evidence, and address all the allegations and issues raised in the Letter of Claim. That is as should be. Others, however, are short, contain bold denials rather than detailed rebuttals, and do nothing to advance the narrowing of issues or the potential for dispute resolution prior to litigation.

The Pre-Action Protocol includes provisions for making offers of settlement. Either party can offer to settle the potential legal claim for compensation on any terms. If a defendant does so, then the offer should comply with Part 36 of the CPR. But the Protocol additionally provides that: *"If an offer to settle is made, the defendant should provide sufficient medical or other evidence to allow the claimant to properly consider the offer. The level of detail necessary will depend on the value of the claim."* This provision is intended to allow the claimant to know whether the offer is made in good faith on the basis of evidence or whether it might just be an attempt to buy them off for an unduly small proportion of the potential compensation to which they might be entitled if they were to bring court proceedings. In practice, defendants are loath to disclose expert opinion evidence at this stage.

The Pre-Action Protocol provides that: *"Litigation should be a last resort. As part of this Protocol, the parties should consider whether negotiation or some other form of alternative dispute resolution ('ADR') might enable them to resolve their dispute without commencing proceedings."* I will discuss the use of ADR after the commencement of proceedings later in this Part. The forms of ADR are the same whenever deployed. My personal view is that more claims could be resolved prior to litigation if legal representatives on both sides were more willing to advise their clients to be pragmatic and to accept risk. Clinical negligence lawyers do not generally like to advise their clients to take risks. It goes against the grain. Too often they gather all the evidence needed to assess the prospects of success in a claim or a defence, and to show with precision the likely level of compensation, before advising their clients to try to resolve the claim by compromise. Earlier resolution, before all the evidence has been gathered, carries the risk that your claimant client will be under-compensated, or that your defendant client will be paying too much. What is certain, though, is that resolving a claim sooner rather than later will save costs and remove a source of stress from the parties and witnesses involved. From the point of view of the NHS as a whole, I would have thought that the gains and losses from earlier resolution, compared with later resolution, would even themselves out. But there would inevitably be a significant saving in costs. From the claimant perspective, early resolution is more problematic. Whilst overall a culture of early settlement might work for claimants as a group, there might well be winners and losers. It is no comfort to an individual claimant to know that whilst they under-settled, another claimant received more than their fair share.

It might be said that a tendency to settle cases early, even those in which liability could be contested, would only serve to encourage more claims, or more claims with borderline merits, to be brought forward, thereby increasing the total costs of litigation to the NHS.

For good or ill, the present tendency is for clinical negligence defendants not to seek to settle a claim before action unless they know full well that they are likely to be found liable in any subsequent litigation. The culture seems to be that if there is a potential defence, the case should be contested irrespective of the overall economics. To this extent the section of the Pre-Action Protocol dealing with ADR reflects wishful thinking rather than current reality.

Re-Assessing the Merits

Once the Letter of Response has been received the claimant and their advisers can re-assess the strengths and weaknesses of the proposed claim. Often the experts who have provided reports of their opinions for the claimant will be asked to comment on the Letter of Response. The pre-action protocol correspondence may have resulted in additional expert evidence being obtained to fill gaps in a party's case. There may be a further conference with Counsel at this stage. Decisions have to be made as to whether there is a worthwhile claim to be brought, against which defendants and with what prospects of success. Some allegations may be dropped. New allegations might emerge from discussions and consideration of the defendant's position. Generally, the claim must now be regarded by Counsel and/or the claimant's solicitor as having more than a 50% chance of succeeding, otherwise the BTE or ATE costs insurer or the provider of public funding will not agree to back the proposed litigation.

The proposed defendant's advisers will also be assessing the merits of the potential claim, the degree to which they are at risk of losing the case if it is litigated, and the likely level of legal costs and compensation if the litigation is brought. As noted, a defendant can make an offer to settle the case or to engage in ADR at this time.

Limitation

As well as considering the prospects of the evidence establishing liability for a particular range of compensation, the parties also need to consider whether the claim is "within time". There is a limitation period within which any clinical negligence claim should be brought. Legal representatives should have considered the question of limitation right at the outset when they were first contacted or when they were first made aware of the potential claim. The limitation period for clinical negligence claims is three years.

There has been a great deal of satellite litigation concerning the limitation period in personal injury and clinical negligence claims. The Limitation Act 1980 sets out what is known as the "primary limitation period" which is, in essence, three years from the date when the cause of action accrued, or the date from which the claimant knew or ought to have known that they had suffered a significant injury that was attributable in whole or in part to the act or omission which is alleged to constitute negligence.

A cause of action in negligence accrues when there has been a breach of duty that has caused injury. If a surgeon leaves a swab inside a patient during an operation on 1 January and it causes an abscess that gives the patient pain beginning on 1 February, becoming serious pain by 8 February, and leading to hospitalization on 15 February, then the cause of action is complete (or it has accrued) by 8 February. Mild pain would probably not be regarded as significant because it would not be reasonable for a claimant to bring a clinical negligence claim only for a few days of mild pain, even if they knew that liability would be admitted and that damages would be paid. By the time the pain is serious then significant injury has been suffered.

However, the patient would not know why they were suffering pain from 1 February or significant injury from 8 February? They would not know that they had a surgical swab in their abdomen. They would not know that their injury was attributable to the negligence of the surgeon on 1 January. Suppose their abdomen is re-opened in theatre on 16 February and the swab discovered. They recover from the anaesthetic and are informed on 17 February that a swab had been left inside them at the previous operation. By then, 17 February, they know or ought to know that they have suffered significant injury attributable to negligence, and they know who was responsible for that negligence. The three year limitation period therefore runs from 17 February, not from any of the earlier dates.

In many clinical negligence cases there is no "smoking gun" such as a retained swab, providing very strong if not definitive evidence of negligence. Retained swabs are an example of what the NHS calls a "never event" – an adverse event affecting patient safety that should never happen given protocols and procedures in place. Very few "never events" are recorded each year. Far more often clinical negligence litigation concerns what you might call "once in a career" or "not very often" events. In those sorts of cases a patient might suffer a significant injury but have no real idea whether it was caused by negligence. Does that mean that so long as they do not know whether negligence caused their injury, the limitation period does not start to run? That could effectively emasculate the provisions of Act in many cases. The Limitation Act 1980 has a solution to prevent that outcome. Section 14(3) provides that:

"For the purposes of this section a person's knowledge includes knowledge which he might reasonably have been expected to acquire—

(a) from facts observable or ascertainable by him; or

(b) from facts ascertainable by him with the help of medical or other appropriate expert advice which it is reasonable for him to seek;

but a person shall not be fixed under this subsection with knowledge of a fact ascertainable only with the help of expert advice so long as he has taken all reasonable steps to obtain (and, where appropriate, to act on) that advice."

A patient cannot turn a blind eye to the possibility that they might have a claim for compensation. They should make reasonable enquiries including obtaining appropriate advice as to whether their injuries might be attributable to negligence. They are not fixed with knowledge of all facts that might have been ascertainable through expert advice, only those facts which were ascertainable by taking reasonable steps to obtain advice.

The three year limitation period does not begin to run, and does not continue to run, for a claimant who lacks capacity by reason of age (under 18) or mental impairment. So, a patient who is incapable of making decisions about litigation because of an episode of psychosis will not have that period of incapacity counted as part of the three year period. A child who suffers injury has until their 21st birthday to bring a claim, because the three year time limit does not begin until they reach their "majority" at the age of 18.

Once the three years is up, the primary limitation period has expired, and a claim brought after that point is "out of time". It is "statute-barred". It is a defence to the claim that it is brought out of time and the court may strike out the claim and award the costs of the litigation to the defendant.

The Limitation Act 1980 does however include an escape hatch for the claimant who is out of time. Under section 33 the court may exercise its discretion to disapply the primary limitation period: *"If it appears to the court that it would be equitable to allow an action to proceed."* The Act goes on to provide some guidance to the courts as to when this discretion can properly be exercised. By section 33(3):

"In acting under this section the court shall have regard to all the circumstances of the case and in particular to—

(a) the length of, and the reasons for, the delay on the part of the plaintiff;

(b) the extent to which, having regard to the delay, the evidence adduced or likely to be adduced by the plaintiff or the defendant is or is likely to be less cogent than

if the action had been brought within the time allowed by section 11, by section 11A or (as the case may be) by section 12;

(c) the conduct of the defendant after the cause of action arose, including the extent (if any) to which he responded to requests reasonably made by the plaintiff for information or inspection for the purpose of ascertaining facts which were or might be relevant to the plaintiff's cause of action against the defendant;

(d) the duration of any disability of the plaintiff arising after the date of the accrual of the cause of action;

(e) the extent to which the plaintiff acted promptly and reasonably once he knew whether or not the act or omission of the defendant, to which the injury was attributable, might be capable at that time of giving rise to an action for damages;

(f) the steps, if any, taken by the plaintiff to obtain medical, legal or other expert advice and the nature of any such advice he may have received."

This is not an exhaustive list of considerations. The courts are required to consider "all the circumstances of the case". The most important consideration is the strength of the case. If the case appears to the court to be fanciful, then it will be slow to exercise its discretion to allow the claimant to pursue it "out of time". If, however, it appears to be a strong case then the court will be naturally more willing to allow it to proceed. However, if a defendant can argue that due to the period of delay "out of time" evidence on which it would have relied to defend the case has become unavailable such that it would be prejudiced in seeking to defend the claim if it were allowed to proceed, then that can be a potent factor in persuading the court against exercising its discretion in the claimant's favour.

Chapter 3: Beginning a Claim

Starting the Litigation Process

Until litigation is under way, there are no claimants and defendants, only people and bodies such as NHS Trusts who may take on those titles. The proposed claimant has raised their grievances and the proposed defendant has answered them. Attempts to resolve the potential claim have failed. A decision has been made to take matters further. All that is left is to begin the litigation.

You will have noticed that even before litigation has begun, a lot of work has been done and that up to this point 75% or more of the work has been done by or on behalf of the claimant. It takes a great deal of investigation and analysis to determine whether a claim should be pursued through the courts. In most complex cases, at least two years will have passed between first contact with the solicitor and the start of litigation. In some cases, it can take longer still. It is not uncommon for the potential defendant to agree that it will not argue that the claim is statute barred under the Limitation Act 1980 if the case is ultimately brought through the courts, so as to enable the parties properly to investigate and analyse the claim.

Most cases which cannot realistically be defended, including the so-called "never events" such as an operation to amputate the wrong limb, will be resolved without the need for litigation. It tends to be the more contentious or complex claims that come to be litigated. Alternatively, one or other of the parties has failed properly to investigate the claim or to take a realistic view of the prospects of them winning it. As it happens, the evidence is that most of the claims that are litigated result in a payment of damages to the claimant. The payment might be for much less than the claimant has sought, but most of these can be regarded as "successful claims". Of those, the great majority will have been resolved by agreement between the parties before the case came to trial. Of the claims that are fought at trial, the success rate for claimant is no higher than 50%.

So, let's look at the process of litigation itself.

Issue and Service of Proceedings

Clinical negligence proceedings in court are begun by issuing a claim form. We no longer have "writs", we have "claim forms". The process of issuing claims is set out at Part 7 of the Civil Procedure Rules (CPR). Proceedings are begun when the court issues a claim form at the request of the claimant. More than one claim can be contained within a claim form if it would be convenient to try two, or more, claims together. A claim form is a "Statement of Case" and must include certain matters as set out in CPR Part 16. These include a concise statement of the nature of the claim and of the remedy sought. The claimant must specify the level of total damages sought, and damages for pain, suffering and loss of amenity, as being within certain brackets. This is not the same as claiming a fixed sum of money, as in a claim for overdue rent or similar – it is an indication of the level of compensation claimed.

Claims can be issued in the County Court or the High Court. There are County Courts all around the country. Clinical negligence claims for damages must not be started in the High Court unless the value of the claim is £50,000 or more. The headquarters of the High Court of England and Wales are at the Royal Courts of Justice, The Strand, London. There are district registries of the High Court around the country. County Courts are local, although with court closures there are fewer and fewer of them. Trials in the High Court are heard, unsurprisingly by High Court Judges, but the cases are managed by judges who are called "Masters" at the Royal Courts of Justice, and "District Judges" at the district registries. Confusingly the management judges of the County Court are also called District Judges and are often the very same individuals who manage High Court claims in the registries. The trial judges in the County Courts are Circuit Judges. In court you address High Court Judges as "My Lord" or "My Lady"; Masters as "Master", Circuit Judges as "Your Honour" and District Judges as "Sir" or "Ma'am". Barristers address each other as "my learned friend", and solicitors as "my friend", which might be thought of as a rather pointed distinction.

Claims for money only, which include clinical negligence claims, to be issued in the County Court should be sent on the required form to the County Court Money Claims Centre as specified in Practice Direction 7A of the CPR. A claim in the High Court can be issued either at the headquarters in London or at any district registry. The choice of venue, at least when issuing a claim, is with the claimant.

An issue fee is payable. This is 5% of the predicted value of the claim for those worth between £10,000 and £200,000, capped at £10,000 for all claims worth £200,000 or more. That is a large sum of money. Remember that, of the costs of litigation for larger cases, £10,000 of the costs of each case goes to the government as a fee. If the NHS ultimately pays the costs of a claim, then it pays a significant amount back to the state. There is a mechanism for seeking remission of the fee for claimants without the means to pay it at the outset of the case. It does not mean that they are exempt from paying the fee, only that they do not have to pay it on starting proceedings.

The issued claim will now have a case number, allocated by the court, and a title. The title is the name of the claimant followed by the name of the defendant(s). So it might be the case of *John Smith v Anne Jones*. Where the claimant is a child under 18, or is an adult who does not have the mental capacity to litigate, then the title will include the name of the person who is acting on their behalf, called a Litigation Friend. So the title for the claimant might be: *"John Smith, a child acting by his Mother and Litigation Friend, Janet Smith"*. In a claim arising out of a death the role of the claimant will need to be specified in the title, for example: *"Janet Smith, Executrix of the Estate of John Smith deceased, on behalf of the estate and on behalf of the deceased's dependants."* The claimant and the defendant are called the "parties" to the litigation. A party may be an individual or a body. A GPs' surgery might be a partnership. It can be sued as: *"Trafford Road Surgery, a partnership"* or in the names of the partners: *"Dr Fred Parkinson and Dr Susan Gill, partners in the Trafford Road Surgery"*. NHS Hospitals come under the management and control of NHS Trusts. So, the defendant would be the name of the Trust, such as: *"South Cumbria Hospitals NHS Foundation Trust"*.

An issued claim form is not brought to the attention of the defendant unless and until it is "served". Service is the term given for providing a document to a party to litigation. There are detailed rules about service in person, by post, by electronic means etc. in CPR Part 6. The claim form must be served on the defendant within four months of issue (CPR Part 7.5). The rule is mandatory and any application to the court to extend the period of service must be made before the four months has elapsed.

The claim form should be accompanied by a document known as the Particulars of Claim. Alternatively, the Particulars of Claim must be served on the defendant within 14 days after service of the claim form provided that the service of the Particulars of Claim is within four months after the date of issue of the claim form. The defendant must also be sent a form on which they can acknowledge service of the claim and indicate whether it is admitted or defended, in whole or in part. Failure to acknowledge service or to defend the claim in time can lead to judgment being entered in favour of the claimant "in default". This means that the court enters judgment for the claimant for damages to be assessed. The claimant has won their case and established an entitlement to damages which the court will determine on a later occasion, by reason of procedural default rather than after a trial of the issues. Naturally, the rules provide for the opportunity for a defendant to apply to the court to set aside a judgment in default, but it is by no means a formality.

The Particulars of Claim is a "pleading". It is a statement of case that sets out the claimant's version of events, the basis of its case that there has been a breach of duty, causation, and injury, loss and damage. CPR Part 16 sets out the requirements of a Particulars of Claim. There are specific requirements that the claimant must state whether they are claiming interest and if so on what basis, and whether they are claiming certain kinds of damages, including provisional damages or aggravated damages. But otherwise the simple rule is that Particulars of Claim must include "a concise statement of the facts on which the claimant relies". In addition, in a clinical negligence claim, they should include a statement of the claimant's date of birth and brief details of their injuries, and must be accompanied by expert medical evidence about the injuries alleged to have been suffered, and a schedule of details of past and future expenses and losses which the claimant claims. In a Fatal Accidents Act claim the Particulars of Claim should include the names and dates of birth of any of the deceased's dependants, and the basis of the dependency claims.

Particulars of Claim, like all statements of case, must be verified with a statement of truth signed by or on behalf of the party making it: *'[I believe] [the (claimant or as may be) believes] that the facts stated in these Particulars of Claim are true.'*

The statement of truth, and the requirements of a Particulars of Claim, indicate that this pleading is a statement of facts. It should set out the basis of the claim in relation to breaches of duty, causation and injury, but it is bad practice to argue the law in Particulars of Claim. It should not include reference to case law. Breaches of statutory provisions should be specified but this pleading is designed to set out the facts on which the claimant's case is based so that the issues between the parties can be identified and narrowed.

See Fig 1 for an example of a Particulars of Claim for a clinical negligence claim. The pleading sets out the identity of the parties, the facts on which the claimant relies, the particulars of the alleged breaches of duty and causation, and of the injury, loss and damage suffered. There is, as required, a statement of the claim for interest and a reference to the attached medical evidence and schedule of loss. The example set out is detailed and describes a cerebral palsy claim. I discuss these sorts of claims in more detail in Part 4, Chapter 1. There is some jargon included in the Particulars of Claim. A cephalic presentation means that the baby's position is head down, breech means that it is feet first. Diachorionic diamniotic twins each have their own amniotic sac. Bradycardia is an abnormally slow heart rate. LSCS is a lower segment Caesarean section, the most common form of surgical delivery of a baby. Meconium is the term used for the stool of an unborn baby. Hypoxic ischaemia occurs when there is a deprivation of oxygen and blood to the baby's brain. Cooling is a form of treatment for certain babies and involves inducing therapeutic hypothermia. A baby's weight, head circumference and other measurements are often expressed by reference to centiles. A baby on the 50th centile is in the middle of the range of measurements. Only 1% of babies will have a higher measurement than a baby on the 99th centile, whereas 99% of babies will have a higher measurement than a baby on the 1st centile.

The Particulars of Claim is long but it is a realistic example of the kind of pleading that is seen in large obstetric negligence cases.

Fig 1 – Particulars of Claim

IN THE HIGH COURT OF JUSTICE   <u>Claim No: K19 1234</u>

<u>QUEEN'S BENCH DIVISION</u>

<u>KINGSTOWN DISTRICT REGISTRY</u>

B E T W E E N :

ALBERT AIREY

**(A Child by his father and Litigation
Friend, ALAN AIREY)**

<u>**First Claimant**</u>

AMANDA AIREY

<u>**Second Claimant**</u>

and

**KINGSTOWN HOSPITALS NHS
FOUNDATION TRUST**

<u>**Defendant**</u>

PARTICULARS OF CLAIM

---

1.   The Parties

1.1   The First Claimant is a child who proceeds by his father and Litigation Friend, Alan Airey.

1.2   At all relevant times the Defendant was responsible for the management and control of Kingstown Hospital ("the hospital") and for the acts and omissions of the midwifery, medical and other personnel at the hospital concerning the management, care and treatment of patients.

1.3   At all relevant times, unless otherwise stated below, the Second Claimant, the First Claimant's mother ("Ms Airey"), was a patient at the hospital, carrying the First Claimant ("Albert"), and the Defendant, its employees and agents owed a duty to both Claimants to exercise reasonable skill and care in the management of the Ms Airey's pregnancy and labour, and the delivery of Albert.

2.   History of Events

2.1   In late 2011 Ms Airey found that she was pregnant. This was her second pregnancy, having previously given birth to a girl by uncomplicated vaginal delivery. An ultrasound scan on 12 December 2011 showed the presence of dichorionic diamniotic twins with an expected date of delivery of 13 June 2012.

2.2   Further ultrasound scans were performed on 15 March 2012 and 14 April 2012. On each scan the twins were of similar size with normal liquor volume. Twin I (Adam) was in a cephalic presentation with Twin II (Albert, the First Claimant) being in a breech presentation.

2.3   On 15 May 2012 Ms Airey underwent a further ultrasound scan at 36 weeks gestation. On this occasion both twins were in a cephalic presentation. Ms Airey was reviewed by Mr Riley, Consultant Obstetrician. It was noted that she had "bilateral ankle oedema ++". It was planned to review her in the antenatal clinic on 15 June 2012 (gestation, 40 +2) with Ms Airey to visit the midwifery clinic weekly in the meantime.

2.4   Ms Airey was seen in the drop-in midwifery clinic:

2.4.1   On 22 May 2012 when it was noted that she was uncomfortable and had been vomiting;

2.4.2   On 29 May 2012 when it was noted that she was feeling very tired and uncomfortable and that she had "bilateral ankle oedema ++";

2.4.3   On 5 June 2012 when it was noted that she was "feeling unwell, very tired and becoming anxious";

2.4.4   On 12 June 2012 when it was noted: "Feeling very tired, uncomfortable and very anxious now that at term. Has appointment in a few days".

2.5 From about 36 weeks gestation Ms Airey was in discomfort carrying her twin babies each of which probably weighed over 6lbs at 36 weeks. She became increasingly restricted in her mobility beyond 36 weeks gestation.

2.6 At 10:45 hours on 14 June 2012 Ms Airey was admitted to the delivery suite at the hospital reporting a history of pain for a few hours. A CTG was commenced at 11:00 hours. Vaginal examination showed that the cervix was effaced, thin, and 3 cms dilated.

2.7 At 11:30 Midwife Lord recorded

"Twin I Cephalic 2/5 palpable

Twin II may be in breech position

Twin I baseline 125 bpm, variability fine, accelerations ↑ 145 bpm, no decelerations, contracting 2:10.

Twin II baseline 130-140 bpm, variability fine, no accelerations, no decelerations. Sister Moorhouse informed".

2.8 Further CTG traces over the next few hours were reassuring for both twins.

2.9 A vaginal examination at 14:00 hours was noted to show that the cervix was 4 cms dilated.

2.10 Vaginal examination at 16:30 hours showed that the cervix was 5 cms dilated.

2.11 At 18:15 hours spontaneous rupture of membranes with clear liquor draining was noted. Vaginal examination was performed and the cervix was recorded as being 9 cm dilated. At 18:50 Ms Airey was noted to have urges to push. The cervix was noted to be fully dilated. The CTG was noted to be reactive with some loss of contact. Sister Moorhouse was called to assist.

2.12 At 19:10 hours Ms Airey gave birth to Twin I (Adam) vaginally and without instrumental assistance. Midwife Lord and Sister Moorhouse were present and managed the delivery.

2.13 Adam was born in a good condition and did not require resuscitation. He was cleaned and wrapped and handed to Ms Airey and then to the father, her husband.

2.14 At 19:15 it was noted that Adam had been born in good condition and "Twin II in breech?"

2.15 Dr Edgar made a note of her attendance at 19:33 hours on 14 June, the note being made in retrospect at 06:40 hours on 15 June. She noted:

"Called to attend twin delivery at 2nd stage after delivery of Twin I.

Twin I delivered spontaneously at 19:10. Good apgars and no resuscitation required.

Twin II breech. Failure to progress after 20 minutes. CTG shows bradycardia.

Called to attend as emergency.

On examination Twin II breech. CTG showed bradycardia.

ECV attempted. Unsuccessful.

For emergency LSCS. Decision at 19:36. To theatre at 19:37.

Anaesthetist arrived shortly after arrival in theatre.

LSCS performed under GA.

Delivery live male Twin II at 19:47 hours.

Apgar 2 at 1, 3 at 5. Flat and pale. HR under 100. No respiratory effort.

Suction to mouth and nose. Initial Bag and Mask by midwife.

HR > 100. Reg arrived. Took over resuscitation. Respiratory effort at 7 minutes."

2.16 The relevant midwifery notes record as follows:

"19:15. Twin I delivered at 19:10. Good condition at birth. No resuscitation required. Examination. Twin II in breech?

19:17 Breech confirmed by Sister Moorhouse.

19:20 FHR 135. CTG reassuring.

19:25 FHR 110. Failure to progress.

19:30 FHR 90. Failure to progress. Bradycarida. DW Sister Moorhouse. Emergency call to Reg.

19:34 Reg attended. Attempted ECV.

19:37 for Crash CS. To theatre."

2.17   In fact, Albert's fetal heart rate dropped to 90 not 110 as noted at 19:25 hours and to 70 not 90 as recorded at 19:30 hours. The CTG trace had been set to record Albert's heart rate at 20 bpm above actual heart rate so as to distinguish his trace from Alec's trace. The maker of the clinical note failed to heed that fact when noting that Albert's heart rate had fallen to between 110 bpm and 90 bpm respectively (it was 20 bpm lower).

2.18   The CTG trace, when the 20 bpm adjustment is made, showed bradycardia from 19:25 hours.

2.19   At 19:37 hours Ms Airey was transferred to the theatre where she was given general anaesthetic. Albert was delivered at 19:47 hours.

2.20   Albert's Apgar scores were 2 at 1 minute and 3 at 5 minutes.

2.21   Umbilical cord gases were recorded as:

Venous: pH 6.60, BE -21.7

Arterial: pH 6.607, BE -25.5 (standard base excess -22.0),

and pH 6.594, BE -25.7 (standard base excess -22.1).

2.22   Five rescue breaths were given and the fetal heart rate increased to 100 bpm. Paediatricians were not in attendance. A midwife provided bag and mask ventilation with a heart rate over 100. There was no respiratory effort until seven minutes.

2.23   At one hour of age Albert was noted to be suffering seizures. In order to undergo cooling he was transferred to Queensfield Royal Infirmary.

2.24   At 8 months of age Albert was noted to have delayed motor development without increased tone. Hearing and vision were normal. Head circumference was between the second and ninth centiles by May 2013.

2.25   A cranial MRI on 8 June 2013 showed high signal on T2 weighted sections in the posterior thirds of the putamina of the lentiform nuclei, regions of high metabolism around the time of fetal maturity and vulnerable to profound circulatory insufficiency. It showed no evidence of any additional damage in the borderzone regions between the cortical distributions of the main cerebral arteries, no evidence of intrauterine brain damage or malformation of the brain.

2.26   Albert has asymmetric dyskinetic (dystonic) 4 limb cerebral palsy with bulbar involvement.

3.   **Breach of Duty**

The midwifery, medical and other personnel at the hospital were negligent in their management, care and treatment of the Claimants in that they:

Before Labour
3.1   Failed adequately or at all to advise Ms Airey of the options for delivery of her twin babies and of the risks and benefits of those options, including elective Caesarean section or induction by 38 weeks.

3.2   Failed to offer Ms Airey the option of an elective Caesarean section or induction by 38 weeks.

3.3   Failed as aforesaid when Ms Airey reached 36 weeks gestation and beyond and when she was in increasing discomfort and unable freely to mobilise.

3.4   Failed adequately to advise Ms Airey of the risks of continuing the labour to term and beyond.

3.5   Failed to obtain Ms Airey's informed consent to continue her labour to term and beyond.

During Labour

3.6　Failed to ensure that an obstetrician was present when Adam was delivered. Alternatively failed to call or ensure the attendance of an obstetrician by 19:25 hours.

3.7　Failed adequately or at all to heed that the CTG monitoring device for Albert's fetal heart had been set at 20 bpm above actual bpm.

3.8　Failed adequately or at all to heed that Albert's fetal heart rate had fallen, in fact, to 90 at 19:25 hours and to 70 at 19:30 hours, before falling even further.

3.9　Failed to heed that Albert was bradycardic from 19:25 hours.

3.10　Failed to call or ensure the attendance of an obstetrician until 19:33 hours.

3.11　Failed to decide to proceed to an emergency Caesarean section:

    3.11.1　By 19:20 hours when labour had failed to progress for ten minutes after the birth of Adam; alternatively

    3.11.2　By 19:30 hours when it was or should have been clear that Albert was bradycardic.

4.　Causation

4.1　Albert suffered brain damage due to hypoxic ischaemia caused by acute profound asphyxia. The period of profound asphyxia probably commenced at about 19:28 hours (as per the timings on the CTG trace) and ended about 1 minute after delivery, i.e. at 19:48 hours: a period of 20 minutes.

4.2　No record was made of a finding of placental separation or cord entanglement at the time of the Caesarean section. No meconium was noted. The umbilical cord gases were similar for the venous and arterial samples. On the balance of probabilities the profound asphyxia was caused by placental separation alternatively by cord entanglement. Similar cord gas levels in the arterial and venous specimens indicate placental separation rather than cord compression. In either case the complication arose after Adam's birth.

214

4.3   But for the negligent antenatal management set out above Ms Airey would have elected to undergo induction by 38 weeks of gestation. She was in significant discomfort, she had restricted mobility and she would have been aware of the risks of complications by continuing the pregnancy to term.

4.4   Induction by or at 38 weeks gestation would, on the balance of probabilities, have resulted in the vaginal delivery of both twins, uninjured.

4.5   Had the twins been delivered vaginally by, at or around 38 weeks gestation, then Albert's brain injury would have been avoided.

4.6   But for the negligent management of the labour and delivery set out above:

    4.6.1   An obstetrician would have been present at the time of Adam's birth and would have noted Albert's breech position, the failure of labour to progress after Adam's birth, and the bradycardia from 19:25 hours.

    4.6.2   A decision would have been made to proceed to an emergency Caesarean section by 19:20 hours, alternatively by 19:30 hours.

    4.6.3   Delivery by emergency Caesarean section would have been effected by 19:30 hours, alternatively by 19:40 hours.

4.7   The period of avoidable delay in delivering Albert has caused or materially contributed to his permanent neurological injuries.

5.   Injury, Loss and Damage

The First Claimant

5.1   Albert was born on 14 June 2012.

5.2   Albert has suffered a permanent and severe brain injury. He has asymmetric dyskinetic (dystonic) 4 limb cerebral palsy with bulbar involvement. He has relative preservation of cognitive function.

5.3   Albert uses his left hand for all tasks, with his right hand being held in a folded, locked position. He cannot fasten or unfasten zips or buttons and has no pincer grip in his right hand. He walks with the aid of tripod sticks. His speech is hard to understand and he uses a communication aid.

5.4 Albert attends school with full time 1:1 support. He appears to have been spared any significant cognitive deficits.

5.5 Although a firm prognosis cannot yet be made because of his young age, Albert will continue to require additional care and assistance throughout his childhood and as an adult. If he is able to work, he will be restricted in the range of work he will be able to perform. He is likely to have specific and additional housing, aids and equipment and transport needs.

The Second Claimant

5.6 Ms Airey was born on 5 May 1982. She experienced vaginal delivery and then attempts at external cephalic version followed by an emergency Caesarean section. Following the delivery of Albert by Caesarean section, Ms Airey came round from anaesthetic to find that her second baby was very unwell and needed to be taken to another hospital. She had to travel to Blackburn Royal Infirmary on 13 April 2010 to see her baby.

5.7 Ms Airey has suffered psychiatric injury as a result of the traumatic experience of having to undergo urgent procedures following the birth of Adam, a crash Caesarean section, of having only one baby with her in the immediate post-natal period and knowing that Albert was very unwell, of seeing him in a life-threatening condition. She has been taking anti-depressants intermittently to treat her condition. She has Post Traumatic Stress Disorder and a Major Depressive Disorder.

5.8 For the avoidance of doubt, Ms Airey claims damages for injury and consequential losses and expenses as a primary victim who has suffered avoidable physical and psychiatric injury. In the alternative, she is a secondary victim who has suffered psychiatric injury as a result of the shocking experience of witnessing the horrifying event of efforts to save the life of her baby from very shortly after the birth of Adam.

5.9 The First Claimant (Albert) relies on the report of Dr Tring, Consultant Paediatric Neurologist, dated 10 August 2016, served herewith.

5.10 Ms Airey relies on the reports of Mr Barnes, Consultant Obstetrician and Gynaecologist, dated 8 September 2016, and Professor Davenport, Consultant Psychiatrist, dated 9 September 2016, served herewith.

5.11 The Claimants have suffered and will continue to suffer consequential losses and expenses and refer to the Schedule of Loss served herewith.

6. Interest

6.1 Further the Claimants claim interest on such sums as shall be found due at such rates and for such periods as the Court shall consider fit pursuant to Section 35A of the Senior Courts Act 1981, including interest on non-recurrent past losses at the full Special Account rate on the grounds that the whole of such loss was incurred within a short time of the alleged negligence.

7. Damages

7.1 The Claimants expect to recover damages for personal injury of more than £1,000 and unlimited total damages.

NIGEL POOLE QC

Statement of Truth

I (the First Claimant's Litigation Friend) believe/the First Claimant's Litigation Friend believes that the facts stated in these Particulars of Claim are true.

I am duly authorised to sign this statement on behalf of the First Claimant.

Full name   :...

Name of Claimant's Solicitor   :Matthews Lane LLP

Signed   :...

Position or office held   :...

Claimant/Claimant's Solicitor

I believe/the Second Claimant believes that the facts stated in these Particulars of Claim are true.

I am duly authorised by the Second Claimant to sign this statement.

Full name : . . . .

Name of Claimant's Solicitor :Matthews Lane LLP

Signed : . . . .

Position or office held : . . . .

Claimant/Claimant's Solicitor

Matthews Lane LLP
New Bank Chambers
York Street
Kingstown

Once the Particulars of Claim are served the defendant has to serve a Defence within 14 days; alternatively, if the defendant serves an "acknowledgement of service", it has then to serve a Defence 28 days after service of the Particulars of Claim.

The purpose of the Defence is to identify those parts of the Particulars of Claim that are admitted, those that are denied and those that are "not admitted". An allegation is denied if the defendant's case is that it is wrong. The defendant needs to have evidence that the allegation is wrong and will be expected to substantiate the denial in the Defence, giving particulars of the denial. An allegation may be "not admitted" if the defendant is unable to admit or deny it but requires the claimant to prove it. For example, some allegations in the Particulars of Claim may not be within the knowledge of the defendant or its witnesses, and so it may decide to require the claimant to prove them rather than admitting them. Once an allegation is admitted, then it is no longer a contested issue in the litigation. It is treated as fact for the purposes of the case. There is no need for the claimant to adduce any evidence to prove an admitted allegation. That is why the court is reluctant to allow a defendant to withdraw an admission – which a defendant may seek to do so only if it has good cause.

A Defence should also set out the defendant's positive case on any issue in the litigation. For example, if the defendant's case is that it was not negligent surgery that caused the claimant's injury but an infection that was due to some non-negligent cause, then that is a positive allegation – not merely a denial or a non-admission – and it should be fully set out in the Defence. Similarly, if the defendant wishes to allege that the claimant's own negligence contributed to their injuries, or that some other person is to blame, that ought to be set out in the Defence. In clinical negligence claims the Defence will be served together with a preliminary Counter Schedule, meeting the case that the claimant has set out in their Schedule of Loss served with the Particulars of Claim. I shall look at the contents of Schedules and Counter Schedules below.

The Defence, being a statement of case, must be verified by a statement of truth.

There are other, subsequent pleadings that the parties sometimes but not always deploy. If a defendant makes positive allegations themselves, for example that the claimant was guilty of contributory negligence, the claimant might well counter those in a pleading called a Reply. Either party might also serve a Request for Further Information of the other party, the rules governing which are set out in CPR Part 18. Where a defendant wishes to join another party to the litigation, alleging that the third party is responsible for the claimant's injuries, they can do so by making a Part 20 claim (under CPR Part 20). That procedure is uncommon in clinical negligence litigation.

Pleadings can be amended, re-amended and re-re-amended but most usually the party making the changes will have to bear the costs of doing so, and the costs of the other party who has to amend, re-amend or re-re-amend their pleading in response.

Chapter 4: Case Management

Court Directions and Applications

Once a Defence has been served the court will send Directions Questionnaires to the parties. Once completed it is common for the court to give
standard directions, without a hearing. This, usually brief, order will allocate the case to an appropriate "track" within the court system, and make
provision for a further Case Management Conference – a hearing attended
by the parties at which detailed directions will be made – together with
directions to file documents setting out what the parties' legal costs have
been to date, and what the likely costs of the litigation will be. The court
will usually carry out a costs budgeting exercise at the Case Management
Conference, limiting the costs that each party will be entitled to recover
from the other, for each stage of the proceedings.

There are many learned books devoted to the question of costs. My judgement is that the reader of this book will not want a detailed analysis of
costs issues in clinical negligence cases: what hourly rate is permissible in
London, whether a barrister should spend three or five hours preparing for
a conference with experts etc. In fact the writer has no appetite to provide
that analysis. It is not that costs are not important, it is just that the law
of costs is a separate area of specialisation. I dare say costs lawyers find it
fascinating.

There are three tracks: the small claims track, the fast track and the multi-track. Clinical negligence claims nearly all fall within the multi-track. The
other two tracks are for simple and relatively low value claims.

The directions given at a Case Management Conference set down a detailed
timetable for the parties to follow. An example of some standard directions,
which may be adapted for each case, is given at Fig 2 below. The parties can
apply to the court for further or other directions as the court proceeds, but it
is expensive to do so. To avoid the need for repeated applications it is now
standard practice to allow the parties to agree short extensions of time to
comply with the court's timetable. However, the courts jealously protect the
timetable set down, in particular the dates fixed for trial. It is very difficult
for a party to persuade the court to shift the date of a trial that has been
fixed in the court's diary.

The court's approach to directions and applications by the parties has
changed dramatically over the years. Lord Wolf oversaw the introduction
of the new Civil Procedure Rules in 1999. The "plaintiff" became "the
claimant", "a subpoena" became a "witness summons", but alongside

those cosmetic changes were more fundamental new rules designed to make the process of litigation more streamlined and effective. As someone who practised for ten years under the old rules, I can safely say that the CPR are a great improvement on their predecessors. The first line of the CPR is:

"These Rules are a new procedural code with the overriding objective of enabling the court to deal with cases justly and at proportionate cost".

The next rule gives the "overriding objective" more substance:

"Dealing with a case justly and at proportionate cost includes, so far as is practicable –

(a) ensuring that the parties are on an equal footing;

(b) saving expense;

(c) dealing with the case in ways which are proportionate –

(i) to the amount of money involved;

(ii) to the importance of the case;

(iii) to the complexity of the issues; and

(iv) to the financial position of each party;

(d) ensuring that it is dealt with expeditiously and fairly;

(e) allotting to it an appropriate share of the court's resources, while taking into account the need to allot resources to other cases; and

(f) enforcing compliance with rules, practice directions and orders."

The overriding objective is to be applied by the court whenever it exercises a power under the rules and whenever it has to interpret any of the rules. Most of the rules within the CPR give the court a discretion to make an order to allow or forbid a party from doing something. So, the overriding objective is an almost constant mantra for those judges who have to make directions and hear applications leading up to the trial of a clinical negligence claim.

CPR Part 3 marked an almost revolutionary approach to the courts' management of cases, allowing, as it does, the court to do almost anything it wants to do, providing that it serves the overriding objective. It can shorten or extend time for the parties to do something, adjourn a case or bring it forward, put a hold on ("stay") the whole claim, order some issues to be tried separately, or exclude them from having to be determined, even to the extent of striking out a claim or defence. The judges have a free hand.

The courts use these wide-ranging powers, and the parts of the CPR dealing with the disclosure of documents, the making of witness statements, and the use of expert evidence, to give "directions" at a Case Management Conference. These orders direct the parties to take certain steps in the litigation at certain times.

One of the important decisions about case management, often taken early in the litigation, is whether to timetable the case through to a trial on all issues – liability and quantification issues – or whether to direct that there be a "split trial", dealing with liability first, and then quantification only if the claimant succeeds in proving liability. This may potentially save costs in certain cases. In some cases the court may be able to identify a specific narrow issue that should be tried first, but more often the first trial will be to establish whether there has been a breach of duty that was causative of injury. If it is needed, then the second trial would be to determine the level of compensation for the injuries found to have been caused by the defendant's negligence. If a split trial is ordered then the directions will, in the first place, be focused solely on the first issue(s) to be tried. In what follows, however, I assume that there is no split trial and that all issues in the case will be heard at a single trial.

Here is an example of the sort of directions that are typically made in a clinical negligence claim.

Fig 2 – Standard Directions

IN THE HIGH COURT OF JUSTICE   <u>Claim No: K19 1234</u>

<u>QUEEN'S BENCH DIVISION</u>

<u>KINGSTOWN DISTRICT REGISTRY</u>

B E T W E E N :

ALBERT AIREY

(A Child by his father and Litigation Friend, ALAN AIREY)

<u>**First Claimant**</u>

AMANDA AIREY

<u>**Second Claimant**</u>

and

KINGSTOWN HOSPITALS NHS FOUNDATION TRUST

<u>**Defendant**</u>

ORDER OF DISTRICT JUDGE SWIFT

Before District Judge Swift sitting at the Kingstown Civil Justice Centre on 23 December 2019

Upon hearing Mr Matthews, solicitor for the Claimant, and Ms Sandhu, solicitor for the Defendant

It is ordered that

(1)   The Claim is allocated to the Multi-Track and is assigned to District

Judge Swift for case management.

(2)   At all stages the parties must consider settling this litigation by any means of Alternative Dispute Resolution (including round table conferences, early neutral evaluation, mediation and arbitration); any party not engaging in any such means proposed by another is to serve a witness statement giving reasons within 21 days of receipt of that proposal. That witness statement must not be shown to the trial judge until questions of costs arise.

(3)   Documents are to be retained as follows:

(a)   the parties must retain all electronically stored documents relating to the issues in this Claim.

(b)   the Defendant must retain the original clinical notes relating to the issues in this Claim. The Defendant must give facilities for inspection by the Claimants, the Claimants' legal advisers and experts of these original notes on 7 days written notice.

(c)   legible copies of the Claimants' medical records are to be placed in a separate paginated bundle by the Claimants' Solicitors and kept up to date. All references to medical notes are to be made by reference to the pages in that bundle.

(4)   Disclosure of documents relevant to the issues of breach of duty and causation and quantification of damages will be dealt with as follows:

(a)   By 4pm on 27 January 2020 both parties must give to each other standard disclosure of documents by list and category.

(b)   By 4pm on 10 February 2020 any request must be made to inspect the original of, or to provide a copy of, a disclosable document.

(c)   Any such request unless objected to must be complied with within 14 days of the request.

(d)   By 4pm on 24 February 2020 each party must serve and file with the court a list of issues relevant to the search for and disclosure of electronically stored documents in accordance with Practice Direction 31B.

(5)   Evidence of fact will be dealt with as follows:

    (a)   By 4pm on 23 March 2020 both parties must serve on each other copies of the signed statements of themselves and of all witnesses on whom they intend to rely in respect of breach of duty and causation and all notices relating to evidence, including Civil Evidence Act notices.

    (b)   For the avoidance of doubt statements of all concerned with the relevant treatment and care of the Claimant must be included.

    (c)   By 4pm on 25 May 2020 both parties must serve on each other copies of the signed statements of themselves and of all witnesses on whom they intend to rely in respect of condition, prognosis and loss and all notices relating to evidence, including Civil Evidence Act notices.

    (d)   Oral evidence will not be permitted at trial from a witness whose statement has not been served in accordance with this order or has been served late, except with permission from the Court.

    (e)   Evidence of fact is limited to 8 witnesses on behalf of each party.

    (f)   Witness statements must not exceed 15 pages of A4 in length, save for the Claimant's statement on condition, prognosis and loss which may not exceed 30 pages of A4 in length.

(6)   Expert evidence is directed as follows.

(7)   In respect of breach of duty and causation the parties each have permission to rely on the following written expert evidence:

    (a)   The Claimants:

        (i)   an expert in Midwifery, namely Mrs Walsh,

        (ii)   an expert in Obstetrics, namely Mr Barnes,

        (iii) an expert in Neonatology, namely Professor Hepworth,

(iv)   an expert in Paediatric Neurology, namely Dr Tring, whose report shall also cover issues of condition and prognosis,

(v)   an expert in Neuroradiology, namely Professor Renard.

(b)   The Defendants:

(i)   an expert in Midwifery, namely Mr Priestley,

(ii)   an expert in Obstetrics, namely Ms Drake,

(iii)   an expert in Neonatology, namely Dr Blowes,

(iv)   an expert in Paediatric Neurology, Professor Mannell, whose report shall also cover issues of condition and prognosis,

(v)   an expert in Neuroradiology, namely Dr Twelves.

(8)   The parties shall simultaneously exchange the reports on breach of duty and causation from the said experts by no later than 4pm on 24 June 2020.

(9)   In respect of condition, prognosis and quantification of damages, the parties each have permission to rely on the following written expert evidence:

(a)   The First Claimant:

(i)   an expert in Physiotherapy, namely Mr Smith,

(ii)   an expert in Care and Occupational Therapy, namely Mr Crowther,

(iii)   an expert in Speech and Language Therapy, namely Ms Little,

(iv)   an expert in Assistive Technology, namely Mrs Sissons,

(v)   an expert in Accommodation, namely Mrs Harwood.

(b)   The Second Claimant:

    (i)   an expert in Psychiatry, namely Dr Hug,

whose reports (both Claimants) must be served by no later than 5pm on 9 September 2020.

(c)   The Defendant:

    (i)   an expert in Physiotherapy, namely Dr Fricker,

    (ii)   an expert in Care and Occupational Therapy, namely Mr Elstub,

    (iii)   an expert in Speech and Language Therapy, namely Ms Jobbings,

    (iv)   an expert in Assistive Technology, namely Miss Davies,

    (v)   an expert in Accommodation, namely Mr Green,

    (vi)   an expert in Psychiatry, in relation to the Second Claimant only, namely Professor Reeves,

whose reports must be served by no later than 4pm on 14 October 2020.

(10)   Unless the reports are agreed, there must be a without prejudice discussion between the experts of like discipline by 4pm on 18 November 2020 in which the experts will identify the issues between them and reach agreement if possible. The experts will prepare for the court and sign a statement of the issues on which they agree and on which they disagree with a summary of their reasons in accordance with Rule 35.12 Civil Procedure Rules, and each statement must be sent to the parties to be received by 4pm on 25 November 2020 and in any event no later than 7 days after the discussion.

(11)   Unless otherwise agreed by all parties' solicitors, after consulting with the experts, a draft Agenda which directs the experts to the remaining issues relevant to the experts' discipline, as identified in the statements of case shall be prepared jointly by the Claimant's solicitors and experts and sent to the Defendant's solicitors for comment at least 35 days before the agreed date for the experts' discussions.

(12)   The Defendants shall within 21 days of receipt agree the Agenda, or propose amendments.

(13)   7 days thereafter all solicitors shall use their best endeavours to agree the Agenda. Points of disagreement should be on matters of real substance and not semantics or on matters the experts could resolve of their own accord at the discussion. In default of agreement, both versions shall be considered at the discussions. Agendas, when used, shall be provided to the experts not less than 7 days before the date fixed for discussions.

(14)   A copy of this order must be served on each expert.

(15)   The parties have permission to call oral evidence of the experts of like discipline limited to issues that are in dispute.

(16)   Any unpublished literature upon which any expert witness proposes to rely must be served at the same time as service of his report together with a list of published literature. Any supplementary literature upon which any expert witness relies must be notified to all parties at least one month before trial. No expert witness may rely upon any publications that have not been disclosed in accordance with this order without the permission of the trial judge subject to costs as appropriate.

(17)   Experts will, at the time of producing their reports, incorporate details of any employment or activity which raises a possible conflict of interest.

(18)   For the avoidance of doubt, experts do not require the authorisation of solicitor or counsel before signing a joint statement.

(19)   If an expert radically alters an opinion previously recorded, the joint statement should include a note or addendum by that expert explaining the change of opinion.

(20)   Schedules of Loss must be updated to the date of trial as follows:

(a)   By 4pm on 9 September 2020 the Claimant must send an updated schedule of loss to the Defendant.

(b)   By 4pm on 14 October 2020 the Defendant, in the event of challenge, must send an updated counter-schedule of loss to the Claimant.

(c)   The schedule and counter-schedule must contain a statement setting out that party's case on the issue of periodical payments pursuant to Rule 41.5 Civil Procedure Rules.

(21)   The trial will be listed as follows.

(a)   By 4pm on 8 February 2020 the Claimants' Solicitors must apply to High Court Listing for a listing appointment for a trial within the trial window and give notice of the appointment to the Defendant.

(b)   Trial: Judge alone; High Court, Kingstown District Registry.

(c)   Category: B.

(d)   Trial window: from 1 February 2021 to 21 May 2021 inclusive.

(e)   Time estimate: 10 days.

(f)   The parties shall file Pre-Trial Check Lists by 8 December 2020.

(22)   Pre-trial directions are as follows:

(a)   There will be a Pre-Trial Review hearing with a time estimate of 1 hour on a date to be fixed after 4 January 2021 but no earlier than 8 weeks before the date fixed for trial.

(b)   If there are no substantial issues between the parties and all parties agree, one party may email the Court to request that the hearing be conducted by telephone and in accordance with Practice Direction 23A Civil Procedure Rules.

(c)   At least 3 clear days before the Pre-Trial Review hearing the parties must file and send to the Court preferably agreed and by email:

(i)   any draft directions;

(ii)   a succinct case summary setting out the remaining factual and legal issues between the parties.

(23) Not more than 7 nor less than 3 clear days before the trial, the Claimant must file at Court and serve an indexed and paginated bundle of documents which complies with the requirements of Rule 39.5 Civil Procedure Rules and Practice Direction 39A. The parties must endeavour to agree the contents of the bundle before it is filed. The bundle will include a case summary and a chronology.

(24) The parties must file with the Court and exchange skeleton arguments at least3 days before the trial, by email.

(25) The parties may, by prior agreement in writing, extend time for a direction in this order by up to 28 days and without the need to apply to Court. Beyond that 28-day period any agreed extensions of time must be submitted to the Court by email including a brief explanation of the reasons, confirmation that it will not prejudice any hearing date and with the draft Consent Order in Word format. The Court will then consider whether a formal application and hearing is necessary.

(26) Costs in the case.

The key steps leading to trial which the standard directions cover are disclosure of documentation, exchange of witness statements, exchange of expert evidence and service of the schedule and counter schedule. These are discussed in the next section.

Note that the trial is expected to last ten working days and the court invites the parties to complete questionnaires which will set out the availability of experts etc, within the trial "window", allowing the court then to fix a definite start date for the trial.

Paragraph 25 allows the parties marginally to extend time for compliance with directions without needing to apply to the court.

"Costs in the case" means that whichever party is ordered to pay the costs of the litigation at the end of the case will have to pay the costs of the directions hearing as part of those costs.

Whilst these standard directions seek to cover all the procedures and steps needed to be followed to ensure the case will be ready for trial on the date to be fixed, there may nevertheless be a need, or wish, for the parties to seek other orders from the court. These cannot be done by an email or telephone request. They have to be sought by making a formal application, notifying the other parties of the nature of the application and sharing with them the evidence on which the party relies in support of the application.

CPR Part 3 covers case management, but other rules govern other specific applications. For example, CPR Part 24 concerns summary judgment and provides:

"The court may give summary judgment against a claimant or defendant on the whole of a claim or on a particular issue if –

(a) it considers that –

(i) that claimant has no real prospect of succeeding on the claim or issue; or

(ii) that defendant has no real prospect of successfully defending the claim or issue; and

(b) there is no other compelling reason why the case or issue should be disposed of at a trial."

This rule allows a court to determine the whole case, or a particular issue, such as liability, without the need for a trial. Where a claim or a defence is manifestly hopeless, the court will not necessarily allow a party to pursue its case all the way to trial. Summary judgments do not feature commonly in clinical negligence litigation. Given that most clinical negligence cases will depend heavily on expert evidence, and given the *Bolam* test, such claims are rarely so "open and shut" as to give rise to a summary judgment. A different power, already mentioned in relation to the court's case management powers under CPR Part 3, is to strike out a statement of case (for example Particulars of Claim or a Defence) or part of it. This has the same effect as summary judgment, but is based not so much on a sober assessment of the merits of the case but on the need to protect the court process from being abused. A party's case may be struck out if it is frivolous, vexatious or otherwise an abuse of the process of the court. So, if a clinical negligence claim has been brought and determined once, the claimant cannot simply have another go! The second claim, if substantially the same as the first, is likely to be struck out. A claim might be struck out as being vexatious if it is being used for some ulterior motive, such as to harass a particular healthcare professional, rather than truly to substantiate a legal right.

Some litigants who make repeated applications that are without merit may be made the subject of "civil restraint orders" (CROs). These can be limited to the particular case (prohibiting the party from making further applications without permission), they may be extended, or they may even become general (meaning that the person needs permission to issue any claim or make any order in any court). These CROs deal with people who are more colloquially known as vexatious litigants.

Other applications that might be made in the course of proceedings include those for interim payments (Part 25) and for an order that the other party disclose a specific document or class of documents (Part 31).

The former allows a claimant, whom the court can be sure is going to recover a substantial sum in damages from the defendant, to be paid a reasonable proportion of the likely final sum "on account". This can be a vital order in favour of a claimant who might have a pressing need for compensation. A claimant might be unable to live in their own house due to their becoming wheelchair dependent. They need alternative accommodation and should not have to wait for months, even years, until the final resolution of their claim in order to receive the money to allow them to move. In cases where compensation for some future losses might ultimately be awarded on a periodical payment basis, then those likely periodical payment damages are kept out of account when considering the likely lump sum that the claimant will be awarded. The interim payment should be a reasonable proportion of the likely lump sum only. Interim payments are not available to claimants where liability remains in dispute.

The parties are obliged to disclose documents in accordance with the CPR and with standard directions (see below). Orders for "specific disclosure" can be sought where a party believes that the other has possession or control of documents and has not disclosed them. The party seeking specific disclosure can specify the documents sought. The party against whom the order is sought will, if ordered to do so, have to provide those documents or give an account of what steps have been taken to locate and produce them.

Disclosure

Each party to litigation has a duty of "disclosure". A party discloses a document by stating that the document exists or has existed. "Document" means anything in which information of any description is recorded. The other party can ask to "inspect" a disclosed document. Ultimately the disclosed documents that are needed will be produced, copied and provided to witnesses, experts and the court.

CPR Part 31 sets out the rules governing disclosure. What is called "standard disclosure" is ordered by the court (see Fig 1). The parties must make a statement, verified by a statement of truth, setting out the documents that exist that are or may be relevant to the issues in the case. The documents are listed and this is known as disclosure by list. This ought to be done before the first Case Management Conference but it is standard procedure for an order for standard disclosure to be made as part of the directions at that first CMC.

The documents which must be subject to standard disclosure are specified in the rules as follows:

"31.6 Standard disclosure requires a party to disclose only—

(a) the documents on which he relies; and

(b) the documents which —

(i) adversely affect his own case;

(ii) adversely affect another party's case; or

(iii) support another party's case; and

(c) the documents which he is required to disclose by a relevant practice direction."

There is therefore a clear legal duty on a party to reveal the existence of documents that are adverse to its case. That duty applies to claimants and defendants equally. It would be a contempt of court to make a false disclosure statement verified by a statement of truth. Nor can a party turn a blind eye to the existence of documents. They must make reasonable searches to find out what documents do exist that might be covered by standard disclosure.

The duty to disclose only applies to documents that are or have been in a party's control. A document is or was in the control of a party if:

"(a) it is or was in his physical possession;

(b) he has or has had a right to possession of it; or

(c) he has or has had a right to inspect or take copies of it."

We have already seen how medical records can be obtained. At the stage of standard disclosure, a party who is or was in control of those records would be bound to disclose them. As time moves on whilst the case progresses, it is likely that new medical records and other documents will be generated. There is an ongoing duty of disclosure on the parties, so they should disclose those newly generated documents as and when they come within their control.

The rules also make specific provision for applications for disclosure before the litigation begins, and disclosure by people or bodies who are not parties to the claim.

Statements and Expert Evidence

I have already discussed the importance of lay witness statements in relation to pre-action preparation. Once the litigation is under way the parties will be able to determine whether they need further lay evidence. Looking at the directions at Fig 2 you will see that there are some specific orders in relation to witness statements. First, the court may order that statements be limited to certain issues. Second, the court will order that a party cannot rely at trial on evidence from a witness whose statement has not been served. Third, the court may (but does not always) limit the number of witnesses and the length of their witness statements. The object of such a direction is to keep the evidence within manageable and reasonable proportions. The more complex the case the more leeway the parties are likely to be given. Restrictions of this kind reveal a lack of trust by the court in the parties' legal representatives. Of course, if it is necessary for a party to call more than, say, eight witnesses, the court will listen to submissions to that effect and would be highly likely to allow more.

At paragraph 5(b) there is an order which on the face of it compels the defendant to serve witness evidence from all the clinicians who had conduct of the "relevant" treatment of the claimant(s). In theory this could cover scores of healthcare professionals. I have already commented that this has always seemed to me to be a standard direction that sits uncomfortably with the basic principle that litigation is adversarial. Why should a party be compelled by the court to serve witness evidence from certain witnesses? On the other hand, as we have just seen, the parties are compelled to reveal the existence of all documents that are both helpful and unhelpful to their case. So, it might be argued, why should an NHS Trust be able to restrict its witness evidence only to those who would be helpful to its defence? If it knows of a healthcare professional who would assist the claimant, should it not be obliged to reveal that evidence, just as it is obliged to reveal an "unhelpful" document?

In certain situations, the court at trial will draw an adverse inference from the absence of a witness. Suppose in the case pleaded above (Fig 1), the defendant did not serve a witness statement from the obstetric registrar Dr Edgar, whose evidence would be obviously important to the case. Dr Edgar would be the "ghost at the feast" at trial. In a case called *Wiszniewski v Central Manchester HA* [1998] PIQR P324 the Court of Appeal articulated four principles that apply in such a situation. The court at trial is not obliged to draw an adverse inference against the party who has not called an obviously important witness, but it may do so. The court should have regard to the following:

(1)   In certain circumstances a court may be entitled to draw adverse inferences from the absence or silence of a witness who might be expected to have material evidence to give on an issue in the case.

(2)   If a court is willing to draw such inferences then the inference may serve to support or strengthen the evidence adduced on that issue by the other party or to weaken the evidence adduced by the party who might reasonably have been expected to call the witness.

(3)   The party that invites the court to make an adverse inference must, however, have adduced at least some evidence on the matter in question, before the court would be entitled to draw the adverse inference. If, in our case, the defendant had no case to answer on the issue on which Dr Edgar might be expected to have been able to give relevant evidence, then no adverse inference could be drawn from Dr Edgar's absence.

(4)   If there is a reason for the missing or silent witness, and if that reason satisfies the court, then no such adverse inference may be drawn. If, on the other hand, there is some credible explanation given, even if it is not wholly satisfactory, the potentially detrimental effect of his/her absence or silence may be reduced or nullified. So, if Dr Edgar has died or has taken a sabbatical to backpack around the world and cannot be located, then that might be a full and reasonable explanation for their absence. If, on the other hand, they had moved to another NHS Trust and the defendant had failed to track them down after making only a half-hearted effort to do so, the court will be much more inclined to draw adverse inferences from Dr Edgar's absence.

The use of paragraph 5(b) in the standard directions (Fig 2) in effect reminds the parties that if they do not serve evidence from the relevant witnesses, adverse inferences may be drawn. In a recent case called *Manzi v*

King's College NHS Foundation Trust [2018] EWCA Civ 1882, the Court of Appeal even suggested that a party dissatisfied that the other side had not served a statement from a particular witness could apply to the court for a direction that if no evidence were served from that witness, adverse inferences could be drawn by the court at trial. The difficulty with doing that is that the drawing of adverse inferences is very much a matter for the trial judge who, at the time of trial, will know of all of the matters relevant to the decision whether or not to draw such inferences, applying the principles laid down in the *Wiszniewski* case.

The court's directions limit the parties as to the expert evidence on which they can rely. The court is enjoined by CPR Part 35 to restrict expert evidence to that which is needed fairly to determine the issues in the case. The parties might decide to seek permission for expert evidence in additional areas, but case management judges are not known for their generous responses to such applications.

Sometimes an expert on whom a party relies becomes unavailable, or unreliable. Experts, like anyone else, might become too unwell to continue in the role or they may die. Others may be able to assist, but they change their minds, or act in a way to cause the party instructing them to lose faith in them. I have even had experts who have faced criminal charges mid-way through a case. What is a party to do?

A series of cases, including one called *Beck v Ministry of Defence* [2003] EWCA Civ 1043, tested the courts' approach in such situations. The position can be summarised as follows:

If, pre-litigation, no-one save for the party themselves (and their representatives of course) knows that Dr A has been instructed, and the party does not like what Dr A has to say, then the party is free, finances permitting, to go to Dr B and ask for their opinion. This is "expert shopping". The courts do not sanction expert shopping for understandable reasons, but pre-litigation there is nothing the courts can do about it. Communications between a party and an expert are confidential ("privileged") and the other potential parties to litigation are not entitled to see them.

Once litigation has begun and a party has nailed their colours to the mast, nominating Dr A as their expert (see Fig 2) then the other parties and the court will know about Dr A if the party later seeks permission to rely on Dr B in their place. The general rule in that situation is that the party seeking permission to change experts must show Dr A's report to the other party. This is an insurance against expert shopping. If the switch in experts is simply due to the fact that, for good reason, Dr A no longer supports the party's case, then that will be exposed. The other party can use Dr A's report to undermine their opponent's case. If, on the other hand, the party has lost faith in Dr A's report for good reason, for example he has refused to answer correspondence or has taken into account some irrelevant evidence, then the party will not lose any advantage by showing that report to the other party. The second party can hardly use Dr A's evidence to its advantage because it will be given very little weight.

If a supportive expert has died or is too unwell to write further reports or to give evidence at court, the party who instructed that expert might seek permission to rely on the written reports alone, or simply seek permission for a new expert, explaining the unavailability of the previous one. The temptation then is for the party to want to rely both on the previous expert and the new one, but that would be unfair on the other party who would have one expert facing two!

If you were paying attention to Fig 2 you will have noticed that the parties' expert reports on breach of duty and causation, and those on condition, prognosis and quantification, were directed to be exchanged simultaneously by 4pm on a certain date. This involves the parties' solicitors agreeing a time and date to send each other the reports. On occasion one party might send theirs to the other in a sealed envelope, not to be opened until the allotted time. Simultaneous exchange of expert reports prevents a party taking advantage of sight of the other side's evidence prior to having to serve its own. The temptation might be for a set of experts to tailor their evidence in the light of seeing the other side's reports. Nevertheless, practice varies around the country. Some courts insist on sequential exchange of expert reports on quantum so that the claimant has to serve their reports first, and the defendant serves theirs in response several weeks or months later. This is meant to allow the defendant to decide whether it needs expert evidence in all areas. It might be persuaded that it need not rely on its own expert evidence on certain issues because it accepts what the claimant's experts have to say. It is incumbent on the claimant to make their allegations and prove their case, so the defendant should be able to see the claimant's cards before playing its own.

Once the parties have exchanged their expert evidence, the standard directions provide that experts of the same disciplines – the midwives, the obstetricians, the neuroradiologists etc – discuss their evidence with each other and produce a joint statement setting out the issues on which they agree and those areas where they disagree, giving the reasons for their disagreements.

Experts' Joint Statements

Lawyers tend towards control freakery. Nothing can be left to chance. But at one of the key points in the history of a clinical negligence claim, the lawyers have to step back and hope for the best. That point is when experts instructed by the parties, who are specialists in the same discipline, put together a joint statement of the issues on which they agree and disagree.

The joint statement must be signed by all the experts who make it, and it is preceded by a discussion, either in person or by telephone or skype etc. No-one else is present at that discussion and so the parties' lawyers cannot control how the discussions progress or how the statement is worded.

The experts' joint discussions and statement are not wholly free of outside interference. The court usually gives standard directions as to the arrangements and timing of such discussions and the production of the statement. The discussion naturally takes place only after exchange of expert reports, and the parties will provide an agenda for the experts to follow. The agenda most often takes the form of a series of questions and so the joint statement sets out each question and its answer. One of the experts should make a note of the discussions and draft the joint statement to send to the other. Once they are agreed on the draft they should sign it and send it to the parties' representatives.

Agendas should begin with a pre-amble advising the experts of the ambit of the discussion. It might look something like this:

"You are required to communicate and, if necessary, meet and to deliver to the parties' solicitors a statement in writing setting out:

(i) matters agreed;

(ii) matters disputed;

(iii) the range of reasonable expert opinion on disputed fact;

(iv) by reference to (iii) above and the facts of the case the justification for the expert views.

Such statement should be prepared and agreed at your meeting or, in the event of discussion at a distance, promptly between you usually before the discussion is concluded. This statement will be produced at court but the contents of your discussion may not be referred to in court unless the parties expressly agree. You are not instructed to reach agreement, but only to comply with the order referred to above.

Where you rely upon published data, guidelines or other documentation, please identify the same and attach copies to your joint statement.

This agenda is intended to assist you to comply with the court's order, but you need not be confined by it and should consider all relevant matters."

In some cases, it may be felt helpful to set out legal tests for negligence and causation, but the questions themselves should not ask "Was the Defendant's conduct negligent?" because that is a question for the judge. Rather, the question should be: *"Did the Defendant act in accordance with a responsible body of paediatric opinion?"* or similar.

The process of agreeing an agenda of questions for a joint experts' discussion can be very tiresome. Many is the time when I have drafted a list of questions only to find them crossed out and replaced by another set by the other party's barrister or solicitor. I am then asked to comment. I might behave reasonably and adopt some of the other party's questions but stick by some of my original ones. A week later I receive another email saying that the other party has not agreed the latest draft. And so it goes on! In some cases, parties give up on trying to agree a single agenda and instead each agree to put their own agendas to the experts. The court is then provided with two joint statements rather than one, and slightly different answers to similar questions. This can prolong the trial, confuse the parties and is unhelpful to the trial judge. The desire of litigators to insist on their chosen questions and not to compromise on the drafting of an agenda is a product of the control freakery I have already mentioned. Some lawyers treat the drafting of an agenda as a dry run at cross-examining the opposing expert witness. In extremis, a party can apply to the court for a direction as to whether a question or series of questions that they object to should be included in the agenda. However, that is a costly solution and not one that the court would ever encourage. If sensible compromise fails to resolve a difference about the questions on the agenda, the more usual solution is to allow the opponent to put the question but to flag up that you object to it.

Chapter 5: Schedule and Counter Schedule

We have already looked at the forms of award for compensation that the courts have the power to make, and at the principles underlying the award of damages. In the course of litigation the parties have to apply those principles to the evidence of loss, preparing schedules listing the heads of damages that are claimed and their position as to the awards that should be made. This is expected to be done from the start of the litigation process.

The purpose of the disclosure of documents, and service of statements and expert reports on condition, prognosis and quantification, is to allow the parties to quantify the compensation that they each say should be paid if the claimant establishes liability. In clinical negligence cases that turn on a period of delay in diagnosis and/or treatment, the proper level of compensation cannot be assessed until it is known beyond what time, if any, the breach of duty occurred. If, for example, decompression surgery to the spine actually took place three days after the patient began to suffer altered sensation and weakness in their legs due to internal bleeding after spinal surgery, then it matters greatly whether, but for the negligent delay in recognising the need for decompression surgery, such surgery would have taken place. Should the decompression have taken place on day one, day two or day three? That will be for the court to decide at trial, or for the parties to agree by way of compromise after negotiation. The avoidable injury, loss and damage will differ considerably depending on when the decompression should have been performed. Decompression on day one might have resulted in a very good outcome for the claimant with no significant neurological injury. Decompression earlier on day three might have resulted in an outcome very similar to the actual outcome. Decompression on day two would have been likely to have produced an outcome for the claimant somewhere between those two extremes. Nevertheless, the parties are expected to set out, in fine detail, their calculations as to the appropriate level of compensation before such issues of causation have been determined. This is done in the form of a schedule from the claimant and a counter schedule from the defendant.

In claims where the claimant is alive, the schedule will fall into three parts: general damages for pain, suffering and loss of amenity; past losses and expenses; and future losses and expenses. If the claim arises out of the death of a patient, then the schedule will cover claims for the deceased's estate for pre-death pain, suffering and loss of amenity and consequential losses; and for the dependants of the deceased for the bereavement award and the financial and services dependency claims. Funeral expenses can be claimed by the estate or for a dependant depending on who paid them. See Part 4,

Chapter 11 for more details on claims arising out of a patient's death.

Practice varies as to the style and layout of schedules – there is no set form – but most will include an introduction setting out the bare facts and key dates; a section on the multipliers used in the schedule, showing how they have been calculated; a statement of the injuries suffered together with a valuation of general damages for those injuries; and then, the list of items claimed as past losses and future losses. Often it is useful to put the detailed calculations of, say, travel expenses, in a separate appendix which might run to several pages. The schedule should also include calculations of interest claimed and a summary showing the totals claimed under each heading and the grand total. Where the claimant is seeking periodical payments for any future losses, usually for future care costs, then that should be made clear in the schedule and reflected in the headings and summary.

Given that the first schedule will be served with the Particulars of Claim, and therefore before the claimant has been able fully to quantify their claim, it is common to find that some heads of claim are marked "TBA" meaning "To Be Ascertained" or "To Be Assessed". This is true also for the first counter schedule served with the Defence, in which the defendant might simply say: "The Claimant is put to strict proof" in relation to many of the heads of claim.

Whilst specific case law should not be included in pleadings such as the Particulars of Claim and Defence, it can be referred to in a schedule. For example, the established case law, at the time of writing, in relation to compensation for the cost of alternative accommodation stems from the judgment in *Roberts v Johnstone*, and this case will often be name-checked in a schedule. The calculations of future loss are highly dependent on the multiplier used, and the correct multiplier depends on the applicable discount rate. Since this discount rate is subject to variation on an order from the Lord Chancellor, the parties will usually expressly reserve their entitlement to amend the schedule should there be a change in the rate.

I have set out, in very short form, a typical schedule at Fig 3. Usually schedules in complex cases such as *Airey v Kingstown*, would run to very many more pages, including appendices. You will have to imagine what is in the appendices I refer to in the example below. Some lawyers use spreadsheet software, others simply type them out with a calculator to hand. I once received one from an opponent that had 64 footnotes. What matters most is that the reader of a schedule (in particular the opposing party and the judge) can easily follow what is being claimed and how it has been quantified. At a JSM or trial, it is very helpful to have a document summarising the heads of claim, the amount for each item set out in the schedule and counter schedule, and then an empty column for insertion of the judge's decision or a compromise amount.

Multipliers are set out in the actuarial tables already mentioned, the Ogden Tables. Tables 1 and 2 set out the multipliers applicable to the lives of males, and females respectively, according to their age at the date of assessment.

The life multiplier in the example given is taken from Table 1 of the Ogden Tables for an eight year old boy and is 89.62. For some of the claims within the schedule, this has to be broken down into multipliers for specific periods within the claimant's life, for example to the age of 18 and then after the age of 18. It is important that the total of the multipliers for these periods is the same as the life multiplier of 89.62. Whilst in my example the multiplier used for the next three years of life (to age 11) is indeed 3, and then from age 11 to 18 I have used 7, a more precise calculation would probably produce multipliers slightly different from those figures. This is an illustration only. Note also that if a claim is made for a one off immediate cost in the future, followed by annual costs, then the multiplier for the future annual costs is not the full life multiplier but 88.62 because the first year's cost is accounted for in the single lump sum element.

The Ogden tables also provide multipliers for loss of earnings claims. Table 9 gives the multiplier for an 18 year old male working until retirement at age 65. Table 11 gives the multiplier for an 18 year old male working until 70. In our example, Albert is only eight. It is assumed he would have worked to age 67. Therefore we use the figures in Tables 9 and 11 to work out what the multiplier should be for an 18 year old working until he was 67, and then adjust the multiplier because Albert is claiming the loss at the age of eight, ten years before he starts working. There is then a further adjustment to be made. Tables 9 and 11 take into account only the risk of mortality, i.e. of Albert dying before reaching retirement age. They do not take into account the chances of his losing his employment and being out of work for periods of time. That risk is accounted for in adjustment Tables A-D within the written introduction to the Ogden Tables. Labour market studies have shown that the most important factors affecting future earning capacity are whether a person has a disability, whether they are presently in work or unemployed, and their educational qualifications. For Albert we have to assume that he would be in work at age 18, would not have been disabled but for the negligence, and would have average educational qualifications (unless his parents were graduates or similar in which case we might assume he would gain a degree himself). Given his age when he starts work (18) and his gender and likely retirement age, Tables A-D give us an adjustment factor. The product of all this information and adjustment is a multiplier for future loss of earnings of 41.5.

Fig 3 – Schedule of Loss

IN THE HIGH COURT OF JUSTICE　　　　**Claim No: K19 1234**

QUEEN'S BENCH DIVISION

KINGSTOWN DISTRICT REGISTRY

B E T W E E N :

ALBERT AIREY

**(A Child by his father and Litigation
Friend, ALAN AIREY)**

First Claimant

AMANDA AIREY

Second Claimant

and

**KINGSTOWN HOSPITALS NHS
FOUNDATION TRUST**

Defendant

FIRST CLAIMANT'S SCHEDULE OF LOSS

---

1. INTRODUCTION

1.1 The First Claimant

1.1.1　Albert brings this action by his Father and Litigation Friend, Alan Airey.

1.1.2　Albert is referred to in this Schedule as "C".

1.1.3   C was born on 14 June 2012.

1.1.4   C is unlikely to have capacity to manage his own affairs as an adult.

1.2   Liability

1.2.1   Liability is in dispute. Trial is listed for 3 May 2021

1.3   Schedule

1.3.1   The schedule is calculated as at 14 June 2020. At that date C will be 8 years old.

1.3.2   Amounts claimed are rounded to the nearest £1.

1.3.3   C will seek permission to revise this Schedule in the light of further evidence or further changes in the law affecting his claim including any change in the discount rate.

1.4   Family

1.4.1   C lives with his mother and father and his two siblings at the family house at Manningham Lane, Kingstown, which is owned by his parents with the assistance of a mortgage.

1.5   Injuries

1.5.1   C has asymmetric dyskinetic (dystonic) 4 limb cerebral palsy with bulbar involvement. He has relative preservation of cognitive function. He uses his left hand for all tasks, with his right hand being held in a folded, locked position. He cannot fasten or unfasten zips or buttons and has no pincer grip in his right hand. He walks with the aid of tripod sticks. His speech is hard to understand and he uses a communication aid.

1.6   Expert Evidence

1.6.1   C relies on expert evidence from Dr Tring, Paediatric Neurologist; Mr Smith, Physiotherapist; Mr Crowther, Care and Occupational Therapy; Ms Little, Speech and Language Therapist; Ms Sissons, Assistive Technology; and Mrs Harwood, Accommodation.

1.7 Life expectancy, Multipliers and PPO

1.7.1   C relies on the expert evidence of Dr Tring who advises that C has normal life expectancy.

1.7.2   The discount rate used in this Schedule is that announced for implementation from 5 August 2019, namely -0.25%. Should the Lord Chancellor make a further announcement or should the law otherwise change, the Schedule will require revision.

1.7.3   Assuming normal life expectancy, the multiplier for life is 89.62 (Ogden Table 1).

1.7.4   Multiplier from 8 to 11: 3

Multiplier from 11 to 18: 7

Multiplier from 18 to 89.62: 79.62

1.7.5   C seeks a Periodical Payment Order in relation to future care and case management.

2. GENERAL DAMAGES FOR PAIN, SUFFERING AND LOSS OF AMENITY

C refers to the evidence of Dr Tring.

General damages to compensate C for his pain, suffering and loss of amenity:

£200,000

Interest

At 2% per annum from date of service of proceedings in June 2017 to the date of calculation: 6%

£12,000

3.   PAST LOSSES AND EXPENSES

3.1   Personal Care and Assistance

3.1.1   C refers to the report of Mr Crowther.

3.1.2   For the sake of economy the breakdown of the value of past gratuitous care and assistance is not repeated in this schedule.

3.1.3   The value of past gratuitous care and assistance is as follows:

Period	Amount	
14.06.12 to 13.06.13	£26,776	
14.06.13 to 04.09.16	£86,380	
05.09.16 to 27.02.17	£21,347	
28.02.17 to 31.03.19	£61,509	
01.04.19 to Date	£44,997	£241,009

3.1.4   C contends that there should be no (25% or other) reduction for gratuitous care because the care given has been in the nature of specialist, nursing care for a severely disabled child.

£241,009

3.1.5   Professional Care: £2,282

£243,291

3.2   Case Management

3.2.1   Parental case management as costed in the report of Mr Crowther:

£12,550

3.2.2   Professional case management: <u>£8,110</u>

                                                                          £20,660

3.3   Travel and Transport Costs

3.3.1   As a consequence of C's disabilities, his family have incurred travelling expenses to numerous appointments at hospitals and clinics, together with therapy appointments. C refers to the report of Mr Crowther:

To and from medical appointments: £2,440

To and from therapy sessions: £2,590

Cost of hiring vehicles: £2,950

                                                                          £7,980

3.4   Therapies

3.4.1   Physiotherapy and Speech and Language Therapy paid by family directly (see Appendix 1):

                                                                          £15,387

3.5   Miscellaneous Expenses

3.5.1   See Appendix 2:

Additional equipment, toiletries, car seat, rain cover, alterations to bedroom and bathroom:

                                                                          £14,250

3.6   Interest

At half the Special Account rate from the first date of loss on recurrent losses and expenses (all past losses)

Total past losses: £314,214

The cumulative Special Account interest from the date of birth (at half the rate because losses have been recurrent since birth):

£314,214 x 3.47% = £10,900

No Credit for interest on Interim Payments (none paid because liability in dispute).

£10,900

4. FUTURE LOSSES AND EXPENSES

4.1 Loss of Earnings

It is likely that C would have worked, but for his disabilities, from the age of 18. It is assumed that he would have enjoyed average earnings. C's case is that although he is only 8, and a firmer view can only be taken after he has been through puberty, on the balance of probabilities C will not be able to enjoy remunerative employment as an adult.

Average earnings: £27,456. Net equivalent £22,208.

Multiplier for earnings from age 18 to age 67 (Ogden Tables 9 and 11), adjusted for contingencies other than mortality and for early receipt (Tables A-D from the Introduction to the Ogden Tables): 41.5

£22,208 x 41.5   **£921,632**

4.2 Care and Assistance

4.2.1   C relies on the expert evidence of Mr Crowther.

4.2.2   C therefore claims for the cost of future employed care from the date of the Schedule to age 11 as set out at page 65 of Mr Crowther's report of February 2019 to include pension contributions of £3,091 pa:

£177,587

Plus term time in-school care £17.50 ph x 20 h x 42 weeks:
£14,700

PPO £192,287

4.2.3   From age 11 to ceasing full time education (to age 18):

£110,000

Plus term time in-school care as above: £14,700

PPO £124,700

4.2.4   From leaving fulltime education (age 18 and over):

PPO £168,000

4.2.5   Lump sum claims:

Cost of DBS registration: **£1,566**

4.3   Case Management

4.3.1   To age 11 (including £1,102 for parental case management):

£12,372 (PPO)

4.3.2   Age 11 to ceasing full time education (age 18) including £1,102 for parental case management:

£13,252 (PPO)

4.3.3   From ceasing full time education (18 and over) including £1,102 for parental case management:

£14,562 (PPO)

4.3.4   Plus lump sum to reflect increased initial years' costs of case management at the beginning of each period:

£6,000 + £3,330 + £3,330 =   **£12,660**

4.4 Occupational Therapy

4.4.1   C relies on the evidence of Mr Crowther: See Appendix 3.

£101,617

4.5 Chiropody

4.5.1   £300 per annum from age 18 x multiplier of 79.62:

£23,886

4.6 Physiotherapy

4.6.1   C relies on the evidence of Mr Smith: see Schedules 5 to 7 of his report.

Initial intensive physiotherapy and equipment:

£7,156

Annual physiotherapy and equipment replacement (after first year):

£1200 x 88.62 =   £106,344

Contingency for future additional physiotherapy in times of particular need:

£8,000

Total   **£121,500**

4.7 Speech and Language Therapy

4.7.1   C refers to the report of Ms Little.

To age 11:   £3,510 per annum x 3   £10,530

From 11 to 18:   £2,500 per annum x 7   £17,500

Provision for remainder of life:

£502 per annum x 79.62   £39,970

                                                                                                    £68,000

4.8   Education

4.8.1   Educational consultant (10 sessions at £100 ph):
                                                                                                    £1,000

4.8.2   Educational Psychology (10 sessions at £175 ph):
                                                                                                    £1,750

4.8.3   Appeal against SEN provision (say 25% chance of £37,500):
                                                                                                    £9,375

                                                                                                    £12,125

4.9   Transport

4.9.1   C relies on the evidence of Mr Crowther.

4.9.2   There are two vehicles that would meet C's reasonable needs. The family's preference, having assessed the options, is for a Mercedes Benz V250.

4.9.3   Cost of Mercedes   £53,630

4.9.4   Replacement of car every five years (cost of new vehicle £53,630, less credit for residual value of replaced vehicle £26,830) = net cost to claimant at an average of £5,360 per annum. Multiplier for life (less first year cost accounted for under 4.9.3 above): 88:

              Replacement costs: £5,360 x 88:   471,680

4.9.5   Annual additional costs of insurance and running costs and AA:

              Insurance: £1,250.33

              AA   £112

Additional running costs of Mercedes as opposed to vehicle he would have had but for the negligence:

£5,010

Total   £6,372.33

Multiplier for additional annual costs: 89.62

<u>£571,088</u>

£1,096,398

4.10 Aids and Equipment

4.10.1   See Appendix 4, in reliance on the evidence of Mr Crowther.

£596,794

4.11 Miscellaneous and Services

4.11.1   C relies on the evidence of Mr Crowther.

4.11.2   Laundry, additional heating and lighting costs, additional clothing and shoes, gardening, DIY and decorating services: see Appendix 4.

£168,212

4.12 Assistive Technology

4.12.1   C relies on the evidence of Ms Sissons.

4.12.2   C refers to Appendix 5.

£198,145

4.13 Holidays

4.13.1   C relies on the evidence of Mr Crowther.

4.13.2   Additional costs of one holiday within the UK and one abroad, to the age of 80 as set out in Mr Crowther's report:

£408,000

4.14   Medical

TBA

4.15   Court of Protection

The Claimant refers to the witness evidence of Mr Dags:

Initial years' costs and one-off costs of writing a will etc:

£27,600

Annual Deputyship Costs thereafter: £9,000 x 86.6:   £797,400

Total: **£825,000**

4.16   Accommodation

4.16.1   C relies on the expert evidence of Mrs Harwood.

4.16.2   C's family's current accommodation is unsuitable for his needs. He requires alternative, single level accommodation due to his disabilities and will do so for the remainder of his life.

4.16.3   Costs of Purchase and Adaptation of Alternative Accommodation

Capital cost of suitable accommodation:

The *Roberts v Johnstone* method of assessing the capital costs of purchasing suitable accommodation is no longer valid if a negative discount rate is used. C reserves the right to claim for the cost of being kept out of his money due to having to purchase alternative accommodation, but in the light of the pending change in the discount rate, he will set out such alternative calculations, if appropriate, in due course. For the purpose of this schedule only no claim is made for the additional capital costs.

255

Alterations: £365,947

Costs of moving as per Mrs Harwood's report:
£38,000

Costs of removing disability related items at end of C's life:
£15,000

Additional annual costs assuming move within 1 year from this schedule:

£5,412 x 88.6: £479,503

Occupational Therapy (additional costs) on advising on adaptations:
£5,490

Additional furniture and furnishings for carers etc:
£17,399

£921,339

(The Claimant will concede credit for accommodation that he might have purchased absent his disabilities, with first purchase at the age of 35 and further moving costs every 15 years if a claim for the capital cost is allowed. Credit as per Mrs Harwood's report: £465,000)

SUMMARY	Lump Sum
Pain, suffering and loss of amenity	200,000
Interest	12,000
	212,000
PAST	
Care	243,291
Case Management	
Parental	12,550

Professional			20,660
Travel and transport			7,980
Therapies			15,387
Miscellaneous Expenses			14,250
Interest			10,900
			325,018
FUTURE			
Loss of Earnings			921,632
Care			
To age 11	192,287	PPO	
Age 11 to 18	124,700	PPO	
Age 18 and over	168,000	PPO	
To age 11	12,372	PPO	
Lump sum			1,566
Case management			
To age 11	12,372	PPO	
Age 11 to 18	13,252	PPO	
Age 18 and over	14,562	PPO	
Lump sum			12,660
Occupational Therapy			101,617
Chiropody			23,886
Physiotherapy			121,500
SLT			68,000
Education			12,125
Transport			1,096,398
Aids and Equipment			596,794
Miscellaneous			168,212
Holidays			408,000

Assistive Technology	198,145
Medical (TBA)	
Court of Protection	825,000
Accommodation	921,339
	5,476,874
	£6,013,892

Counsel: Robert Delves

Statement of Truth

I believe/the Claimant's Litigation Friend believes that the facts stated in this Schedule of Loss are true.

Signed:

Chapter 6: Resolution without Trial

A claim that is the subject of litigation must come to an end (eventually). Some are discontinued by the claimant: they throw in the towel. A few are struck out by the court. Others are concluded by a judgment of the court after a trial. Most, however, are resolved by agreement between the parties.

Settlement and Alternative Dispute Resolution

Whilst the process of litigation is directed towards resolution of the case by a judge at trial, the vast majority of claims do not reach trial – they are resolved without any determination of the substantive issues by a judge. Some cases are never litigated at all – that is, proceedings are never issued – either because the party proposing to make a claim decides not to do so, or because the proposed claimant and defendant come to an agreement about the payment of damages and costs which means that there is no need for litigation. Of those claims that are issued at court, and therefore become the subject of litigation, still the great majority are not tried. Some are discontinued when it becomes apparent that the claim will fail at trial. Many more are resolved by an agreement by the defendant to make a payment to the claimant.

Resolution by agreement can be reached by a number of different routes.

Offer and Acceptance

A party bringing or defending a case may feel "locked in" to the litigation, but there is nothing to stop them speaking to or writing to the other side to the proceedings and seeking to resolve their differences. They can come to an agreement on individual aspects of the claim or the whole of the claim. A claimant's solicitor can pick up the telephone and suggest to the defendant's solicitor that they can resolve this case if the defendant pays £50,000 and the claimant's reasonable costs. This might be accepted by the defendant, in which case a contract is entered into and the claim has been compromised by agreement, or they might reject that offer and make a counter offer of, say, £30,000 plus costs. Or they might reject the offer and make no counter offer at all. This process can be done verbally or in writing, but if, after some haggling, an agreement is reached it is binding. The parties would be wise to put the agreement in writing and inform the court promptly of the agreement. It is common to talk of "full and final settlement" of a claim; that is a settlement that cannot be revisited and that covers the whole of the claimant's entitlement to claim damages arising out of the subject matter of the litigation.

An offer made by letter or verbally, and which is not a Part 36 offer (see below) remains open for the other party to accept unless and until it is withdrawn. Once the offer is accepted, and that acceptance has been communicated to the offeror, then the deal is done.

Such settlement discussions are usually carried out "without prejudice". A party making an offer should make it plain that the offer is confidential or "without prejudice". Such an offer, and the discussions that follow, cannot be made known to the judge who decides the case at trial. A party can offer to settle the case for £50,000 but then claim £200,000 at the trial, provided the offer has not been accepted. The defendant is not permitted to say to the judge at trial: *"The claimant is claiming £200,000 but we know they would have settled for £50,000."* "Without prejudice" negotiations are kept secret from the judge.

There are formal rules about written offers and acceptance, referred to below, but the parties do not have to choose to abide by the mechanisms set out in the court rules. The advantages of following the court procedures when making offers is that the rules provide for penalties if the offers are not accepted when they ought to have been. Offers made outside the rules, for example verbal offers, do not generally have consequences in terms of costs. Obviously, a defendant who is ordered to pay £200,000 damages after trial will kick themselves for not having accepted a verbal offer to settle the case for £50,000, but there will not be any additional penalties imposed upon them for their mistake. In contrast, offers made in compliance with the court rules do have the potential to lead to additional consequences.

Part 36 Offers

The CPR provide for a mechanism for making written offers to settle. These come under the provisions of Part 36 of the CPR and are therefore known as Part 36 offers. Either party can make a Part 36 offer. Such offers are usually made to resolve the whole of a claim, but need not be: offers can be made in respect of specific issues, such as liability alone. Hence, a Part 36 offer could be made by a defendant to pay 75% of the damages, whatever those damages are ultimately assessed or agreed to be.

Provided that the rules under Part 36 are complied with, a Part 36 offer is automatically available for acceptance for 21 days. If accepted, then the case is over. The settlement has been reached on the terms set out in the written offer which has been accepted by the other party. If the offer is not accepted then it raises a risk for the party to whom the offer was made. A claimant who proceeds with their claim in the face of a Part 36 offer but does not do better than that offer at trial will have to pay the defendant's costs from the time when they should have accepted the offer – 21 days after the offer was made. Given that those costs may well include the costs of the trial, that can be a very heavy penalty on the claimant for not accepting what turned out to be a good offer. If a claimant makes a Part 36 offer which is not accepted by the defendant, and then does at least as well as that offer at trial, then the rules provide for various financial penalties to be imposed on the defendant for not having accepted the claimant's reasonable offer.

Part 36 offers can therefore be brought to a judge's attention in relation to the issue of the costs of the litigation. They must not, however, be mentioned to a judge before judgment on the substantive case. They are relevant only to costs.

Part 36 offers can be made at any time. They are an important tool for litigators to put pressure on the opposing party to settle rather than to continue the litigation.

ADR

Some jargon: ADR stands for alternative dispute resolution, meaning any mechanism for resolving the litigated dispute other than through judicial determination or court process. This is usually done at a JSM or joint settlement meeting, otherwise known as an RTM or round table meeting. The alternative is to agree to mediation or, much more rarely, arbitration.

A JSM or RTM is quite simply a meeting of the parties with their lawyers at which they enter into negotiations to seek to resolve the litigated claim.

A mediation is a meeting with an independent person, the mediator, who has no power to compel the parties to negotiate or resolve the claim, but who can facilitate discussions to achieve those ends.

An arbitration is the closest form of ADR to a court trial. The parties agree to argue their case before an independent person, the arbitrator, and to be bound by the decision of the arbitrator on the issues they agree to leave to them to decide.

The courts now require the parties to litigation to engage in ADR. That does not mean that the ADR will succeed in resolving the claim – there are still clinical negligence trials, albeit not many of them – but it must be tried unless there is good reason not to do so. A party that unreasonably refuses or fails to engage in ADR may well be penalised in costs at the end of the litigation.

By far the most common form of ADR in clinical negligence claims is a

JSM or RTM. Mediation is becoming more common since NHS Resolution instigated a mediation scheme. Arbitrations are extremely rare.

A JSM can be held at any stage of the litigation. There is a tendency for the parties to want to see all the other side's evidence before discussing settlement, but that point will be reached quite late on in the litigation, and after a lot of costs have been incurred. There is no set form for a JSM but typically the claimant will attend with their solicitor and barrister and will take one room at the premises where the meeting is held. The defendant's solicitor and barrister will take another room, sometimes joined by a representative from the defendant NHS Trust, or someone from NHS Resolution. If it is a case funded by the MPS or MDU, rather than by NHSR, then typically a representative from the relevant funding body will attend. I have never known an individual healthcare professional, even those who are named defendants, to attend a JSM. The usual process is for the lawyers to meet in a third room to discuss the case. When representing claimants at JSMs I do not encourage my clients to come with me when I speak to the lawyers for the defendant, but they are of course entitled to do so. I have been at a JSM when the defendant's barrister had to negotiate in front of the claimant. I did not think that their presence was helpful to the claimant or to the negotiation process. Some might argue that it is important that the claimant "takes ownership" of the litigation, including the negotiations at a JSM, but usually a claimant will never have been involved in trying to negotiate a resolution of a clinical negligence case, they will have a distinctly personal perspective on the issues being negotiated, and the defendant will feel constrained in what they can say in front of the claimant (or if they feel unconstrained, they may say things that are upsetting to the claimant).

Whether or not the claimant is directly involved in the face to face negotiations at a JSM, they are certainly involved in the decision-making. Indeed, they make the decisions. The barrister and solicitor give advice but ultimately the decision as to what offer to make, or what offer to accept, is for the claimant. The claimant gives authority to their lawyer to make an offer or to accept an offer. The lawyers cannot make or accept offers without being given such authority. The position is the same on the defendant's side except that the person who makes the decisions about offers and acceptance is not an individual who was directly affected by the events giving rise to the claim. It is not the allegedly negligent surgeon, for example, who conducts the negotiations or who gives authority to the lawyers who do conduct the negotiations. The person who does make the decisions is the one who holds the purse strings: the claims handler at NHSR, the MPS or the MDU. They will of course take into account the advice of the lawyers, and the views of any relevant healthcare professionals or representatives from the Trust involved, if any, but the decisions are theirs to make.

Different lawyers have different styles of negotiation: some are very detailed in their approach, some use a broad brush. Some make numerous offers and counter offers, others cut straight to the chase! One well-known QC from Manchester was known to make a single "take it or leave it" offer at JSMs. Much more commonly the parties haggle until one says that they are making a final offer. It is a professional requirement on barristers conducting such negotiations to be honest. That is, I would not be permitted to say that my client will only accept £1,000,000 and not a penny less if they have told me that they would accept £900,000. That said, offers and counter offers can be carefully worded, and the experienced lawyer is attuned to the differences between *"that is my final offer"*, *"I cannot advise the claimant to accept anything less"*, *"that is the best we can do today"*, and *"that is the limit of my authority"*. That last phrase is commonly used by lawyers for defendants who have been told in advance of the JSM the upper limit of what they can offer. It does not necessarily mean that the authority could not be extended on request or further discussion.

Negotiations at a JSM are "without prejudice". They cannot be divulged to the trial judge nor to any court determining costs.

At a mediation, the mediator exercises control over the process. Typically, the mediator will have been provided with the case papers and they may speak to the solicitors for each party in advance. At the meeting itself, the mediator will speak privately with each opposing team and let them know about the mediator's role and talk through the process for the day's mediation. Then, usually, everyone participating will meet in a single room and introduce themselves and perhaps say something about the case and why they are at the mediation. This does give an opportunity for a claimant to speak directly to representatives for the defendant. I have participated in mediations where the healthcare professionals alleged to have been negligent have attended. Their attendance in what was a very sensitive case was very welcome to the claimant and it helped to lead to an agreed resolution of the claim. After this plenary session the mediator will then usually visit each team and ask questions designed to identify the key issues that need to be addressed. And so the process of negotiation begins, but through the auspices of the mediator.

The mediator has no power to make decisions in the case, or to compel agreement. Their skill is in teasing out the strengths and weaknesses of each party's case, in pointing out consequences of stances or decisions, and in encouraging dialogue. Mediations tend to take longer than JSMs but I believe that in appropriate cases, particularly those that are sensitive and where the claimant may want more than just a monetary solution, they can be very valuable. A claimant might want an apology, some information about how a negligent practitioner has been dealt with, or reassurance about how systems have been improved in the light of the failings in their particular case. None of these matters are strictly the subject of litigation, but they can be aired at a mediation.

The vast majority of mediations and JSMs conclude in one day. In very complex cases, or claims involving multiple claimants, they might be arranged to take place over more than one day.

If the parties come to terms of agreement at a mediation or at a JSM, then the terms are usually recorded and they become binding on the parties.

Claimants Without Capacity

Some claimants lack the mental capacity to litigate – due to injury, illness or disability they cannot sufficiently understand, weigh up and make decisions about information relevant to the litigation, even with appropriate help. As we have seen, a person who lacks the capacity to litigate is appointed a litigation friend to conduct the litigation on their behalf. However, the litigation friend cannot conclude a settlement without the approval of the court. Any settlement of a claim by a person without capacity to litigate, reached through ADR, is not binding on the parties unless or until the court has considered the settlement and given its approval for it as being in the best interests of the claimant. The defendant's position is irrelevant to the court. A judge is only concerned with the interests of the party who lacks capacity.

Part 21 of the CPR sets out the procedures to be followed and the matters for the court to consider when a case has been settled on behalf of a party without capacity. Firstly, the agreement reached between the parties is not effective before the court has approved it. Therefore, if something significant were to occur between settlement and approval, one or other party may no longer choose to abide by the agreement. Suppose a claimant was run over by a bus and killed two weeks after their claim for future losses and expenses were settled for £1 million. The claim would survive for their estate but it would obviously be worth nothing like £1 million, given their death. The beneficiaries of their estate cannot seek to enforce the settlement agreement which had not been approved by the court, because it was not binding until approval.

The second important point about such settlements is that the court has to be satisfied that the settlement is in the claimant's best interests. Thus, the court is free to disagree with the advice given by the claimant's lawyers, or a decision made by the litigation friend. The court might disagree with the form of the settlement or the size of it. It might disagree with the proposals for how to deal with the sum to be recovered. In large cases the commonest form of order, upon approval being given, is that the money recovered is paid into the Court of Protection. A person, called a "deputy", is appointed by the Court of Protection to have responsibility for managing the money recovered, but they are answerable to and must account to the Court of Protection. They must file accounts and may have to make applications to the court for permission to use the money in certain ways. Both the need for the settlement to be approved, and the need for oversight of the use of the money recovered, give the claimant protection. In fact, they are known as "protected parties".

Deputies may be professional or "lay". A family member might make a suitable lay deputy. The costs involved in using a professional deputy are very considerable in the larger claims, and they can be claimed as a head of damage within the claim itself. So, in claims where all the other heads of damage amount to say £3 million or more, the costs of using a professional deputy and the costs of the Court of Protection itself might amount to £350,000 or more.

When smaller sums are recovered by settlement, the court might well sanction payment out of the money into a trust or the use of some other mechanism that is less formal and costly than the Court of Protection, but which still provides safeguards to ensure the money is used in the claimant's best interests.

Children under the age of 18 are, in effect, treated in the same way as adults who lack capacity to litigate. The settlement of a claim on behalf of a child must be approved by the court. This is so even where most of the money is recovered by an adult, but only a small sum is recovered on behalf of a child. In many claims under the Fatal Accidents Act 1976, the dependants of the deceased will include a spouse or co-habiting partner, and their children. They may recover damages to be apportioned between or amongst them. Even if the adult partner receives, say, £200,000 and a child £5,000, still the court's approval is required for the settlement insofar as it affects the child.

Chapter 7: Trial

The standard directions (Fig 2) envisage trial of the claim and, in preparation for trial, a Pre-Trial Review hearing (PTR). These pre-trial hearings give the court the opportunity to ensure that everything is in place for the trial itself. If a witness will need to give evidence by video link, then arrangements can be made. If a particular expert can only attend trial on the third and fourth days, then the trial timetable can be varied accordingly. If there are late applications by a party to adduce further evidence, then the court can be asked to make an order to that effect. The court will usually ask whether the parties have sought to resolve the case by means of ADR. The judge hearing the PTR may or may not be the judge who eventually tries the case but whoever it is, they must not be told of any offers or negotiations, only whether there has been a JSM or mediation. If there has been no attempt to resolve the case through ADR, the court will want to know why, and may make a further order that the parties hold a JSM prior to the date fixed for trial.

As part of the standard directions, the court will order the parties to prepare a trial bundle – this is an indexed and paginated set of documents that the court will need to have in order to determine the case at trial. It will comprise the pleadings, witness statements, experts' reports and joint statements, and the schedule and counter schedule. Too often, parties also include every single page of the medical records in their possession and control. The fact is that at trial there are usually only relatively few pages from the medical records that the court needs to scrutinise. Best practice is for the parties to agree a core bundle of medical records, copied for the judge and for use by witnesses in the witness box. A full set of medical records can then be on hand should it be needed. Similarly, there may be hundreds of pages of pay slips, receipts and other documents relevant to the quantification of losses and expenses. Not all of them need to be copied several times. A core bundle of the essential documents will suffice.

To ensure that a witness attends court for the trial, the solicitors for each party may issue a witness summons which is a formal document requiring the appearance of the witness at court on a particular day or days. Some witnesses, such as the claimant themselves, will not require a witness summons. For others, the solicitors may think it worthwhile issuing a summons rather than risking the witness deciding to do something else on the big day. Failure to comply with a summons without good reason can lead to penalties being imposed on the witness.

The court will also order the parties to provide written opening submissions, sometimes called "skeleton arguments", in advance of the trial. These will be prepared by the barristers representing the parties at trial. They typically summarise the issues to be determined, highlight the key evidence that supports the party's case, refer to the relevant statutes and case law, and set out concise arguments as to why the court should find in their favour. As well as ensuring that these written submissions and documents are prepared, the solicitors will be making practical arrangements to ensure that every witness and expert will be at court at the right time, and the barristers will be preparing their cross-examination of the witnesses, and scrutinising the medical records and other evidence in minute detail.

All is now ready for the trial.

Assume that the trial in question is that of *Airey and Airey v Kingstown Hospitals NHS Foundation Trust*. Assume also that Mrs Airey's claim has been resolved by agreement prior to trial, and that, after a JSM, the parties have agreed the quantification of the child's claim but still cannot reach agreement as to whether the defendant is liable for those damages or not. Therefore, the trial judge only has to determine a single issue – is the defendant liable to compensate the First Claimant, Albert Airey, for the injuries he has suffered? There is no dispute that the defendant, its employees and agents, owed Albert a duty of care. It *is* disputed that there was any negligence (breach of duty) or that his injuries, loss and damage were caused by any negligence on the part of the defendant.

The judge hearing the case at trial is Mrs Justice Kewley. Counsel for the First Claimant is Mr Delves. Counsel for the Defendant is Ms Greenwood. In the light of the agreement as to the quantification of damages the parties notified the court at the PTR that the estimated length of trial was reduced to five days. The timetable for trial is as follows:

Day 1   Opening by Mr Delves

                  Evidence from Mrs Airey

                  Evidence from Mr Airey

Day 2   Evidence from the Defendant's witnesses:

                      Midwife Lord

                      Sister Moorhouse

Dr Edgar

Mr Riley

Day 3   Expert evidence from:

Mrs Walsh and Mr Priestley, midwifery experts

Mr Barnes and Ms Drake, Obstetric Experts

Day 4   Expert Evidence from:

Professor Hepworth and Dr Blowes,
Neonatologists

Dr Tring and Professor Mannell, Paediatric
Neurologists

Day 5   Closing submissions

The parties' neuroradiologists have come to agreement on all the relevant issues in their joint statement, so their evidence will be read by the court without the need for the experts to be called and questioned at trial.

You will notice that there is no space in the trial timetable for judgment. That is because it is highly unlikely that Mrs Justice Kewley would give a judgment at the trial itself. There will be a lot of evidence to sift and scrutinise. Typically, a judge hearing such a case will "reserve" judgment, giving it in writing some days or weeks after the evidence has been heard. Judgments given immediately and verbally at the end of the evidence are called "extempore" and are rare in clinical negligence cases in the High Court. In less complex cases in the County Court it is more common for the judge to "hand down" judgment on the day after the evidence has been completed. The proceedings at which the judge gives their judgment verbally are recorded and the lawyers can take notes of the judgment. More experienced and confident judges may even give their judgment without a prepared script or note but in a clinical negligence case that will be uncommon.

Mrs Justice Kewley sits "on the bench"; usually, in fact, a chair behind a long desk on a raised platform that is separated from the rest of the courtroom. She wears a simple, long black gown with red "tabs" around her neck. There is no gavel on the bench. Judges in England and Wales do not use gavels. Bizarrely half of all articles about litigation that appear in the press or social media are illustrated by stock images of gavels. The other half are illustrated by pictures of tiny weighing scales of the kind used by drug dealers, but not, curiously, by judges. What you will see on the judge's bench are the trial documents arranged in a series of numbered ring binders. She has a red, hard-backed notebook or a computer notebook for recording her notes of the evidence. Being a High Court Judge she has a personal clerk who is akin to a PA. Her clerk may appear in court before the trial begins, and each subsequent morning, to ensure that everything is in place. The judge looks out, and slightly down, on the rest of the courtroom. Immediately in front of her she can see the back of the court clerk, who deals with the court administration, ensures orders are properly drawn up and logged on the court system, and whose responsibilities include making sound recordings of the trial proceedings, from which a transcript can be written up if later required. The court associate also faces out to the courtroom. A third assistant to the court is the usher. The usher wears a short black gown and looks after the witnesses and the parties, ushering them into court for the start of proceedings, and ushering them out at the close of the day. They ensure the water jugs are filled, that seating is in place, that a bible or other holy book is ready for the use of witnesses taking an oath. They lead witnesses to the witness box, provide boxes of tissues for those who become upset, turn up the right page in a bundle of records if the witness is struggling to find it. They oil the wheels.

To the judge's left is the witness box. Across the body of the court room, parallel with the judge's bench, are Counsels' benches. Traditionally QCs ("silks") take the front row, and non-QCs ("juniors") the second row. These days QCs often represent parties to litigation without the assistance of a junior barrister. If there are no QCs present, then the junior barristers will use the front row. Any QC appearing against a junior who were to insist on that junior sitting on the second row would rightly be considered to be an oaf. However, these are the old traditions and some like to abide by them!

Whilst the judge does not wear a grey horsehair wig, the barristers do. Barristers also wear black gowns and white tabs. QCs have heavier gowns (not necessarily silk!) and, under their gowns, either a special long sleeved, short-bodied garment called a "bum-freezer" or a tailcoat and waistcoat. Why barristers still wear horsehair wigs for clinical negligence claims is a mystery to me. Members of the bar voted to maintain this tradition several years ago. I was in the minority who voted to dispense with wigs. What a picture we make!

The solicitors in the case sit on the rows behind Counsel. The claimant will usually sit beside their solicitor. A key healthcare professional involved for the defence might sit with their solicitor. Experts might take up seats on that row also. Other witnesses and members of the public might take up seats closer to the rear of the court.

Unlike in criminal cases, witnesses can remain in court before and after they have given evidence. If, rarely, there is a real basis for thinking that a witness might be influenced to tailor their evidence according to what they have heard other witnesses have said, the parties may agree or the court may direct that those witnesses should remain out of court until they are called to give their testimony. The courts are open to the public. If the judge considers it appropriate, subject to any representations from the parties and from members of the press, an order can be made that there be no reporting of the proceedings that would identify the claimant or a particular witness. Such anonymity orders are not uncommon where the claimant is a child, but otherwise they are rare. The principle that justice should not only be done, but be seen to be done, is a very strong one.

The parties and their legal teams will usually have met for a conference several weeks before the trial, and they meet again in a "conference room" within the court building for an hour or so before going into the court room. The usual sitting hours are from 10:30am to 1:00pm and from 2:00pm to 4:30pm. However, the working day for the legal representatives usually also involves early morning preparation, meeting at court from about 9:00am, meeting over the lunch hour, and a post-hearing meeting for an hour or so followed by evening preparation for the next day.

Shortly before 10:30am the parties enter the court room and set themselves up. At 10:30am the usher asks if everyone is ready and moments later calls out: "All rise". Everyone who is able to do so stands for the judge as she enters through a door behind the bench, walks to her chair, bows, acknowledging the bows of Counsel facing her, and sits down. The court clerk calls on the case: *"The matter of Airey and Kingstown Hospitals NHS Foundation Trust"*. The judge looks up: *"Yes, Mr Delves?"* and the trial is underway.

Although the court has ordered written opening submissions to be provided, Counsel for the claimant will make opening oral submissions too. They usually begin:

> *"My Lady, I appear for the claimant. My learned friend Ms Green-wood represents the defendant. This is a trial of liability only in a clinical negligence claim. Quantum has been agreed. Your Ladyship should have the trial bundle in the form of six ring binders ......"*

If there are some practical matters – an ill witness, some additional documents to be added etc. – these are sometimes referred to as "housekeeping". Some judges prefer just to listen, others are more interventionist, but judges are enjoined not to "enter the fray". They must not act in a way in which they appear to be taking sides or to be preventing a fair hearing for all parties. On the other hand, their duty is to keep the trial to the planned timetable and to ensure that valuable court time is not wasted with irrelevant questioning or, heaven forbid, extreme verbosity from the advocates.

Defence Counsel will not usually make an opening speech.

Once the claimant's Counsel's opening submissions are complete, the first witness is called, usually the claimant.

All witnesses called to give evidence will take up their position in the witness box. If they are able, they stand to say the oath or affirmation. An oath to tell the truth, the whole truth and nothing but the truth (without *"so help me God"* which is not heard in our courts) will be given whilst holding the holy book relevant to the witness' faith. No less important is the alternative for those of no faith, or those who would prefer not to swear on a holy book: the affirmation: *"I sincerely and solemnly declare and affirm that I shall tell the truth, the whole truth and nothing but the truth."* Once that is over with the judge will usually ask the witness to sit down if they wish. They will have the ring-binders containing the trial documents with them in the witness box, and a glass of water in front of them ready to be knocked over as they nervously reach for one of those ring-binders.

The first stage of a witness' evidence is called "examination in chief". Counsel for the party that relies on and has called the witness asks them their name and address, identifies their witness statement within the trial bundle and asks them whether the contents of the statement are true. The witness may want to correct one or more errors in their statement(s) at this point. That might be the end of the examination in chief, but with permission of the judge, supplementary questions can be asked by way of clarification and amplification. A barrister must not "lead" a witness during examination in chief. A leading question is one that strongly suggests the answer. If the question is a formality ("are you a registered nurse?") or is about a matter that is not disputed, then it is unobjectionable to ask a leading question. If, on the other hand, the matter in hand is disputed or controversial, then the questioner must not lead the witness. You cannot ask: *"Had you been warned of the risk of paralysis you would not have elected to undergo the spinal surgery, would you?"* You may ask: *"Had you been warned of the risk of paralysis, what would you have decided to do?"*

The second, and usually longest, stage of a witness' evidence is "cross-examination". This is when the barrister for the other party asks questions of the witness. These questions may be leading. Indeed, it is a good technique to suggest the answers to the witness: *"You very much wanted to have this spinal surgery to cure your pain didn't you? You would have elected to go ahead with it even if warned of the very small risk of paralysis. Isn't that right?"*

Witnesses worry greatly about being cross-examined. We have all seen courtroom dramas on the screen, or read about them in books. I am pleased to say that I have never had to give evidence in court, but the advice I give to clients and to witnesses is to take your time, answer each question as it comes rather than second-guessing where the questioning is leading, speak up, do not speak too fast, do not be afraid to say if you really cannot remember something, never be argumentative with the other party's barrister, and, most importantly, always tell the truth. As in life generally, giving evidence in court gets very complicated if you start telling lies.

In fact, very few witnesses, I believe, come to court to tell bare-faced lies. Nor have I ever encountered that very rare moment when a witness metaphorically holds up their hands and admits that their whole case has been built on a tissue of lies. More commonly some witnesses find themselves in difficulty by what my old pupil supervisor used to call "gilding the lilly". They embellish slightly, adding some new detail for emphasis. An experienced cross-examiner will focus on that slight exaggeration, contrast it with what the witness has said or written previously and, before they realise what has hit them, their credibility will be lying helplessly in tatters on the floor.

A cross-examiner must not intimidate or bully a witness. The judge should intervene if they believe that is happening. In any event, judges are, contrary to popular opinion, human beings. They know that many witnesses will be anxious, some will be forgetful, others inarticulate. They take all of these sorts of matters into consideration. A hectoring barrister cross-examining a timid witness will rarely impress the trial judge. A concession given in response to a line of courteous, probing questions carries much more weight with a judge than an exasperated admission from a witness who has faced increasingly hostile questioning from a booming-voiced QC.

Good advice to a young advocate is to decide in advance of cross-examining a witness: (i) which parts of their evidence are acceptable to you? Do not ask questions about those matters unless you are very, very sure that you can extract even more favourable evidence by probing further; and (ii) which parts of their evidence do you want to challenge? When challenging a witness about their evidence, decide whether you think their evidence is deliberately or inadvertently misleading. Far more often it will be the latter rather than the former. The approach you take to cross-examination will be very different depending on whether you are seeking to expose a witness as dishonest, or trying to suggest that they may be mistaken. It is said to be a golden rule of advocacy never to ask a question to which you do not know what the witness will answer. I confess that I do that all the time! How can you be sure what a witness you have never spoken to before will say? However, I would rarely ask questions out of curiosity – you have to have a plan that you hope will lead to answers being given that will help your case or damage the other party's case.

One duty that the cross-examiner has is to put their case to the witness. The rule is that an advocate cannot make a closing submission that, for example, a witness has misled the court about the time when they noted the patient's blood pressure, if they have not put that to the witness, thereby giving them an opportunity to deny it or otherwise to respond. This "rule" can lead to some pedestrian cross-examination along the lines of: *"I put it to you, Mr Briggs, that...."*.

Once the witness has survived cross-examination, the third stage of their evidence is "re-examination" when the first Counsel has a second opportunity to ask them questions. Having been very restricted in what they can ask "in chief", the barrister does not get much more leeway in re-examination. They can only ask questions about matters that were raised in cross-examination and, again, they must not lead the witness. For advocates there is always a risk involved in re-opening questions that the witness feels they have already dealt with. Relaxing after their cross-examination they might let slip some nugget that will help the other side. When asked whether they have any re-examination questions, a confident reply: *"No questions in re-examination, my Lady"* will, the advocate hopes, convey the impression that the witness' evidence has gone as well as expected and that there is no damage to be repaired.

The witness' function is not necessarily finished after questioning by the advocates. The next thing that will be asked is: *"Does you Ladyship have any questions?"* Many judges will ask questions during the main body of the witness' oral evidence. Whether they do or not, they will be invited to ask questions to follow the advocates' examinations. I have noticed over many years at the Bar that witnesses often lower their guard when answering questions from the judge. As such, a simple question from the judge can elicit crucial evidence that the advocates have failed to unearth. If the witness says something of importance to the judge at this stage, the judge will usually ask the advocates if they have any follow-up questions.

And then the ordeal is over for the witness. If the questioning of a witness is incomplete by the time the lunchbreak ("the short adjournment") comes, or by the end of a day, then they are given a warning by the judge that they must not talk to anyone else about their evidence. Indeed, witnesses will often sit alone in the court café (if there is one) forlornly eating a sandwich whilst everyone else associated with their side of the case shares a table at the other end of the room. But once their evidence is completed, they can say what they like about what they went through, and to anyone they like. It is very rare for a witness to be called back after they have completed their evidence. If they are called back they will be reminded that they remain "on oath" or "under affirmation". If the claimant completes their evidence they will usually want to stay in the court room to watch the rest of the trial. Other witnesses may be given permission to leave the court room and the court building. They are "released" by the judge.

The process of giving evidence is effectively the same for the expert witnesses, except that they will confirm that the opinions they have given in their reports are their true opinions, rather than referring to "statements". Cross-examining experts is not an easy task. Quite obviously they know a lot more about the subject at hand than the lawyer questioning them. Each expert ought to have been asked to provide a CV setting out their qualifications and experience that allow them to offer expert opinion in the particular case. Sometimes it is necessary to explore an expert's knowledge. The most famous ever question to an expert in court was put by Sir Norman Birkett QC during a criminal trial, to an expert engineer:

> *Q: What is the coefficient of the expansion of brass?*

The exchange continued:

> *A: I beg your pardon?*

> *Q: Did you not catch the question?*

> *A: I did not quite hear you.*

> *Q: What is the coefficient of expansion of brass?*

> *A: I am afraid I cannot answer that question off-hand.*

The exchange went on, and the jury's confidence in the expert was undermined because he could not give a straight answer to the question. This was an advocate's trick. But in clinical negligence cases it is often necessary to check the experience of the expert at trial. It is surprising, but some-times an expert offering an opinion on a certain procedure turns out not to have performed one, or that they have relied on an out of date edition of a textbook when writing their report. These sorts of deficiencies should have been rooted out by the time the case has come to trial, but sometimes they are not.

Remembering that in relation to the issue of breach of duty the *Bolam* test is most often applied, the experts are not being asked simply to tell the court what they would have done in the situation faced by the defendant's health-care professionals, but rather what a reasonable body of practitioners would have considered acceptable, the judge has a difficult task when faced with conflicting opinion on that very point. A very helpful summary of the ap-proach that judges ought to consider in such cases was given by Mr Justice Green, as he then was (currently he is a judge in the Court of Appeal and therefore Lord Justice Green), in *C v North Cumbria University Hospitals NHS Trust* [2014] EWHC 61 (QB). I quote it in full because it so nicely describes the judicial function in many clinical negligence cases that turn on disputed expert opinion on breach of duty:

> *"i) Where a body of appropriate expert opinion considers that an act or omission alleged to be negligent is reasonable a Court will attach substantial weight to that opinion.*
>
> *ii) This is so even if there is another body of appropriate opinion which condemns the same act or omission as negligent.*
>
> *iii) The Court in making this assessment must not however delegate the task of deciding the issue to the expert. It is ultimately an issue that the Court, taking account of that expert evidence, must decide for itself.*
>
> *iv) In making an assessment of whether to accept an expert's opinion the Court should take account of a variety of factors including (but not limited to): whether the evidence is tendered in good faith; wheth-er the expert is "responsible", "competent" and/or "respectable"; and whether the opinion is reasonable and logical.*
>
> *v) Good faith: A sine qua non for treating an expert's opinion as valid and relevant is that it is tendered in good faith. However, the mere fact that one or more expert opinions are tendered in good faith is not per se sufficient for a conclusion that a defendant's conduct, endorsed by expert opinion tendered in good faith, necessarily accords with sound*

medical practice.

vi) Responsible/competent/respectable: In *Bolitho* Lord Brown Wilkinson cited each of these three adjectives as relevant to the exercise of assessment of an expert opinion. The judge appeared to treat these as relevant to whether the opinion was *"logical"*. It seems to me that whilst they may be relevant to whether an opinion is *"logical"* they may not be determinative of that issue. A highly responsible and competent expert of the highest degree of respectability may, nonetheless, proffer a conclusion that a Court does not accept, ultimately, as *"logical"*. Nonetheless these are material considerations. In the course of my discussions with Counsel, both of whom are hugely experienced in matters of clinical negligence, I queried the sorts of matters that might fall within these headings. The following are illustrations which arose from that discussion. *"Competence"* is a matter which flows from qualifications and experience. In the context of allegations of clinical negligence in an NHS setting particular weight may be accorded to an expert with a lengthy experience in the NHS. Such a person expressing an opinion about normal clinical conditions will be doing so with first hand knowledge of the environment that medical professionals work under within the NHS and with a broad range of experience of the issue in dispute. This does not mean to say that an expert with a lesser level of NHS experience necessarily lacks the same degree of competence; but I do accept that lengthy experience within the NHS is a matter of significance. By the same token an expert who retired 10 years ago and whose retirement is spent expressing expert opinions may turn out to be far removed from the fray and much more likely to form an opinion divorced from current practical reality. *"Respectability"* is also a matter to be taken into account. Its absence might be a rare occurrence, but many judges and litigators have come across so called experts who can *"talk the talk"* but who veer towards the eccentric or unacceptable end of the spectrum. Regrettably there are, in many fields of law, individuals who profess expertise but who, on true analysis, must be categorised as *"fringe"*. A *"responsible"* expert is one who does not adapt an extreme position, who will make the necessary concessions and who adheres to the spirit as well as the words of his professional declaration (see CPR35 and the PD and Protocol).

vii) Logic/reasonableness: By far and away the most important consideration is the logic of the expert opinion tendered. A Judge should not simply accept an expert opinion; it should be tested both against the other evidence tendered during the course of a trial, and, against *its internal consistency. For example, a judge will consider whether the expert opinion accords with the inferences properly to be drawn from the Clinical Notes or the CTG. A judge will ask whether the expert has addressed all the relevant considerations which applied at the time of the alleged negligent act or omission. If there are manufacturer's or clinical guidelines, a Court will consider whether the expert has addressed these and placed the defendant's conduct in their context. There are 2 other points which arise in this case which I would mention. First, a matter of some importance is whether the expert opinion reflects the evidence that has emerged in the course of the trial. Far too often in cases of all sorts experts prepare their evidence in advance of trial making a variety of evidential assumptions and then fail or omit to address themselves to the question of whether these assumptions, and the inferences and opinions drawn therefrom, remain current at the time they come to tender their evidence in the trial. An expert's report will lack logic if, at the point in which it is tendered, it is out of date and not reflective of the evidence in the case as it has unfolded. Secondly, a further issue arising in the present case emerges from the trenchant criticisms that Mr Spencer QC, for the Claimant, made of the Defendant's two experts due to the incomplete and sometimes inaccurate nature of the summaries of the relevant facts (and in particular the Clinical Notes) that were contained within their reports. It seems to me that it is good practice for experts to ensure that when they are reciting critical matters, such as Clinical Notes, they do so with precision. These notes represent short documents (in the present case two sides only) but form the basis for an important part of the analytical task of the Court. If an expert is giving a précis then that should be expressly stated in the body of the opinion and, ideally, the Notes should be annexed and accurately cross-referred to by the expert. If, however, the account from within the body of the expert opinion is intended to constitute the bedrock for the subsequent opinion then accuracy is a virtue. Having said this, the task of the Court is to see beyond stylistic blemishes and to concentrate upon the pith and substance of the expert opinion and to then evaluate its content against the evidence as a whole and thereby to assess its logic. If on analysis of the report as a whole the opinion conveyed is from a person of real experience, exhibiting competence and respectability, and it is consistent with the surrounding evidence, and of course internally logical, this is an opinion which a judge should attach considerable weight to."*

The usual form is for the trial judge to hear from experts in pairs – the claimants' midwifery expert followed by the defendant's midwifery expert, then the parties' obstetric experts etc. This gives the court the advantage of focusing on the issues covered by those two experts, rather than hearing their evidence several days apart. One recent fashion takes this even further. It is called "hot-tubbing". Cast out of your mind romantic thoughts of a cold, clear night in Scandinavia. Imagine instead two experts giving evidence at court simultaneously and being asked the same question in turn. This, so the theory goes, can lead to a more inquisitorial and less adversarial process, better designed to reach the truth, or at least some common ground.

Once the expert evidence is over with, then all the evidence has been heard and Counsel will make their closing submissions. These might be oral submissions only, or a combination of written and oral submissions. Defence Counsel goes first, leaving the last word to the claimant's barrister. This is their opportunity to persuade the judge that Mrs Walsh was more reliable than Mr Priestley, or that Dr Blowes had provided particularly telling evidence in relation to causation. As an advocate I have always tried to have in mind what my closing submissions will be, well before the first witness is called. Obviously the submissions given have to reflect the evidence as it was given, not as I would have wanted it to be, but it is more persuasive for the court to see that the fundamentals of a party's case have been stated in opening submissions, supported by the evidence during the trial, and then re-stated in closing submissions. I want to try to present a consistent, clearly articulated case, leading the judge on an easy path to giving judgment for my client. The way to that judgment must be made clear and all obstructions removed.

Submissions end and Mrs Justice Kewley informs those left in the courtroom that she will reserve judgment.

Styles of judgment differ from judge to judge but the format is usually as follows:

(i)   An introduction identifying the nature of the case, the parties and the issues to be determined.

(ii)   A statement of the relevant legal principles.

(iii) A review of the evidence given and the judge's findings on the evidence. The judge must decide "on the balance of probabilities" what happened.

(iv)   A review of the expert evidence, and a discussion of which expert evidence the judge prefers to rely on and why.

(v)   Conclusions about the issues to be determined incorporating and further consideration of the legal principles and the application of the facts to those principles.

(vi)   A final conclusion as to who has won and lost, and an expression of sympathy for the claimant if their claim has been defeated.

It is uncommon, whether the judge is giving an extempore judgment in court, or a reserved judgment in writing, to declare who has "won" the case at the beginning of the judgment. Some believe that leaving it to the end of a judgment to deliver the "verdict" is a tease, causing unnecessary further anxiety to already stressed litigants. In a written judgment handed out to the parties, this is not really a problem – anyone can turn the pages to the final paragraph and see what the ultimate result is. Or the party will have been told the result by their lawyer before they have an opportunity to read the full judgment. When judgments are delivered for the first time in court, in the presence of the parties, a good reason for not declaring the conclusion at the outset is that no-one will take in the rest of the judgment. It is rather like being given a significant diagnosis by a doctor: once you hear the bad news, the rest of what the doctor says is just "white noise". Whatever the preference, the usual format of judgments in clinical negligence cases is along the lines set out above.

Judges who "reserve" their judgments to be given in writing at a later date should provide their judgments within three months of the hearing. On occasion judges have been reprimanded for not doing so and, on even rarer occasions, trials have had to be re-heard because a judgment has been given so late that one or more of the parties justifiably have no confidence in the judge's ability to have remembered the evidence as it was given at trial. Thankfully 99.99% of judgments are given within time. The process adopted is for the judge to send a written draft of the judgment to the legal representatives for them to make suggested changes for obvious errors or typing mistakes. This is not an opportunity for them to put forward new arguments or to seek to persuade the judge to come to a different conclusion. The judgment remains strictly confidential at this stage and must not be shared with anyone else. Once the corrections have been submitted, the judge "perfects" the judgment and formally "hands it down". This can be done in court without anyone else present.

The parties then have to decide on any consequential orders. In our case of *Airey v Kingstown*, if judgment were given in favour of the claimant, then the order would be something like:

"1. Judgment for the First Claimant in the agreed sum of £3 million, the said sum to paid into the Court of Protection to the credit of the deputyship account of ....

2. The Defendant shall pay the Claimant's costs to be assessed on the standard basis if not agreed.

3. The Defendant shall pay the sum of £200,000 on account of the Claimant's costs by no later than 4 pm on [date]..."

If the defendant were to have won, the order would be to dismiss the claimant's claim. Any costs orders would depend on the funding arrangements, offers that had been made etc.

Usually, but not always, these consequential orders are agreed or determined by the judge without the need for a further hearing. However, the actual assessment of costs involves a whole new process not unlike the full litigation process described above and, in the absence of settlement, culminating in a trial of the issue of the appropriate award of costs for the case. It can take one to two years after the end of the clinical negligence litigation before costs are resolved.

The losing party can appeal a judgment after trial. CPR Part 52 deals with the rules of appeals. An appeal from the judgment of Mrs Justice Kewley would be to the Court of Appeal, Civil Division. The party first needs to obtain permission to appeal. This can be given by the trial judge herself, and if refused, by the Court of Appeal by a single judge of that court who will usually decide whether to grant permission on a review of the papers alone. If permission is refused on paper then the appellant could ask for an oral permission hearing. The test that the courts apply when deciding whether to grant permission to appeal is whether the court considers that the appeal would have a real prospect of success or there is some other compelling reason for the appeal to be heard. Nothing feels quite as hopeless as losing a case and then saying to the trial judge that they should grant permission to appeal because the appeal would have a real prospect of succeeding. Judges usually listen to such submissions with good grace and then refuse them. The losing party, now the "appellant" can then issue a notice to appeal in the Court of Appeal within 21 days.

If permission is granted then the Court of Appeal, sitting at the Royal Courts of Justice, The Strand, London, will hear from Counsel who will have served written grounds of appeal, a response, and skeleton arguments. The appeal hearing will usually last no more than one day, possibly two. It is not a re-hearing of the trial. No witnesses will be called and the parties cannot introduce new evidence except in very narrow circumstances and then only with the permission of the appellate court. Three judges of the Court of Appeal will determine the appeal. They only allow appeals where the trial judge has made a material error of law, or if there was some procedural or other irregularity that renders the trial unjust. Errors of law can encompass "perverse" findings on the evidence.

For litigants unlucky enough to lose in the Court of Appeal, there is one further avenue – appeal to the Supreme Court. This is the highest court in the land and it picks and chooses which cases it permits to be brought before it. Only cases of wider public importance will be heard. Very few clinical negligence cases reach this court. Anyone can visit the Supreme Court, which is situated on Parliament Square just opposite the Houses of Parliament. There are two courtrooms upstairs, and an interesting exhibition and nice café in the basement. You can even purchase Supreme Court merchandise. It is well worth a visit.

Of the thousands of clinical negligence cases brought each year, it is unlikely that more than one of them will end up in the Supreme Court. But, for that one case, the Supreme Court really does mark the end of the road.

Part 4: Particular Claims

In this Part I shall discuss eleven particular kinds of clinical negligence claim. I shall focus on some of the common features and problems that arise within each field of litigation. Whole books could be written on birth injuries, primary healthcare claims and the other areas of claim addressed in this Part. I cannot provide much depth of detail, but I hope the reader will be able at least to dip their toes in the water.

Chapter 1: Birth Injuries

Cerebral Palsy

Half of the cost of clinical negligence to the NHS is accounted for by birth injury claims. As in the hypothetical case of *Airey v Kingstown* in Part 3, babies who suffer from deprivation of oxygen in labour and around the time of their birth can suffer from cerebral palsy which, depending on its severity, can lead to a lifetime need for care and assistance.

Cerebral palsy is an umbrella term describing a group of permanent conditions that affect movement and co-ordination, and sometimes cognitive function, and are caused by an insult or injury to the brain occurring before, during or soon after birth.

In these cases, because the baby was injured when inside their mother, the experts and lawyers have to piece together different sources of evidence to work out what happened. The evidence will include MRI brain scans, blood samples, clinical evidence of the baby's condition at birth, traces made by cardiotocograph ("CTG") monitors, and examination of the young child to determine the nature of their disability.

Neuroradiological evidence from an MRI scan will demonstrate the distribution of damage to the infant brain. The pattern of damage will indicate whether it was likely to have been suffered at or around the time of birth, or perhaps whether it is due to a congenital malformation. If the latter, then it will not have been due to negligence. Two kinds of pattern often play a part in litigation: a so-called "watershed" pattern usually said to be consistent with a period of prolonged partial hypoxia ischaemia, and a basal ganglia–thalamus pattern (BGT) predominantly affecting bilaterally areas known as the central grey nuclei and perirolandic cortex. This pattern is thought to be associated with an acute period of profound hypoxic ischaemia.

Hypoxic ischaemia occurs when the baby's brain tissue is deprived of oxygen. Hypoxia at or around the time of birth (perinatal) can lead to a number of serious medical conditions, such as Hypoxic Ischaemic Encephalopathy (HIE) and brain injuries related to birth asphyxia. Partial hypoxic ischaemia describes a situation where there is some brain oxygenation, but the supply of oxygen is reduced. Profound hypoxic ischaemia occurs when there is a cessation of oxygenation – it is cut off completely or almost completely. Whilst prolonged partial hypoxic ischaemia can occur over a period of hours, acute profound hypoxic ischaemia is likely to cause death in a baby if it lasts for more than about 25 to 30 minutes. Animal studies indicate that a baby can survive a period of up to ten minutes of acute profound hypoxic ischaemia and then recover intact. Therefore, most children who suffer cerebral palsy due to acute profound hypoxic ischaemia at the time of their birth, and who survived, underwent a period of between ten and 25 to 30 minutes of severe deprivation of oxygenation to the brain.

The neuroradiological evidence is therefore crucial in some cases in identifying a pattern of brain damage typical for a baby who has survived a period of up to 25 to 30 minutes of acute profound hypoxic ischaemia at or around the time of their birth. Alternatively, it might show a pattern typical for a longer period of partial hypoxic ischaemia.

A paediatric neurologist giving expert evidence in a birth injury case involving cerebral palsy will examine the child and describe and categorise the nature of their disabilities. Difficulties encountered by children with cerebral palsy may include:

–   Deficits in gross motor function such as walking and mobilising, standing, sitting, gripping and handling etc. In severe cases the child will not be able to lift their heads when lying in a prone position, or to roll over. They may not be able to sit without support, let alone to walk and run.

–   Reduced fine motor skills required to use a pen or pencil, to operate a keyboard or switches, to pick up and use a knife and fork.

–   Problems with speech and with swallowing.

–   Learning difficulties.

–   Behavioural difficulties.

–   Hypersensitivity to noise.

–   Impairment of sight and/or of hearing.

–   Problems with toileting.

The impairment of movement and mobility typically takes one of three forms:

Spastic cerebral palsy: the child has very tight tone in their arms or legs, making movement difficulty. They may have stiff and jerky movements and, with age, their muscles may contract. This is the most common form of cerebral palsy affecting about three-quarters to four-fifths of individuals with cerebral palsy. A child with quadriplegic spastic cerebral palsy will suffer it in all four limbs. Hemiplegia means that the arm and leg on one side of the body is affected. Diplegia is when both legs are affected but the arms are either unaffected or only mildly affected.

Athetoid (or "dyskinetic") cerebral palsy: this is characterised by uncontrolled limb movements caused by muscle tone which varies from tight to very loose. This may produce twitching or writhing movements which the child cannot control.

Ataxic cerebral palsy: this is usually a milder form of cerebral palsy where the child has difficulty with balance, spatial awareness and experiences unsteady movements.

Paediatric neurologists will be able to identify the kind of cerebral palsy that the child has. They will be able to assess the degree of "bulbar involvement" which affects speech and swallowing, and other deficits such as learning difficulties and bladder and bowel function, impairment of senses etc. They can usually then advise as to how the child's presentation fits with the neuroradiology and other evidence to suggest a likely causal mechanism. Certain kinds of presentation will be associated with an acute period of profound hypoxic ischaemia, others with prolonged partial hypoxic ischaemia.

When a baby is born the midwifery or medical staff will usually ascribe to it an Apgar score from 1 to 10, at one minute, five minutes and ten minutes of life. This is a rough assessment of the clinical condition of the newborn child, and is named after its originator Virginia Apgar, an anaesthetist working in New York who developed the system in the 1950's to assess the effect of anaesthesia on babies. I have seen it claimed that Apgar actually stands for Appearance, Pulse, Grimace, Activity, and Respiration. Not sure about "grimace"! Clinicians assess heart rate, respiratory effort, muscle tone, response to stimulation, and skin colour and give a mark from 0 to 2 for each. A healthy baby will score 8 to 10 out of 10. The lower the score, the worse the clinical condition of the baby. Alongside the Apgar score, other neonatal/paediatric records will show whether the baby required resuscitation and how that was managed, if they suffered seizures in the hours after birth, whether they had cooling (a modern neonatal "treatment" that can mitigate the effects of brain injury), and whether there was an impact on other organs. All of this evidence will be relevant to the determination of whether the child's cerebral palsy was likely to be due to a profound insult at or about the time of birth.

If there is reason to believe that a new-born baby has suffered deprivation of oxygen then samples of blood should be taken from the umbilical cord for analysis for "blood gases". Both venous and arterial cord blood samples should be taken. Oxygen and nutrients cross the placental membrane from maternal arterial blood and reach the fetus via a single large umbilical vein. The fetus extracts oxygen and nutrients from the blood and then returns blood to the placenta via two umbilical arteries. When an unborn baby suffers from deprivation of oxygen they may produce excessive lactic acid: "metabolic acidosis" occurs and is demonstrated by the blood sample results. If the arterial cord blood samples show metabolic acidosis (pH < 7.0 and base excess < −12.0 mmol/L) then this indicates hypoxia at or around the time of birth. In the case for which I gave an example of a Particulars of Claim, the acidosis was more severe, with a base excess of more than −20, indicating a severe case of acidosis. The extent of the acidosis may give the experts clues as to the severity and duration of a period of hypoxic ischaemia.

Other findings that may be included in the medical records, and that may give clues as to the how and why the baby has been born in a poor condition and gone on to suffer from cerebral palsy, may be found in an operation note for a Caesarean section or the obstetric or midwifery notes following vaginal delivery. It may be that the cord was found to be around the baby's neck, or to be knotted, or the placenta is found to have come away from the uterus ("abruption") or that the uterus was itself damaged. Sometimes defects or abnormalities with the placenta are noted either by the clinicians or on a histopathological examination. This might reveal evidence of infection affecting the placenta which had affected the amniotic fluid ("chorioamnionitis"). Such findings might well explain why the oxygen supply to the fetal brain was disrupted.

If labour has progressed in a hospital setting then it is likely that the midwives and obstetricians will have monitored the baby electronically using CTG. This device "listens" to the fetal heart rate and records the uterine contractions. It produces a trace on paper which looks rather like a graph. The trace follows the fetal heart rate over time. It is part of the training of midwives and obstetricians to interpret a CTG trace. The traces produced are helpful in litigation not only in determining whether earlier or different action should have been taken by those managing the labour, but also as to what was happening to the fetus during the minutes and hours before delivery. There are four features of the trace that clinicians should look for: the fetal heart rate, the variability of the heart rate, and decelerations and accelerations in the rate. Abnormalities in these features may lead to the concern that the CTG trace is suspicious of fetal distress, or that it is "pathological".

The following table is from *"Intrapartum care: NICE guideline CG190 (February 2017)"* © National Institute for Health and Care Excellence 2017.

Description	Feature		
	Baseline (beats/min	**Baseline variability (beats/ minute)**	**Decelerations**
Reassuring	110 to 160	5 to 25	None or early Variable decelerations with no concerning characteristics* for less than 90 minutes
Non-reassuring	100 to 109† OR 161 to 180	Less than 5 for 30 to 50 minutes OR More than 25 for 15 to 25 minutes	Variable decelerations with no concerning characteristics* for 90 minutes or more OR Variable decelerations with any concerning characteristics* in up to 50% of contractions for 30 minutes or more OR Variable decelerations with any concerning characteristics* in over 50% of contractions for less than 30 minutes OR Late decelerations in over 50% of contractions for less than 30 minutes, with no maternal or fetal clinical risk factors such as vaginal bleeding or significant meconium

Abnormal	Below 100 OR Above 180	Less than 5 for more than 50 minutes OR More than 25 for more than 25 minutes OR Sinusoidal	Variable decelerations with any concerning characteristics* in over 50% of contractions for 30 minutes (or less if any maternal or fetal clinical risk factors [see above]) OR Late decelerations for 30 minutes (or less if any maternal or fetal clinical risk factors) OR Acute bradycardia, or a single prolonged deceleration lasting 3 minutes or more

Abbreviation: CTG, cardiotocography.
* Regard the following as concerning characteristics of variable decelerations: lasting more than 60 seconds; reduced baseline variability within the deceleration; failure to return to baseline; biphasic (W) shape; no shouldering.
† Although a baseline fetal heart rate between 100 and 109 beats/ minute is a non-reassuring feature, continue usual care if there is normal baseline variability and no variable or late decelerations.

As well as monitoring the CTG trace, the midwives and/or obstetricians will be assessing the progress of labour with vaginal examinations, palpation of the mother's abdomen etc. During the first stage of labour the cervix dilates. Once it is fully dilated then the second stage of labour begins. The first stage can take many hours or be rapid. The second stage usually takes less than two hours. As labour progresses the baby descends and the midwives and obstetricians can feel how far it has descended by reference to a pair of bony prominences in the mother's pelvis known as the ischial spines, which acts as a marker post. The level of concerns raised by the trace together with knowledge of the progress of labour will mandate certain decisions: for example, for a midwife to alert an obstetrician, to review the trace in 15 minutes or half an hour, or to proceed immediately to an urgent Caesarean section. An operative delivery (Caesarean section) might take longer than assisted vaginal delivery using forceps or ventouse (a vacuum device attached to the baby's head) if labour is advanced. On the other hand if the cervix is only 3 cms dilated, the baby has not descended very far, but the CTG trace indicates that it is in significant distress and may be hypoxic, then it is more likely that a decision will be taken to transfer the mother to theatre for a Caesarean section. It is generally accepted that it ought to take no more than half an hour from the decision to proceed to an emergency (sometimes known as a Category 1) Caesarean section, to the delivery of the baby in theatre.

The CTG trace, records from the labour and of the delivery, neonatal observations, histopathology, blood gas results, paediatric neurological assessment and neuroradiological findings will all combine to suggest a mechanism whereby the baby suffered neurological injury and cerebral palsy. Of course, in some cases there are robust disputes about the correct interpretation of the evidence.

In these cases, timing is everything. Some claims depend on whether it was a breach of duty to have failed to decide to proceed to an emergency Caesarean section only five minutes before the actual decision to do so was taken. Those five minutes can make the difference between a baby who suffered ten minutes of acute profound hypoxia ischaemia and made a full recovery, and one who suffered for 15 minutes and has a lifelong disability.

Where there is a breach of duty that has caused the period of damaging hypoxic ischaemia to be longer than it should have been, but the baby would even so have suffered cerebral palsy without that negligent delay, then a difficult task falls on the experts to advise as to whether the outcome would have been materially better for the child in the absence of the negligence.

I have talked about children with cerebral palsy in this chapter, but claims can brought within three years of a person's 18th birthday, and at any time if the claimant has always lacked the mental capacity to litigate. So, some cerebral palsy claims are brought by adults. This means that some midwives and obstetricians may be asked to account for their actions many years after the events in question.

Whenever the claim is brought, the parties have to deal with what are permanent and usually very serious injuries or disabilities. Cerebral palsy covers a wide range of disability, but in most cases the parties will need to obtain expert evidence as to the claimant's lifelong care needs and requirements for equipment. In more severe cases they will also instruct experts in physiotherapy, speech and language therapy, accommodation and assistive technology (the use of eye-gaze technology, large switch operated games and computers, environmental controls etc.) Equipment needed might extend to powered wheelchairs, ceiling mounted hoists, sleep systems and cars that can accommodate a wheelchair and equipment.

Periodical payment orders are more common in serious cerebral palsy claims than in most other kinds of clinical negligence case. The claimant may need to be assured that they can afford a certain level of nursing or other care for the rest of their lives. They cannot guarantee state provision at a level they need, they cannot risk running out of money from a single lump sum payment, and they want to be "inflation proof". Sometimes the claimant's life expectancy may be uncertain (none of us know how long we are going to live, but experts might differ significantly in their opinions as to a claimant's life expectancy in a cerebral palsy case). If the care costs are, say, £200,000 per annum and there is a five year difference between the parties' experts' views of likely life expectancy, then that could make a difference of £1 million to a lump sum payment of damages. If the future costs of care are paid by way of annual periodical payments of £200,000 for as long as the claimant lives, then the risk of over-payment or under-payment is removed.

It is not just the individual child who is affected by their cerebral palsy – there is also a huge impact on their family. Sometimes the strain on the family is so great that relationships break down. For all parents of children with cerebral palsy, whether caused by clinical negligence or not, their lives change forever. The same is true for the child's siblings too. However, the law operates to compensate the child, not their parents, brothers, sisters or grandparents. If a parent puts their career on hold to look after a child with severe disabilities, then the court does not compensate that parent. The courts do, however, seek to assess the appropriate level of compensation for the care given by family members to the claimant. One measure of that level of care might be by reference to a parent's lost earnings but more usually compensation for family care is assessed by reference to the number of hours of additional care given, and the application of a notional hourly rate. There is no compensation to the family for the anxiety and distress caused to them by reason of having a severely disabled child.

In substantial claims the "care regime" to be funded by the compensation is usually based on a model of care within a family setting – or at least in a private home – rather than in an institution or publicly funded residence. This means that the home has to be fully equipped and adapted for an individual who may spend most of their day in a wheelchair and be unable to transfer from the chair to a toilet, bed, car or shower without the help of two carers and/or a mechanical hoist. They might need help with all toileting, feeding (whether via their mouth or a tube), dressing and undressing and daily activities. They might need a carer to be present in the house at night, or sometimes to be awake close by in case they need immediate help. I have heard one judge describe the arrangements as being akin to building and operating a small private hospital. Such claims can therefore cost the NHS £5 million or more. In the highest cases, and where the claimant lives into old age, the total cost can exceed £20 million.

Shoulder Dystocia

The well-known consent case of *Montgomery v Lanarkshire* concerned shoulder dystocia and the lost opportunity to avoid the risk of it occurring, but most claims arising out of this obstetric emergency relate to the management of it once it arises. Shoulder dystocia occurs during delivery when the baby's shoulder becomes stuck behind the mother's pubic bone. It is an obstetric emergency requiring calm but purposeful management. It occurs in about 1 in 150 vaginal births. Risk factors for it include maternal diabetes, maternal obesity, induction of labour and previous pregnancies complicated by shoulder dystocia.

It is not preventable but if the risk of shoulder dystocia is thought to be sufficiently high the mother may be offered, and may elect to have, a Caesarean section rather than attempt vaginal delivery.

Once encountered, after the head has been delivered, there are various recommended steps that the obstetrician or midwife managing the delivery should take. They include asking the mother to stop pushing and re-positioning the mother on her back with her legs pushed outwards and up towards her chest (this is known as the McRoberts manoeuvre). The legs are held in that position by the assisting midwives whilst a third midwife tries to delivery the baby. Supra-pubic pressure is applied by pressing with hands on the mother's abdomen just over the pubic bone. This will normally then release the stuck shoulder and the shoulders will be delivered. Some obstetricians and midwives will consider making a cut to enlarge the vaginal opening (an episiotomy). If these steps do not release the shoulder, then there are other techniques that can be deployed including reaching into the vagina manually to try to release the shoulder.

The mistake that can be made when shoulder dystocia is encountered is for the midwife or obstetrician to pull too hard or too long on the baby's head to try to deliver it. This excessive traction can stretch the network of nerves in the baby's neck causing what is known as obstetric brachial plexus injury. If this damage is severe and permanent it can cause significant disability in the affected arm.

The Royal College of Obstetricians and Gynaecologists produced a fact sheet in 2013 advising that:

> *"About one in ten (10%) babies who have shoulder dystocia will have some stretching of the nerves in the neck, called brachial plexus injury (BPI), which may cause loss of movement to the arm. The most common type of BPI is called Erb's palsy. It is usually temporary and movement will return within hours or days. Permanent damage is rare. It is important to remember that BPI can occur without shoulder dystocia. BPI can also occur in babies born by caesarean section. Sometimes shoulder dystocia can cause other injuries including fractures of the baby's arm or shoulder. In the majority of cases, these heal extremely well. Even with the best care, in a very few cases, a baby can suffer brain damage if he or she did not get enough oxygen because the delivery was delayed by shoulder dystocia."*

In the more severe cases people with Erb's palsy have an arm with very little useful function.

There have been a relatively large number of clinical negligence claims by or on behalf of children born with Erb's palsy following shoulder dystocia during delivery. Naturally it is not common to find a midwifery note recording that the baby's head was subjected to a good long pull when its shoulder became stuck. So, claimants have to persuade the court using other evidence that the injury was caused by excessive traction. You will have noted that the Royal College advised that brachial plexus injury can occur even with Caesarean section births. That suggests that it can occur without excessive traction being applied, if we can be sure that at an operative delivery excessive force cannot be applied to the nerves in the baby's neck (which some would dispute). There is a theory that during a vaginal delivery, the natural forces of maternal propulsion pushing the baby out can, when the baby's shoulder becomes stuck, cause brachial plexus injury. It is important, in this context, to differentiate between the anterior shoulder and the posterior shoulder. The "maternal propulsion" theory applies to damage to the "posterior shoulder", that is the shoulder facing the mother's rectum. Cases such as *Rashid v Essex Rivers Healthcare NHS Trust* [2004] EWHC 1338 (QB) and *Sardar v NHS Commissioning Board* [2014] EWHC 38 (QB) demonstrate the importance of this finding of fact. Thanks to the considerable work of Professor Tim Draycott from Bristol, the current thinking is that if the anterior shoulder is injured after shoulder dystocia, and if the injury is sufficiently severe to cause permanent disability, then it is very likely that the injury could have been avoided with the exercise of reasonable care when managing the shoulder dystocia. Such permanent injuries seem to be capable of being eradicated when proper training is given to those managing deliveries.

Chapter 2: Wrongful Birth

This is an unfortunate label given to clinical negligence claims where the outcome that was within the scope of duty of the defendant to prevent was the birth of a child, or of a child with a particular condition or disability. This might come about due to a negligently performed sterilisation or vasectomy, negligent advice or information, or a failure to identify and inform an expectant mother of a fetal abnormality. Some of these might more accurately be called "wrongful conception" cases – it was the act of conception that was meant never to happen. In others the conception was not attributable to negligence (at least not that of a treating clinician) but the fact that the pregnancy resulted in a live birth was caused by negligent clinical management.

Discussion of these kinds of claim may upset some readers, but the assumption behind the claims is not that the child who is born is unloved, but rather that the choice of the parent not to have that child has been taken away by someone else's negligence. Some might find the whole notion of wrongful birth claims to be repugnant, others that such claims are merely an example of the courts upholding an individual's right to autonomy over their bodies and their rights to a private and family life free from the unwarranted interference of others.

In common with other clinical negligence claims, claimants in wrongful birth cases have to prove the existence of a duty of care, breach and causation, but there are some unique and striking features of wrongful birth claims that require particular attention.

The first unusual feature of wrongful birth claims is that they are not claims for personal injury. Whilst the mother might well have a claim for her injuries, as explained below, the claim for the wrongful birth of a child is itself a claim for "economic loss". The child does not bring the claim. The parent who has the additional costs of bringing up and looking after the child is the claimant. If a child with spina bifida is born to a mother who would have terminated the pregnancy in the second trimester had she known of the condition whilst the baby was in utero, then if the reason she did not know of the condition was that a sonographer missed an obvious abnormality on an antenatal scan, there is no claim on behalf of the child for their lifelong disability. Instead there is a claim for the mother for having to give additional care and support to that child because of the child's disability.

The second unusual feature of wrongful birth claims is that the courts have refused to countenance awarding more than a nominal and fixed level of damages where the "wrongful birth" is of a healthy child. Three landmark judgments decided only a few years apart laid down the principles to be applied.

In *McFarlane v Tayside Health Board (Scotland)* [1999] UKHL 50, the House of Lords considered the case of a healthy child born to parents after negligent advice had been given about the effectiveness of a vasectomy. In *Parkinson v St James and Seacroft University Hospital NHS Trust* [2001] EWCA Civ 530, a mother who had undergone a negligently performed sterilisation gave birth to a child with severe disabilities. In *Rees v Darlington Memorial Hospital NHS Trust* [2003] UKHL 52, a mother with a severe and progressive visual impairment chose to have a sterilisation. It was performed negligently and she gave birth to a healthy child.

As analysed by Lord Bingham in *Rees v Darlington*, the House of Lords in *McFarlane* had three options:

> *"(1) That full damages against the tortfeasor for the cost of rearing the child may be allowed, subject to the ordinary limitations of reasonable foreseeability and remoteness, with no discount for joys, benefits and support, leaving restrictions upon such recovery to such limitations as may be enacted by a Parliament with authority to do so.*
>
> *(2) That damages may be recovered in full for the reasonable costs of rearing an unplanned child to the age when that child might be expected to be economically self-reliant, whether the child is "healthy" or "disabled" or "impaired" but with a deduction from the amount of such damages for the joy and benefits received, and the potential economic support derived, from the child.*
>
> *(3) That no damages may be recovered where the child is born healthy and without disability or impairment."*

Application of conventional principles would probably have supported the first option, but the House of Lords in *McFarlane* chose the third. It is fair to say that the five judges in the House of Lords reached that conclusion by different routes but, as Lord Bingham later observed, all relied on considerations of legal policy. What troubled these very senior judges was the idea that the birth of a healthy child could be considered to be a liability or burden. Lord Millett put it this way:

> *"In my opinion the law must take the birth of a normal, healthy baby to be a blessing, not a detriment. In truth it is a mixed blessing.*

It brings joy and sorrow, blessing and responsibility. The advantages and the disadvantages are inseparable. Individuals may choose to regard the balance as unfavourable and take steps to forgo the pleasures as well as the responsibilities of parenthood. They are entitled to decide for themselves where their own interests lie. But society itself must regard the balance as beneficial. It would be repugnant to its own sense of values to do otherwise. It is morally offensive to regard a normal, healthy baby as more trouble and expense than it is worth."

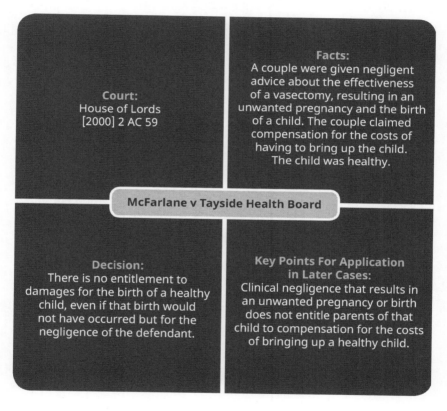

Court:
House of Lords
[2000] 2 AC 59

Facts:
A couple were given negligent advice about the effectiveness of a vasectomy, resulting in an unwanted pregnancy and the birth of a child. The couple claimed compensation for the costs of having to bring up the child. The child was healthy.

McFarlane v Tayside Health Board

Decision:
There is no entitlement to damages for the birth of a healthy child, even if that birth would not have occurred but for the negligence of the defendant.

Key Points For Application in Later Cases:
Clinical negligence that results in an unwanted pregnancy or birth does not entitle parents of that child to compensation for the costs of bringing up a healthy child.

Casenote 8

As some have put it, there is a "deemed equilibrium" in bringing into the world a healthy child. There are financial consequences but there may ultimately be financial advantages. There may be unquantifiable benefits as well as hardships. The only fair approach is to assume that these costs and benefits will even out. The birth of a healthy child is not something that should be the subject of an award of compensation.

This approach was tested in more difficult circumstances in *Rees v Darlington*. Here the mother's own disability meant that having a child, which was precisely what she wished to avoid when she chose to have a sterilisation procedure, might more readily be regarded as a burden. However, the House of Lords maintained the policy adopted in *McFarlane* and determined that no compensation should be paid for the birth of a healthy child, even though the mother was disabled. Nevertheless, the court chose to introduce a "conventional sum" of £15,000, payable whether or not the child is disabled. As Lord Millett put it in *Rees*, this is:

> "*a modest conventional sum by way of general damages, not for the birth of the child, but for the denial of an important aspect of their personal autonomy, viz the right to limit the size of their family. This is an important aspect of human dignity, which is increasingly being regarded as an important human right which should be protected by law. The loss of this right is not an abstract or theoretical one.*"

This conventional sum has not changed since the *Rees* decision in 2003. Arguably it should be increased to reflect inflation.

In *Parkinson v St James and Seacroft*, the child was born with a severe disability. In that case the court was bound by the *McFarlane* decision but found that the circumstances were sufficiently different, when the child is born with significant disability, that a different solution should be found. It allowed compensation not for the birth of the child itself, nor for the "ordinary" costs associated with bringing up that child, but for the additional costs caused by the child's disability.

In all such claims there is also a potential claim by the mother for the injury caused to her by having to carry the child through pregnancy and to give birth. If the pregnancy, labour or birth cause further injury such as a perineal tear or deep vein thrombosis, then those are injuries for which claims can be made according to orthodox principles. Compensation would encompass general damages for the injuries and any consequential loss and expense.

I conducted a wrongful birth case where a disabled mother gave birth to a disabled child. This was a combination not previously considered by the courts. It gave rise to questions about what additional costs the mother had incurred, and would incur, as a result of the child's disabilities, given that she herself was disabled. What assistance would she have needed had the child not been disabled, and was it necessary to offset the cost of that assistance against the costs she would now incur given that her child was disabled? The court approved a settlement of the claim (approval being required because the claimant mother lacked capacity to litigate) and so these and other issues were not tested in court.

In Part 2 I mentioned a recent wrongful birth case, *Khan v MNX* [2018] EWCA Civ 2609, in which the Court of Appeal held that a doctor who negligently misinformed a woman that she was not a carrier of haemophilia, was liable only for the additional costs attributable to the subsequent child having haemophilia, not those due to his also having autism. The claimant had asked whether she was a carrier of haemophilia. The doctor arranged for the wrong test and so wrongly advised her that she was not a carrier. The woman went on to become pregnant and gave birth to a child who did have haemophilia, but also had severe autism. The Court of Appeal held that the defendant doctor was liable only for the costs associated with the haemophilia because it had not been within the scope of duty of the doctor to advise about the wider risks of pregnancy or congenital disabilities or other potential conditions that might affect a baby, such as autism. Liability did not extend to all disabilities affecting the child even though arguably the child would not have been born but for the negligence of the doctor.

In relation to compensation for the "wrongful birth" of a disabled child, the court has to determine what the additional costs will be, beyond those that would have been incurred had the child been born without the disability. This raises the question of the period of time in the future which should be covered by the claim. Defendants have argued that such claims should only last for the period of childhood, up to the child's age 18. But if a child has a significant disability that will mean that they continue to be dependent on parental care beyond 18, perhaps even for life, then the courts have favoured compensation awards for that longer period.

Another issue that has been raised is who is entitled to make the claim for compensation for wrongful birth. Most obviously the mother can claim, but if the father is also likely to incur additional costs due to the child's disability, then the father will seek compensation too. Suppose that the parents live apart but the child spends equal time with each of them? Each house might need adaptations and equipment. In some cases the father might be the only parent who will have to meet the additional costs. Indeed if the father is not included, and the mother dies during the litigation, then there might be problems in continuing the claim – particularly if the father would be "out of time" for starting a claim himself.

What has sometimes troubled me about wrongful birth claims is that the child is effectively removed from the centre of the case. In claims where the child's injuries are compensated there are significant protections to ensure that compensation is used in their best interests. The settlement of a child's claim is subject to the court's approval. It has to be authorised by a judge who has read the evidence and advice from Counsel. Usually the money is paid into an account on trust for the child or it is managed under the auspices of the Court of Protection. No such safeguards exist to protect the child in wrongful birth claims. It would be comforting to believe that all parents will use the compensation recovered for the additional costs of bringing up a disabled child, for the benefit of that child, but they have no legal obligation to do so. Suppose a couple recover £2 million in a wrongful birth claim. Then suppose that five years later the mother dies and the father re-marries. He decides to start a new life in Australia and leaves the child with his sister in England, or gives the child up into local authority care. Alternatively, he might find a residential setting for the child funded by the state. He still has the lion's share of the £2 million compensation but for the rest of the child's life he will not be using it for the child's benefit.

Alternatively, since the compensation is designed to compensate the parent, it is calculated to last for as long as the parent lives. Suppose the parent is known to have a shortened life expectancy because of some congenital heart defect. The compensation for the wrongful birth may be calculated on the basis of a 15 year period only, whereas the disabled child might be dependent on care for another 50 years. It seems that periodical payment orders are not suitable for wrongful birth claims for economic loss.

Once compensation is paid there is no obligation on the claimant parent recovering that compensation to use it in any particular way, and no obligation to spend it on care and equipment for the child.

Of course, I do not wish to suggest that parents in these cases are uncaring. I have been deeply touched by witnessing the incredible dedication of many parents of disabled children in these cases, often in the most difficult circumstances. However, the law in this area surely requires re-consideration. Whereas I believe most observers would think that the purpose of the wrongful birth compensation should be to benefit the disabled child, currently the law does nothing to ensure that that is the case.

Chapter 3: Accident and Emergency

NHS Accident and Emergency departments have become our country's crisis centres. 24 hours a day they have to deal with patients critically injured in accidents on the road, at home or at work, victims of crime, patients with drug and alcohol addictions, patients with mental health problems, and those who have self-harmed, vulnerable adults, the homeless, elderly patients and injured and sick children. They deal with every part of the body and mind. And those attending will very often be anxious, sometimes agitated, and mostly in need of urgent attention.

It is difficult to imagine a more challenging environment in which to work. Important decisions have to be taken in an instant, there is little to no control over the number of patients needing help, or the kind of conditions and injuries that they will be suffering.

And yet, as in all areas of human endeavour, mistakes are made and avoidable injuries caused.

The first point of contact with the emergency medical services for many is through a 999 call. A call handler – usually someone without medical qualifications – will deal with the call, following a computerised protocol or algorithm that has been developed to prioritise patients. This is the first element of triage within the emergency care system. The call handler may also have to give advice to the person who is with the patient to help them keep the patient alive, or prevent them from deteriorating before the emergency services reach the scene. An ambulance is dispatched to the patient. Not all personnel arriving by ambulance to attend on a patient will have medical or paramedic training. The system will have determined what level of personnel will be required for each call.

In *Kent v Griffiths* [2000] EWCA Civ 3017, the Court of Appeal found that the London Ambulance Service was liable to pay compensation to a patient. A doctor had been with the asthmatic patient. The doctor called for an ambulance and the call handler advised as to a time of arrival. Twice further the doctor called to chase up the ambulance and was reassured. In fact, the ambulance arrived 40 minutes after the initial call. The ambulance record was falsified to indicate an earlier arrival time. The doctor's evidence was that, had she been told that the ambulance would take 40 minutes to arrive, she would have arranged for some other means of taking the patient to hospital, and the patient would have arrived and received effective emergency treatment earlier. The ambulance service had been negligent in advising the doctor that the arrival time would be significantly earlier, and the patient suffered injuries because of the avoidable delay caused.

When ambulance personnel arrive at the patient, they have to decide on the priorities at the scene. This is a further exercise in triage, sometimes called "field triage". In certain cases, an air ambulance is used. These are not all operated by the NHS; some are operated by charities or private organisations. The personnel attending on the patient have to take steps to keep the patient safe, decide whether treatment is required at hospital, decide which hospital is best suited to receive the patient, inform the hospital of their imminent arrival, and ensure the patient's safety during transit.

Some patients are brought to A&E by ambulance, others are taken by family members or get themselves to the emergency department. Those needing urgent life-saving treatment will be dealt with immediately. Others, and those who walk into the department are usually clerked in, and then wait to be "triaged", usually by a triage nurse.

Triage is the name for a system of prioritisation of patients with a variety of illnesses and conditions. It is necessary when resources within the hospital do not match the demands, and so prioritisation of need is required. This is more or less always the case within NHS A&E departments. Triage allows the hospital to identify which patients need immediate attention, which ones should be seen urgently, and which can wait a while longer. In England and Wales, and in many countries elsewhere in Europe, the Manchester Triage System is commonly used. Triage ought to be carried out by a properly trained and experienced A&E practitioner. Patients should be assessed within 15 minutes of arrival and the triage process ought to be capable of being completed within five minutes. Patients are categorised as having immediate need of care, or very urgent, urgent, standard or non-urgent need. Corresponding colour categorisations are red, orange, yellow, green and blue. Red categorisation means that there should be no wait to have medical attention; orange means to be seen within ten minutes; yellow one hour; green two hours; and blue four hours. So, all patients ought to receive attention within four hours.

Patients who then undergo monitoring and care are sometimes assessed using National Early Warning Scores (for adults) and Paediatric Early Warning Scores (for children). These systems allocate scores to vital signs such as blood pressure and temperature. If the scores reach certain thresholds they indicate an early warning that the patient may be deteriorating and in need of further medical assessment.

It would be foolish for a litigant to believe that they have a good case simply because they had been an "orange" patient, but had been seen after 15 minutes rather than ten minutes. The courts are not unaware of the pressures on A&E departments. It will not necessarily be negligent to fail to see a patient within the timescales indicated by a particular triage system. Nevertheless, a failure to recognise a feature of the patient's presentation, and thereby to fail to ensure that they receive the urgent medical attention they need, might well result in a claim if avoidable injury ensues.

In 2019 the Supreme Court considered a case called *Darnley v Croydon Health Services NHS Trust* [2018] UKSC 50 concerning a busy A&E department.

Mr Darnley had been struck over the head when out at night. He attended the A&E department of what was then known as the Mayday Hospital, accompanied by a friend. They went up to reception and the receptionist, a person who had no healthcare qualifications, told him wrongly that he would have to wait four to five hours to be seen because the department was so busy. With a head injury, he should have been seen, under national guidelines, within 15 minutes, and he would in fact have been seen within 30 minutes that night. Mr Darnley said that he felt as though he might collapse and was told that if he did so he would then be attended to. This might not have been received as particularly reassuring. In any event Mr Darnley decided after 19 minutes that it was not worth waiting any longer and he left. He did not tell staff that he was leaving. He went home and later collapsed due to a bleed on the brain. He was taken to hospital for surgery but it was too late to save him from permanent, severe, neurological injury.

At trial, before HHJ Robinson, and on appeal to the Court of Appeal, the claimant lost his case. The trial judge did find that if he had been given correct information about waiting times, the claimant would have stayed. He would have been seen within about 30 minutes and he would have been under medical management when he suffered his bleed. He would then have been treated immediately within the hospital and he would have avoided the long-term neurological injury that he suffered. However, the trial judge found, and the Court of Appeal, by a majority, agreed, that it was not within the duty of care of the receptionist to advise the claimant as to waiting times. The fact that she did so was as a matter of courtesy not a matter of legal obligation. Lord Justice McCombe disagreed – he would have found the defendant liable to the claimant, but he was outnumbered by his two fellow appeal judges.

Counsel for Mr Darnley had urged the Court of Appeal to adopt the same line as had been taken by the same court in the earlier case of *Kent v Griffiths* [2000] EWCA Civ 3017; [2001] QB 36 referred to above. If the ambulance service call handler's misinformation to a patient could lead to a finding of liability, so should a receptionist's misinformation to Mr Darnley. The Court of Appeal rejected that comparison.

The Supreme Court overturned the decision of the Court of Appeal and readily found that the Trust was liable for Mr Darnley's avoidable injuries. First, the Supreme Court held that:

> *"It has long been established that such a duty is owed by those who provide and run a casualty department to persons presenting them-selves complaining of illness or injury and before they are treated or received into care in the hospital's wards. The duty is one to take rea-sonable care not to cause physical injury to the patient."*

The imposition of a duty of care on a hospital in relation to the care of patients within the A&E Department was not a novel proposition – it was in accordance with well-established case law.

Second, it mattered not whether the Trust chose to meet its duty of care by allocating particular roles to a "civilian" or a healthcare professional:

> *"The duty of the respondent trust must be considered in the round. While it is not the function of reception staff to give wider advice or information in general to patients, it is the duty of the NHS Trust to take care not to provide misinformation to patients and that duty is not avoided by the misinformation having been provided by reception staff as opposed to medical staff. In this regard, it is simply not ap-propriate to distinguish between medical and non-medical staff in the manner proposed by the respondent."*

Interestingly this approach was the same as that adopted by a High Court Judge, Mr Justice Foskett, in another case brought against the same Trust for negligence by a receptionist in the same A&E department. In that case, *Macaulay v Croydon Health Services NHS Trust* [2017] EWHC 1795 (QB), a patient left the department having been assured that it was all right for him to leave, whereas in fact he was required to wait for a blood test. Had the test been performed it would have raised concerns leading to further inves-tigation and effective treatment. The judge responded to the defendant's argument that it would be unreasonable responsibility on the receptionist by saying that the fault was with the system as a whole. The case:

> *"involves the "system" failing (i) to identify the fact that an impor-tant test had not been done on [the claimant] and (ii) to alert him to*

or to reinforce the desirability of making himself available for it to be carried out."

Court:
Supreme Court
[2018] UKSC 50

Facts:
Mr Darnley attended A&E with a head injury but was told wrongly that he would have to wait 4-5 hours to be seen. He left after 19 minutes. Had he stayed he would have been seen in 30 minutes. At home he collapsed with a bleed on the brain and suffered serious permanent neurological injury.

Darnley v Croydon Health Services NHS Trust

Decision:
The Trust assumed responsibility for the claimant when he was clerked in to A&E. He was negligently given misinformation on which he foreseeably relied when he decided to leave. This was causative of his neurological injury. It is well established that hospitals owe duties of care to patients in A&E. It matters not that the function was allocated to a receptionist rather than a healthcare professional. The defendant trust was liable.

Key Points For Application in Later Cases:
Once a patient has been clerked in, the NHS Trust has assumed responsibility for them. NHS Trusts have to operate a safe system, and cannot avoid liability by devolving responsibility to staff who are not healthcare professionals. Liability may extend to patients who choose to leave the hospital even without telling staff.

Casenote 9

However, whereas Mr Justice Foskett appears to have looked at both the existence of a duty of care and the question of whether there was a breach of duty, at a Trust level, the approach of the Supreme Court in *Darnley* on breach was a little different. In relation to the standard of care and breach, it held:

"the legitimate expectation of the patient is that he will receive from each person concerned with his care a degree of skill appropriate to

the task which he or she undertakes. A receptionist in an A & E department cannot, of course, be expected to give medical advice or information but he or she can be expected to take reasonable care not to provide misleading advice as to the availability of medical assistance."

The Supreme Court focused on the standard of care relevant to the role, being the first point of contact for patients attending an Emergency Department. It did not appear to apply the *Bolam* test to the performance of that role by the receptionist. Rather it expressed a view of what it was reasonable to expect from someone performing that role, namely that they would not give misleading information or advice about the availability of medical assistance. However, the court did not examine breach by reference to the conduct of the Trust as a whole, but by reference to the conduct of the particular individual. It might have been different had the finding been that the Trust ought not to have deployed a non-medically qualified person as the first point of contact, but that was not an issue in the case – the claimant accepted that it was reasonable to have the receptionist as first point of contact.

It was of interest that the Supreme Court in Mr Darnley's case did not seem troubled by the fact that he left the department without telling anybody. The court said that, as the trial judge had determined, it was predictable that having been given the misinformation about waiting times, the patient would leave early rather than wait four to five hours to be seen. His departure was one of the things that was a foreseeable consequence of the negligence.

Many A&E departments will have leaflets that they can hand to patients such as Mr Darnley attending with a head injury that does not appear to require immediate attention. Written material can inform the patient of the importance of being seen by a nurse or doctor following a head injury, and that there is a risk of deterioration. Many patients are aware of the fact that they should be seen promptly if they have a serious injury but may have to wait a number of hours for minor problems. So, Mr Darnley might have believed that he must have only a minor injury (although he had only spoken to a receptionist).

NHS hospitals might be concerned that if they owe a duty of care to protect a patient once they are clerked in at an A&E department, then they have to take positive measures to advise patients not to leave, or to try to get them back into the hospital if they do leave. This might well be regarded as an additional layer of responsibility for an already much stretched department.

In other cases involving A&E departments, liability findings have been made for failures to monitor patients who are suicidal and who abscond, and patients who suffer a serious deterioration whilst waiting to be seen by a doctor. But most claims against A&E departments are made by patients who have been seen, examined, and then wrongly reassured and discharged when in fact they have an unrecognised but serious condition or injury. Decisions may be made not to perform an x-ray that would have revealed a fracture, or not to perform a scan that would have shown a brain haemorrhage. There are many cases, sadly, where signs of sepsis are missed and the patient later suffers serious, even fatal collapse. In all these cases the claimants have to establish what would or should have happened had the necessary investigations been performed and diagnosis made.

Chapter 4: Cosmetic Surgery
and Private Healthcare

Private Healthcare

In this Chapter I shall focus on cosmetic surgery provided within the private sector. Private healthcare provision covers many more areas than cosmetic surgery – most fields of clinical practice, from obstetrics to psychiatry are offered by the private sector – but the same principles about contractual obligations as are discussed below in relation to cosmetic surgery, apply to any private provision.

The fact that treatment is given privately usually means that the provider owes a duty to exercise reasonable care and skill both in tort, and under contract. The duties co-exist and are unlikely to be materially different in nature or extent. The fact that a patient is paying for treatment does not, by itself, raise the standard of care they are entitled to expect. If, however, they are paying a premium price with the reasonable expectation of exceptional care, then the standard of skill and care that the provider is obliged to exercise may well be higher than would otherwise be the case.

Principles of legal policy, such as the bar on claiming compensatory damages for the "wrongful birth" of a healthy child, are not altered by reason of the fact that the clinical advice or treatment was given within the private sector.

It follows that just about all of the core principles and procedures discussed in this book will apply to claims arising out of private clinical care, as they do to state-funded clinical care. The cosmetic surgery industry, however, raises some particular issues all of its own.

Cosmetic surgery

Cosmetic surgery is big business. It is a fast growing, profit-making industry that actively promotes and sells surgery as a luxury service. The essentially commercial nature of cosmetic surgery puts pressures on patients and providers that are unlike those within other fields of healthcare provision.

It is in the interests of providers within this industry to generate custom but cosmetic surgery is always elective. There is always the option of not having cosmetic surgery. Excepting extreme cases involving severe psychiatric illness or disorder, no-one would die or suffer disability if they did not have cosmetic surgery. Individuals choose to become patients. You do not choose to have kidney stones but you do choose to have a facelift. There is rarely a healthcare need to undergo cosmetic surgery; rather there is a desire to do so. That desire for surgery has a psychological or social origin. From a commercial point of view, the goal is to create and encourage that desire to undergo surgery. It would be a poor business that discouraged potential customers.

The desire to undergo surgery is promoted by advertising, marketing and use of the media. Over the years cosmetic surgery has been normalised. Celebrities used to hide the fact that they had undergone a nip and tuck. There was a stigma associated with it. Now it is commonplace, some celebrities positively boast of the number of operations they have had, and cosmetic surgery has entered the mainstream. I once had a client who complained that her breast augmentation was not sufficiently obvious: *"If I am spending that amount of money, I want people to know about it."* Conspicuous consumption!

It is beyond my abilities and the scope of this book to analyse the ways in which our culture has contributed to the growth of the cosmetic surgery industry, but it clearly serves the purposes of that industry: (i) to have more people dissatisfied with their appearance; (ii) for cosmetic surgery to be more widely accepted as normal; and (iii) to have encouraged the belief that the benefits of cosmetic surgery far outweigh the risks.

Slick advertising promotes the services on offer. Sales personnel are engaged, sometimes on commission, to talk through the options for surgery with potential patients. Contracts are sometimes entered into before any contact with a healthcare professional, credit arrangements are often available, and large sums of money are paid; sometimes credit facilities are agreed.

The image that many people have of the provision of cosmetic surgery is far removed from reality. The very language used by some within the industry encourages the belief that cosmetic surgery is unlike other kinds of surgery. Patients are "customers", hospitals are "clinics", and operations are "procedures".

The first point of contact for someone enquiring about cosmetic surgery is often a patient co-ordinator or guide who, typically, has no clinical qualifications but is trained in the art of selling. The patient may be told that a particular surgeon is the best in the business and it so happens that a space in their schedule next month has just come free. The patient might be offered a discount if they elect to have more than one procedure. Sales techniques are deployed because this is a business.

These features make the provision of cosmetic surgery far different from surgical provision within the NHS. Patients seek surgery to fulfil a desire rather than a physical need. They are encouraged to have the surgery, and they enter into commercial transactions to secure the surgeon's services. How do these differences affect litigation arising out of cosmetic surgery?

Contracts
The first distinctive feature of cosmetic surgery litigation is that it will usually involve an allegation of breach of contract. A negligent surgeon who causes avoidable injury is liable in negligence whether or not they were being paid to perform the operation. However, they may also be liable in contract. If the surgeon has promised to perform the surgery in return for the payment to them by the patient for the service, then a contract will have been entered into between surgeon and patient. Contracts have terms, and one of the terms that will either have been written down, or will be implied, is that the surgeon will exercise reasonable care and skill in performing the contracted service, including the surgery itself.

More commonly, in my experience, the patient enters into a contract with a provider – a clinic or business that offers cosmetic surgery and other services. The clinic engages the surgeon to perform the surgery, as well as engaging a theatre nurse, an anaesthetist and so on. The patient pays a single sum of money to the clinic. In such cases there is undoubtedly a contract between the patient and the clinic but there is often a dispute about the nature of the contract and its terms and conditions. Many clinics argue that their only contractual role is to introduce the patient to the surgeon. The surgeon is an "independent contractor" for whose negligence the clinic is not liable. The patient should look to the surgeon for redress if the surgeon has acted negligently, not to the clinic.

This would not present too much of a problem for patients seeking redress were it not for the fact that sometimes the surgeon is not effectively insured, difficult to track down or uncooperative. Some clinics engage surgeons who are based abroad for half the year or more. The surgeons do not have professional indemnity insurance of the kind provided by the MDU or MPS in England and Wales. I have known surgeons who have insurance that is effective only if the claim is made under the policy within the period during which the premium is paid. So, if the patient comes forward with a claim in February 2017 and the surgeon's certificate of insurance expired in December 2016 then there is no indemnity even if the negligence occurred in 2016. In other cases, the insurer has been contractually entitled to terminate the insurance policy after one claim has been made in the relevant period. So if the patient making a claim is the second person to do so, they may find that the policy has been cancelled and the surgeon has no insurance cover. Other insurance contracts I have seen have expressly excluded cover for negligent advice or pre-operative counselling. Even when a surgeon does have stand-ard professional indemnity protection, that cover might be avoided by the relevant indemnifying organisation because of the conduct of the surgeon or other reason. Sometimes cover has been refused in cases where a single surgeon has faced multiple claims. In still other cases the surgeon goes to ground or does not co-operate with their insurer.

So, for a variety of reasons, the aggrieved patient might have to look to the clinic for redress. In those cases, it is necessary to look at the contractual terms and to determine what obligations the clinic owed to the patient. The mere fact that the surgeon was not an employee of the clinic does not nec-essarily mean that the clinic was not liable for the negligence of the surgeon. We have seen that in some situations one person might be vicariously liable for the negligence of another. Alternatively, the clinic might be considered to have a non-delegable duty to the patient such that it is liable for the negli-gent performance of the surgery, even though it was the surgeon themselves who made the mistakes.

If a patient has paid for their surgery on credit, then the credit company might owe a contractual duty to the patient under the Consumer Credit Act 1974.

What is crucial in cosmetic surgery litigation is to examine the contrac-tual arrangements, the relationships between patient, clinic, creditor and surgeon, and to determine what obligations arose to the patient and when.

Advertising and Salesmen's Claims

Advertising and claims by sales personnel can bring a dimension to cos-metic surgery litigation that is absent from the usual claims against NHS providers. In contract law, the courts may have to decide whether a claim made by one party to the contract, designed to be relied upon by the other party, constitutes a term of that contract. Suppose an advert for a cosmetic surgery clinic says that: *"We use only the best surgeons!"* Can the claimant in a subsequent case brought against the clinic assert that it was a term of the contract that the surgeon who operated on them was "the best"? Proba-bly not! The advertising was not sufficiently precise to be relied upon as a warranty. It was clearly a boast rather than the equivalent of a contractual promise. It might be different if the claim in advertising named a particular surgeon and claimed that he had a 100% success rate or something similar. If the legal claim is against the surgeon and the advertising claim had been made on their behalf, they might be deemed to be bound by the advertising claim themselves, even though they did not make it. For those purposes the clinic placing the advertisement might be regarded as acting as the surgeon's agent.

In clinical negligence law, claims by the clinic and its sales personnel might well affect the standard of care which the patient was entitled to expect. The *Bolam* test means that patients are entitled to expect a standard of care and skill that all reasonable bodies of surgeons would consider acceptable. If a patient is told that Mr Spoon is the very best breast augmentation surgeon in England, then the patient might reasonably contend that they expected more than reasonable care from a competent surgeon. They were entitled to expect a particularly high standard of care. The court might then judge the care given by reference to that higher standard.

Consent to Treatment

A very common feature of cosmetic surgery litigation is that of informed consent. Pre-operative advice is always important, but in cosmetic surgery cases it is a potential minefield for the practitioner. First, as already observed, the patient is electing to undergo surgery. They do not have a physical need for it. Nothing terrible will befall them if they do not proceed. Hence, the balance of risks and benefits is necessarily different from, say, an operation to remove a malignant tumour. There is no real "balancing exercise". You either have the surgery with all the attendant risks, or you do not have it in which case you stay exactly as you are.

The first task for the surgeon is to discern what the patient desires. This is not the usual diagnostic process leading to a conclusion about what the patient needs from a medical perspective. Instead it is an exploration of what the patient believes needs changing, and how they want it to change. There is no such thing as a perfect nose. What does the patient think is unsatisfactory about their nose, and how would they like it to look?

Has the patient thought through the consequences of getting what they seek? I had one client who had enormous breast implants inserted and suffered from a bad back and balance problems. She undoubtedly got what she asked for, but was adequate pre-operative advice given about the possible consequences of providing it?

It is always important that pre-operative information is given in circumstances that allow the patient fully to assess and weigh that information before deciding whether to consent to treatment. In too many cosmetic surgery cases that have crossed my desk, the patient has already paid a deposit, sometimes even the full price, for a procedure before meeting the surgeon to discuss the proposed surgery. They naturally feel committed to going ahead. This is a sales technique that ought not to be used.

The *Montgomery v Lanarkshire* principle requires the surgeon to take reasonable care to make the patient aware of the material risks of the proposed procedure and of reasonable alternative and variant treatments. One of the alternatives to cosmetic surgery is always to walk away and do nothing, or at least to avoid surgery but to alter diet or levels of exercise. One alternative might be to have psychological therapy. This is not a flippant observation. If the desire to undergo surgery stems from dissatisfaction with your own appearance, then there might be two obvious solutions. One might be to alter the appearance. The other might be to remove the dissatisfaction. Therapy might bring about a change of mindset, allowing the patient to be satisfied with their appearance and so avoid the risks and costs of cosmetic surgery. As for the material risks, it might be difficult to identify any risks, however minimal, that might be immaterial to a patient who has no need for the operation.

Some patients seek cosmetic surgery because they have a psychological disorder known as Body Dysmorphic Disorder, or because they are depressed or have some other mental illness. BDD is a mental health condition whereby the individual has a distorted perception of their own appearance. They can become fixated with one aspect of their appearance. Cosmetic surgery is rarely a cure for BDD. Sadly, as soon as surgery alters that feature, their BDD causes them to fixate on another aspect. They will rarely, if ever, be satisfied with their appearance. They may seek multiple operations and may be very insistent on surgeons proceeding with operations on them. Patients who are depressed might seek cosmetic surgery as a trigger to jolt them out of their depression, when what they would really benefit from is treatment for the depression.

Although there are some signs of improving practice, very unfortunately I have seen many cosmetic surgery cases over the years where the surgeons and clinics have not carried out even a cursory psychological assessment of the patient, and in some cases have not troubled even to obtain general practitioner records which would have revealed a relevant history of mental illness.

There is clearly a tension at play here. The healthcare professional has a duty of care to advise a patient of all the material risks or alternatives to surgery and so forth. But the commercial imperative for the business is to make the sale. The drive to make money would naturally lead to the patient being encouraged to elect to proceed with the surgery rather than to go away and think about it, to try counselling, or to have less expensive, non-surgical treatment. For regulated healthcare professionals there should be only one way to go when the path of duty diverts from the path of profit.

A Poor Outcome

One standard warning to a patient contemplating cosmetic surgery is that there is no guarantee that the surgery will create the outcome they desire. There is no doubt that some patients have unrealistic expectations. As noted, some expectations are distorted by a mental health condition. In many other cases the expectations are unrealistic because of misleading images in the media, advertising and promotional material. Even if the consent process is managed properly, some patients will be dissatisfied with the outcome.

Beauty may be in the eye of the beholder, but in cosmetic surgery litigation there has to be an objective assessment of the result of treatment. If the outcome is within a reasonable range of what might have been expected, then the outcome itself cannot be the grounds for complaint. However, just because the outcome is outside the range expected by the patient, it does not follow that the surgery was negligently performed. Nor does it follow that just because a cosmetic surgeon acting as an expert witness thinks that, say, a rhinoplasty ("nose job") produced an unacceptable cosmetic result, the operation was necessarily negligently performed. As Counsel for a claimant I would want to know from the expert witness what the surgeon did wrong in the operation – did they remove too much cartilage, did they fail to rasp a bone or to perform an "infracture" (which is exactly what you think it is)? Merely saying that the outcome was poor will rarely cut much ice with a judge at trial.

Causation

Many cosmetic surgery claims are based on an alleged failure to warn of risks and/or to obtain informed consent to the procedure. The outcome of the surgery was not what was desired and unnecessary surgery was performed. Complications may have arisen which, whilst being non-negligent consequences of the surgery, would have been avoided had the surgery not gone ahead. But, as in all cases where the patient alleges that they were not adequately warned of risks or given sufficient information to make an informed decision whether to go ahead with the procedure, the cosmetic surgery claimant has to establish causation. This can be particularly difficult in cosmetic surgery cases because often the claimant had been particularly motivated to undergo surgery. By the time an individual has decided to go to a clinic and to discuss the possibility of cosmetic surgery, they may already have been very keen to go ahead with a procedure. They are likely to have done some research themselves online or through talking to someone who has had a similar operation to the one they are contemplating. They took positive steps to seek an opportunity to undergo the surgery. So, when a claimant who has suffered visible keloid (raised) scarring after a face lift tells the court that, had they been warned of the very small risk of such scarring, they would not have elected to undergo the operation, the court will be sceptical. Is this just a case of buyer's remorse? Wasn't the patient so motivated to have a facelift that knowledge of a small risk of raised visible scarring would not have put them off?

Compensation

Cosmetic surgery claims are rarely of large value. In some awful cases negligent cosmetic surgery has caused death or severe disability. Denise Hendry, whose case made headline news, suffered very serious injury because of negligent liposuction during which her bowel was perforated. Tragically she later died of complications of those injuries. Other physical injuries that may be caused by negligent cosmetic surgery include, for example, breathing problems after rhinoplasty, or infection and tissue necrosis following breast augmentation. More often, thankfully, the injury is itself cosmetic only; it is limited and it can be improved or corrected with further surgery. That is not to understate the impact of negligent cosmetic surgery. Many patients put great faith in their cosmetic surgeon. They believe that the surgery will not only improve an aspect of their appearance but it will make them more confident, have more self-esteem, restore the health of their relationships, and bring them new work opportunities. The gap between those hopes and the reality of the outcome of a negligently performed operation can be enormous and psychologically very damaging.

It is nearly always necessary to obtain expert evidence, not only on the prospects and costs of revision surgery, but also on the psychological impact of the negligence.

Contrary to what most claimants expect, it might not be possible in a negligence claim to recover the fee they paid for the negligently performed operation. Suppose a patient pays £5,000 for an operation. If the negligence was in the performance of the surgery, and it can be corrected with a revision operation, then, but for the negligence, they would have had a successful operation at the same cost. They should recover general damages for the injury and consequential losses and expenses including the cost of revision surgery. But they would have incurred the £5,000 even without the negligence. In a claim for breach of contract, the claimant might have a better argument for return of the money, particularly if they derived no gain at all from the operation that they paid for.

Cosmetic surgery provision is regulated but regulation has only slowly developed whereas the industry itself has rapidly grown. Arguably, much tighter regulation is required to protect patients from the worst excesses, and in particular to ensure that there is a person, be it the clinic or the surgeon, with the means to pay compensation when liability against them is established.

Chapter 5: Delay in Diagnosing Cancer

Members of the public are conditioned to believe that the earlier a cancer is detected, the better the outcome for the patient. That is why we have screening programmes and why we are encouraged to self-examine and to go to a doctor at the first sign of any potential problem. As a result, any avoidable delay in diagnosing cancer is naturally regarded as nothing short of a disaster for the patient. It may surprise many non-healthcare professionals, therefore, that the NHS defends many negligence claims for delay in diagnosing cancer on the basis that the delay made no difference to the patient.

These claims are particularly complex on the issue of causation, especially when it comes to proving reduced life expectancy. Many a litigation battle has been fought on that issue.

The first issue, however, is breach of duty of care. This may happen at a hospital, for example at a breast clinic, but typically cases for delay in diagnosing cancer are brought against primary healthcare providers. General Practitioners and practice nurses are not expected to diagnose cancer but should recognise the need to refer patients for specialist assessment as to whether they have cancer.

There are national guidelines for the referral of patients with suspected cancer. They are available online on the NICE website and are updated every few years. The guidelines cover the most common types of cancer including lung and breast cancer. They envisage immediate referral (*"go to hospital now, I am calling them to tell them you will be arriving soon"*), urgent referral with the patient being seen within two weeks, and non-urgent or routine referral. For each kind of cancer covered by the guidance, threshold criteria for referral are set out. These are evidence-based. The guidelines for breast cancer, in short form, are currently:

> *"Refer people using a suspected cancer pathway referral (for an appointment within 2 weeks) for breast cancer if they are:*
>
> *aged 30 and over and have an unexplained breast lump with or without pain or*
>
> *aged 50 and over with any of the following symptoms in one nipple only: discharge; retraction;*
>
> *other changes of concern.*

> *Consider a suspected cancer pathway referral (for an appointment within 2 weeks) for breast cancer in people:*
>
> *with skin changes that suggest breast cancer or*
>
> *aged 30 and over with an unexplained lump in the axilla.*
>
> *Consider non-urgent referral in people aged under 30 with an unexplained breast lump with or without pain".*

These are guidelines. They do not have the force of law. However, if the guideline is expressed in what appears to be mandatory terms, such as "Refer [urgently] people aged 30 or over with an unexplained breast lump", then a GP who notes an unexplained breast lump in a woman aged 45 but does not refer her has some explaining to do. Where the guidance is to "consider referral" then the GP has more room to exercise judgement. That said, if the guidelines set a clear threshold for referral that is not met in a patient's case, then the patient will have a tough task persuading a court that the GP was negligent in failing to refer. The guidelines indicate urgent referral for a man with a prostate-specific antigen (PSA) level that is above the age-specific reference range. If the patient's PSA was just below that level, then it will be difficult to establish that it was negligent not to refer them to a urology clinic within two weeks.

Guidelines cannot cover every possible set of circumstances. So, GPs ought to take into account family history, personal medical history including previous cancers, and so on. Furthermore, the decision whether to refer does not end the GP's role. Even if the GP decides that referral is not warranted, they may want to give "safety netting" advice to the patient about returning for further assessment, for example if they notice certain further changes in the breast, or if an area of lumpiness does not resolve after their next menstrual cycle. A borderline PSA level might mandate a repeat test in three or six months, even if it does not mandate urgent referral.

In most delay in diagnosing cancer litigation, there has been a failure to refer, leading to a period of months or years before later referral and diagnosis. The claimant has to prove that the negligent failure caused them injury. Typically the injuries to consider are: (i) pain and discomfort during the period of delay; (ii) the need for more extensive treatment than would have been required on earlier referral; (iii) the likelihood of future, avoidable deterioration, illness, disability and treatment; (iv) psychiatric injury; and (v) reduced life expectancy.

In order to prove any or all of those consequences, the claimant has to establish all the links in the chain of causation. The claimant has to establish: (i) that on earlier referral, the cancer would have been diagnosed earlier; (ii) what the size, grade and stage of the cancer would have been on earlier diagnosis; (iii) what treatment would have been offered on earlier diagnosis; (iv) what treatment the claimant would have elected to undergo, and when that treatment would have been administered; and (v) what the outcome of such earlier treatment would have been.

The parties will usually instruct an oncologist or other specialist in the type of cancer under consideration to advise as to the likely features of the cancer at the time when referral should have been made. The national guidelines are helpful to establish that an urgent referral would or should have led to the patient being seen by a specialist within two weeks. The court will need to know whether investigations by the specialist would have resulted in diagnosis. If the cancer were a tumour but too small to be detected at that time, then diagnosis would not have been likely. Since, by definition, there were no investigations because there was no referral, the experts have to work out what features the cancer would have had, and therefore what would have been found, had investigations been performed. The evidence available will include the assessment by the General Practitioner, the claimant's own evidence, and, importantly, the findings on actual diagnosis months or years later. By a process of interpolation, the experts calculate the likely size of, say, a breast tumour at the time when the patient ought to have been subject to specialist assessment. They interpolate from the size of the tumour as it was on actual specialist assessment.

Suppose a breast tumour has been detected, excised and examined. The histopathologist examining the excised tissue will have measured it and recorded a pathological size. Assuming a spherical shape, the volume of the excised tumour can be calculated using the formula Volume = $4/3 \, \pi r^3$, where "r" is the radius. If a certain doubling time is assumed, which might be 80 days for breast cancer, then the likely volume of the tumour at an earlier date can be calculated. This might give you a reliable pathological tumour size at the date when earlier specialist assessment ought to have been performed, but expert evidence would be needed to advise whether a tumour of that size, and in the position it was likely to have been at the relevant time, would have been detectable on clinical examination and/or mammogram or ultrasound examination.

A key assumption lying behind the process of interpolation just described is the doubling time, but experts often disagree as to the likely doubling time which is not uniform for all breast cancers, let alone for all cancers of whatever kind and whether primary or secondary.

As well as trying to work out the likely size of any tumour at the time when it ought to have been diagnosed, the experts will advise as to the likely grade and stage of the cancer. It is important to know the cell type (such as adenocarcinoma or squamous cell carcinoma), whether the cancer would have been confined to a particular organ or would have spread beyond it, whether the cancer would have spread to lymph nodes near to the primary tumour, or to other organs or parts of the body. The grade of a cancer refers to the extent of the abnormality of the cancer cells and how aggressive they appear to be. Tumour cancers are often described by reference to the TNM staging system. T stands for the main tumour and a score is given depending on its size and extent. N refers to the nearby lymph nodes and a score is given according to how many are affected. M refers to metastases – has the cancer spread to other parts of the body. So T1, N1, M0 might mean that the tumour is not the smallest it could be, but has not yet progressed to higher levels, at least one lymph node is involved but there are no distant metastases.

Some cancers, including blood borne cancers, are not staged in this way. There is no primary tumour. However, in appropriate cases, the experts will give opinions as to the likely TNM of a cancer at the time when it ought to have been diagnosed.

There are two obvious reasons why it is necessary to know what the stage and grade of the cancer would have been at the time when it ought to have been diagnosed. First, the stage and grade would have dictated the treatment that would have been offered to the patient. Second, the stage and grade would, together with the treatment undergone, indicate the likely prognosis. I have drawn a distinction between the treatment likely to have been offered and the treatment that the patient would have elected to undergo, because not all patients follow recommendations, and sometimes there is a choice to be made which will be left to the patient without a particular steer from the clinician. Some women will opt for mastectomy over a wide local excision of a malignant lump. Others will choose the less invasive surgery. Some patients will elect to have adjuvant chemotherapy even though it is likely to bring about only a marginal benefit whilst others will decline the offer in order to avoid the side-effects of that treatment.

Perhaps the most difficult part of litigating delay in diagnosis of cancer cases is that of establishing the effect of earlier treatment on life expectancy. The starting point is to compare life expectancy following actual diagnosis and treatment – as it is in fact – with life expectancy as it would have been following earlier diagnosis and treatment. The treatment that would have been given may well be different from the treatment as it has been and will be. The cancer may have been at a different stage at the earlier point in time than it was at actual diagnosis. But those are minor complexities compared with the assessment of life expectancy itself.

Oncologists talk to their patients about life expectancy but when they do, they tend to discuss the percentage chances of surviving for five years or ten years. When a patient survives five years following diagnosis, it might be said that they have been "cured". For litigators, information that a claimant has a 45% chance of surviving five years from actual diagnosis but would have had a 65% chance of surviving five years from earlier diagnosis is not particularly helpful. How does that translate into a calculation within a schedule or an assessment of compensation? How long will they need care for? How many more years would their children have had a parent to look after them if the parent, now deceased, had been diagnosed earlier?

There is another problem with assessing life expectancy by reference to a chance of survival. The House of Lords addressed it in the case of *Gregg v Scott* [2005] UKHL 2.

A delay in diagnosis reduced Mr Gregg's chance of a cure from non-Hodgkin's lymphoma from 42% to 25%. A cure was regarded as ten years of disease free survival. Initially, the evidence had been that the chance of cure, in the absence of the negligence, was over 50% and the only claim he brought was for loss of a cure. As subsequently the evidence changed to an opinion that in the absence of the delay there would have been only a 42% chance of cure, he altered his claim to one for damages for a reduced chance of a cure. He did not bring claims for injury caused by more invasive treatment, psychological injury or anything else. The House of Lords said that, whilst a claimant might be able to establish that on the balance of probabilities he would have been cured and now would not be or that he had lost an ascertainable number of years of life, the claim he had brought did not entitle him to compensation. There is no award of damages for the loss of a chance of a cure.

The court summarised the issue as follows (changing some of the statistics for the sake of the illustration):

> "A patient is suffering from cancer. His prospects are uncertain. He has a 45% chance of recovery. Unfortunately his doctor negligently misdiagnoses his condition as benign. So the necessary treatment is delayed for months. As a result the patient's prospects of recovery be-

come nil or almost nil. Has the patient a claim for damages against the doctor? No, the House was told. The patient could recover damages if his initial prospects of recovery had been more than 50%. But because they were less than 50% he can recover nothing."

This case was interpreted in some quarters as meaning that unless a claimant can prove that their prospects of cure went from above 50% to below 50% as a result of the negligent delay, they had no case. That was an unreasonably simplistic interpretation. As Baroness Hale explained in her judgment in the case, it may be possible to obtain expert evidence of median life expectancy. The median is different from the mean average. The median is the "man in the middle". On the balance of probabilities the individual

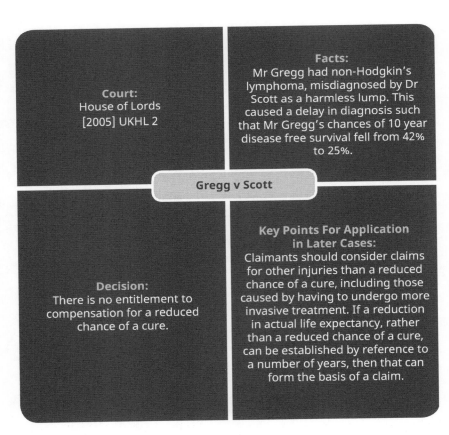

Court:
House of Lords
[2005] UKHL 2

Facts:
Mr Gregg had non-Hodgkin's lymphoma, misdiagnosed by Dr Scott as a harmless lump. This caused a delay in diagnosis such that Mr Gregg's chances of 10 year disease free survival fell from 42% to 25%.

Gregg v Scott

Decision:
There is no entitlement to compensation for a reduced chance of a cure.

Key Points For Application in Later Cases:
Claimants should consider claims for other injuries than a reduced chance of a cure, including those caused by having to undergo more invasive treatment. If a reduction in actual life expectancy, rather than a reduced chance of a cure, can be established by reference to a number of years, then that can form the basis of a claim.

Casenote 10

will live to the median age of the group of people with their cancer (of the same grade, stage etc). On the balance of probabilities they will not live beyond that age. Comparison of median life expectancy with and without the negligent delay will give you a reduction in life expectancy in the form of a number of years.

This approach came to the rescue of the claimant in *JD v Mather* [2012] EWHC 3063 (QB). This was a malignant melanoma case. Mr Justice Bean found that even without the negligent delay, the claimant had a less than 50% chance of being cured. On that basis he had no claim to damages. However, he allowed the claimant to rely on evidence of median life expectancy and found there to have been a reduction of three years. Damages were to be assessed accordingly.

Applying *Gregg v Scott* as misinterpreted, you could have a reduction of 48% in the chances of a cure, from 99% to 51% and have no claim, but have only a 2% reduction, from 51% to 49% and be able to claim for the loss of a cure. That would be manifestly at odds with reality. So the better option is to consider the effect of a negligent delay in diagnosis on the claimant's median life expectancy.

All well and good? Well, not quite. There are significant problems with the parties looking at median life expectancy.

First, data is not readily available for all cancers showing 5, 10, 15 or 20 year survival.

Second, if the chances of cure following actual diagnosis are above 50%, then, as a matter of statistics, median life expectancy is not ascertainable. You need more than 50 of your sample of 100 people with the same cancer to die before the five year or ten year "cure" date.

Third, many expert witnesses are uncomfortable with giving an opinion as to median life expectancy. Although this is a mathematical analysis of data that they have at their disposal, they are not used to giving an opinion of median life expectancy.

Fourth, time marches on. As happened in Mr Gregg's case, so in any case where you seek to rely on median life expectancy: the evidence can change as the case progresses. So, a claimant might have a two years median life expectancy at the start of the litigation but still be alive at trial three years later. Sadly, the reverse can happen, and a claimant may die earlier than the statistics predicted. Not only does this change actual life expectancy (you either know the claimant has died, in which case there is no need to specu-late, or you know that the use of median life expectancy is not valid in their case because they have outlived it) but also it calls into question the validity of the figure for median life expectancy had they been diagnosed earlier. If you have a claimant who has outlived the median after actual diagnosis and treatment, would it be fair to say that they would probably have outlived the median on earlier diagnosis too? Or if they have died earlier than expected, would they have died earlier than the median on earlier diagnosis?

In some cases, the defendant contends that poor life expectancy following actual diagnosis of cancer is because of an underlying feature of the cancer that would have become apparent at the same time and in the same way even after earlier diagnosis and treatment. Where claimants have a poor life expectancy because of metastases, defendants sometimes say that those metastases would have been present earlier, even if in undetectable form (micrometastases). Those micrometastases would have resisted the likely treatment and would have developed into overt metastases just as they did, causing the same consequences for the claimant. In several cases in which I have been involved, the NHS has contended that the claimant would have been likely to die at exactly the same time with or without the significant delay in diagnosing and treating their cancer.

The state of the law is such that, in a delay claim where the patient has died of cancer and the evidence is that, but for the delay they would probably have been cured, the temptation is to assert that the deceased would have had a normal life expectancy in the absence of the negligence. That may not accord with reality: a 51% chance of surviving five years after cancer is not necessarily a guarantee of a normal life expectancy.

The consequences of proving reduced life expectancy are two-fold. First, the claimant might be able to make a so-called "lost years" claim for net loss of earnings or income during the period when they will not be alive but would have been earning but for the negligence. Second, the dependants of a claimant who then dies prematurely because of negligent delay in diag-

nosis might have a Fatal Accidents Act claim for the loss to them of their reliance on the deceased for the period when he or she would otherwise have been alive.

Difficult decisions have to be made when a claimant with terminal cancer and a short life expectancy is bringing a personal injury claim. As noted earlier in this book, if a personal injury claim is concluded during the claim-ant's life, then their family cannot later bring a claim if the claimant dies prematurely as a result of the negligence. So, the claimant and their family have to decide how to manage the claim and the potential for a Fatal Accidents Act claim. The courts are usually willing to give directions to expedite such claims, so that evidence is gathered and exchanged and the case heard earlier than would be the norm. There are also means of taking oral evidence from a "dying claimant" before the actual trial. Legal representatives have to consider all these options.

Chapter 6: Psychiatric Care

Very few clinical negligence claims concern a failure to alleviate or improve a mental health condition. It is rare to find allegations that a psychiatrist should have increased this medication or provided that treatment to a patient and that, had they done so, the patient would have endured less suffering or had a better quality of life. I suppose that it is very difficult to prove that the outcome for a patient would have been markedly better in one case compared with the other. Sadly, most negligence claims arising out of psychiatric care involve acts of serious self-harm or suicide. In these cases, patients who are or have been under the care of a mental health service, whether as in-patients or in the community, or who are otherwise under the care of healthcare professionals, have hurt or killed themselves in circumstances which they contend ought to have been prevented.

Such claims may arise in any healthcare setting. I have had claims for clients who have self-harmed whilst in Accident and Emergency departments, in secure psychiatric units, or at home. They might be long-term patients with an established diagnosis of a particular condition or they might have only recently made first contact with a mental health service. They might have self-harmed previously or they might not.

Claims arising out of self-harm or suicide sometimes concern the physical environment – windows that are not secure, access points allowing patients to abscond too easily, or ligature points in a bedroom within a unit. In other cases, it is the decision to admit or not to admit an individual as an in-patient that is in issue, or the regime of observation of a patient whilst in hospital that is alleged to have been inadequate. In other cases, insufficient advice has been given to the family of a patient who were trying to look after them at home.

At the root of many of these cases is the assessment of risk: was an adequate assessment made of the risk that a patient might attempt to die by suicide, abscond from hospital or cause themselves serious self-harm? Was the assessment adequately acted upon? But for failings in the assessment and management of risk, would the injury or death have been avoided?

Whereas an untreated infection will be likely to cause certain kinds of damage, the human mind is perhaps less predictable. Indeed, it is the very unpredictability of behaviour that can give rise to a risk of harm. Many patients suffering from mental illness might be considered to be at risk of harming themselves, but it would be unacceptable to lock all of them up in secure wards without access to their own possessions, just to keep them

331

"safe". How do healthcare professionals assess risk and decide on appropriate measures to manage that risk?

Mental health care seems to generate a lot of pro-forma documentation. "Care Pathway" records can be voluminous. They will generally include a section on the risk of suicide or self-harm. Analysis of the patient's history and presentation will allow the professional to record whether they are agitated, hallucinating (hearing voices or seeing things that are not there), whether they are under the influence of drugs, whether they have carers at home, whether they have self-harmed recently or in the past, whether they have ongoing thoughts that they may want to harm themselves or to take their own lives and so on. In cases in which I have been involved, there has often been an important distinction drawn between "suicidal thoughts" or "ideation", and "actively suicidal", but when explored in evidence, the distinction has not always been easy for the healthcare professionals to articulate. Some professionals have said that if a patient is not "actively suicidal" they are not at high risk, but they regard "actively suicidal" as meaning "in the act of trying to kill themselves." That seems to set the bar for intervention rather too high. On the other hand, mental health teams cannot put every patient who has ever had a thought of suicide on constant watch.

Common sense dictates that in these cases "risk" cannot be quantified with any precision. It would be surprising if an expert said that the patient was at a 45% risk of killing themselves. A more realistic view is that patients can be assessed as being at a low, medium, high or very high risk. However, how would you categorise a 1 in 20 risk of a patient killing themselves in the next 48 hours? Is that a low risk, a very high risk or somewhere in between?

For the purposes of litigation, the question is at what level the risk ought to have been assessed at the time, not knowing what was going to happen. If a case has come to court, it is because the patient has in fact harmed themselves or died by suicide. It can wrongly seem to be inevitable that harm or suicide was going to occur but that retrospective knowledge should not be allowed to prejudice opinion as to what, prospectively, the proper assessment of risk should have been. Some patients cause themselves serious harm having never done so before and not having expressed any intent to do so. Others who have a long history of self-harm, and who express intent, do not then go on to self-harm again after the clinical assessment. The clinician has to make an adequate assessment of risk in all the circumstances – they are not expected to see into the future.

Once the assessment of risk is made, the question is how to manage it. Again, the fact that a patient has gone on to self-harm or to die by suicide does not prove that the management of risk was inadequate. The claimant will have to prove that there were negligent acts or omissions in their management that caused the harm to occur. An important part of management of an in-patient assessed as being at risk of self-harm or suicide is observation. Typically, hospitals and units operate different levels of observation from perhaps hourly to constant and within arm's length. If observations are, say, every 15 minutes, then there ought to be a record on which staff enter their initials every 15 minutes to show that they have observed the patient and that they are safe and well. This record might include some other details such as where the patient was, whether they were asleep or awake, interacting with others, watching television etc.

Whilst it might be thought to increase patient safety to observe every 15 minutes, the very routine of regular observations gives a patient who is intent on self-harming or taking their life a predictable gap between observations when they know they are not going to be observed. That is not to say that the only safe regime of observation is constant, one to one observation. But the use of regular, intermittent observations has to be seen for what it is. The observation regime should be re-evaluated in the light of any material incidents, disclosures by the patient or changes in their condition and behaviour, and in any event every 24 hours or so.

One of the measures that mental health teams can take in appropriate circumstances is to detain a patient under the Mental Health Act 1983. It is difficult to envisage many circumstances in which it would be considered to be negligent not to have detained a patient but it could happen. The statutory provisions regarding detention form a set of powers rather than obligations. In *S v South West London and St George's Mental Health Trust* [2011] EWHC 1325 (QB) the claimant claimed damages for personal injury for detention after an alleged misdiagnosis of bi-polar disorder but the court found that there had been no negligence. In one case in which I was involved, *Rabone v Pennine Care NHS Trust* [2012] UKSC 2, the Trust had admitted that it had negligently allowed their patient, Melanie Rabone, to go home on "leave" having been an in-patient for a week. She was not being detained under the Act but was a so-called "voluntary" patient. As such she was technically free to leave at any time, but the Trust accepted that had she tried to leave against advice, then she would probably have been detained under the Act. She only left to go home because it had been negligently advised that she should do so.

Where the alleged breaches of duty involve failures to protect someone who is clearly suffering an acute mental health crisis, it may be easier to establish that, but for the negligent failures to observe, to remove sharp objects from the patient's room etc., the subsequent suicide or serious self-harm would probably not have occurred. In other cases, it can be very difficult to prove causation. The course of an untreated disease or traumatic injury is more predictable, perhaps, than the future actions of an individual suffering from a mental health condition. That is why claims arising out of a negligent failure to offer therapy, or to increase this or that medication, will often fail: the claimant cannot prove that the alternative course of treatment would have prevented their suicide attempt or serious self-harm.

The case of *Rabone v Pennine* also illustrates the use of the Human Rights Act 1998 in claims which might usually be seen as fitting squarely within the law of clinical negligence. Melanie Rabone took her own life during the short period of leave from hospital. As noted, she should not have been allowed leave to go home. Negligence was admitted but the only claims that could be made in a clinical negligence claim were for funeral expenses and a small sum to represent her pre-death pain, suffering and loss of amenity. She was 24 years old when she died and as such her parents had no entitlement to a bereavement award under the Fatal Accidents Act 1976. Accordingly, they brought a claim under the Human Rights Act as well as in negligence. They contended that the Trust, a public authority, had failed to take reasonable steps to protect their daughter's life when it had an obligation to do so under Article 2 of the European Convention on Human Rights. Article 2 obliges states in certain circumstances to take action to protect the lives of its citizens. It is established that states should put in place laws and systems of care to fulfil this obligation but, in some cases, there is a particular "operational" obligation to protect individual citizens where it is known, or ought to be known, that their lives are at real and immediate risk. This particular obligation typically arises where a citizen is detained by the state, for example in prison. However, Melanie Rabone was not detained; she was a voluntary patient. Nevertheless, the Supreme Court found that in her case the level of control over her and her vulnerability were such that the operational obligation arose and that it was contravened. Her risk of suicide or serious self-harm was real and it was present and ongoing at the time that she was wrongly allowed home.

This operational obligation under Article 2 of the Convention may arise in cases where the NHS is caring for and, to an extent, controlling a patient with a mental health condition that puts their life at risk. It is unlikely to arise in cases where the NHS is looking after a patient with a purely physical illness, condition or impairment.

In cases where the patient has self-harmed or taken their own lives, the harm was at their own hand. The hospital authority or community mental health team might have owed a duty to assess and manage the risk but they did not directly cause the harm. The fact that the patient took action to harm themselves will not prevent negligent failures of the healthcare team being causative of the subsequent injury or death, but it might give rise to allegations of contributory negligence.

I have addressed the question of contributory negligence in Part 2. It is particularly controversial in the field of psychiatric care. One of the key purposes of the care given to a patient will be to keep them safe from self-harm or suicide. Acts of self-harm by the patient are a manifestation of the very illness or condition which the defendant is responsible for managing. The suicide or incident of self-harm is the result of a negligent failure of care (if it were otherwise the question of contributory negligence would not arise). So, how can it be justifiable to blame the patient, at least in part, for the injury or death?

In Part 2 I referred to the case of *Reeves v Commissioner of Police of the Metropolis* [1999] UKHL 35 in which a finding of contributory negligence was indicated, but that was not a healthcare case.

In another important case, *Corr v IBC Vehicles Ltd* [2008] UKHL 13, a man who suffered a head injury due to his employer's negligence suffered a long and distressing aftermath to the injury culminating in his suicide. The case went to the House of Lords where it was determined that the employer remained liable for all the injuries caused including the suicide, but that a finding of contributory negligence was appropriate.

Lord Mance said:

> "[64] ...a nuanced approach is appropriate, and the existence of a spectrum can and should be recognised. At one extreme is a case such as Reeves where (surprising though it might seem) the evidence was that Mr Lynch was of sound mind when he killed himself. In those circumstances, the suicide could be said to be a purely voluntary act, and one can see how the principle of personal autonomy could be invoked to justify the view reached by Morritt LJ. Nonetheless, your Lordships House decided that there were, in reality, two proximate causes of the death, namely the negligence of the police and Mr Lynch's choice to kill himself and it was effectively impossible to say, at least on the facts of that case, that the suicide was more attributable to one cause than to the other.

> "65. At the other extreme, in my view, would be a case where the

deceased's will and understanding were so overborne by his mental state, which had been caused by the defendant, that there could be no question of any real choice on his part at all, because he had effectively lost his personal autonomy altogether. In effect, in that type of case, the deceased does not really appreciate what he is doing when he kills himself, and he has no real control over his action. In such a case, as the deceased would have had no real choice, there would therefore be no real "fault" on his part for his suicide; consequently there would be no reduction for contributory negligence.

"66. In my judgment, there will be cases in the middle, where the deceased, while not of entirely sound mind, can be said to have a degree of control over his emotions and actions, and will appreciate what he is doing when he kills himself. In other words, there will be cases where a person will have lost a degree of his personal autonomy, but it will not by any means have been entirely lost. In one sense, of course, it can be said that anybody that kills himself has been driven to it, because his natural instinct for self-preservation has been overcome by an irresistible urge to die. However, if that analysis were correct, there would have been no contributory negligence in Reeves, because that argument would apply equally when the deceased's mental state was entirely unimpaired."

Useful though these judgments are to the correct analysis of whether a claimant or deceased patient was guilty of contributory negligence when they harmed themselves or took their own life, they were not judgments in clinical negligence cases. More recently, in part of her judgment that did not contain rulings necessary to determine the case ("obiter" remarks) Mrs Justice Whipple did consider contributory negligence in the case of an attempted suicide in *PPX v Aulakh* [2019] EWHC 717 (QB). The claimant had hanged himself but survived with serious neurological injury. The allegation of negligence was that his GP had made a negligent assessment of his condition and failed to refer him to the crisis team within the community. The judge found that the GP had not been negligent, but that had the GP been found liable, she would have found that the claimant had been guilty of contributory negligence such that his damages should have been reduced by 25%. She referred to both *Reeves* and *Corr*, but because her remarks were not directed to the central issue in the case, her comments were brief and there was no detailed analysis.

Arguably, *Reeves* and *Corr* are materially different from a case where a patient is being treated as an in-patient or within the community as someone at risk of suicide and self-harm (or ought to be being managed in that way).

The defendants in such cases not only have a responsibility for the patient's safety but they are specifically responsible for managing the condition that creates a risk of suicide or self-harm. In such cases, where the defendant alleges contributory negligence, the court will consider whether the claimant was so overwhelmed by their mental health condition at the time that they took action to harm themselves and that they did not have capacity to make decisions about their own health and welfare. So, if the expert opinion is that at the relevant time the claimant did not have such capacity, then a finding of contributory negligence will be unlikely. But that still leaves a lot of cases where a patient has self-harmed or taken their own life when they were capable of making that decision for themselves but were very unwell. The correct analysis of contributory negligence in that kind of case is one that will doubtless be considered by a higher court at some time in the future.

Chapter 7: Neurosurgery

Brain and spinal injuries form the basis of many of the higher value clinical negligence claims. We have already looked at one form of brain injury claim – cerebral palsy – but the neurosurgery-based claims usually concern unrecognised brain injury or delay in operating on deteriorating brain or spinal conditions.

A classic clinical negligence situation arises where an individual presents to a GP or to A&E with a history of having suffered a sudden onset of the worst headache they have ever had – a feeling like being hit with a sledgehammer. They might later develop a stiff neck, nausea and vomiting, sensitivity to light and blurred or double vision. That group of symptoms and complaints suggests a subarachnoid haemorrhage which is bleeding on the surface of the brain. It might be due to a ruptured aneurysm. This is a medical emergency and if it is missed, the patient can die or develop long term neurological complications that might have been avoidable with earlier diagnosis and management. The GP or A&E doctor on recognising the possibility of a subarachnoid haemorrhage should organise a brain scan as a matter of urgency.

A subdural haematoma is a serious condition where blood collects between the skull and the surface of the brain. This may follow a blow to the head which causes a headache that keeps getting worse. The patient might suffer nausea and vomiting, confusion, irritability and drowsiness. The patient with a recognised subdural haematoma might undergo surgery by way of a craniotomy, removing part of the skull to allow access to the brain to remove the haematoma, or by drilling a hole through the skull to drain the haematoma.

Bleeding into the brain can cause raised intracranial (inside the skull) pressure, but so can other causes such as a tumour, a blockage of the flow of the fluid around the brain, or even an unidentifiable cause – the patient can have idiopathic (of unknown cause) intracranial hypertension. Raised intracranial pressure can cause headaches, reduced consciousness, death of parts of the brain, distortion of the brain and ultimately death.

Intracranial pressure can be measured and the patient's level of consciousness can be monitored. Consciousness level is usually assessed using the Glasgow Coma Score (GCS) which runs from 3 to 15. The healthcare professional assesses eye opening (is there none, is it in response to pain or is it spontaneous?), verbal response (none, confused or fully orientated), and motor response (from none to "fully obeys commands"). Even a score of

13 to 14 might give rise to some concern, but a dip to 10 or below is serious.

An example of a clinical negligence claim arising out of a brain injury is the case of *John v Central Manchester & Manchester Children's University Hospitals NHS Foundation Trust* [2016] EWHC 407 (QB).

The claimant fell down some stairs on returning home from a night out. He was found by a neighbour two hours later, slumped in vomit and unable to say anything intelligible. Upon arrival at hospital just before 07:00 he was resuscitated and a CT scan arranged. In fact, the scan was not undertaken for another six hours 15 minutes. It showed an acute subdural haematoma that required urgent neurosurgery. Arrangements were made for the claimant to be transferred to a different hospital for surgery. Whilst awaiting the ambulance of transfer the claimant had a seizure and had to be stabilised. The ambulance was sent away and a second one requested. Eventually the claimant made it to the second hospital where he underwent a craniotomy. He had a further seizure after the surgery and developed a post-operative infection. He required further surgery to relieve raised intracranial pressure.

The judge, Mr Justice Picken, found that the defendant had been guilty of two periods of negligent delay. The first was in performing the CT scan; the second was in summoning a second ambulance after the claimant had been stabilised after his first seizure. The judge also found that the claimant had suffered a period of raised intracranial pressure and that the delays made a material contribution to his injury.

One consequence of brain injury can be epilepsy or the risk of epilepsy. Where epilepsy is suffered then it is an injury that can be "quantified" in the usual way. Where the claimant has an increased risk of suffering epilepsy in the future due to the defendant's negligence then it is common for the claimant to claim provisional damages, i.e. damages on the assumption that they will not later suffer epilepsy but an entitlement to claim further compensation if they do later suffer epilepsy due to the defendant's negligence.

Neurosurgical cases involve the spine as well as the brain. Clinical negligence cases involving the spine usually concern the failure to recognise some changes that are compressing the spinal cord. Compression might be caused by natural spinal degenerative changes, tumour, haemorrhage or infection. Depending on the level of the spine affected, this compression may cause reduced sensation and power in the arms or legs, numbness and altered sensation in the "saddle area" between the legs, and bladder and bowel problems. A form of spinal compression with which experienced clinical negligence litigators are familiar is Cauda Equina Syndrome (CES).

The cauda equina (horse's tail) is a collection of fine nerves that run from the base of the spinal cord. If compressed they may cause neurological dysfunction in the form of so-called "red flag" signs and symptoms such as bilateral nerve pain or altered sensation down the back of the legs, numbness in the saddle area and bladder and bowel problems. Cauda Equina Syndrome giving rise to red flag signs and symptoms requires very urgent neurosurgical attention to decompress the affected nerves. This is an emergency whilst the CES is "incomplete", meaning that the patient has not yet gone into urinary retention whereby they cannot pass water at all. If the affected spine is not decompressed within hours then CES can become complete and the patient goes into retention. They can then suffer permanent loss of bladder and bowel function, sexual dysfunction and serious mobility problems.

As can be imagined, a person who presented to a healthcare professional with "red flag" signs and symptoms and was not treated as requiring immediate neurosurgical attention, and who then goes on to require a wheelchair for mobility and a permanent catheter, might well want to sue for negligence. So, there are quite a few CES cases that pass through the courts each year. They are "knife edge" cases where the difference of an hour here and there can make all the difference to whether liability is established.

An example of how the courts approach claims of deterioration due to CES can be found in *Oakes v Neininger, Borwn and Greater Manchester Ambulance Service* [2008] EWHC 548 (QB). The claimant had suffered from back pain and a urinary problem for some years but the back pain increased and he consulted his GP. After a disturbed night and difficulty in urinating an ambulance was called to the claimant's house. The crew believed he had sciatica and arranged for a second GP to attend who agreed. Later a second ambulance crew was called out but did not recommend that the claimant should go to hospital. Still later the claimant lost control of his bladder and a third GP attended and arranged for urgent specialist attention. The claimant went to hospital and was diagnosed with CES, undergoing decompression surgery but being left with serious bladder and bowel function, loss of sexual function, impaired walking and poor balance. The claimant successfully sued the first GP, the second GP and the second ambulance crew. He failed against the first ambulance crew.

The first GP was found to have been negligent because the claimant had advised him about pain down both legs and whilst the GP had not been obliged to make an urgent referral, he should have given proper advice to the claimant that if he developed any urinary problems, as he did, he should seek immediate specialist help. The court held that, but for the negligence of the three defendants, the claimant would have undergone decompression whilst still in the CES incomplete stage, whereas because of the negligence he went on to the CES retention (or complete) stage. Had he been treated in the incomplete stage he would probably have enjoyed a good recovery.

Chester v Afshar [2004] UKHL 41 was discussed in Part 2 but it is useful to mention it again here because it was a case of Cauda Equina Syndrome following neurosurgery. Miss Chester had back pain and was advised by Mr Afshar, a neurosurgeon, to have surgery to her spine. The surgery carried with it a small (1% to 2%) unavoidable risk of causing CES. Mr Afshar did not warn Miss Chester of that risk but her evidence was that had she been warned she would not have gone ahead with the operation as soon as she did, but would have taken time to consider the risks and benefits and other options. She was unable to say that she would have elected not to undergo the surgery. As it is, she went ahead with the surgery, the complication arose and she was left with permanent disability due to CES. The defendant contended that, on the evidence, the claimant was unable to prove that but for the negligent failure to warn her of the risk, she would have avoided having the surgery that inevitably gave rise to that risk.

The application of ordinary principles of causation would have defeated Miss Chester's claim but the majority of judges in the House of Lords were prepared to bend the ordinary principles and to find that Mr Afshar was liable. Lord Steyn said, *"Her right of autonomy and dignity can and ought to be vindicated by a narrow and modest departure from traditional causation principles."*

As I mentioned in Part 2, Lord Hoffmann was dismissive of the claimant's case.

Over the years since *Chester v Afshar* was decided, several courts have taken the opportunity to narrow the circumstances in which it might be applied, and, more recently, frankly, to cast doubt on it. In *Duce v Worcestershire Acute Hospitals NHS Trust* [2018] EWCA Civ 1307, Lord Justice Leggatt said that it was high time for the Supreme Court to reconsider the principle set out by the majority of judges in *Chester v Afshar*. He described the *Chester* decision as "problematic", observing that:

> *"In law as in everyday life A's wrongful act is not normally regarded as having caused B's injury if the act made no difference to the probability of the injury occurring. In such a case the fact that the injury would not have occurred but for the wrongful act is merely a coincidence."*

Neurosurgery to the spine often involves small risks of very serious compli-cations. Patients often face difficult decisions whether to continue with con-servative, non-surgical management of back pain or to elect to undergo an operation. The importance of warning those patients of material risks prior to their electing to have surgery is particularly acute in such cases. This was illustrated in *Hassall v Hillingdon Hospitals NHS Trust* [2018] EWHC 164 (QB), in which the claimant was awarded damages of £4.4 million after she had been left permanently paralysed as a result of spinal surgery. Al-though the surgeon had used reasonable care and skill when performing the surgery, he had not obtained the claimant's informed consent before the surgery. The risk of paralysis was very small but Mr Justice Dingemans held that: *"if she been told that not having conservative treatment was an option, and that surgery carried a risk of 1 in 500 to 1 in 1,000 of permanent paralysis, [the claimant] would have opted for conservative treatment."*

Chapter 8: Care of the Vulnerable

For obvious reasons most claimants in clinical negligence cases are not fully fit and well at the time of the alleged breaches of duty. Most are undergoing clinical care because they are unwell. However, particular consideration needs to be given to claimants who are vulnerable or who have underlying, permanent conditions that give rise to the need for care and support irrespective of any additional injury caused by clinical negligence.

Vulnerability might arise because of learning difficulties, dementia, old age, young age, disability or countless other reasons. Of course, the vulnerability of someone with dementia in a nursing home is very different from that of a young adult amputee. Each claimant is an individual and their own circumstances, limitations, abilities and characters need to be taken into account in each case. However, there are some common themes that are worth consideration.

First, patients who have an existing disability or limitation on their ability to live independently tend to receive less compensation than those who are not so restricted. This is because compensation is paid for the additional losses and expenses caused by injury. In *Reaney v University Hospital of North Staffordshire NHS Trust* [2015] EWCA Civ 1119 the claimant had contracted transverse myelitis at the age of 61 leaving her paralysed below the mid-thoracic level. Her needs would have been met initially by a few hours care each week rising to over 31 hours of care per week after she reached the age of 75. That care regime would have allowed her to live largely independently but, during her hospitalisation, she suffered some deep pressure sores which led to infection in her bones, hip dislocation, serious leg contractures and increased lower limb spasticity. As a result, she was unable to use a standard wheelchair and was left with a large area of skin that was prone to breakdown. Accordingly, she needed 24 hour care from two carers. The defendants admitted that the pressure sores were caused by their negligence. At trial the judge found the defendants liable for all the claimant's care needs. The defendants appealed and the Court of Appeal overturned the judge's decision: the defendants were liable to meet only the increased care needs. If the defendants' negligence caused her to have care and other needs which were substantially of the same kind as her pre-existing needs, then the damage caused by the negligence was only that due to the additional needs. If the needs caused by the negligence were qualitatively different from her pre-existing needs, then those needs were caused in their entirety by the negligence.

It does not help the claimant that the care needs that they would have had, irrespective of the negligence, might have been paid for by the state, whereas after the negligence they are likely to pay for all of their needs themselves (theoretically out of the damages awarded to them in the claim). The defendants are only liable for the costs that are for additional needs created by their negligence.

Second, and in contrast, sometimes a claimant's pre-existing disability can lead to a higher level of compensation than would otherwise have been the case. If an eye surgeon negligently causes blindness in the patient's right eye, they can expect to face a larger damages claim if the patient was already blind in their left eye than if they had previously had good vision in both. A claimant who was previously a wheelchair user but, due to the defendant's negligence, loses function in their hands, may well suffer much greater loss and expense than someone who was previously fully ambulant. They may now need a powered wheelchair, help with transferring in and out of it, and to and from bed etc.

Third, where the patient is a child or an adult who lacks capacity to make decisions about their own treatment, then careful consideration needs to be given in relation to those decisions. For children, there will usually be a parent or guardian who will make decisions on their behalf. Healthcare professionals also rely heavily on the parents or guardians of young children to help to give a history of the presenting complaints, to describe symptoms and so on. In all but exceedingly rare cases, healthcare professionals and parents agree on a course of action to treat and care for a child. This is testament to the trust that parents have in the professionals, the communication skills of those professionals, and the ability of people, sometimes under extreme stress, to work together in the interests of the child patient. Every now and then, however, there are profound disagreements and the courts become involved. These are not clinical negligence cases but applications for the court to determine whether a proposed course of action is in the best interests of the child. The proposed action might involve the withdrawal of life-sustaining treatment. Unsurprisingly, some parents find that they cannot agree that the withdrawal of treatment, with the likely consequence that their child will die, is in the child's best interests. Cases such as those include Alfie Evans *(Alder Hey Children's NHS Foundation Trust v Evans* [2018] EWHC 308 (Fam) and *Evans & Anor v Alder Hey Children's NHS Foundation Trust & Ors* [2018] EWCA Civ 805). The test for the court, the "gold standard", is what is in the best interest of the child. As Baroness Hale expressed it in *Aintree University Hospital NHS Trust v James* [2013] UKSC 67:

> *"[22] Hence the focus is on whether it is in the patient's best interests*
> *to give the treatment rather than whether it is in his best interests to*

withhold or withdraw it. If the treatment is not in his best interests, the court will not be able to give its consent on his behalf and it will follow that it will be lawful to withhold or withdraw it. Indeed, it will follow that it will not be lawful to give it. It also follows that (provided of course they have acted reasonably and without negligence) the clinical team will not be in breach of any duty toward the patient if they withhold or withdraw it." ...

"[39] The most that can be said, therefore, is that in considering the best interests of this particular patient at this particular time, decision-makers must look at his welfare in the widest sense, not just medical but social and psychological; they must consider the nature of the medical treatment in question, what it involves and its prospects of success; they must consider what the outcome of that treatment for the patient is likely to be; they must try and put themselves in the place of the individual patient and ask what his attitude towards the treatment is or would be likely to be; and they must consult others who are looking after him or are interested in his welfare, in particular for their view of what his attitude would be."

It is not the function of the courts in such cases to uphold the rights of the parents whatever the consequences for the child. Some of the comments about the *Alfie Evans* case from around the world suggested that parents should have an absolute right to dictate the treatment decisions concerning their child. The state, it was alleged, was taking those rights away and effectively terminating the life of a child rather than doing everything to keep them alive.

Much of the reaction against the judgments in the *Alfie Evans* case seemed to assume that any decision other than to do everything to keep him alive was immoral and unjustified. However, this is not the position usually adopted by the courts or indeed by moral philosophers or the church. In one of his judgments in the case Mr Justice Hayden quoted from an open letter from His Holiness Pope Francis in 2017:

"It thus makes possible a decision that is morally qualified as withdrawal of "overzealous treatment". Such a decision responsibly acknowledges the limitations of our mortality, once it becomes clear that opposition to it is futile. "Here one does not will to cause death; one's inability to impede it is merely accepted" (Catechism of the Catholic Church, No. 2278). This difference of perspective restores humanity to the accompaniment of the dying, while not attempting to justify the suppression of the living. It is clear that not adopting, or else

> *suspending, disproportionate measures, means avoiding overzealous treatment; from an ethical standpoint, it is completely different from euthanasia, which is always wrong, in that the intent of euthanasia is to end life and cause death. Needless to say, in the face of critical situations and in clinical practice, the factors that come into play are often difficult to evaluate. To determine whether a clinically appropriate medical intervention is actually proportionate, the mechanical application of a general rule is not sufficient. There needs to be a careful discernment of the moral object, the attending circumstances, and the intentions of those involved. In caring for and accompanying a given patient, the personal and relational elements in his or her life and death – which is after all the last moment in life – must be given a consideration befitting human dignity. In this process, the patient has the primary role."*

An adult with capacity can make decisions for themselves. A baby cannot. It does not follow that the parents of the baby have an absolute right to make all decisions for their child. The courts serve to protect the interests of the child, rather. Likewise, the court may be called upon to make decision in the best interests of an adult who does not have the capacity to make decisions about their own treatment. These decisions are obviously difficult and sensitive, but there is no hard and fast rule that treatment must always be given whatever the circumstances, nor that the wish of healthcare professionals to withdraw treatment (if that is the case) must always prevail. Each case will turn on its own facts after careful consideration of all relevant circumstances and putting the interests of the patient first.

For adults who lack the mental capacity to make a decision, there is a range of provisions that may allow their wishes to be put into effect. Many people give power of attorney to others. Appointing an attorney to make decisions about your medical care and treatment can only be done whilst you have the capacity to make the appointment but once made, it lasts so that if you lose capacity your appointed attorney can make those decisions on your behalf. This appointment is now called a "lasting power of attorney". You can appoint more than one attorney to act jointly (having to take decisions together) or jointly and severally (allowing some of the decisions to be taken individually).

Individuals can also make advance decisions. These documents will set out their wishes for their treatment or management in the event of certain circumstances arising. For example, you might make an advance decision not to have life sustaining treatment or not to be resuscitated. If you have made an advance decision and later give lasting power of attorney to someone then you should specify whether the advance decision is to be respected by the attorney. Advance decisions should be made in writing, signed and the signature witnessed. You must have full mental capacity and be over 18 when you make the advance decision. You should specify clearly which treatments you wish to refuse, explain the circumstances in which you wish to refuse them, state that you have made the decision of your own accord and without any harassment or pressure from anyone else, and you should not do or say anything to contradict the advance decision.

You cannot make an advance decision that someone should assist you to die by suicide or should kill you. It remains unlawful to assist suicide and "mercy killing" is murder.

I have already explained that compensation recovered by a claimant who does not have the mental capacity to litigate and to manage the proceeds of litigation will be managed on their behalf under supervision of the Court of Protection. If the claimant's lack of capacity is not due to the negligence, but pre-existed the negligence, then it remains the case that their compensation will have to be managed on their behalf. If a claimant is injured due to clinical negligence they will need to claim the costs associated with the management of the money as part of the claim, even though the defendant did not cause the incapacity.

Fourth, the care and management of some vulnerable adults involves a deprivation of their liberty. The European Convention on Human Rights gives citizens a right to freedom of movement, but if you are the subject of a care regime that effectively prevents you from leaving a care home as you please, then your liberty is being curtailed, even if it might be in your interests for that to be so. The Mental Capacity Act 2005 introduced Deprivation of Liberty Safeguards (DOLS) which took effect from 2009. Amendments to the Act in 2019 replaced these with Liberty Protection Safeguards. A responsible authority may authorise care or treatment that restricts a person's freedom where to do so is in their best interests. A case decided in 2019 demonstrates the importance of complying with the law concerning deprivation of liberty and the safeguards in place. The case was *Esegbona v King's College Hospital NHS Foundation Trust* [2019] EWHC 77 (QB).

Mrs Esegbona was admitted to Kings College Hospital on 20 October 2010 with pulmonary oedema due to left-sided heart failure. She suffered hypoglycaemic episodes requiring intensive care treatment including intubation. She was transferred out of the ICU to a ward on 14 January 2011. She was confused and had cognitive impairment and communication difficulties. She was seen by a psychiatrist who advised that she needed an assessment of her capacity but no assessment was ever carried out even though there were subsequent, repeated recommendations to the same effect. Mrs Esegbona wished to go home and her family was prepared to look after her at home. She still had a tracheostomy and so home-care was fraught with risk but the indications within the judgment are that her family had the personal resources to cope. Mrs Esegbona did not want to have her tube in place and sought to self-extubate whilst in hospital, necessitating emergency intervention. Her tube became blocked on another occasion. Eventually, on 14 June 2011 Mrs Esegbona was transferred to a nursing home, Wilsmere House, but the nursing home was not informed of the difficulties with her tracheostomy, her wish to be at home, and the previous events of self-extubation and blockage. About a week after the transfer she self-extubated again, this time fatally.

The court found that the Trust had been negligent in failing to give sufficient advice to the nursing home. Had it done so then Mrs Esegbona would have been under one to one supervision or kept within sight of a nurse at all times. Her self-extubation would have been avoided. The Trust was held liable for damages for her pre-death pain, suffering and loss of amenity in the sum of £3,500.

The court also found that the defendant Trust had kept the family out of the planning for discharge. It had not carried out an assessment of mental capacity and had not undertaken any assessment of best interests. Deprivation of Liberty Safeguards under the Mental Capacity Act 2005 had not been followed. Mrs Esegbona's retention at the hospital was found to have been unlawful for the period from 15 February 2011, when an assessment of her capacity and deprivation of her liberty ought to have occurred, until 14 June 2011, when she was transferred to the nursing home. The defendant had been guilty of false imprisonment over that period. The court rejected the defendant's argument that even if correct procedures had been followed it was obvious that Mrs Esegbona would have been retained in hospital until a suitable placement in a nursing home had been found, as was the case. The court awarded damages of £130 per day – over £15,000 – for false imprisonment. It also awarded aggravated damages of £5,000. In most similar cases a claim would be brought under the Human Rights Act but there is a time limit of one year for bringing claims under that Act, which might explain why the claim was brought for the tort of false imprisonment (which has a six year time limit) rather than under the Act.

The case underlines the importance of NHS Trusts and others in a similar position identifying when decisions are being made or proposed that affect the liberty of a vulnerable individual who may lack mental capacity in relation to those decisions. The NHS must act lawfully and in accordance with the liberty protection safeguards.

Chapter 9: Primary Healthcare

General medical practitioners, GPs, see dozens of patients each day. They have perhaps ten to 15 minutes allocated for each one. They do not know how a patient will present, what the history will be or what level of communication skills the patient will have. They have to act as inquisitor, detective, counsellor and guide. The television series: *GPs Behind Closed Doors*, set in my home city of Bradford, provides a fascinating insight into the role of a general medical practitioner. Many of those attending have very minor ailments. One patient was shown presenting with a spot which his diligent GP squeezed for him! But in amongst the majority is the odd case where there is a serious underlying condition behind the presentation. Just like the goalkeeper called upon to make one save during a ninety minute game, the GP has to be constantly alert.

Naturally, as a clinical negligence barrister, I see the cases where the GP dropped the ball. I cross-examine GPs on the basis that they missed obvious signs of cauda equina syndrome or early stages of meningitis. But how many patients had they seen with back pain or with headaches that had no sinister underlying cause?

In the past general practitioners have tended to be represented by a Medical Defence Organisation. That remains the case at the time of writing, but the new Clinical Negligence Scheme for General Practice, operated by NHS Resolution, may, if the MDOs agree that their members should join it, mean that GPs and others who work with them to deliver primary healthcare within the NHS will be backed by the NHSR in litigation.

General Practitioners tend to work in partnership at surgeries or healthcare centres, working alongside practice nurses and, sometimes, therapists, to deliver primary healthcare. In my experience the great majority of clinical negligence claims against primary healthcare professionals do not concern harm done by them directly through the administration of treatment, but rather the harm done by their failure to recognise the need for treatment, or the need to refer a patient for more specialist care.

As we have seen in relation to delay in diagnosing cancer, there are national guidelines to help general practitioners and practice nurses make evidence-based decisions about when to refer a patient for specialist investigation and management for suspected cancer. There are many other guidelines for the management of a range of problems from headaches to diabetes.

A study for the Medical Protection Society conducted by The Health Foundation looked at 50 clinical negligence claims against general practices over a three-year period. 28% of the cases involved a delay in diagnosis or treatment of a patient with cancer. 30% were judged to be 'never events' and 85 distinct system issues were identified. Just under half of cases involved a failure to notify patients of an abnormal test result and 36% involved a test result not being actioned by a doctor.

Failures to follow up test results will often lead to litigation where the test results should have mandated referral. This is a recurrent theme in litigation, as the study showed. A patient is advised by the GP to have, say, a blood test. The results will come back from the laboratory to the surgery with abnormal results usually marked by an asterisk, or written in bold or otherwise highlighted. There has to be an adequate system in place at the surgery, properly deployed, to review incoming results, note abnormalities and to take appropriate action which will include communication with the patient. The individual GP might not be to blame for a "missed" test result: it can be the system that is deficient. But the GP is not only responsible for their own acts and omissions when dealing directly with patients – they often run the surgery in partnership with others and have responsibility for the proper functioning of the systems in place.

One frequent bone of contention is when a patient is asked to return for further tests or advice but they fail to do so. What is the duty on the primary healthcare professional to "chase" the patient and ensure that they return? Sometimes the practice will maintain that a letter for a follow up appointment was sent but the patient maintains that it did not arrive. Sometimes the patient misses an appointment, perhaps not realising its importance. There is no neat answer to where responsibility lies. "It depends" is not a very appealing answer for a lawyer to give, but it truly does depend on the exact circumstances before it can be determined whether the GP might be responsible for the failure to take reasonable steps to secure the re-attendance of a patient. If, for example, there is a test result showing an alarmingly high PSA result (raising the possibility of prostate cancer) for a patient who had gone to their GP with urinary problems, then a standard letter to the patient saying, *"Your recent test results have been received, please make an appointment to see a GP"* might not be regarded as adequate. NICE Guidelines would suggest that the patient should be referred to a urologist to be seen within two weeks but there is no sense of urgency in the letter. On the other hand, there are limits to the extent to which a general practice can be expected to request a patient to re-attend.

A related problem that affects many clinical negligence actions against primary healthcare providers is the advice given. It is sometimes said that GPs apply the rule of three – on the third attendance for the same problem they will refer the patient to a specialist. Of course, that is a crude generalisation but it is nevertheless true that GPs will often assess the patient as being well enough not to require specialist intervention, but having the potential to deteriorate or to need specialist help if their condition does not improve. There are subtle but important differences between advice to *"come back if worse"*, and to *"come back again if does not improve"*, or to *"come back if still concerned."* In some cases, it is negligent for a GP not to give a specific date to return for review, rather than leaving it to the patient to make their own mind up about whether and when to return. Advice about what symptoms to look out for – those which might indicate a deterioration in the patient's condition requiring urgent specialist attention – is very important, just as important sometimes as giving the patient some tablets for their pain, or some antibiotics for a suspected bacterial infection. Sometimes the patient is putting on their coat ready to leave when the GP gives that sort of advice and it may not be fully understood. Court cases can turn on these small details.

Such are the demands on general practice that sometimes GPs conduct consultations by telephone. In *Payne v Jatoi* [2018] EWHC 871 (QB) Mrs Justice Lambert was satisfied that the GP had acted reasonably when not diagnosing a fractured hip after a telephone "triage" of the claimant who had suffered a fall at home. General practices also make increasing use of practice nurses. The standard of care expected should be that appropriate to the role so it is no defence that the person carrying out the role was a nurse rather than a medical practitioner. Practice nurses who are deployed to carry out assessments of skin lesions of breast lumps etc should be properly trained and experienced and ought to follow the same guidelines as general practitioners.

Locum GPs may be employees or agents of the practice such that the practice is vicariously liable for their negligence, or they might be employed by an NHS body, or they might be sued individually if they are indemnified by a Medical Defence Organisation. The new Clinical Negligence Scheme for General Practice would cover the negligence of locums. In *Brayshaw v The Partners of Apsley Surgery and O'Brien* [2018] EWHC 3286 (QB) Mr Justice Martin Spencer found that the GP partners were not vicariously liable for the acts of a locum GP, later erased from the medical register for misconduct, who had advised a patient with mental health problems to eschew medication and to put her trust in God. The court held that notwithstanding the claimant's lack of credibility on a number of issues, the locum GP had been negligent and had caused injury thereby. However, the partnership was not vicariously liable for that negligence: the locum worked at other practices as well as the defendant's surgery; the locum was not delivering medical care when seeking to evangelise and therefore not acting on behalf of the practice in that respect; and the locum had mostly acted away from the surgery premises when acting negligently.

This very short review highlights the fact that alongside claims directed at individual failures by primary healthcare professionals, to which the *Bolam* test would apply, there are others that are directed at the systems in place at a GP practice. Failures in the way appointments, tests, call-backs and referrals are managed can lead to avoidable harm to patients. The *Bolam* test does not seem well suited to assessing whether such system failures were negligent.

Chapter 10: Other Healthcare Professionals

Members of the public come into contact with a whole range of healthcare professionals other than medical doctors and nurses but it is fair to say that the vast majority of clinical negligence claims arise from medical and nursing care. There are lawyers who specialise in dental negligence claims, which does demonstrate the existence of a flow of claims against dental practitioners, but the number is still relatively very small. I have conducted claims against physiotherapists and osteopaths, but I can count them on the fingers of one hand from 30 years of clinical negligence practice. Pharmacists have particular duties that have been explored in a very few reported cases. Counsellors and psychotherapists can certainly face claims for negligence, but reported court judgments are hard to find.

A common approach to the standard of care to be expected for non-medical healthcare professionals is for the courts to look at guidelines and standards published by professional bodies. In the cases of *Horton v Evans and Lloyd's Pharmacy Ltd*, and *D and P v Cardiff & Vale NHS Trust*, mentioned below, the court used those standards to set the bar for expectations for the conduct of the defendant. Arguably, this reliance on standards set by the profession itself becomes more questionable with therapists such as chiropractors when some medical professionals would question the validity and usefulness of the therapy itself. There might, in such cases, be a more significant role for the court's own scrutiny of the rationality of the standards set by the profession itself. That was the approach taken in *Shakoor v Situ* [2001] 1 WLR 410 mentioned in Part 2. The court looked at the standards set by the "profession" and then at whether those standards were themselves acceptable by reference to standards of orthodox medicine.

Dentists

General Dental Practitioners have to be as alert as GPs to the need to refer to specialists for suspected cancer. In *Drabble v Hughes* (unreported), a judgment of Recorder Sweeting QC sitting as a Deputy High Court Judge, a dentist was found not to have been negligent in failing to refer a patient to an oral surgeon. The patient had a longstanding white patch on the lower left side of her mouth which had been kept under observation by her dental hospital until, after several years, the hospital discharged her on the basis that she would be reviewed at routine checkups, writing to her general dental practitioner, the defendant, accordingly. Five years later the defendant did refer the claimant to an oral surgeon who identified a tumour which required surgical excision, radiotherapy and chemotherapy. The claimant alleged that she had complained about changes in the colour and appearance of the patch a year earlier but the court did not accept her evidence, noting that the dentist had been well aware of the need for vigilance following the 2004 referral letter, he had reviewed the white patch on the gum regularly and had recorded the presence of the patch and the medical history in the dental records. There had been no significant change in the appearance of the patch which warranted an urgent referral. This case shows the importance of keeping good records.

Just like doctors, dentists have to obtain the informed consent of their patients to treatment. In *Parry v Day* [1996] 7 Med LR 396 the allegation was that the claimant's dentist had failed to do so. The claimant claimed to have suffered loss of feeling in her lip and gum due to nerve damage sustained during extraction of a wisdom tooth. She alleged that the defendant ought to have recognised that the extraction would be extremely difficult and that there was a high risk of nerve damage which he ought to have warned her about, advising her also that there were alternative treatments available. The court held that, although the claimant suffered residual numbness, it was not possible to say how the nerve was damaged, that the extraction had been straightforward and that at the relevant time (1990) it had not been "necessary" to explain potential complications or alternative treatments when performing a straightforward extraction because it ran contrary to the thinking of the majority of the dental profession at the time to frighten every patient with excessive warnings. This might not be a finding were a similar case to come to court now, following *Montgomery v Lanarkshire*. In any event, the court found, there had not been a foreseeable risk of nerve damage with the extraction of this tooth, and therefore there could have been no need to warn of such a risk.

Interestingly in *Parry v Day* the court held that if the claim had succeeded, damages would have been £1,000. The costs of bringing that claim would have been hugely disproportionate to the likely damages had it succeeded.

There is one kind of claim against general dental practitioners that is unusual to find in litigation against doctors and nurses, and that is a claim for over-treatment. In *Appleton and others v Garrett* [1996] PIQR P1, eight claimants were patients of the defendant. They alleged that the defendant had grossly over-treated them between 1981 and 1988. The defendant had been struck off the dental register in 1989 following a disciplinary hearing concerning over-treatment, and negligence was admitted. The court hearing the damages claims had to decide whether the defendant was liable for the tort of trespass to the person. Such was the gross over-treatment and the absence of informed consent in the case that Mr Justice Dyson (later to become a judge of the Supreme Court) held that it must have been obvious to the defendant that the over-treatment was unnecessary, he had withheld information deliberately and in bad faith knowing that the patients would not have consented to treatment had they been given proper advice that the treatment was unnecessary, and there was exceptional and blameworthy behaviour to justify a finding that the defendant had been guilty of trespass to the person. The defendant had acted for the purpose of financial gain and it was proper to award aggravated damages to the claimants for their feelings of anger and indignation. On top of the damages awarded for the injuries themselves they were awarded a further 15% of those sums each by way of aggravated damages.

This was an extreme example, but there have been other claims in negligence arising out of alleged over-treatment by general dental practitioners.

Opticians

Few patients will sue their opticians for issuing the wrong prescription for the lenses for their spectacles. The more relevant risk is of litigation arising out of the failure to detect or suspect a more sinister or serious problem on an examination. In *Thomas Murphy v Gillaine Seymour and another*, 2005, Judge Goldstein found the defendant optician liable for failure to refer a patient to a specialist where his symptoms should have alerted her to the existence of reticular disturbance. The optician had initially advised that the claimant had an early cataract. Two years later the patient returned with near total loss of vision in the affected eye. On referral a large melanoma was diagnosed and the eye had to be removed.

In a striking criminal legal case an optometrist who failed to identify signs of a brain condition in an eight year old schoolboy, Vincent Barker who died months later, was convicted of gross negligence manslaughter. Her conviction was overturned on appeal in a judgment reported at *Rose v R* [2017] EWCA Crim 1168.

Expert opinion evidence on images of the boy's eyes was that they showed papilloedema: swelling of the optic disc. This was probably due to hydrocephalus, a build up of fluid in the brain. He did not have symptoms often associated with hydrocephalus such as headaches and sickness. It was alleged that Ms Rose had been grossly negligent in failing to carry out an adequate examination and in failing to refer the patient for specialist opinion. Had she done so then he would, ultimately, have been diagnosed with hydrocephalus which could have been treated, preventing his death.

Ms Rose told police that she had begun the examination using an ophthalmoscope but that Vincent had been resistant, and so she had relied on photographs of the back of the eye.

The Court of Appeal found that the conviction had been unsafe because it was not right to take into account, when considering whether the defendant was guilty of gross negligence, consequences of their actions that would only have been reasonably foreseeable to them had they carried out the appropriate examination:

> *"We conclude that, in assessing reasonable foreseeability of serious and obvious risk of death in cases of gross negligence manslaughter, it is not appropriate to take into account what the defendant would have known but for his or her breach of duty. Were the answer otherwise, this would fundamentally undermine the established legal test of foreseeability in gross negligence manslaughter which requires proof of a "serious and obvious risk of death" at the time of breach. The implications for medical and other professions would be serious because people would be guilty of gross negligence manslaughter by reason of negligent omissions to carry out routine eye, blood and other tests which in fact would have revealed fatal conditions notwithstanding that the circumstances were such that it was not reasonably foreseeable that failure to carry out such tests would carry an obvious and serious risk of death. For these reasons, this appeal is allowed and the conviction is quashed."*

This principle is applicable to the conduct of all healthcare professionals.

Pharmacists
Dispensing pharmacists have a solemn responsibility to ensure that the right drugs are given in the right quantity to the right patients.

In *Wootton v J Docter Limited* [2008] EWCA Civ 1361 the Court of Appeal addressed a problem of causation following negligence by a pharmacist who dispensed the wrong contraceptive pill to the claimant, who later became pregnant. The individual pharmacist had been a self-employed locum and was found to have been negligent at trial. Where a dispensing pharmacist makes a clear error, selecting and dispensing the wrong drug, and when there is a material difference between the drug prescribed and the drug dispensed, then it will be difficult to defend an allegation of negligence. That is why pharmacies have strict protocols and safety netting procedures in place.

In fact, the claimant lost her claim in that case and the Court of Appeal upheld the trial judge's decision. As a result of the negligent error the claimant took exactly the same quantity of oestrogen but took 100mcg less of progesterone. The court held that the evidence showed that this did not materially increase the risk of contraceptive failure and the claimant could not prove that her pregnancy resulted from the change in pills.

The dispensing pharmacist's duty goes beyond merely following instructions from a medical practitioner. In *Horton v Evans and Lloyds Pharmacy Ltd* [2006] EWHC 2808 (QB) the court decided that when dispensing a prescription, a pharmacist was required to consider whether the medication prescribed was suitable for the patient and, where there had been a change to the strength or dose of the patient's medication, the pharmacist should consider whether the doctor had really intended to prescribe what was written down or had made a mistake. A pharmacist was found to have been negligent for failing to question the correctness of a prescription. The claimant sued their GP and the pharmacist Lloyds who employed a particular pharmacist (G). She had been mis-prescribed some medication for a minor problem. By the time the case came to trial the only issue for the judge to decide was whether the pharmacist had been negligent and had caused the claimant her injuries. The judge did not have to decide whether the prescribing GP had also been negligent. Over a long time, the claimant had taken one 0.5mg tablet of dexamethasone a day but on one occasion her GP had provided a prescription for 28 4mg tablets, and had omitted to specify the dosage. Lloyds' computerised system showed that the same branch had dispensed dexamethasone to the claimant on seven previous occasions. G noticed that the strength of the tablets was greater than in the past and did look up the medication to discover that 4mg was within the usual therapeutic range for a daily dose. Consequently, he did not question the prescription with the GP. In fact, 4mg tablets were not available so G dispensed 56 2mg tablets. Some three weeks later, whilst on holiday in the United States, the claimant asked another doctor for a repeat prescription and was given 90 4mg tablets. She eventually became unwell due to an overdose. The court found that a pharmacist (at the time) was required by the Royal Pharmaceutical Society of Great Britain's Code of Medicines, Ethics and Practice to consider whether the medication being prescribed was suitable for the patient. Given also that the claimant had previously had a lower dose tablet from the same pharmacy, G ought to have asked whether the GP's prescription was a mistake and checked with the GP. In fact, Lloyd's Pharmacy had a branch procedures manual that covered that very situation. G failed to follow the procedures in place and to act as would any reasonable body of pharmacists. The doctor in the USA had not been negligent and the pharmacy was liable for the deterioration in the claimant's condition caused by her taking the increased dosage. Compensation was later assessed by the court at over £1.4 million.

Psychologists and Counsellors

Psychologists and counsellors have to be acutely aware of the need for specialist referral, of the importance of maintaining confidentiality, and of respecting boundaries. In *D v P and Cardiff and Vale NHS Trust* (unreported, 2008) a defendant clinical psychologist entered into a consensual sexual relationship with a former patient who had been suffering from borderline personality disorder. The High Court Judge held that the psychologist's conduct was to be judged by reference to the psychological society's guidelines which prohibited any sexual relationship between a psychologist and an existing client or with a former client for at least two years after discharging them. The guidelines also placed a burden on a therapist to show non-exploitation of the former client where there was a sexual relationship starting more than two years after the end of the professional relationship. In this particular case, the sexual relationship had begun three years eight months after the psychologist had discharged their patient from a course of counselling. The therapist had not known that their former client had a borderline personality disorder. The claimant had in fact made positive moves to form the sexual relationship and there had been no exploitation by the defendant. Thus, the judge found, there had been compliance with the professional guidelines and no negligence. In any event, the claimant failed to prove causation of any injury. The court held that there was no evidence of the claimant suffering a recognised psychiatric injury resulting from the relationship or that the relationship adversely affected or aggravated her personality disorder.

The issue of causation will be difficult for many claimants who allege negligence by their counsellor or psychologist. Whilst such therapy may improve a claimant's condition, it will be difficult to prove that inadequate therapy has caused avoidable harm.

Physiotherapists

The claims against physiotherapists in which I have been involved have all involved failures to recognise "red flag" signs of cauda equina syndrome (see "Neurosurgery" above). I can vouch for the fact that physiotherapists can cause their patients to suffer pain, but it would be unusual for negligent physiotherapy to cause lasting damage serious enough to make it worthwhile to bring a clinical negligence claim.

Medical practitioners may refer patients for physiotherapy but the fact that the patient has already seen a doctor does not preclude the physiotherapist from having a duty to make their own assessment of the patient's needs. If the patient will not benefit from physiotherapy or needs referral to a specialist medical practitioner, then the physiotherapist has a duty to act accordingly. A failure to recognise the need for urgent specialist attention, for example when a patient has signs of developing cauda equina compression, could result in delay in decompression and permanent neurological injury.

Chiropractors and Osteopaths

If you look at medical "malpractice" litigation in the United States of America, you will not have to look for long before finding accounts of large claims against chiropractors where patients have suffered strokes following neck manipulation. Osteopaths also sometimes adopt the same technique. I know from personal experience of similar claims in England and Wales but perhaps none have yet reached trial because there seems to be a shortage of judgments on the issue. The allegation is that neck manipulation can cause arterial damage and stroke. In 2001, members of the Association of British Neurologists were asked to report cases referred to them of neurological complications occurring within 24 hours of neck manipulation over a 12-month period. This was reported in the Journal of the Royal Society of Medicine 94:107-110, 2001. There were 35 reported cases which included seven strokes involving the vertebrobasilar artery and two strokes involving a carotid artery. None of the 35 cases were reported to medical journals. It is surely of concern that there had been no prior reporting of these incidents.

In the Journal of Neurology in 2009, Reuter and others reported 36 patients with vertebral artery dissections following chiropractic neck manipulation after a nationwide survey of neurological departments in Germany over a three-year period. Symptoms consistent with vertebral arterial dissection had occurred within 12 hours of manipulation in 55% of those patients.

In 2003, a coroner's jury in Canada found that a patient had been killed by a stroke following a chiropractic neck manipulation and recommended that patients be warned of the risk of stroke following high neck manipulation. In 2016 a model in the USA, Katie May, died following a stroke due to a tear in the left vertebral artery after neck manipulation by a chiropractor. Newspapers in Britain have covered several stories where patients of chiropractors have alleged that they have suffered arterial tears and strokes following neck manipulation.

Claims that neck manipulation causes stroke are strongly disputed. It is argued that stroke can occur following normal activity such as doing household chores or sneezing and that the fact that arterial damage and stroke have followed neck manipulation is coincidental. I am sure that there are many patients who will swear that they have benefited greatly from such treatment.

In 2012 the NHS website published a comparison of differing views as to the risks of neck manipulation that had been canvassed in the British Medical Journal. Experts had argued for and against the use of neck manipulation. On the one side, it was concluded that: *"the evidence supports manipulation as a treatment option for neck pain, along with other interventions such as advice to stay active and exercise."* On the other side, authors argued that: *"The potential for catastrophic events and the clear absence of unique benefit lead to the inevitable conclusion that manipulation of the cervical spine should be abandoned as part of conservative care for neck pain."*

Arguably patients who may be offered neck manipulation by a chiropractor or osteopath should at least be advised that there is, or is thought by some experts to be, a very small risk that neck manipulation can cause arterial tears and stroke, with potentially life changing consequences. Even if a risk is very small in absolute terms, it may be material to patients if the consequences of the risk materialising are very serious, and the claimed benefits of the proposed treatment might be achievable through some other form of treatment.

Chapter 11: Claims Arising
from Deaths of Patients

The core principles of establishing liability in clinical negligence litigation apply to claims arising from the death of a patient just as they do to claims arising out of injuries to living patients. The claimant has to prove not only that the defendant caused the injury, but that it also caused the death of the patient. This element is proved even if the negligence more than minimally brought forward the death of the patient. The principles governing the quantification of so-called fatal claims are however very different.

If a patient who has suffered an injury due to clinical negligence subsequently dies of unrelated causes then their claim for compensation for their injuries, loss and damage survives for the benefit of their estate. Clearly there can no longer be any future losses and expenses because the person has died. However, the value of their claim at the date of their death is the value of the claim that the estate can bring. The entitlement of the estate to bring such a claim is provided for by the Law Reform (Miscellaneous Provision) Act 1934. The estate can claim general damages for the pain, suffering and loss of amenity suffered by the deceased as a result of the negligence and the consequential losses and expenses.

If a patient who has suffered an injury due to clinical negligence is likely to die prematurely as a result of that injury, or the negligence that caused the injury, then they can bring a claim, whilst they are living, for loss of income during what are called the "lost years". Conceptually this is an odd head of claim. The claimant may have a shortened life expectancy of say 30 years, and therefore a shortened working life of say ten years. They will not "enjoy" the net earnings they would have received during those ten years. They are entitled to claim the loss of earnings for those "lost years" and in some cases loss of pension from the "lost years" after retirement age. The claims have to be adjusted for the fact that they will not have to incur expenses in generating that income, and for the fact that they will receive the money now, rather than from the age of, say, 55. These "lost years" claims do not extend to other forms of loss, only to lost income. They provide some compensation for reduction in life expectancy. There is no free-standing claim for having your life reduced because of another's negligence, only a claim for lost income in the "lost years".

Claimants who know that they are dying, or that they have a shortened life expectancy due to the negligence of the defendant, have some difficult decisions to make in terms of litigation. If a patient fully resolves their own injury claim whilst they are alive, then that precludes their loved ones from bringing a claim after they die (see below for Fatal Accidents Act claims). It might be possible that their relatives would have a larger claim arising out of their death than the value of their own personal injury claim. If so, it might be worthwhile not concluding their own claim whilst they are alive, thereby allowing their relatives to bring a claim that could be of greater value, after they die. On the other hand, if liability is disputed or the value of the relatives' future claim is uncertain, they may choose to proceed with their personal injury claim whilst they are alive, and whilst they can give evidence in the case. There are competing advantages and disadvantages of different courses of action that the dying claimant may take. In those cases it is important to involve the family in the decision-making, because their entitlement to claim damages will be affected by the decisions that are made.

If a patient who has suffered an injury due to clinical negligence subsequently dies as a result of that injury, or the negligence that caused the injury, then two kinds of claim result. The first is the claim, already mentioned, brought on behalf of the deceased's estate for the damages that the deceased would have been awarded for their injury, loss and damage the moment before they died. If the death was caused by the defendant's negligence and the estate incurred funeral expenses, then the estate can claim to be reimbursed for those expenses by the defendant. The second claim is that which arises out of the death: it is a claim by those who were dependent on the deceased. The claim is brought under the Fatal Accidents Act 1976 on behalf of those dependants.

The Fatal Accidents Act 1976 provides that the following people are dependants:

(3) In this Act "dependant" means—

(a) the wife or husband or former wife or husband of the deceased;

[(aa) the civil partner or former civil partner of the deceased;]

(b) any person who—

(i) was living with the deceased in the same household immediately before the date of the death; and

(ii) had been living with the deceased in the same household for at least two years before that date; and

    (iii) was living during the whole of that period as the husband or wife [or civil partner] of the deceased;

    (c) any parent or other ascendant of the deceased;

    (d) any person who was treated by the deceased as his parent;

    (e) any child or other descendant of the deceased;

    (f) any person (not being a child of the deceased) who, in the case of any marriage to which the deceased was at any time a party, was treated by the deceased as a child of the family in relation to that marriage;

    [(fa) any person (not being a child of the deceased) who, in the case of any civil partnership in which the deceased was at any time a civil partner, was treated by the deceased as a child of the family in relation to that civil partnership;]

    (g) any person who is, or is the issue of, a brother, sister, uncle or aunt of the deceased.

(4) The reference to the former wife or husband of the deceased in subs.(3)(a) above includes a reference to a person whose marriage to the deceased has been annulled or declared void as well as a person whose marriage to the deceased has been dissolved.

[(4A) The reference to the former civil partner of the deceased in subs.(3)(aa) above includes a reference to a person whose civil partnership with the deceased has been annulled as well as a person whose civil partnership with the deceased has been dissolved.]

(5) In deducing any relationship for the purposes of subs.(3) above—

    (a) any relationship [by marriage or civil partnership] shall be treated as a relationship by consanguinity, any relationship of the half blood as a relationship of the whole blood, and the stepchild of any person as his child, and

    (b) an illegitimate person shall be treated as the legitimate child of his mother and reputed father.

(6) Any reference in this Act to injury includes any disease and any impairment of a person's physical or mental condition.

The number of amendments to this part betrayed by insertions of subsections such as (aa) and (fa) arises from changing attitudes to cohabitation, and changing laws as to family life including the introduction of civil partnerships.

Those who were dependants of the deceased are entitled to damages for the loss of dependency. This can be a financial dependency or a non-financial dependency. Examples of a financial dependency would be the loss of that part of the deceased's income that would have contributed to the household expenses. Examples of non-financial dependency might be the loss of the deceased's time decorating the house and performing DIY tasks.

A dependant can only claim damages for the period of time during which they would have been likely to have remained dependant on the deceased. So, for a child aged ten at the date of their father's death, they might have a claim for a period of 8 years if they were likely to have left school at 16, set themselves up in work and lived independently. Alternatively they might have a claim to the age of 25 if, for example, they were likely to have been supported by their late parent through university, a post-graduate course, and in the first couple of years thereafter when they began to set up themselves in a new home and in a new career. Many parents would continue to support their children over a much longer period, for example by contributing payments for their weddings or other family celebrations, helping them buy a first car or even a first house. The loss of these contributions is a loss of dependency.

There are two rules of thumb used to assess the level of dependency on the deceased's income. These are used to take into account the fact that the deceased would have used some of their income exclusively for themselves, or partially for their own benefit. They come from the case of *Harris v Empress Motors Ltd* [1984] 1 WLR 212. Where the only dependant is the deceased's spouse/cohabitee, it is assumed that the deceased would have spent one-third of their net income on themselves and two-thirds on their spouse/cohabitee or on their joint expenses. Where the dependants are the surviving spouse/cohabitee and one or more children, then it is assumed that the deceased would have spent one-quarter of their net income on themselves personally and three-quarters on their family for so long as the children would have been in education.

The financial dependency might have varied over time, not just because of changing family situations, but also because of changes in income. The prospects for promotion have to be considered, as well as the likely retirement ages of all concerned, including the deceased, and the likely pensions.

A multiplier/multiplicand approach is taken to this calculation, as it is for the non-financial dependency.

Non-financial dependency can have a higher value than financial dependency. Indeed in some cases it is the entirety of the dependency claim. A non-working parent might have been likely to spend many hours a day looking after their children had they remained alive and well. The courts attempt to put a value on these lost "services" such as cooking, cleaning, providing transport, doing the laundry etc. The usual method is similar to that used to calculate past care and assistance for an injured person, i.e. the court applies an hourly rate to the number of hours of services the deceased would have been likely to provide for the benefit of the surviving members of the family.

Even experienced lawyers sometimes make the mistake of valuing dependency by reference to the costs that have been incurred by the surviving members of a family, rather than by reference to the financial and non-financial contributions that the deceased would have made. The cost incurred, such as in hiring a nanny to "replace" the services of a deceased parent, might be evidence of the value of the lost services but it is not necessarily a recoverable expense just because it has been incurred since the death of the patient concerned.

The duration of a dependency will depend on the likely life expectancy of the deceased (but for the negligence) and of the dependant.

By section 3(3) of the Fatal Accidents Act the prospect of a widow remarrying in the future is to be disregarded. Anomalously there is no such provision in respect of widowers.

Another anomaly is provided by section 4 of the Fatal Accidents Act which provides:

"In assessing damages in respect of a person's death in an action under this Act, benefits which have accrued or will or may accrue to any person from his estate or otherwise as a result of his death shall be disregarded."

Thus if the employer of the deceased pays out a widow's pension, for example, that is a benefit that has to be disregarded. This provision arguably leads to over-recovery of compensation by surviving families in some cases.

After a recent change in the law, the multiplier is now calculated from the date of the assessment of damages.

It is common also for the dependants to claim a small sum, usually no more than £5,000, by way of damages for the loss of the irreplaceable love and affection that the deceased would have given the surviving dependant.

In addition there is an entitlement to compensation for being bereaved. This is not, in truth, a compensatory award, but rather a fixed sum, set by Parliament under the 1976 Act, which is the same in every case. There is a narrow band of people who are entitled to claim Bereavement Damages. By section 1A of the Act they are the wife or husband of the deceased and where the deceased was a minor who was never married, their parents if they were legitimate and their mother alone, if they were illegitimate. In *Smith v Lancashire Teaching Hospitals NHS Trust & Ors* [2017] EWCA Civ 1916, the Court of Appeal held that section 1A of the Act, which excludes those who have cohabited for more than two years from the scope of awards of bereavement damages, was incompatible with the European Convention on Human Rights. The government has introduced an Order to change the law accordingly.

The current level of bereavement award is £12,980. You might think they could have rounded it up!

Claims arising out of the death of a patient due to clinical negligence can be brought in respect of any person who lived. Therefore a stillborn baby never lived, in the eyes of the law, and so there cannot be a Fatal Accidents Act claim, or an estate's claim arising out of their death. There are other claims that can be, and are, made as a result of a negligently caused stillbirth.

The total dependency has to be apportioned amongst the dependants. The usual practice where there is a family with young children is that the largest part of the award will be apportioned to the surviving spouse, with relatively small proportions being paid out to the children. It is the surviving parent who will shoulder the burden of bringing up the children in the future. Where a child recovers compensation through a Fatal Accidents Act claim then the approval of the court will be required for any settlement of the claim. The money recovered for the children is usually paid into a court account until they are aged 18.

Epilogue: The Future of Clinical Negligence

Having looked at how the civil justice system deals with clinical negligence, it is natural to ask whether the current approach is sustainable. Does it deliver justice? Is it affordable? Should it be replaced with an alternative mechanism for compensating injured patients?

The Culture of Blame

One commonly held belief is that the civil justice system has succumbed to a compensation culture: parasitic lawyers are killing the NHS by burdening it with speculative and exaggerated claims. The facts suggest otherwise. Over the five years to 2019, whilst the number of patients treated by the NHS has risen, the number of clinical negligence claims received by NHS Resolution has fallen. Patients are now less likely to make a claim than they used to be. Of the claims concluded by NHS Resolution in 2018-19, 56% were resolved with payment of damages to the claimant. It does not follow that the 44% that were concluded without payment of damages were wholly without merit. We have seen how many hurdles a claimant has to overcome to prove a clinical negligence claim. A significant number of claims will fall by the wayside after expert investigation but before formal proceedings have begun. 88% of claims that were concluded without payment of damages were resolved without the need for litigation. Typically those claims will not have cost the NHS very much money to defend. Most of them will have been funded by conditional fee agreements, under which the supposedly greedy lawyers will have been paid no fees for the work they did on behalf of their clients.

Once claimants have committed to litigating their claims, they tend to be successful. Of those claims in which court proceedings were started, over 80% resulted in the payment of damages by the NHS. Thus, four out of five clinical negligence claimants were justified in litigating their claims against NHS Trusts.

There has been no surge in clinical negligence claims in recent years, and there is no evidence of the widespread misuse of litigation to bring speculative claims. Nevertheless some commentators argue that it is too easy to bring a clinical negligence case and that we have to find ways of restricting the number of compensation claims. In contrast, others have argued that the *Bolam* test is too deferential to healthcare professionals and presents too high a barrier for claimants to overcome. Many politicians, journalists and doctors contend that compensation payments are far too high, but often claimants and their families consider the damages awarded to be inadequate. Do we have the balance right, or are there changes that ought to be made?

Sir Rupert Jackson, retired Lord Justice of Appeal and a very influential judicial figure within the civil justice system, gave a speech on 19 May 2019 entitled, *"Medical Errors: Sanctions and Compensation – Is There Another Way?"* He pointed to a survey reported by the Health Service Journal in March 2019 to the effect that a quarter of NHS staff say that within the preceding month they have witnessed an error that could have harmed patients or service users. He also referred to increasing demands on the NHS. He proposed a new test for liability to pay compensation:

> *"Let there be a new statutory test for liability in the medical context, namely whether the patient has suffered 'reasonably avoidable injury'. If the injury was reasonably avoidable, then the fact that the doctor had been on a twelve-hour night shift and had numerous other patients to treat is neither here nor there. The relevant health trust or private hospital is liable. If this objective test is adopted, then (a) the patient is better protected and (b) the investigation of liability is depersonalised."*

Sir Rupert accepted that this could lead to a higher number of compensation claims than under the current system, but he proposed that costs and compensation could be controlled by introducing a new tribunal system to determine such claims and tariff systems for determining the level of compensation:

> *"The costs of litigating before the tribunal should be lower than the costs of litigating in court. The process of assessing damages can be simplified. The Clinical Chamber could have scales for assessing future care costs. Defendant health trusts could do more to assist the tribunal by producing care plans for individual cases, hopefully agreed by claimant representatives ... this would enable an equitable distribution of the available compensation amongst all deserving claimants, in place of the present system in which a smaller proportion of deserving claimants recover higher damages."*

If the test for entitlement to compensation were to become whether a patient had suffered "reasonably avoidable injury", then there would have to be some mechanism for determining which patients fell within, and which outside, that category. It is not self-evident that a patient with cauda equina who undergoes spinal decompression but is left with bowel and bladder dysfunction and reduced power and sensation in their lower limbs, has necessarily suffered a reasonably avoidable injury. Suppose that with good care they could have had surgery 48 hours earlier and have enjoyed near normal function for the rest of their lives. With average care they could have had surgery 24 hours earlier and had about 50% more function than they now have. With just about acceptable care they could have had surgery 12 hours earlier and been 20% better off. Have they suffered "reasonably avoidable injury" and if so, what is the extent of the injury that falls to be compensated?

If it were possible to say of every patient who begins their "patient journey" in a particular set of circumstances that there was a standard expected outcome, then that would make life a lot easier for clinical negligence parties, lawyers and experts. The fact is that it takes a lot of investigation and scrutiny, as well as expertise, to work out the likely outcome for a patient had they had reasonable treatment, and therefore whether there was an avoidable injury and, if so, what that injury was. So, questions of causation would surely remain under Sir Rupert Jackson's proposed new test for entitlement. And what is the difference between an avoidable injury and a reasonably avoidable injury? Is a "reasonably avoidable injury" one which was avoidable with reasonable care? If so, it is in effect the same question as is currently asked.

Sir Rupert Jackson's proposal is not wholly dissimilar to a form of no-fault compensation such as that operated in New Zealand. Many highly regarded jurists have proposed abolishing the fault-based tort system for compensating for personal injuries. Lord Sumption did so in a speech to the Personal Injuries Bar Association in 2017 – the equivalent of speaking in favour of Christmas to an audience of turkeys. A central argument in favour of a no-fault compensation scheme is that it is better able to achieve distributive justice: all those who suffer injury are treated alike. If a child is born with cerebral palsy and requires lifelong care and assistance, why should compensation at the levels awarded by the civil courts be paid only to those who can prove that their condition was caused by the negligent clinical management of their delivery?

One of the main arguments against no-fault compensation schemes for injuries to patients is that they remove one of the incentives for higher standards of clinical practice – the fear of being sued. Some argue that it is a "good thing" that healthcare professionals are afraid of litigation. They will improve their practice so as to avoid being sued. For me this is unconvincing. Firstly, most professionals will be motivated to protect their patients and act in accordance with good clinical standards without the "stick" of possible litigation hovering over them. In any event they have the threat of professional regulatory sanctions, or the loss of employment as a corrective to falling standards of conduct. Secondly, practices that are designed to avoid litigation are not necessarily practices that are in the best interests of patients.

Whilst it is important to identify and learn from individual errors, clinical negligence litigation is not a useful tool for improving the standards of healthcare professionals. Seldom do individual practitioners have to account for themselves in a court of law even when they have fallen far below the standards required of them. Negligence claims are designed to compensate the injured, not to correct the standards of practice of the defendant.

The conceptual difficulty that I have with a no-fault compensation scheme for NHS patients is that it targets only one part of the system for dealing justly with those who have suffered personal injury, i.e. those who have suffered harm as a result of clinical negligence. If the point is to treat all people with the same disability equally, why should there be a scheme directed solely at NHS patients? Under the current tort system, the core principles of compensation are, with some adjustments, the same for all who are negligently injured, whether they were a patient, a pedestrian or a factory worker at the time of the injury. If you remove the need to establish negligence, why have any compensation scheme at all? Everyone with the same disability would be treated equally, whether it was caused by clinical negligence, another form of negligence, pure accident, criminal assault, genetic disorder, disease or illness.

The main practical objection to a no-fault compensation scheme for NHS patients, it seems to me, is that either it would be unaffordable, or that it would be affordable only by very significantly reducing the levels of compensation paid to the injured. If you pay the current, judicially determined, levels of compensation to all patients whose outcomes are worse than they should have been, then the costs would be enormous. If you paid the same levels of compensation to all people with the same disabilities, however caused, it would be even more unaffordable.

Is it justified to have in place a system of compensation that depends on proof of negligence? I would argue that it is. Whilst none of us can expect an entirely smooth path through life, harm suffered due to negligent conduct or criminal behaviour is beyond the bounds of what we should have to tolerate. The law of negligence sets limits to what acts and omissions should be tolerated. Stray beyond those bounds thereby causing harm and your victim should be entitled to redress. That seems to me to be principled and in accordance with what most citizens would accept as a fundamental part of the rule of law.

Since the core purpose of clinical negligence law is to compensate the wronged claimant rather than to punish or correct the defendant, it is regrettable that the law is viewed as pitting patient against doctor. As we have seen, this is a misconception since the most common defendant in clinical negligence claims is an NHS Trust rather than an individual professional. Nevertheless I would suggest a further step towards depersonalising the law of clinical negligence, moving the target further away from blaming individual practitioners and re-directing it to the system as a whole. This could be achieved by making the NHS itself the sole defendant in claims brought for clinical negligence within the NHS. It would be unnecessary for claimants to sue individual healthcare practitioners or bodies within the NHS. If an NHS patient claimed they had suffered injury as a result of negligent treatment, they would not have to decide which NHS body or practitioner to sue – they would sue the NHS. This would remove the jeopardy that claimants face in having to identify who within the NHS was responsible. A patient who goes to their NHS GP practice and is seen by a nurse and then a doctor may wonder why they have to sue both when the GP and nurse blame each other for missing clinical signs that should have led to the patient's referral for specialist assessment and treatment. The patient relied on the NHS, so why should they have to risk losing a claim against the nurse, or the GP, if it is clear that at least one of them was negligent? Both were working for the NHS.

Allowing injured patients to sue the NHS as a single organisation would also remove the excessive costs and inequality caused by multiple defendants each instructing their own lawyers and experts. If a GP delayed referring a patient for suspected breast cancer and the hospital to whom she was referred negligently misinterpreted a mammogram, then instead of suing both the GP and the hospital Trust, the patient could sue the NHS. There would be one defendant, one team of lawyers, one set of experts.

This innovation would also help to focus attention on improving systems of care. Poor systems increase the risk of individual error. Good systems protect against them. Within the NHS, systems of care cannot be isolated to individual practitioners, small groups or even single Trusts. Many negligence claims turn on failures of communication between different parts of the NHS. It makes sense that the NHS as a whole should be liable when NHS patients are injured as a result of failings within the NHS. It would encourage the NHS to improve its systems of care and help to reduce the adverse impact of a culture of blame.

Abolishing the *Bolam* Test

Should the *Bolam* test survive? There is an argument that the test for negligence should be the same for all defendants, whether or not they are professionals: did the defendant take reasonable care? The courts should decide the standard of what patients, pedestrians, employees and everyone else is entitled to expect. Why should healthcare professionals be treated any differently from HGV drivers?

In 2015, when he was a Lord Justice of Appeal, Sir Rupert Jackson delivered the Peter Taylor Memorial Lecture to the Professional Negligence Bar Association, arguing that the *Bolam* test may well disappear from clinical negligence litigation. He was not then proposing the new test referred to in his 2019 speech referred to above, but he said that the special status of professions, in particular medicine, was under threat:

> *"Professional persons are no longer generally seen as a class of individuals superior to other workers, driven by higher ideals and meriting protection. ....The operation of the Bolam test is illustrated most clearly in the medical field. There are numerous reported cases where doctors have made mistakes with grave consequences, but have nevertheless escaped liability on the basis of Bolam.... Such cases make chilling reading, if one focuses on the individual case rather than the issues of principle which are at stake."*

He noted the *Montgomery* decision in the Supreme Court: the *"invaders have broken through the castle walls on Bolam"*. He predicted that:

> *"The argument will be that the ordinary principles of tortious liability should apply to the professions in the same way that they apply to everybody else. There is no reason for the courts to accord special protection to the professions."*

The *Bolam* test, which is still rigorously applied to questions of investigation, diagnosis and treatment, is considered to represent a high obstacle for claimants to overcome. It is commonly thought to be more difficult to prove that a doctor failed to act in accordance with any responsible body of relevant practitioners than it is to show that they failed to act with the level of care that the court believes a patient is entitled to expect. I am not so sure that that is so. If the court sets the standard of care to be exercised by doctors, would it be higher or lower than the standard that the profession sets for itself or tolerates from those within the profession? In any event it is not necessarily unjust to continue with a test of negligence just because another test would make it easier, or harder, for claimants to prove their claims.

The *Bolam* test sets the parameters within which healthcare professionals can operate. It allows some leeway for the exercise of professional judgement whilst setting limits beyond which a practitioner should not stray. In contrast the rules of the road are laid down and all road users depend on strict adherence. There is little room for a difference of opinion about whether it is safe to drive through a red traffic light.

Furthermore, in my view the *Bolam* test demonstrates a proper respect for the medical and allied professions by judges who do not operate within that world, and who do not have the experience and qualifications of the professionals upon whom they are sitting in judgment. How could a judge determine whether complex brain surgery was performed to a reasonable standard without hearing evidence from a brain surgeon? Would they rely on a Google search?

In my view *Bolam* should remain as the test for setting standards for the performance of investigations, diagnosis and treatment by healthcare professionals. It is also still of some relevance to obtaining a patient's informed consent, even though the question of what risks are material to a patient is rightly seen as a matter to be judged by reference to what a particular patient wants to know, rather than what a doctor thinks they need to know.

Nevertheless, following *Bolitho*, the *Bolam* test does require the court to consider whether the practice adopted was rational. Does the professional's decision-making withstand logical scrutiny? And perhaps the courts have been too slow to override established medical practice when that practice is illogical. Case law warns judges not to be too hasty to impose their own standards over those of the profession, but perhaps they should be more sceptical and more willing to set a standard by what ought to be done rather than always accepting what is done.

If it were possible to sue the NHS, rather than having to sue individual practitioners or trusts, then that would contribute to what is already a greater emphasis on the adequacy of systems in place at NHS hospitals and GP surgeries. Whilst the NHS would be vicariously liable for the negligent acts and omissions of individual professionals working for it, the increased focus on systemic failings will naturally lead the courts away from applying the *Bolam* test to the standards of care of individual professionals. It seems likely that if, as in *Darnley v Croydon*, the courts increasingly ask what the duty of care was on an NHS Trust, as opposed to what the duty of care was for an individual professional, then *Bolam* does not necessarily give the answer as to whether that duty of care was fulfilled. Instead a judge will weigh up the risks and benefits of certain procedures and actions, assess the foreseeable consequences, and determine whether the systems in place fell below an acceptable standard. However, perhaps curiously, the Supreme Court in *Darnley* did focus on the individual role within the system when determining whether the standards of care to be expected of someone carrying out that role, were met. Therefore, for now, if the role demands professional skill and care, then the *Bolam* test will continue to apply (save for *Montgomery* type cases). If the role does not demand professional skill and care then the ordinary, non-*Bolam*, test of negligence will apply.

The *Bolam* and *Montgomery* tests have not opened the floodgates to litigation. The number of clinical negligence claims is currently falling even though the number of patient interactions within the NHS is rising. The chances of any one patient interaction leading to a claim have diminished considerably over time. This is perhaps surprising given that we live in an age where people are more aware of their rights to use the courts, solicitors use advertising and marketing techniques to generate work, and the conditional fee system allows many people who could not otherwise afford to bring cases to have access to the justice system. Even so, the number of clinical negligence claims is not obviously disproportionate to the number of doctor-patient interactions.

Reducing Patient Harm

Everyone would benefit, and there would be fewer claims, if there were a reduction in the number of incidents of avoidable patient harm. It should not be shocking to suggest that the way to reduce the costs to the nation of clinical negligence litigation is to reduce the number of incidents of harmful negligence. And yet most of the headlines decrying the size of the NHS bill for clinical negligence focus on reducing the availability of compensation to those negligently harmed rather than on reducing the harm caused. Avoidable patient harm is not a "given". Of course, there will always be mistakes but a determined focus on improving systems of care and a patient safety culture would surely pay dividends both for patients and for taxpayers.

The NHS has recently launched an initiative to improve patient care but this has already been looked at in detail some years ago by Sir Robert Francis QC when he chaired the Inquiry into Mid Staffordshire NHS Foundation Trust and identified some of the core systemic problems that resulted in poor patient care. The Executive Summary of the Report of the Mid Staffordshire NHS Foundation Trust Public Inquiry [February 2013] concluded:

> "The negative aspects of culture in the system were identified as including:
>
> • A lack of openness to criticism;
>
> • A lack of consideration for patients;
>
> • Defensiveness;
>
> • Looking inwards not outwards;

- *Secrecy;*

- *Misplaced assumptions about the judgements and actions of others;*

- *An acceptance of poor standards;*

- *A failure to put the patient first in everything that is done.*

"It cannot be suggested that all these characteristics are present everywhere in the system all of the time, far from it, but their existence anywhere means that there is an insufficiently shared positive culture.

"To change that, there needs to be a relentless focus on the patient's interests and the obligation to keep patients safe and protected from substandard care. This means that the patient must be first in everything that is done: there must be no tolerance of substandard care; frontline staff must be empowered with responsibility and freedom to act in this way under strong and stable leadership in stable organisations."

Former Prime Minister Theresa May later used that same phrase *"strong and stable leadership"* causing it to be the subject of ridicule, but the report's emphasis on patient-centred care, openness, leadership and willingness to change was widely accepted when the report came out.

In contrast, one powerful strand of opinion later to emerge in response to cases such as that of Jack Adcock and Dr Bawa-Garba has been to resist openness and to protect healthcare professionals from scrutiny. This has led to the move to create "safe spaces" for doctors and others where they can give their accounts of events that may have caused serious patient harm, without the patients or their families having access.

My own experience dealing with patients and their families who have chosen to explore the possibility of suing the NHS tells me that an open system of dealing with complaints which encourages trust that: (i) failings have been identified and acknowledged; and (ii) lessons have been learned and improvements put in place, would go a long way to reducing the number of claims and to early and cost-effective resolution of those claims that do progress to litigation.

Far too many patients seek the help of lawyers because they "want answers" when the state could have used its resources to give those answers and to save both the patient and their clinicians time, money and stress.

If a patient has died unexpectedly, or they have suffered serious and unanticipated injury, then there ought to be a system of immediate investigation that is manifestly open, determined to identify any failings, and the ways in which the system can be improved to try to prevent those failings from recurring. Such investigations should not be directed at punishing healthcare professionals but if they reveal evidence suggesting possible regulatory or even criminal offences, then the relevant authorities would have to be informed. The public is unlikely to have trust in any system that suppressed evidence of serious wrongdoing.

Whoever fed professionals the line that they should admit nothing when something goes wrong, has a lot to answer for. Openness and good communication with patients and their families is much more likely to bring down the number of claims rather than increase it. And candour can help reduce patient harm. If professionals become more open to admitting mistakes, and investigating them thoroughly, then they will become more open to changing practice and improving the systems within which they work. To bring this about healthcare professionals and other staff need to be supported, so that when things do go wrong they can admit mistakes and point out the errors of others and of the system without fear that it will count against them. When healthcare professionals raise concerns they are called "whistleblowers". This term implies that the act of raising concerns is exceptional and that most colleagues keep quiet even when they know something is going wrong. Surely, the process of raising concerns should be commonplace – however else will improvements be made if the clinicians treating patients and working within the system are not supported to point out deficiencies and suggest positive changes?

So both patients and their families, and professionals and staff need to be supported. This support needs to be in place at a very early stage for it to have benefits.

Early and open investigations can therefore lead to improved patient safety. Likewise, early appraisal of the merits of a claim and defence that might be litigated will help reduce legal costs.

The pre-action protocol allows four months for potential defendants to clinical negligence litigation to investigate the allegations against them and it is very common for that time to be extended by agreement to 12 months or more. But those grievances ought to have been the subject of proper investigation and report, even before patients consider instructing a lawyer and before a Letter of Claim is sent. In cases where there have been what are now called "serious untoward incidents" independent expert evidence could be used to allow proper investigation and reporting. Patients and their families could have a say in which experts are involved in the initial report. Once the report is issued, a panel of independent mediations could be available to explore how any remaining grievances might be resolved.

Clearly a process of that kind would be more expensive than the current system of complaint handling and incident analysis. But it might well bring about savings by resolving grievances without the need for intervention from lawyers, let alone litigation.

A focus on early, independent evaluation and mediation could also speed up the litigation process if it did nevertheless ensue. Potential claimants could be discouraged, through an amended protocol, from notifying any claim or bringing any action unless and until that independent report had been published, and an opportunity for mediation explored. However, if at that stage no resolution were reached, then defendants might be allowed only three months to respond to a Letter of Claim and with no expectation of extensions to that time limit. The pre-action protocol process ought to take no more than a few months as a final attempt to avoid litigation. It should not mark the start of serious and lengthy attempts to investigate and resolve grievances.

One product of clinical negligence litigation which I fear is not currently utilised as well as it might, is the host of independent expert investigations into systemic and individual errors within the NHS and the private sector. Most claims are resolved by compromise. What happens to the thousands of expert reports that are produced every year when litigating those claims? Often they are put into storage, and then the confidential waste bin. Tens of thousands of hours of careful scrutiny which could be used to advance learning are wasted. Clearly if that considerable resource were to be used to improve systems and practices, then it would have to be carefully handled so as to protect confidentiality, but it should be possible for a team of researchers to collate the material and learning from clinical negligence claims in order to identify patterns, recurrent errors and ways to improve. I am aware that NHS Resolution has taken to engaging clinicians to look into what can be learned from claims so as to improve patient safety. This is a very welcome development and one that could be built upon. As well as looking at individual cases, it should be possible to look for patterns within clinical negligence claims. Is there a disproportionate number of claims that arise out of a failure to make key decisions at weekends or bank holidays? Are systems for communicating blood test results leading to failures to follow up patients who need further investigation?

One pattern that has been found by researchers to emerge from an analysis of claims is that a small number of professionals are responsible for a disproportionate number of claims. Research by Marie Bismark and others in Australia revealed that 3% of Australia's medical workforce accounted for 49% of complaints and 1% accounted for a quarter of complaints. There is no reason to suppose that the figures would be wildly different in the UK. This evidence shows that targeting training and supervision of the "repeat offenders" could significantly reduce complaints and claims arising out of patient safety incidents.

The Patient Experience Library was started to collate patient experiences of the NHS. It is intended to provide a data base to assist in learning so as to improve standards of care. In a similar way, the expert and other evidence gathered at considerable cost for the purpose of litigation, could be used to enhance learning within the NHS.

An emphasis on improving patient care through changes in leadership and culture, openness in dealing with complaints and explaining what has gone wrong, early and sincere attempts to resolve disputes, and a determination to learn from past incidents of clinical negligence, could all lead to significant reductions in clinical negligence litigation. But the figures show that the rising costs of clinical negligence litigation to the nation in recent years are due not to an increase in the number of claims, but from the increasing levels of compensation paid out in those claims.

Reducing Compensation Awards

One way to limit the compensation paid to those harmed by clinical negligence would be to introduce a tariff system in place of judicial awards. This was Sir Rupert Jackson's proposal. It would effectively place the level of awards in the hands of the government. The Medical Defence Union has run a not dissimilar campaign for some years now. It says:

> *"When the MDU paid the first million pound compensation award in 1988, it caused a sharp intake of breath among doctors. Today, multi-million pound damages payments for clinical negligence claims are common. We should not stand by and watch compensation awards running unchecked to many millions of pounds. Reform of personal injury law needs to happen."*

The MDU proposes:

(i)   Repealing section 2(4) of the Law Reform (Personal Injuries) Act 1948

> *"One reason care costs are so expensive is because a 1948 law still applies. Personal injury defendants must disregard NHS care when paying compensation. This means public bodies like the NHSLA have to fund private care so billions of pounds from NHS funds, goes to the independent sector."*

(ii)   Health and Social Care Packages

> *"The MDU also advocates that an independent body should define the health and social care package that provides an appropriate standard of care for all patients regardless of the cause of the patient's care needs. Compensating bodies such as the MDU should be required to fund a package of care that would provide the standard of care defined in the care package."*

(iii)   Capping loss of earnings

> *"If people who are negligently harmed are high earners they can receive millions of pounds in compensation for loss of future earnings. It is possible to award financial compensation on a more equitable basis. For example, in many states in Australia the maximum amount a person can claim for loss of earnings is three times the national average salary. That is fairer and we suggest a similar system is adopted here."*

These measures would involve government intervention to restrict damages for clinical negligence claims.

As explained in Part 1, clinical negligence litigation is part of the system of compensating individuals carelessly injured by others. Many would question the justice in a system that would award different levels of compensation to individuals suffering the same injury, depending on whether they suffered that injury in a hospital as opposed to at work or on a road. That said, the government has already introduced legislation to introduce lower awards of compensation for people who suffer a certain kind neck injury in road traffic accidents. However, the fact that the principle of even-handedness has already been breached once does not mean that it would be just to do it again. Patients who suffer serious harm due to negligent treatment might well ask why they should be compensated less than if they had suffered an identical injury through some other (negligent) mechanism.

A tariff-based system for clinical negligence also would impose rules and limits restricting the entitlement of patients to compensation they would otherwise recover.

Many would argue that it would undermine the whole of the common law system for compensating individuals who have suffered harm due to negligence to impose a tariff system for one area of negligence whilst retaining a judicial assessment of damages for other areas.

If the public's view is that compensation awarded by the courts for injury, however caused, is much too high, then a tariff-based system reducing the amounts paid for all injuries, however caused, would at least have the virtue of consistency. Furthermore, there is no right or wrong figure for damages for the injuries themselves. It is not a human right to recover £100,000 rather than £50,000 for an amputated limb. A tariff-based system may be very rough and ready, but it is not inherently less just than the present judicial system for compensating individuals for their pain, suffering and loss of amenity.

A tariff-based system for damages for pain, injury and loss of amenity would ultimately be under the control of the government rather than the judiciary. Given that the defendant in most clinical negligence claims is the state run NHS, this means that the defendant would be restricting the compensation paid to those it had harmed.

Different considerations apply to caps or tariffs for compensation for consequential losses and expenses. These have a precise monetary value. If you cap loss of earnings claims, then it will reduce compensation below the losses that the negligence has actually caused. A high earner who misses a year from work because of negligence will presently recover more for loss of earnings than a low earner who is unable to work for the same period. Suppose the former earns £80,000 a year and the latter £15,000 per year, and average net earnings were £20,000. If loss of earnings were capped at three times average earnings then, even after compensation, the higher earner would lose £20,000 over the year. The lower earner would be awarded the same sum. The higher earner does not necessarily have £20,000 to spare. They might have arranged their affairs – mortgage, HP on their car etc, so as to live within their means at £80,000 per annum. They could well be put into financial difficulties by a sudden 25% cut in those earnings (after the compensation) which was through no fault of their own. And suppose that they are unable ever to return to work. Over 20 years of loss of earnings they lose out on £400,000 of income they would otherwise have had. Again, many would argue that it would be unjust to cap loss of earnings for NHS patients who have suffered avoidable injury, but not for victims of other forms of negligence.

As for the MDU's first two proposals, the upshot would be that patients injured by negligence by the NHS would have to rely on the NHS or some other arm of the state to care for them in the future. There would be several implications. First, whilst there would be a potential saving in compensation payments, there would be an increased cost to the NHS and the state caused by having to meet claimants' needs. It is not cost free for the NHS (or another arm of the state) to provide lifelong care for the individual. And the cost would not only be for nursing care and care assistants but for therapists, aids and equipment and accommodation. It is not self-evident that the true cost to the state of providing lifelong care, support and accommodation for someone with cerebral palsy will be significantly lower than the sorts of sums currently recovered through compensation. After all, some argue that the private sector is more efficient in providing such services than the public sector. The "saving" in compensation payable by the NHS is not necessarily a saving to the taxpayer. Someone has to house and look after the injured individual. It is simplistic for the MDU to complain that the legal system requires billions of pounds to be paid by the NHS to the independent sector. If it is the NHS that has to provide the care, accommodation and equipment, then the state will spend billions of pounds in doing so.

The second implication is the removal of individual autonomy. From an individual's perspective the kind of regime proposed by the MDU would entail the removal of freedom of choice. They would not be able to live where and with whom they chose. They would not be able to say that they do not want to be looked after by a particular carer and want to change to another. They would have to take their services from the state, and, if the regime is taken to its furthest point, they would have to take the package of services deemed appropriate for them. Indeed, the proposals would risk removing claimants from their families and placing them in accommodation that is not their own home, away from those who love them. What would be the test and who would be the arbiters of a reasonable level of care and accommodation for all patients regardless of the cause of their needs? Is this shorthand for treating all persons with disabilities and care needs the same as those who currently depend entirely on state benefits?

It is of course true that a claimant who succeeds in their clinical negligence claim, and is properly represented, will probably be able to afford a higher standard of support, equipment and accommodation than a claimant who was born with the same disabilities but which were not caused by another's negligence. State provision might pay for a standard wheelchair for the one, whilst negligence compensation might fund a powered wheelchair with e-motion wheels for the other. Looked at in terms of distributive justice, that might well be unfair. Why should one disabled person have greater benefits/compensation than another? But is the answer to take away the better provisions from one of those individuals until they are both in receipt of the same? This is not a rhetorical question – it is the subject of much debate.

The third implication of the MDU's proposal is for the security of provision. If a claimant is given a sum of money through compensation, then they have to use it to meet their needs for the rest of their lives, but they are not dependent on a public body maintaining services and support at an appropriate level for decades to come. If instead claimants were compelled to rely on the NHS or a local authority to make provision for them, where would be the guarantee that the level of state provision agreed shortly after the injury occurred, would be maintained in 30 years' time? How could the individual have the security of knowing that there would be no cutbacks to the services following changes of government or economic conditions?

Some years ago there was a series of court cases in which defendants challenged the fairness of claimants not having to account for the receipt of benefits and publicly funded services. There is a system for accounting for benefits that have been received for five years from the injury, and which are attributable to that injury. This is through the Compensation Recovery Unit. However, once a case is concluded, and compensation received, a claimant may seek publicly funded care, services and accommodation. Defendants contended that compensation awards should be reduced to take into account the receipt of such services, and the likely receipt of them in the future. The courts were reluctant to do so, not least because of the lack of any guarantee that appropriate publicly funded services would be available for the remainder of a claimant's life. However, it would be possible to introduce a law requiring that claimants who did avail themselves of publicly funded services to meet needs for which they have received compensation, should have to account for the benefit of those services. The object is to prevent "double recovery" – the claimant's needs being met both by the compensation payments and the receipt of state-funded services or benefits.

One consequence of the current principle of compensation is that the "true cost" of negligent errors is exposed. Actually, as I have observed earlier, the true cost of negligence within the NHS is probably understated by the total bill for compensation because a large number of patients who could bring claims do not do so. However, for those claims that are brought, the high cost of compensation serves to demonstrate the true impact of the avoidable mistakes that are made. A child who suffers severe cerebral palsy at birth will need millions of pounds of care and assistance, equipment, therapies and accommodation if they are to be supported to have as independent and worthwhile a life as is possible given their condition. If the system of compensation is changed in order to reduce the levels of compensation, then this will disguise the true impact of negligence within the system. To some the high cost of clinical negligence is an incentive to reduce levels of compensation. To others it should be an incentive to reduce the number of errors.

As I have noted often in this book, half the cost of clinical negligence to the taxpayer is caused by birth injuries. Reduce the number of children born with cerebral palsy due to clinical negligence and the costs bill would be cut significantly. More importantly, fewer children and families would have their lives blighted. That is not to say that it is easy to achieve such a goal, but surely it is worth a concerted effort, and a substantial investment, to improve obstetric services so that fewer adverse outcomes occur. The NHS has a very good record for obstetric patient safety but an NHS Resolution report in 2017 by Michael Magro noted that the rate of avoidable cerebral palsy births had been constant for about ten years. Jeremy Hunt, then Secretary of State, announced in 2015 an ambition to reduce the rate of stillbirths, neonatal and maternal deaths and brain injuries that occur during, or soon after, birth by 50% by 2030. That is a laudable ambition but it remains to be seen whether this will be achievable. If the number of cerebral palsy births due to negligence were halved, then the overall clinical negligence bill would be reduced by about 25%.

Are the objections to changes to the system for awarding compensation simply a plea to maintain the status quo? Not necessarily.

The principle of compensation for negligence is to put the claimant back in the position they would have been in but for the injury. Whilst it is recognised that money cannot achieve this, nevertheless claimant lawyers are always looking for new ways in which to ensure that their clients are adequately compensated under that guiding principle. Technological advances and an awareness of the possibilities to help people with disabilities in new and interesting ways, such as the use of eye-gaze technology, ever more sophisticated prosthetic limbs, even powered exoskeletons, tend to increase the levels of compensation in high value cases. The costs of providing nursing and other care at home tends to rise faster than general inflation. New medical treatments become available in the private sector. And so there is an inexorable rise in levels of compensation to the extent that the MDU can justifiably point out that levels of award can double in a few years.

What can be done? Should a claimant who has lost a leg due to someone else's negligence "make do" with a mid-market prosthesis rather than having a more expensive one that more nearly brings them closer to the level of mobility they would have had they not had the amputation? For some, the difficult answer to that question might well be "yes".

Lord Woolf Master of the Rolls giving the judgment of the Court of Appeal in *Heil v Rankin et al.* [2000] EWCA Civ 84 at paragraphs 22, 23 and 27:

> ".. the aim of an award of damages for personal injuries is to provide compensation. The principle is that 'full compensation' should be provided. ... This principle of 'full compensation' applies to pecuniary and non-pecuniary damages alike. ... The compensation must remain fair, reasonable and just. Fair compensation for the injured person. The level must also not result in injustice to the defendant, and it must not be out of accord with what society as a whole would perceive as being reasonable".

In *Whiten v St George's Healthcare NHS Trust* [2011] EWHC 2066 (QB) Mrs Justice Swift said at paragraph 5 that:

> "The claimant is entitled to damages to meet his reasonable needs arising from his injuries. In considering what is "reasonable", I have had regard to all the relevant circumstances, including the requirement for proportionality as between the cost to the defendant of any individual item and the extent of the benefit which would be derived by the claimant from that item."

Warby J in *Ellison v University Hospitals of Morecambe Bay NHS Foundation Trust* [2015] EWHC 366 (QB) considered the interpretation of this principle:

> "18. Ms Vaughan Jones [for the Defendant] also relied on a proposition in the same paragraph of Swift J's judgment, that the relevant circumstances include "the requirement for proportionality as between the cost to the defendant of any individual item and the extent of the benefit which would be derived by the claimant from that item". I accept, and I did not understand it to be disputed, that proportionality is a relevant factor to this extent: in determining whether a claimant's reasonable needs require that a given item of expenditure should be incurred, the court must consider whether the same or a substantially similar result could be achieved by other, less expensive, means. That, I strongly suspect, is what Swift J had in mind in the

passage relied upon.

19. The defendant's submissions went beyond this, however. They included the more general proposition that a claimant should not recover compensation for the cost of a particular item which would achieve a result that other methods could not, if the cost of that item was disproportionately large by comparison with the benefit achieved. I do not regard Whiten as support for any such general principle, and Ms Vaughan Jones did not suggest that Swift J had applied any such principle to the facts of that case. She did suggest that her submission found some support in paragraph [27] of Heil v Rankin, where Lord Woolf MR observed that the level of compensation "must also not result in injustice to the defendant, and it must not be out of accord with what society would perceive as being reasonable."

20. Those observations do not in my judgment embody a proportionality principle of the kind for which the defendant contends, and were in any event made with reference to levels of general damages for non-pecuniary loss. Ms Vaughan Jones cited no other authority in support of the proportionality principle relied on. I agree with the submission of Mr Machell QC for the claimant, that the application to the quantification of damages for future costs of a general requirement of proportionality of the kind advocated by Ms Vaughan Jones would be at odds with the basic rules as to compensation for tort identified above."

Some would argue for a change in approach so that the courts should consider the proportionality of additional cost to the benefit from an item that could achieve a result that other methods could not. For example, equipment might allow a claimant to open and close curtains, windows and doors using eye-gaze technology. Suppose that there is no other means of achieving this benefit for the claimant and suppose the lifelong cost were £100,000. Would that be proportionate to the benefit to the claimant? I am not suggesting that it would or would not be proportionate, but you can see how the imposition of a test of that kind could reduce compensation that might otherwise be paid in some cases without inflicting undue hardship on claimants. The cost of providing for fundamental needs would virtually always be considered reasonable and proportionate if there is no other means of providing them. But the costs of advanced equipment or treatment might not be.

Adding a requirement that compensation for the cost of an item or service will only be awarded insofar as the expenditure would be proportionate to

the gain to the claimant from use of it, even when there would be no other means of meeting the claimant's particular need, would probably limit
some damages awarded for aids and equipment, assistive technology, transport, holiday costs, even accommodation. But in nearly all large clinical
negligence claims, the most costly head of claim by far is for future care.
If a claimant needs a single support worker for 14 hours a day and ten
hours at night to ensure that they are dressed and undressed, fed, washed,
toileted, stimulated, taken out, attend for therapies and treatment, and are
kept safe, then the total annual cost will exceed £100,000. One carer cannot
provide all that support, so a team is needed. The team will need managing.
There will be training costs, employer's national insurance to pay (which
goes back to the government), costs of recruitment when one of the carers
leaves, holiday cover, weekend and bank holiday rates, food for the carers,
and several other add-on costs.

The parties rely on care experts to advise as to the hours of care required in
the future, and the cost of providing that care. As with all disputes involving
expert evidence, care experts are typically instructed by each party and they
ultimately produce a joint statement of the issues on which they agree and
disagree. Whereas experts in other fields often do reach some agreement on
some matters, it is my experience that care experts too often say that there
is no room for compromise and simply repeat the evidence given in their
original reports. That is surprising because there must surely be a range of
possible costs for a certain kind of care regime.

Once evidence establishes: (i) that the defendant's negligence has caused
injuries that will result in the claimant needing a certain level of care in
the future; (ii) the likely cost of providing that care to the claimant in the
private sector, and (iii) that the claimant is entitled to choose to live in their
own home and to choose their own carers, then under the principle that the
defendant should make good the harm they have caused, claimants are entitled to compensation for the true costs of the care they will require. Forcing
claimants to be housed and cared for by the state carries with it all sorts of
objections, as referred to above. The principle that compensation for negligently caused injury should do no more and no less than make good, so far
as money can, the losses and expenses suffered means that the true financial
cost of clinical negligence is exposed. If you read of a child with severe disabilities being compensated £10m or more, that is a statement of the cost of
the negligence, not a windfall to the child. However, if the claimant's care
requirements and level of independence can be fully met and be guaranteed
for life, but at lower cost, then it would be difficult to see any injustice to the
claimant if the defendant were ordered to fund that lower cost package of
care. One possible way of achieving this might be for bodies representing

claimants, and NHSR and other "stakeholders", to agree a tariff or a range of care costs that would apply to clinical negligence awards. Just as legal costs are budgeted by the court, so it might be possible for care costs to be managed to avoid the kind of inflation that has occurred over recent years.

In many road traffic and employers' liability claims, the defendant insurer offers to arrange and pay for treatment, therapies, care and so on in the early stages after an accident. There is a Rehabilitation Code under which the defendant can help the claimant to mitigate the effects of their injuries. This is of benefit to all. It is currently rarely, if ever, used in clinical negligence cases, but a similar code or practice could be adapted to clinical negligence litigation so as to reduce suffering, encourage rehabilitation and therefore to reduce the compensation that the claimant ultimately requires.

A Just System

Through these and many other initiatives, the costs of clinical negligence to the country can be managed and even reduced. But it would surely be reckless, in the pursuit of cost savings, to cast aside the whole system of clinical negligence law and to seek to build a brand new structure.

When the principles and procedures of clinical negligence litigation are properly understood, it is apparent that they are designed to compensate the injured, not to punish those who have made errors. Liability mostly falls on the institutions that provide healthcare rather than on individual practitioners. Far from creating an open season for disgruntled patients to bleed money out of the NHS, clinical negligence law puts considerable obstacles in the way of a potential claimant.

The law of clinical negligence is the product of many years of experience and learning. It has been stress-tested through the resolution of tens of thousands of cases. It strives to achieve a fair balance between the competing interests of claimants and defendants and for the most part succeeds in achieving that goal. The basic principles of clinical negligence law are easy to understand yet they are sufficiently comprehensive and flexible to cover a myriad of different circumstances in which healthcare professionals interact with patients. It is hubristic to believe that this huge, refined body of law could be improved by devising and implementing an alternative system from scratch. Of course there are flaws in the current law and procedures, but the common law has been adapting and improving for many decades. We are fortunate to have inherited the civil justice system that we have. We should not discard it but should continue to develop it so that it continues to serve us all. In any system of justice there will be winners and losers. The quality of justice is not found in the results of individual cases but in the fairness of the processes that led to those results. If justice involves a fair, equal and balanced process, then clinical negligence law is justice in action.

Glossary

Word or phrase	Definition
Adversarial	The process of litigation where two or more parties are opposing each other. The court adjudicates between them rather than taking the lead to inquire into what occurred.
Adverse inferences	Negative conclusions drawn by the court, including from a party's silence or failure to provide evidence.
Alternative Dispute Resolution (ADR)	Resolving a dispute without the need for court proceedings.
Arbitration	A form of ADR where the arbitrator makes a decision which is binding on the parties.
Authority	A judgment of the higher courts which lawyers may bring to the attention of another judge in a later case.
Balance of probabilities	Standard of proof in negligence and other civil claims where the claimant has to prove that something is more likely than not to be true.
Barrister	A type of lawyer who mostly specialises in courtroom advocacy and litigation.
Beyond reasonable doubt	The criminal standard of proof where the prosecution has to establish that a crime has been committed beyond reasonable doubt.
Bolam test	Principle named after *Bolam v Friern Hospital Management Committee* [1957] 1 WLR 582 which says: "If a healthcare professional acts in accordance with the practice of a reasonable body of relevant professional opinion, they are not negligent."
Breach of contract	Failure to honour a legally binding agreement.
Bundle	An indexed and paginated set of documents that the court will need to have in order to determine the case at trial.

Word or phrase	Definition
Burden of Proof	The obligation that rests on one party to prove their case.
Citation	Reference to a reported judgment.
Civil law	The branch of law that regulates private transactions and disputes and provides redress for the the wrongs done by people to each other.
Civil Procedure Rules (CPR)	A set of rules governing the detailed procedures to be followed when bringing or defending civil claims, including clinical negligence claims.
Civil restraint order (CRO)	A court order preventing a person from making an application without the permission of the court.
Claim	A formal assertion of a legal right, for example to compensation for injury caused by negligence.
Claimant	The person bringing the claim (formerly Plaintiff).
Clinical negligence	Failure by a medical professional or organisation to take adequate care of a patient.
Closing submissions	Concluding statement summarising a party's argument at trial.
Common law	Law that is judge-made.
Compensation	The money a defendant is ordered to pay to a claimant they have injured. It is designed to put the injured party back in the same position they would have been in had the defendant not been negligent.
Compensation Recovery Unit	A Government organisation that recovers social security benefits paid to claimants out of the compensation paid by defendants.
Conditional fee agreements	Agreements whereby the claimant does not pay a fee to their lawyer unless they win the case. Sometimes called 'no win no fee' agreements.
Conference	A meeting between a party to litigation, their legal representatives and, often, expert witnesses.

Word or phrase	Definition
Contract law	Branch of law dealing with cases involving breach of contract.
Contributory negligence	A defence that the claimant was partly responsible for their own injury.
Coroner's inquest	An investigation into a death if the cause of death is unknown, or the death was violent or unnatural, or sudden and unexplained.
Costs	Lawyers and experts' fees, court fees and other expenses incurred in bringing or defending a case.
Costs in the case	Whichever party is ordered to pay the costs of the litigation at the end of the case will have to pay the costs of the directions hearing as part of those costs.
Counter schedule	Alternative schedule of loss produced by the defendant. See also *Schedule*.
County Court	A court which deals with civil (non-criminal) matters of low and moderate value and complexity.
Court of Appeal	The court which hears appeals against both civil and criminal judgments from the Crown Court, High Court and County Court.
Court of Protection	Part of the court system that is concerned solely with the best interests of persons who do not have the capacity to make decisions for themselves about their own welfare, or about their finances.
Criminal law	The branch of the law that is concerned with unlawful conduct deserving of punishment.
Cross-examination	Questioning of a witness called by a party to litigation by the legal representative of another party.
Crown Court	The court that deals with serious criminal cases as well as appeals from criminal cases in the magistrates' courts.
Damages	Compensation.

Word or phrase	Definition
Defence	Case presented by the defendant to rebut the claim against them.
Defendant	Party defending the claim.
Deprivation of Liberty Safeguards (DOLS)	A system designed to regulate how a responsible authority may authorise care or treatment that restricts a person's freedom where to do so is in their best interests. Now called Liberty Protection Safeguards.
Deputy	Someone appointed by the Court of Protection to manage the affairs of, including the compensation received by, a person who lacks capacity to do so for themselves.
Disclosure	Stating that a document exists or has existed.
Domestic legislation	Laws created or authorised by legislative bodies in the UK.
European Convention on Human Rights	An international agreement comprising Articles that protect fundamental human rights such as the right to life (Article 2), freedom from torture (Article 3); right to a fair trial (Article 6), and the right to family and private life (Article 8).
European Court of Human Rights	International court established by the European Convention on Human Rights to uphold and enforce the convention rights.
Evidence	Information presented to the court to advance or defend a civil claim or criminal prosecution.
Examination in chief	Questioning of a witness by the legal representative of the party who asked them to give evidence.
Expert witness	A person giving evidence to the court who, by reason of their specialist knowledge, qualifications and experience, are entitled to give opinions on issues in the case.
Extempore judgments	Court decisions, and the reasons for those decisions, given immediately and verbally at the end of the evidence.

Word or phrase	Definition
Fast-track claims	Claims for damages of between £10,000 and £25,000.
Fatal Accidents Act 1976	Legislation which permits certain people to bring claims for the losses they have suffered as a result of the death of another.
Financial dependency	The loss of monetary support that a deceased person would have given to another had they not died.
Gross negligence manslaughter	A crime committed when exceptionally negligent conduct causes the death of another person.
Hearsay evidence	An out of court statement offered to prove the truth of the matter asserted.
High Court	The Senior Courts of England and Wales which deal, amongst other things, with negligence claims of high value and complexity.
Hot-tubbing	Two experts giving evidence at court simultaneously and being asked the same question in turn.
House of Lords	Until 2009 the highest court in the UK (now the Supreme Court).
Human Rights Act 1998	An Act which incorporates into UK law the rights contained in the European Convention on Human Rights.
Inquisitorial	Investigation of the facts of a case led by a tribunal, such as a Coroner, rather than by a contest between parties.
Instructing a solicitor	Formal engagement of a solicitor to act for a person in relation to a claim or other matter.
Interim payment	Payment on account made when the court is satisfied that the claimant will ultimately recover a substantial sum in damages from the defendant.
Interlocutory proceedings	Court hearings that precede the trial of the claim.

Word or phrase	Definition
International law	Laws and standards generally accepted by a group of countries.
Issuing proceedings	Filing a claim at court.
Joint and several liability	Where multiple parties can be held liable for the same injury, loss or damage.
Joint settlement meeting (JSM)	A meeting of the parties with their lawyers at which they enter into negotiations to seek to resolve the litigated claim. Also known as a Round Table Meeting.
Lay magistrates	People from the local community who are involved in the judicial process but who are not legally qualified.
Leading question	One that strongly suggests the answer.
Legal aid	Public funding to cover the legal costs of a person involved in court proceedings or a claim.
Legislation	Laws created by Parliament.
Letter of Claim	A formal letter written to the defendant to inform them about a person's intention to issue a claim at court. Formerly called Letter before Action.
Letter of Notification	Notification to the proposed defendant that the claimant intends to send a Letter of Claim.
Letter of Response	A reasoned response from the defendant having received the Letter of Claim.
Liberty Protection Safeguards	A system designed to regulate how a responsible authority may authorise care or treatment that restricts a person's freedom where to do so is in their best interests. Formerly called Deprivation of Liberty Safeguards.
Limitation period	Period of time within which a claimant has to bring a claim. For clinical negligence claims the limitation period is 3 years.
Litigation	Process of bringing or defending a civil claim in court.

Word or phrase	Definition
Magistrates Court	A lower court which holds trials for summary offences and preliminary hearings for more serious ones.
Mediation	A form of ADR involving a meeting with an independent person, the mediator, who has no power to compel the parties to negotiate or resolve the claim, but who can facilitate discussions to achieve those ends.
Multiplicand	Annual expense or loss.
Multiplier	The figure by which the multiplicand must be multiplied to produce a single lump sum sufficient to meet those annual payments for the period needed.
Multi-track claims	Claims for damages of over £25,000
No win, no fee agreements	See *Conditional fee agreements.*
Non-delegable duties	A duty of care which cannot be assigned to someone else.
Non-financial dependency	The loss of support other than monetary support that a deceased person would have provided to another had they not died.
Ogden Tables	A set of tables containing multipliers for calculating future losses and expenses.
Opening submissions	The speeches made by legal representatives of the parties to litigation at the beginning of a trial.
Overriding objective	The first rule and cornerstone of the Civil Procedure Rules, requiring the courts to deal with cases justly.
Part 36 offers	Written offers to resolve litigation made under the provisions of Part 36 of the CPR.
Particulars of Claim	Formal court document in which the claimant sets out their claim.
Parties	Persons joined in litigation, including the claimant and the defendant.

Word or phrase	Definition
Periodical payment orders	Orders for future losses to be paid on an annual (or other regular) basis rather than by way of a single lump sum.
Personal injury law	The branch of law relating to injury to a person caused by another person's wrongful act, including negligence.
Plaintiff	The old word for claimant.
Practice direction	Detailed procedural provisions which accompany the Parts to the Civil Procedure Rules.
Pre-action protocol	A process setting out a standard for the conduct of a proposed civil claim which the courts expect to be followed.
Pre-trial review hearing (PTR)	A hearing held shortly before the trial of a claim giving the court the opportunity to ensure that the necessary preparations are in place for the trial itself.
Primary legislation	See *Statutes*.
Privileged communications	Confidential communications between a party and their expert or lawyer which they are not under a duty to disclose.
Professional negligence	Failure by a professional to perform to the standards expected of them.
Provisional damages	A form of compensation award where the claimant has a real chance of suffering a serious deterioration in their condition.
Public funding	See *Legal aid*.
Queen's Counsel (QC)	A title awarded to a certain high level barristers. Also known as "silks".
Re-examination	The third stage of a witness' evidence when the legal representative of the party who relies on the witness has a second opportunity to ask them questions.

Word or phrase	Definition
Request for further information	A written request by one party for clarification of the other party's case.
Reserving judgment	When a judge takes some days or weeks to give a full judgment in writing rather than delivering their decision immediately at the end of a trial hearing.
Rights of audience	An entitlement to represent a client at court.
Round table meeting (RTM)	See *Joint Settlement Meeting*.
Satellite litigation	Further legal action arising from the original claim.
Schedule	Document itemising the heads of loss claimed.
Secondary legislation	Subordinate law, also called Statutory Instruments, which do not need to be passed as an Act of Parliament.
Service	Delivery of court documents such as the claim form, pleadings and written evidence, to the other party.
Similar fact evidence	Evidence of past conduct that tends to prove that a party is likely to have again acted in the same way.
Skeleton argument	Written submissions drafted by legal representatives to outline the law, and the key evidence relevant to issues in a case to be heard at court.
Small claims track	Claims for damages of less than £5,000.
Solicitor	Lawyer who manages the case for the client but who may instruct a barrister to represent the client at court.

Word or phrase	Definition
Standard of proof	The level of proof required for a judicial finding to be made. The standard could be the balance of probabilities (for civil cases) or beyond reasonable doubt (for criminal cases).
Statutes	Acts of Parliament.
Summary judgment	A court judgment made without the need for a trial.
Supreme Court	The highest court in the UK which hears the most important cases.
Tort law	The branch of law concerned with civil wrongs.
Variable periodical payments	Future losses which are paid periodically rather than as a final award and on the assumption that the claimant will not suffer a serious deterioration in their condition, but with an entitlement to apply to the court for a variation in the periodical payments should that deterioration occur as a result of the defendant's negligence.
Vicarious liability	Where an employee or agent of the defendant is negligent in carrying out an activity on behalf of the defendant, and the defendant is liable for harm caused by that individual's negligence.
Without prejudice	Confidential. The term is applied to correspondence, negotiations or evidence which cannot be revealed to the court or anyone else other than the other party to the litigation.
Witness statement	Document recording the evidence of a person, signed by a statement of truth.
Witness summons	Order for a witness to attend a trial.
Wrongful birth	Where the outcome that was within the scope of duty of the defendant to prevent was the birth of a child, or of a child with a particular condition or disability.

Index